REAL FREEDOM FOR ALL

WHAT (IF ANYTHING) CAN JUSTIFY CAPITALISM?

PHILIPPE VAN PARIJS

CLARENDON PRESS · OXFORD

Oxford University Press, Great Clarendon Street, Oxford OX2 6DP

Oxford New York
Athens Auckland Bangkok Bogota Bombay
Buenos Aires Calcutta Cape Town Dar es Salaam Delhi
Florence Hong Kong Istanbul Karachi
Kuala Lumpur Madras Madrid Melbourne
Mexico City Nairobi Paris Singapore
Taipei Tokyo Toronto Warsaw

and associated companies in
Berlin Ibadan

Oxford is a trade mark of Oxford University Press

Published in the United States
by Oxford University Press Inc., New York

First published 1995
First issued in paperback 1997

British Library Cataloguing in Publication Data
Data available

Library of Congress Cataloging in Publication Data
Parijs, Philippe van, 1951–
Real freedom for all : what (if anything) can justify capitalism?
/ Philippe Van Parijs.
— (Oxford political theory)
Includes bibliographical references and index.
1. Social justice. 2. Capitalism—Moral and ethical aspects.
3. Guaranteed annual income. 4. Income. 5. Basic needs.
6. Liberty. I. Title. II. Series.
JC578.P37 1995 330.1—dc20 94–44910
ISBN 0–19–827905–1
ISBN 0–19–829357–7 (Pbk.)

Printed in Great Britain
on acid-free paper by
Bookcraft (Bath) Ltd.
Midsomer Norton, Avon

For Sue

PREFACE

Work on this book started in the rainy spring of 1977, as I was settling down in a small green commune within hitching distance of Bielefeld University. What exactly is fundamentally wrong, I wanted to find out, with the capitalist societies we live in? From a close reading of *Das Kapital*, my search gradually broadened, as I moved on to Berkeley and then to Oxford, into an attempt to survey critically old and new economic indictments of capitalism. When I returned to Belgium in 1980, I discovered with excitement John Roemer's novel approach to the theory of exploitation. This prompted me to widen further my critical survey to encompass ethical condemnations of capitalism. Around 1985 the outcome became, under the title *What (If Anything) is Wrong with Capitalism?*, what I believed to be a full draft of the whole book. In fact, I had only a very preliminary version of its last two chapters.

Three intellectual developments conspired to prevent the book from achieving rapid completion along these lines and to impose instead its present, unexpected structure and character. First, I became convinced that it was only by taking so-called neo-liberal thought, and above all the libertarian defence of capitalism, as seriously as it deserves that the Left could ever hope to regain the ideological nerve which it so badly needed in order to reach beyond purely defensive struggles. Secondly, as a result of thinking about radical strategies for fighting unemployment in Western Europe, I hit upon a simple idea—here called basic income—that I later discovered had already been discussed and advocated by others under a variety of labels. Rather suspicious at first, I grew increasingly confident of its importance and of its crucial relevance to the question of the legitimacy of capitalism. Finally, I was persuaded that the book would be far better organized if from the outset I spelt out the conception of justice to which I gradually realized I could subscribe. In the process of doing so, I came up against unsettling difficulties which compelled me to delve into liberal theories of justice to an extent I had not anticipated.

Some stepping stones along this long and tortuous road have formed separate publications. The most recent among them are earlier versions of (parts of) chapters 2 to 4: 'Basic Income Capitalism', *Ethics*, 102/3 (April 1992), 465–84; 'Equal Endowments as Undominated Diversity', *Recherches économiques de Louvain*, 56/3–4 (1990), 327–56; 'Why Surfers Should be Fed: The Liberal Case for an Unconditional Basic Income', *Philosophy and Public Affairs*, 20/2 (spring 1991), 101–31. I am very grateful to the publishers and editors for allowing me to use the material contained in these articles. In addition, the critical explorations of Anglo-American political philosophy and of Marxist social thought which form the substance of *Qu'est-ce qu'une société juste?* (Paris: Le Seuil, 1991) and *Marxism Recycled* (Cambridge: Cambridge University Press, 1993), respectively, have been precious ingredients in—though also to some extent unwelcome digressions from—the preparation of this book.

Along the road, I have accumulated many debts. Johannes Berger and Andrew Glyn guided my first steps. Thanks to Ian Steedman and Hillel Steiner, Robert van der Veen and Percy Lehning, Erik Wright and Steven Lukes, work on the book benefited greatly from the exceptionally productive periods I spent at the Universities of Manchester (1983), Amsterdam (1985), and Wisconsin (1990) and at the European University Institute in Florence (1990–1), where I wrote the final full draft. However, most of the work was done in Louvain-la-Neuve. As a senior fellow of the Belgian National Fund for Scientific Research, I wrote the bulk of the preliminary drafts in the friendly and stimulating surroundings of the University of Louvain's economics department. And after returning from Florence to Louvain's newly created Hoover Chair of economic and social ethics, I used all my spare time to make the thousands of local improvements which I felt the book could not do without, and also to do some further thinking on the argument's overall significance and on what I believed to be its most vulnerable steps. To all those who enabled me to enjoy these environments and benefit from them as much as I did, I am extremely grateful, not least among them to the Hoover Chair's secretary Annick Dabeye, who —along with OUP's competent editorial staff— efficiently helped me through the final stages.

Further, I cannot imagine what this book would have looked like had I not joined, in 1981, what later became known as the September Group. The Group's ambition to combine unflinching intellectual rigour and a passionate commitment to the values characteristic of the radical Left, the tremendous stimulation provided by its annual meetings, the pains it took in subjecting to its critical scrutiny some ancestor of most chapters of this book, have deeply affected both its form and its content. To all present members of the Group (Pranab Bardhan, Sam Bowles, Bob Brenner, Jerry Cohen, John Roemer, Hillel Steiner, Robert van der Veen, and Erik Wright) and not least to its two former members (Jon Elster and Adam Przeworski), I am deeply grateful for what I have learned both from their own work and from their comments on mine.

In addition, earlier versions of one or more chapters benefited from helpful written comments by Dick Arneson, Christian Arnsperger, John

Baker, Wendy Carlin, Ian Carter, Andrew Glyn, André Gorz, Sue James, Jeroen Knijff, Anton Leist, David Miller, Gérard Roland, Ian Steedman, and three anonymous readers, and from stimulating oral reactions from audiences to which they were presented in Amsterdam, Antwerp, Barcelona, Beijing, Berlin, Bristol, Brussels, Cambridge (Mass.), Canterbury, Chicago, Davis, Florence, Geneva, Ghent, Leuven, Liège, London, Louvain-la-Neuve, Madison, Madrid, Montevideo, Montreal, New York, Paris, Pisa, Plios, Siena, and Thessaloniki. Brian Barry, Louis Gevers, Erik Schokkaert, and Susan Strange deserve special thanks because they served as thorough discussants on at least one occasion, and so do several cohorts of my MA students in economics, who were subjected to different stages of various chapters. Among all these comments, some have forced me to clarify my formulations. Others have led me to work out further important twists in my argument. Others still have left me with the nagging feeling of an unresolved difficulty to which I, or someone better equipped or more ingenious than I, should one day return. But I have learned from all of them, and am most grateful to their authors for having taken the trouble to make them.

Finally, Rebecca, Jonathan, Benjamin, and Sarah were all born at some point in the course of the long preparation of what at home was simply called 'the book' (somewhat confusingly, as I unwittingly wrote and unexpectedly published three other books over this period). Each of them displayed some understanding for the peace I needed to work on it, and now and then politely enquired into how far it still was from completion. None of them, I am sure, will regret that it is finally out of the way. Nor will, I am even more certain, their mother. Combining the lonely writing of a lengthy theoretical text with a (fair?) share in the running of a large household—and a number of other things besides—was never easy. It even repeatedly seemed impossible. That it proved possible in the end I undoubtedly owe in part to having stubbornly resisted some of the demands the family made on me, but to an incomparably greater extent, in countless ways, and more than to anyone else on Earth, to Sue.

P. V. P.

CONTENTS

Introduction

One: Our capitalist societies are replete with unacceptable inequalities. Two: Freedom is of paramount importance. This book is written by someone who strongly holds these two convictions. And it is primarily addressed to those who share them with him. One of its most central tasks, therefore, is to provide a credible response to the libertarian challenge, that is to the claim that these two convictions are mutually exclusive, or that taking freedom seriously requires one to endorse most of the inequalities in today's world—and more.

In the first chapter, I shall tackle this challenge head on by scrutinizing the claim that pure capitalism—or pure socialism—is bound to provide the best embodiment of the ideal of a free society. In the process, I shall spell out what I believe to be the most defensible interpretation of this ideal: real-libertarianism, or real-freedom-for-all.

In Chapter 2, I shall state my claim that the regime that would best embody this ideal under current conditions is the regime that could afford, and would actually implement, the highest sustainable unconditional income, subject to the constraint that everyone's formal freedom should be protected. The prima-facie argument in support of this claim is straightforward enough. But the close connection it asserts between the real-libertarian ideal and the institution of an unconditional income is open to powerful objections which Chapters 2 to 4 aim to formulate and refute.

Moreover, even if this close connection can be upheld, the argument may still fail to justify the regime that sustainably maximizes the level of the unconditional income. For real-freedom-for-all is unacceptable as a conception of social justice, so it may be argued, because it fails to take properly into account the most important component of the ethical critique of capitalism: the condemnation of exploitation. Chapter 5 aims to express and refute the most salient variants of this very different and no less serious type of objection.

Supposing real-libertarianism provides a defensible conception of the just society and justifies the introduction of an unconditional income at the highest sustainable level, should one opt for capitalism or for socialism? Current common wisdom generates a strong presumption that capitalism is characterized by far greater economic efficiency. Might socialism none the less be preferred on real-libertarian grounds? This is the topic of the final chapter, which will close with a sketch of the key intellectual tenets of what I believe is needed for progressive hope and action in today's world.

The sequence of these six chapters forms a complex but, I hope, clear and coherent argument. In order to make the thread easier to follow, each chapter opens with a prologue that briefly and informally summarizes the content of the chapter. I have given each of these prologues the form of a dialogue. This is not just a way of symbolically expressing a deep continuity with a 2,500-year-old—and yet suprisingly congenial—style of philosophizing. Nor is it merely a way of forcing me to be somewhat less stiff and dense than in the rest of the text. The dialogue form also proves a very natural way of presenting arguments persistently prompted and stimulated by actual and virtual discussion partners in the academic community and beyond. A contribution to political philosophy such as this one is in the end nothing but a very stylized account of a conversation conducted in a small corner of the large democratic forum.*

The end-product of this conversation can be described in a number of distinct ways. It consists in a sympathetic but unindulgent evaluation of the left-wing critique of capitalism after the rough times it recently went through, in both thought and reality. It constitutes an attempt to represent and sort out, for myself and for my readers, the intricate web of arguments and counterarguments on the legitimacy of capitalism, which has been growing steadily in the last two decades as the result of the cross-fertilization of economic theory and political philosophy. It purports to spell out the implications of the combined ideals of liberty and equality in the context of a technologically sophisticated, ecologically threatened society. Above all, though unexpectedly, it provides the most sustained, systematic ethical case for a radical reform—the introduction of an unconditional basic income—which I believe to be far more than a mere abstract possibility in the economic and political context of contemporary Europe: a central component of what is urgently needed to save the 'European model' by taking it one step further.

---

* This suggests one interpretation for the names of the two characters in the dialogues: Δ for Demos, and Φ for Philosopher. Unless Δ rather stands, less pompously, for David, and Φ for Philippe? As a conscientious series editor, David Miller persuaded me to help my readers get a more synthetic grasp of the argument. I hope he will forgive me for (fictitiously) involving him more than he expected in my attempt to meet his wish.

CHAPTER 1

Capitalism, Socialism,
and Freedom

PROLOGUE

Δ *European communism has collapsed. The high tide of neo-liberalism has come
   and gone, leaving a deep mark. The old debate between capitalism and socialism can never be the same again. Hasn't the case for socialism become so weak
   that it is not worth bothering with?*

Φ Our first task, to avoid misunderstandings, is to define capitalism and socialism. Unoriginally, I propose to distinguish capitalism from socialism in terms
   of whether the bulk of a society's means of production is privately or publicly
   owned. And I distinguish them from slavery and collectivism by stipulating
   that they both require that people are not owned by other people or by society but, in some sense, own themselves (§ 1.1).

Δ *Your point of departure is that, in a post-communist, post-neo-liberal world,
   the ideal by reference to which the relative merits of capitalism and socialism
   must be assessed is that of a free, or perhaps a maximally free society. Should it
   not be obvious at once that this will lead to a justification of capitalism?*

Φ It shouldn't. To start with, a number of people have argued that, as a matter of
   logical necessity, a free society, understood as a society whose members all
   enjoy to the greatest extent the freedom to shape their destiny, can only be a
   democratic socialist society. The appeal of this argument rests, I believe, on a
   confusion between freedom and power, and the implied picture of a free society is altogether implausible as an ideal (§ 1.2). But the very fact that some
   people have argued this way suffices to indicate that the conclusion you suggest cannot be taken for granted.

Δ *A symmetrical argument is at the heart of contemporary libertarianism's apol-
   ogy of capitalism. It does not seem to rest on such a confusion and is intuitively
   quite appealing.*

Φ It too loses its appeal once you notice that it rests on a distinct, but equally fatal confusion. Libertarians persuasively argue that no consistent formulation of the ideal of a free society can help giving a crucial role to a consistent system of private property rights. But by no means does it follow that only capitalism, let alone only pure capitalism, can be just. For there are many ways in which such a system of rights can be generated apart from the 'purely historical' one which libertarians favour. And it is easy to think up highly repressive states of affairs perfectly consistent with a full respect of property rights, as construed by libertarians (§ 1.3). Put differently, libertarians rightly stress the importance of formal freedom, but formal freedom does not exhaust the real freedom that must feature in any defensible ideal of a free society. Once we are fully aware that 'real-freedom-for-all' is what really matters, the discussion of capitalism versus socialism appears in a very different light.

Δ *What is exactly the difference between formal and real freedom?*

Φ The first thing to be clear about is that both formal and real freedom are aspects of individual freedom: collective freedom—typically, at the level of a political entity—is only instrumentally relevant to both of them, and so is personal participation in the exercise of this collective freedom (§ 1.4).

Δ *Does this mean that even real freedom is sheer negative freedom?*

Φ It certainly is 'negative freedom' (an ambiguous expression I don't like to use), if the contrast is with political participation, the so-called 'liberty of the ancients'. It also is, in the sense that it is a freedom to do 'whatever one might want to do', rather than a freedom to do what is dictated by moral duties or autonomously chosen preferences (§ 1.5).

Δ *Where lies the difference then?*

Φ The difference appears as soon as you focus on the question of what freedom is a freedom from, or of what obstacles are, as a matter of definition, freedom-restricting. Formal freedom can only be restricted by coercion, broadly understood as the (threat of a) violation of a person's rights, her ownership of herself included (§ 1.6). But real freedom can be further restricted by any limit to what a person is permitted or enabled to do. Both a person's purchasing power and a person's genetic set-up, for example, are directly relevant to a person's real freedom. Unlike formal freedom, in other words, real freedom is not only a matter of having the right to do what one might want to do, but also a matter of having the means for doing it (§ 1.7).

Δ *So, a free society, according to the ideal you find defensible, is one in which everyone possesses both the right and the means to do whatever she might like to do?*

Φ Not quite. It is, first of all, a society whose members are all formally free: there is a well-enforced structure of property rights which includes the ownership of each by herself. And it is, secondly, a society in which opportunities—

access to the means for doing what one might want to do—are distributed in maximin (or, more pedantically still, leximin) fashion: some can have more opportunities than others, but only if their having more does not reduce the opportunities of some of those with less. In other words, institutions must be designed so as to offer the greatest possible real opportunities to those with least opportunities, subject to everyone's formal freedom being respected (§ 1.8). This provides, I believe, a far more plausible and attractive formulation of the ideal of a free society than the one put forward by libertarians of the standard kind.

Δ *Are you claiming that a free society, as you characterize it, is also a just society?*

Φ Yes I am, and this turns me into a real-libertarian, a believer in the claim that real-freedom-for-all (as explained) is all there is to social justice. You look perplexed, sceptical? I am not surprised. This was all very abstract, and what we must do next is look at the institutional implications of real libertarianism.

1.1 *Capitalism versus socialism*

Freedom is of paramount importance: we want—or at any rate many of us want—our society to be a free society. But can, or even must, such a society be a capitalist society? Or can, or even must, such a society be a socialist society? The answers to these questions crucially hinge on what constitutes a defensible interpretation of the ideal of freedom. But they also depend on how capitalism and socialism are being defined. It is to the former and more important issue that the bulk of this chapter is devoted. In this section, however, I shall give explicit definitions of capitalism and socialism which will, I hope, minimize misunderstandings and clumsy talk in a way that does not beg the question in favour of either the pro-capitalist or the pro-socialist position, indeed in a way that gives both of them the best chance of being proved right.

Unoriginally, *capitalism* will here be contrasted with *socialism* in terms of private versus public ownership of society's (non-human) capital, of its (material) means of production. *Private ownership* is ownership by individual people in their personal capacity, or by voluntary associations of such people. *Public ownership* is ownership by political communities or their representatives, whether at the national or subnational level. Note, first, that these two categories are not collectively exhaustive, at least if the concept of ownership is extended so as to cover *common ownership*, simply defined as access for all, unrestricted by any set of rules. They *are* exhaustive, however, if one prefers to speak in the latter case—as I shall—

of unowned rather than of commonly owned assets.[1] Note, further, that the private/public divide does not coincide with the distinction between *individual* and *collective* ownership. It is perfectly possible for private ownership to be collective, as when shareholders jointly own a company or workers a co-operative. It is also conceivable, though hardly likely, for public ownership to be individual, for example, if only one citizen were left in some political territory.

Private and public ownership of the means of production are obviously a matter of degree in terms of *scope*, that is, in terms of the proportion of society's capital governed by either regime. They are also a matter of degree in terms of *depth*, that is, in terms of the degree to which either regime applies to each particular component of that capital. The depth of private ownership is diminished, for example, if the product of the use of private capital is subjected to taxation, if there is an obligation to re-invest any profits made, to install anti-pollution devices, to hire people irrespective of their race or sex, or if means of production can only be owned by the workers who operate them. Symmetrically, the depth of public ownership is lessened if public capital can be leased to private individuals or collectives for a significant period of time, or if part of the profits made by using that capital can be appropriated by such individuals or collectives. I shall speak of a *pure capitalist economy* only if there is *full* private ownership of *all* means of production, and of a *pure socialist economy* only if there is *full* public ownership of *all* means of production. I shall speak, more broadly and more loosely, of *capitalism* if the bulk of the means of production is essentially privately owned, and of *socialism* if the bulk of the means of production is essentially publicly owned. This allows, no doubt, for a sizeable grey area, but its existence need not bother us at this stage.[2]

Private ownership of capital, however, is not the only feature that needs to appear in our definition of capitalism. In tune with Marx's well-known passage on the proletarians' 'twofold freedom', I shall stipulate in addition that, under pure capitalism, each person *fully owns herself*.[3] Capitalism differs from slavery in so far as it does not allow human beings to be owned and sold by other human beings, on a par with animals and inanimate objects. I shall analogously define pure socialism as requiring full self-ownership.[4] Unlike what I shall call a *collectivist* society, a socialist society does not own its human capital, only its material capital. Like the ownership of the means of production, self-ownership is a matter of degree. Its *scope* varies depending on how large a proportion of a society's membership enjoys it, while its *depth* varies as a function of what each person is allowed to do with herself. The more people are sentenced to prison or subjected to conscription, for example,—and the longer their sentence or service, the less the scope of self-ownership. And the more the citizens' freedom of movement is restricted, or the more repressive the legislation on sexual behaviour, the less the depth of self-ownership. I shall talk of capitalism (respectively, socialism), rather than slavery (respectively, collectivism) when 'most' members of a society 'essentially' own themselves. Here again, there is a grey area, which need not worry us at this stage.

There is no point in discussing these stipulative definitions at length. The use to which they are being put in subsequent sections will tell us whether or not they have been judiciously chosen. I will make only one comment about the proposed definition of capitalism. Under this definition, every part of society's capital can be owned (1) by the individual who operates it (self-employment); or (2) by the collectives of workers who jointly operate it (worker-ownership); or (3) by individuals or collectives distinct from those who operate it (waged labour). The dominance, or indeed the exclusive presence, of any of these three forms of private capital ownership is perfectly compatible with our definition of capitalism, and even of pure capitalism, *providing* it is not the result of institutional restrictions on what private owners can do with their capital. And a systematic tendency to such dominance—for example, to the dominance of waged labour—is therefore fully relevant to the discussion of capitalism. A regime can be indicted because of some features it systematically tends to possess, even if these features are not logically entailed by its definition. On the other hand, if the dominance of some particular form of private ownership *is* the result of such an institutional restriction, we may well have entered the grey area lying between capitalism and socialism. One may question, for example, whether in a *co-operative* economy, in which all means of production *must* be owned by the worker or group of workers which operates them, capital can still be said to be 'essentially' owned by the individuals or collectives that are their private owners. Whether such a private-ownership economy can still be called a capitalist economy, in terms of the above definition, is debatable. For present purposes, however, all that matters is that pure capitalism involves no such restriction and is therefore, it would seem, a far more promising candidate for an a priori claim to incorporate the ideal of a free society. But what is a free society?

1.2 Pure socialism as the free society

As I turn from the problem of defining capitalism and socialism to that of characterizing a free society, my aim is no longer just to provide an unambiguous, convenient terminology. I want to clarify what we have or should have in mind when we say that freedom is of paramount importance, or use the notion of a free society to describe an ideal we think is worth pursuing. The task, therefore, is not to identify what is usually called, or what could conveniently be called, a 'free society', but rather to determine how the latter is to be defined if it is to represent an ethically appealing goal. Rather than proposing a full characterization straight away, I shall let its components emerge gradually, as I scrutinize a number of arguments that have been put forward in order to establish that a free society is bound to be capitalist, or—more surprisingly, perhaps—that it is bound to be socialist, and thereby to settle the matter on an a priori basis.

Let us begin by looking at the a priori case for socialism. One promising point of departure is the suggestion that a free—or maximally free—society is to be conceived as a maximally *democratic* society, a society that subjects everything to collective decision-making and gives each of its members an equal power in the decisions it takes. If this suggestion were adequate, a thoroughly democratic form of collectivism, of public ownership of both people and capital, would stand a good chance of being the best expression of the ideal of a free society. But it cannot be adequate. To understand why, it suffices to reflect on the following two situations. In situation A, each of us can decide for herself whether to scratch her nose. In situation B, we decide together, in perfectly democratic fashion, whether nose-scratching is permissible. Assuming (plausibly) that variations in nose size can be deemed irrelevant, it can be said that in both situations the weight of each person in decision-making is identical. But surely the freedom to scratch (or not to scratch) one's nose is not. Each of us enjoys this freedom in situation A. But there is no such freedom in situation B, where scratching is subjected to collective approval. Denying this would amount to conflating someone's freedom and her power, her weight in the decision process. Demanding that people be equally or maximally free is not the same as demanding that they be given equal or maximal power. Democracy, no doubt, matters on many counts. It may even empirically turn out to be a necessary condition for realizing a free society.[5] But, as the nose-scratching example should have made plain, a (maximally) democratic society cannot plausibly be said to coincide by definition with a society of (maximally) free people.[6]

The example does more than warrant the rejection of one suggestion. It also points to another, namely that a society of free people is one which leaves each of its members to decide what does and does not happen to herself. However democratic, one is thus encouraged to say, a society cannot be free if it does not grant each of its members something like *self-ownership*. That individuals do *not* own themselves, and that society, or the State, has property rights over them, has unambiguously been maintained by many political philosophers, including the founding fathers of the subject.[7] Self-ownership is not a perennial idea. It is a modern idea, and one that remains controversial.[8] If one wishes to attack it, however, one has to do so on grounds other than liberty. Those who are serious about wanting a free society cannot help requiring that each person be granted ownership of herself in the sense sketched above (§ 1.1) and further clarified below (§ 1.8).[9]

It directly follows, given our definitions (§ 1.1), that neither slavery nor collectivism are compatible with a free society. But nothing, so far, prevents a free society from being either capitalist *or socialist*. That even pure socialism should be consistent with self-ownership might be challenged on at least two grounds. First, it does not allow people to perform waged labour. Indeed, it does not even allow people to engage in any productive activity on a self-employed basis or for their own consumption. Pure socialism requires full public ownership of all means of production. This means that only consumption goods can be privately owned, and hence that even a self-employed shoe cleaner could not use her own brush as a means of production, to provide services to her customers. Though true, this cannot disqualify pure socialism as a potentially free society on the basis of anything that has been said so far. The restriction that follows from the definition of pure socialism is a restriction on what may be done with external objects—they cannot be used as means of production—not a restriction on what people may do with themselves.[10]

Secondly, it may be objected that public ownership of the means of production requires an authoritarian procedure for allocating labour,[11] and hence the systematic violation of the dimension of self-ownership involved in occupational choice.[12] The quickest way of substantiating this objection relies on the assumption that socialism equalizes incomes and on the conjecture that income equality is bound to clash with self-ownership. The latter claim, it is worth emphasizing, is a conjecture and not an analytical truth. Self-ownership, as understood here, is weak enough to be consistent with the absence of any differential reward to talents and is therefore conceptually compatible even with pure equality. The claim, therefore, must be construed as the factual claim that, *if* one wishes to achieve an acceptable level of allocative efficiency, one can have either self-ownership or income equality but not both.[13] But even if this claim turns out to be factually correct under all circumstances, by no means does it follow that minimally efficient socialism needs to violate self-ownership. The public ownership of the means of production does not entail any specific pattern of income distribution, and freedom-based attacks on egalitarianism are therefore not *ipso facto* freedom-based arguments against socialism. The public ownership of capital does not prevent whatever institution is in charge of allocating labour from using wage differentials as incentives, if required, for the purpose of achieving an efficient allocation. There is no obvious reason for supposing that some sort of labour market mechanism would be unable to reconcile the public ownership of capital, the workers' self-ownership, and a reasonable level of allocative efficiency.[14]

Can one go beyond this and argue that an exclusive concern with the freedom of all must lead to the choice of pure socialism, as defined? After all, a society of maximally free people must not only entitle each of them to decide what happens to herself, for there is little, if anything, that one can do using nothing but oneself. A society of maximally free people must also give each of them maximum access to external objects. And how can such maximum access be guaranteed to all people, unless all external objects are publicly owned, with each person given an equal weight in the decision-making process? A free society, on this view, is a society which combines full self-ownership with full and fully democratic public ownership of the external world, including of course all means of production. A free society, therefore, must be purely socialist.[15]

This argument fails for a reason strictly analogous to, though distinct from, the one that led to the rejection of collectivism. How can each of us possibly be said to be free if she cannot breathe, eat, move, let alone preach or demonstrate without the approval of the political community which owns everything in the world around us except ourselves?[16] Like the redistribution of decision-making power over people, the redistribution of decision-making power over external things is no zero-sum affair in terms of freedom. The freedom for each of us to wear a skirt or launch a vegetarian café is not the same, depending on whether each of us has the right to decide for herself or whether instead collective decisions settle the matter. It is, therefore, not just private ownership of oneself, but also private ownership of external objects that is required in a free society.

Is there any conceivable way of salvaging this a priori freedom-based case for socialism? A first possibility consists in challenging the assumption that public ownership requires the use of an external object to be subjected to majority approval: much autonomy could be left to individuals in the use they make of publicly owned assets. But this will not do. Either such autonomy is not mandated by the institutions, and then this defence of pure socialism is worth no more than the attempt to reconcile pure capitalism with a concern for the propertyless by claiming that adequate private charity will be forthcoming. Or such autonomy is mandated by the institutions in the form of private rights (short of full ownership) over publicly owned external objects (long-term leases on houses or land, for example), but then one has already moved away from pure socialism. And it is hard to see why the impure form of socialism thus generated could a priori be said to be better than any form of capitalism at guaranteeing to all maximum access to external objects.

A second possibility consists in pointing out that there are things that can be done with jointly owned property but which could not be done if the latter were turned into smaller private holdings. If our back gardens became a large, jointly owned lawn, we may lose the freedom to sunbathe in them unseen by neighbours, but we would gain the freedom to use them as a single soccer pitch. Hence private property does not unequivocally expand our freedom to do things we might want to do, and full public ownership, so the objection goes, cannot be dismissed as flatly as it has just been. One might think of replying that nothing would prevent private owners, if unanimous, from combining their resources for some common purpose, and thereby achieving through voluntary co-operation what a public-property regime would achieve through collective decisions. But such a reply would be unfair, for under public ownership, collective decisions need not be taken unanimously. And if a lesser majority is sufficient, there are options—such as using the back gardens as a soccer pitch—that will be available in a public-ownership regime under circumstances in which they would not be available under private ownership—in the example, because of the *de facto* veto power of some neighbours with an aversion to soccer. But there is no need for such a reply to defeat the second rescue strategy. It is enough to point out that the converse of the claim on which it rests is no less true: there are things that can be done under private ownership which could not be done under a public-ownership regime—whatever the decision-making rule adopted: keeping one's back garden for intimate sunbathing, for example, may be made impossible by simple-majoritarian public ownership, while turning half the back gardens into a small soccer pitch may be made impossible by unanimitarian public ownership.[17]

Thus, neither strategy manages to salvage the a priori claim that a free society must be purely socialist. As I do not believe any other strategy can do the trick, it is now time to turn to the opposite position and scrutinize the libertarians' fervently advertised claim that a free society must be a capitalist, indeed a purely capitalist society.

1.3 Pure capitalism as the free society

For a libertarian, a free society is—as a first approximation—a society whose members are all 'permitted to run their own lives as they wish'.[18]

But this is an unsatisfactory formulation, since by running her life as she wishes one person may easily prevent another from running hers as she wishes. A coherent formulation of the libertarian position therefore requires an essential reference to property rights in order to deal with the lack of pre-established harmony between the wishes of different people. Hence, a free society should be characterized, more cautiously, as a society whose members can all do what they wish to do *with what they legitimately own*. But this is still not enough. If the latter addendum were not further specified, a free society would be consistent with collectivism and slavery. All that is required so far is that property rights be defined and enforced. This is, no doubt, a necessary condition for a free society. For what would society be like in the absence of both pre-established harmony and property rights? Brute force would determine who controls what and whom. Clashing wishes would be 'reconciled' by letting those of the strongest prevail over those of the weakest. Surely this cannot be a free society, a society in which *all*, weak and strong, are free to run their lives as they wish. A legal or customary framework of property rights and a system of effective sanctions are necessary, though not sufficient, if this is to be achieved. For this reason, libertarians rightly claim, there can be no liberty without property.

On the other hand, as collectivism and slavery blatantly illustrate, there can be property without liberty. Libertarians, therefore, demand that the above characterization of a free society be further specified as follows: 'a society whose members can all do what they wish to do *with themselves* and with whatever external object they legitimately own'. Even this expanded formulation, however, is still short of what is needed to support the claim that a free society is bound to be purely capitalist. Any variety of capitalism or socialism would do, providing the associated system of property rights is well defined and respected. If they are to come up with an a priori justification of capitalism, libertarians need to characterize a free society, even more specifically, as a society whose members can all do what they wish to do with themselves and with whatever external object they own *by virtue of an uninterrupted chain of voluntary transactions starting from some initial unrestricted private appropriation of objects previously unowned*.[19] Under this specification, it looks likely that libertarians will have no difficulty showing that in a free society all means of production must be and remain unrestricted private property, that is, that only pure capitalism is compatible with the libertarian ideal.

Note that by moving from the first and most general characterization of a free society to the third and most restrictive one, we have moved from the requirement that the distribution of holdings, in a free society, should be governed by an entitlement principle in a weak sense, to the requirement that it should be governed by an entitlement principle in a far stronger sense.[20] *Entitlement principles in the weaker sense* are perfectly compatible with a designing of property rights aimed at achieving some distributive objective. The latter can be effectively pursued *ex ante* through a restrictive definition of property rights, and not just *ex post* through the violation of unrestricted property rights. Being prevented from using a piece of land one 'owns' as a means of production, or as a means of production operated by hired workers, for example, is fully consistent with an entitlement principle in this sense. The property rights one has over the plot of land need not include the right to use them in this way. *Entitlement principles in the stronger sense,* on the other hand, rule out this sort of designing. For the structure of property rights is then no longer viewed as a control variable on which one must act in order to achieve some aim, for example, the aim of a free society, but as a parameter which the ideal of a free society consists in respecting.[21] It is on the plausibility of some entitlement principle in this stronger sense that the strength of the libertarians' a priori defence of pure capitalism depends.

As spelt out above, the strong entitlement principle to which libertarians appeal clearly requires that a satisfactory solution be given to the problem of original appropriation, that is, that a defensible criterion be specified for the legitimate appropriation of previously unowned external objects. But, one may wonder, is not the choice of this criterion bound to be arbitrary? All libertarians may be willing to subscribe to Locke's (1690: bk. ii, § 25) claim that 'all the fruits [the Earth] naturally produces, and beasts it feeds, belong to mankind in common'. But can this mean only that natural resources are entirely up for grabs (Kirzner 1978), or also that they are open to private appropriation subject to the proviso that no one should be made worse off as a result (Nozick 1974), or that they are available for private appropriation subject to all non-appropriators getting a fair share in the benefits (Brody 1983), or perhaps even that they are equally owned by all (Steiner 1981). Depending on which of these propositions is deemed correct, private property rights will turn out to be absolute or limited instead by more or less comprehensive tax schemes. In the absence of a decisive argument in favour of the first of these propositions, the libertarian justification of pure capitalism is, therefore, on very shaky ground.

Note, however, that the argument as stated so far does not threaten the libertarian case for (less than pure) capitalism. The regime that would end up being justified under any of the four interpretations of legitimate original appropriation listed above is still unambiguously capitalist. Let us now add one further interpretation: if the Earth really 'belongs to mankind in common', then there must be public ownership of all natural resources, as well as of anything they enable people to make, including all produced means of production.[22] We are then back to the public ownership of the world, as discussed above (§ 1.2) in connection with pure socialism. This interpretation can no doubt be rejected, as it has been there, on the ground that it is blatantly at odds with our intuitive conception of a free society. But this is no legitimate ground in a libertarian perspective, for appealing to it amounts to judging the structure of property rights by the associated consequences. If one wishes to stick to an entitlement approach in the strong sense, one must find another, consequence-independent reason for selecting one criterion of original appropriation rather than another. Failing this, it is no more arbitrary or implausible to interpret the 'common ownership' of the Earth as its joint ownership by all, than as the private ownership of its components by whoever cares or manages first to put her hands on them. And the strong entitlement justification of pure socialism is then exactly as strong—and as weak—as the strong entitlement justification of pure capitalism.

The difficulty libertarians experience in finding a non-arbitrary criterion of original appropriation is serious enough. But it is just one reflection of the fundamental defect that lies at the very core of the libertarian approach. To capture this defect in its simplest form, just think of an island which happens to be owned, for whatever reason fully consistent with the libertarian characterization of a free society given above, by one of its inhabitants. Providing it is difficult or expensive enough to leave the island, the owner can impose on the other inhabitants any condition she fancies. If they are to be allowed to earn their livelihood, they may have to work abysmally long hours, for example, or give up their religion, or wear scarlet underwear. On a libertarian account, as presented above, such a society would not cease to be free.[23] On any intuitively defensible interpretation of the ideal of a free society, on the other hand, this is plain nonsense. What lies at the root of this clash between so-called libertarianism and what we feel is implied by a genuine concern with people's freedom?

One guess—and at the same time an attempt to defuse the threat presented by this clash—is that a libertarian's maximally free society is a society in which the aggregate of individual freedom is maximized, not one in which all are as free as possible. The extent of private property is crucial to this understanding of the libertarian ideal, but its distribution is not. If this understanding were correct, however, there would be no reason for libertarians to be bothered with granting people self-ownership. Full private ownership of selves would be sufficient. But if mass slavery is repulsive to a libertarian, so must be the tale of the island owner. In either case, it is false for most people that they are 'permitted to run their own lives as they wish'. If distributive considerations are relevant in one case, they must also be relevant in the other. Libertarians cannot consistently appeal to some notion of aggregate freedom to make sense of their endorsement of the island owner's despotic rule.

The real root of the clash is different. In the process of working out a coherent conception of a free society, libertarians have been led—sensibly—to giving a key role to property rights. But as a result of doing so, they have also been misled—far less sensibly—into adopting an altogether implausible *moralized* conception of freedom. According to such a conception, my freedom is only restricted when my rights are violated. From this it follows, for example, that I remain fully free when I am rightly imprisoned or when my rightful endowments leave me no option but to starve. More generally, such a moralized conception of freedom implies that the perfect enforcement of the 'right' structure of property rights (somehow assumed to be given 'naturally', prior to any social arrangement) means total freedom for all—since all are allowed to do anything they wish with what they legitimately own—and not just one particular allocation of freedoms and unfreedoms, which makes me unfree to hold your ankle while making you free to run away, for example, or which makes me free to grow pumpkins in my garden while making you unfree to trample them.[24] This is why a libertarian had to call the island of our tale a free society, however despotic its owner's rule. Such counterintuitive implications clearly make the moralized conception of freedom untenable, and 'libertarianism' a misleading label. Libertarians should rather be called rights-fetishists, and their alleged freedom-based case for capitalism, pure or otherwise, is worth no more than the freedom-based case for socialism rejected in the previous section.

1.4 Individual versus collective sovereignty

If the arguments of the previous two sections are correct, there is little prospect in trying to show on a priori grounds that capitalism or socialism, whether pure or not, is a better embodiment of the ideal of a free society: the most promising attempts to do so have each been shown to rely on an unacceptable interpretation of that ideal. Among these failed attempts features the so-called libertarian case for pure capitalism. If we want to work out a powerful response to the challenge presented by libertarianism, however, we need to go far beyond these purely negative moves. We need to spell out the notion of freedom that has been implicitly appealed to throughout the discussion so far, show the coherence of the associated ideal of a free society and derive its institutional implications. This I shall now do (in §§ 1.4 to 1.6), while locating the notion I have appealed to among the most significant notions of freedom to be found in the large and often confusing literature on the subject. Much of the confusion has been generated by the great variety of meanings that have been attached to the distinction between positive and negative freedom, and an important task will therefore be to clarify in which senses the conception of freedom implicit in the previous discussion is 'positive', and in which other senses it is 'negative'.

A preliminary step in this undertaking is the explicit acknowledgement that the expression 'free society' is a misnomer. Taking the expression at face value implies that it is society itself that is and ought to be the subject of freedom. A free society, on this account, might be characterized, for example, as one that can determine its fate according to its wishes, one that is not just independent from outside powers, but also in full control of itself. There is no a priori reason why a free society, in this sense, should grant *its members* much freedom, however this freedom is defined. Suppose, for example, that there is nothing like an army of citizens—or indeed a society of soldiers—to protect a society against external threats.[25] Unless patriotic feelings are so strong that most people will spontaneously make themselves available for the defence effort, society's freedom then requires compulsory conscription—presumably a blatant restriction of individual freedom.[26] To reduce the tension, one may wish to point out that a society's freedom from subjection to foreign powers is a factual precondition for the freedom of its members. But even if this were true[27] the tension would remain, for in order to make a society free, or as free as possible, one would often need to make its members unfree, or less free than they could be, for reasons that do not reduce to the need to take care of external threats. On the background of realistic informational and motivational assumptions, it is clear that a society could only be really free to equalize income while maintaining a high level of effort, for example, if it significantly restricted its members' freedom of choice about the level and nature of their productive activities.[28] Maximal freedom for society as a whole is bound to clash with the maximal freedom of its individual members.

Thus a free society, taken literally, and a society of free people are two different things, and, on many occasions, two conflicting things.[29] Which should we choose? Surely, a social order which maximizes 'societal freedom', that is, removes more obstacles in the way of society's achievements than any other, including through the enslavement of its members, does not provide an adequate interpretation of the ideal of a free society we are trying to spell out. What we must mean by a (maximally) free society is a society whose members are (maximally) free. It may conceivably be argued that a society's members cannot be free, or maximally free, unless society itself possesses the freedom to do or prevent certain things. Indeed, we shall see much later (§ 6.7) that one instance of this claim is of central—and perhaps decisive—importance in the debate between capitalism and socialism. The ideal, however, remains a society of free individuals, to which the freedom of society is no more than a means.

On the other hand, even a conception of freedom as individual freedom may make the individual's relationship to the political life of the society considered a matter of definition. According to one such conception, a person's freedom is nothing but her weight in the decisions being taken over people's lives, and a society whose members are maximally free will then naturally be conceived of as a thoroughly democratic society. This is precisely the conception that was mentioned and rejected above in connection with the defence of pure socialism (§ 1.2). To use Mill's (1859: 62) characterization of the two negations of despotism (or the government of all by one), individual freedom does not consist in the government of all by all, but in the 'government of each by himself'. A second conception of individual freedom which also involves a definitional connection with political life is the so-called 'freedom of the ancients'. According to Benjamin Constant's (1819: 275–6) famous distinction, the 'freedom of the ancients' consists in 'active and constant participation in collective power', whereas the 'freedom of the moderns' is but 'the peaceful enjoyment of private independence'.[30] Clearly, a society of active citizens may conceivably be a factual condition for the rise or viability of a free society in the sense implicit in the earlier discussion.[31] But it does not enter its definition any more than democracy does. If either of the two conceptions just mentioned is understood to characterize 'positive' freedom, the ideal of a free society, in what I take to be its most defensible interpretation, is definitely on the side of 'negative' freedom, of individual sovereignty, as opposed not just to collective sovereignty (societal freedom) but also to individual participation in collective sovereignty.[32]

1.5 Freedom to what ? *Duty, autonomy, and potential desire*

This choice is not without consequences—it excludes, for example, as we have seen, the a priori case for socialism discussed above—but it still leaves many options open, including some which have also been characterized in terms of 'negative' versus 'positive' freedom. For example, negative freedom is sometimes defined as *freedom from* some obstacle, while positive freedom is defined as *freedom to* do certain things. Such a contrast, however, does not make much sense, as the freedom *from* some obstacle (interference, impediment, prohibition, force, etc.) in the presence of which freedom vanishes is always also the freedom *to* perform some activities in the performance of which the exercise of freedom consists.[33] The only use for this distinction is to point out that the emphasis may be on the 'obstacle' side or the 'exercise' side of freedom, depending on the context. But in all its variants, freedom as individual sovereignty is both a freedom *from* and a freedom *to*.

A far more significant contrast comes to the fore as we ask what this freedom is supposed to be a freedom *to*, for all along we have been talking, when explicating the ideal of a free society, about its members being free *tout court*, rather than, say, free to snort, to flirt, or to shirk. What is meant, one may first conjecture, is their freedom to do anything they want to do. As Voltaire (1766) puts it: 'When I can do what I want, there is my freedom.' But this cannot be right. If freedom consists in not being prevented from doing what one wants to do, why could one not make someone freer by adjusting what she wants to what she has, rather than what she has to what she wants? On this definition, in other words, someone could be made free, or her freedom could be increased, through an appropriate manipulation of her preferences, whether by others or by herself. And although it cannot be ruled out that such manipulation may make the person happier, it is obviously counterintuitive to admit that it may also increase her freedom. Any characterization of a person's freedom that makes essential reference to her wants would seem to give rise to this 'contented-slave' objection.[34]

There are at least three ways in which one might try to solve this difficulty. One can plausibly be traced back to Rousseau (1762). A person's freedom, on this view, consists in her not being prevented from doing what she wants to do, but only on condition that what she wants to do is what she ought to do, to wit, serve the public interest or conform to the general will. If our freedom is to be increased, therefore, our tastes may not be changed in any arbitrary way in order to fit what we are not prevented from doing, but only in a way that makes them conform to this normative criterion. A free society is then a society in which no one is prevented—whether by internal inclinations or by external interference—from doing what she must. The conception of a free society that was implicit in our earlier discussion is clearly not of this normative type. It does not assert the existence of an analytical link between freedom and civic virtue. Indeed, the very appeal of the ideal of a free society is arguably rooted in the observation that people profoundly disagree about what counts as virtue or vice and in the conviction that they will keep doing so. Freedom, therefore, must be the freedom to do good or evil. Again, this does not rule out that there may be an instrumental link. One may conceivably make the case, as Machiavelli did, that people will not retain their individual freedom for long unless they display civic virtues.[35] But the (putative) empirical fact that people will soon be prevented from doing what they want to do unless they want to do (at least part of) what they ought to do is quite distinct from—and has no bearing on—the (alleged) conceptual fact that people are only free if they are not prevented from doing what they want to do *and* want to do what they ought to do.

There is a second way of ruling out that want-manipulation may increase freedom, which avoids any appeal to a normative criterion. It rests on the distinction between wants which are imposed and wants which are chosen by the person concerned. Freedom does not simply consist, on this view, in not being prevented from satisfying one's tastes. It also requires that one should have shaped these tastes oneself, rather than have them shaped, whether consciously or not, by outside agents. Freedom, in this sense, requires *autonomy*.[36] But this second strategy will not do either. For one thing, it still seems stuck with the following sort of counterintuitive implication: of two otherwise identical slave societies, the one whose slaves have adjusted to their miserable situation through deliberate character planning comes closer to the ideal of a free society than one in which slaves live under identical circumstances but remain discontented. More fundamentally, it faces a fatal dilemma. One can only choose one's wants on the basis of further, second-order wants. Hence, either one gets caught in an infinite regress, or one stops on the way by decreeing that some wants are 'authentic' and thereby reverts to the first, normative strategy.

The first and, to some extent, the second strategy just described can both be viewed as attempts to solve the 'contented-slave' problem by appealing to something that has sometimes been called 'positive freedom'.[37] There is a third strategy that can claim to remain true to the spirit of the 'negative-freedom' approach. It stipulates that being free consists in not being prevented from doing not just what one wants to do, but whatever one *might* want to do.[38] Want-manipulation, whether by the slaves themselves or by anyone else, on this view, cannot make a society of contented slaves any freer than an otherwise identical society. At the same time, this view allows us to discriminate between a society that prevents its members from doing something they would all like to do and one that prevents them from doing something no one could seriously want to do.[39] No doubt, the characterization of the counterfactual that defines what a person 'might want to do' needs to be refined—and it will be as we proceed. But the ideal of a free society that is being spelt out is now further clarified: the individual sovereignty by reference to which it is to be understood is the freedom to do whatever one might want to do.

1.6 Freedom from what? Two notions of coercion

Still, none of the clarifications adduced so far explains why the a priori argument for capitalism was rejected above. If we are to understand why this argument failed, we need to ask what obstacles count as freedom-restricting, what freedom consists in not being prevented *by*. The a priori case for capitalism, as we shall see, requires a narrow characterization of these obstacles, one that allows in particular for a sharp distinction between unfreedom and inability.

As mentioned earlier (§ 1.3), a minimal and pretty uncontroversial feature of anything that can be called a free society is a system of well-defined and effectively enforced property rights or entitlements (in the weaker sense of the term). No society can be free if its members can constantly be prevented from doing what they might want to do by the arbitrary use of force or threats. If this were the case, the freedom of its weaker members would unavoidably be small indeed. And a free society has been understood throughout as a society whose members are *all* free, or as free as possible. I shall in the sequel assume that whatever institutional set-up is being discussed satisfies this condition of rights security, and ask what set-up of this sort has the strongest claim to embodying the ideal of a society of free people. Though in one way very strong—never a thug in your street, never a thief in your bag—this condition is also very weak. It can in principle be satisfied, for example, by both slavery and collectivism, as these regimes have been defined.[40]

So, the next question is: what are the obstacles which the institutional framework of a free society should abolish, or at least minimize. One prominent issue—the key issue according to such authors as Hayek or Buchanan—is whether or not only *coercion* can count as a freedom-restricting obstacle. What is coercion? According to one prima-facie plausible account, coercion is the restriction of a person's opportunity set, relative to what she is legitimately entitled to. Coercing someone into doing (or not doing) something then consists in making her do (or not do) it by the use of force or threats, that is, by (credibly) suppressing from the range of options open to her some options she has a right to choose. Bullying someone in the street, threatening to take someone's life, to burn down her house, to tarnish her reputation by slander, or to jeopardize the promotion she is entitled to: these are all cases of coercion.[41] By defining coercion in this way, however, one fails to discriminate among different institutional set-ups that satisfy the security condition stated above. A non-coercive society in this sense is nothing but a society with a perfectly enforced system of rights. But it would—unacceptably—be consistent with a very repressive but law-abiding system of slavery.

Could then coercion not be interpreted, secondly, not as a constraint on people's actions stemming from the (threat of a) violation of whatever rights happen to prevail under a given institutional set-up, but rather, more broadly, as the (threat of a) transgression of a framework of rights which comprises the right of self-ownership?[42] And this is indeed a second element which the above discussion (§ 1.2) has explicitly recognized as an essential ingredient in the ideal of a free society. Note that self-ownership is here to be understood in a sense that is weak enough to be consistent with the impossibility of actually doing anything with oneself, owing, for example, to not being entitled to stand anywhere; but at the same time in a sense that is strong enough to exclude not just slavery or feudal bondages, but also compulsory schooling or military service and the imposition of lump-sum taxes on people's talents. I shall later take up the question of whether some restrictions of self-ownership may be justified for the sake of strengthening the other features of a free society, and there will be room for significant disagreements on this score. But that institutional restrictions of self-ownership are freedom-restricting is hard to dispute. The genuinely controversial issue is whether there is anything else, apart from coercion in the second and broader of the two senses just mentioned, that can be said to restrict freedom.

1.7 Formal freedom versus real freedom

Two positive answers to this question have featured in our earlier discussion (§ 1.3). The standard libertarian answer can be construed as further extending the concept of coercion (or of aggression) to cover institutional violations of pre-existing rights in external objects: 'The libertarian creed rests upon one central axiom: that no man or group of men may aggress against the person or property of anyone else' (Rothbard 1973: 23). But this position, it was argued above, degrades a genuine concern with people's freedom into an obsession with alleged natural rights, and only owes whatever prima-facie plausibility it may have to a confusion between the weak and the strong notion of entitlement. Another answer was suggested as an alternative to the libertarian view. It asserts that security and self-ownership, though necessary to freedom, are not sufficient for it, because doing anything requires the use of external objects which security and self-ownership alone cannot guarantee.

The move proposed in this second answer has been fiercely resisted by those among the advocates of pure capitalism who claim to give freedom a prominent place, whether or not they share the standard libertarian stance just recalled. Thus, Friedrich Hayek (1960: 17) complains about the 'confusion of liberty as power with liberty in its original meaning', which 'inevitably leads to the identification of liberty with wealth': 'whether or not I am my own master and can follow my own choice and whether the possibilities from which I must choose are many or few are two entirely different questions.' 'Even if the threat of starvation to me and perhaps to my family impels me to accept a distasteful job at a very low wage, even if I am "at the mercy" of the only man willing to employ me, I am not coerced by him or anybody else' (ibid. 137), nor therefore unfree, since freedom is nothing but freedom from coercion.[43] James Buchanan's formulation hardly differs: 'Whether or not an individual has the ability or power to undertake the activity that he is at liberty to undertake is a separate matter, and it can only confuse discussion to equate liberty with ability or power or to extend its meaning to include these qualities.' Freedom, he insists, is 'negative liberty': 'an individual is at liberty or free to carry on an activity if he or she is not coerced from so doing by someone else, be this an individual or a group.' According to proponents of a conception of what he calls 'positive liberty', on the other hand, 'if someone lacks the means to take a round-the-world cruise, then that person is not at liberty to take the cruise, even though no individual or institution is constraining such travel. We believe this to represent a serious conceptual confusion.'[44]

Thus, in the language of Hayek and Buchanan, (appropriately labelled) 'negative liberty' consists in the 'absence of constraint by individuals or institutions', whereas (misleadingly labelled) 'positive liberty' is a matter of power, ability, means, wealth, or size of the opportunity-set. As it stands, however, this distinction does not stick. It is, surely, the social institution of private property (or, as the case may be, of public property) that prevents those who 'lack the means' of taking a round-the-world cruise from getting on to the boat. Moreover, no refining of the definition could make nonsense of the following intuitions: if I am penniless, I am not really free to join the cruise; if I have no option but to starve or to accept a lousy job, I am not really free to turn the latter down. I shall call *opportunity* the third component of freedom which these examples point to. The exact nature of this component clearly requires further clarification, but no semantic trick, *à la* Hayek or Buchanan, should blind us to its existence.[45] I shall use the term *real freedom* to refer to a notion of freedom that incorporates all three components—security, self-ownership, and opportunity—in contrast to *formal freedom*, which only incorporates the first two.[46] Unlike the formal freedom, the opportunity, and hence the real freedom, to do whatever one might want to do can only be a matter of degree. The ideal of a free society must therefore be expressed as a society whose members are maximally free—in a sense to be specified shortly—rather than simply free.

It is worth emphasizing that the choice that has just been made amounts to selecting the broadest possible characterization of freedom-restricting obstacles consistent with the view that lacking freedom is being prevented from doing some of the things one might want to do (§ 1.5). Abstracting for the time being from the time dimension,[47] any restriction of the opportunity-set is relevant to the assessment of freedom. For example, I can lack the real freedom to swim across a lake despite my being the full owner of myself, not just because I would not be granted permission by the private owner of the lake, but also because my lungs or my limbs would give in before reaching the other side. And this would be the case whether or not this physical inadequacy resulted from deliberate action by other human beings, whether or not other human beings played any role in bringing it about, and also whether or not they could do anything to remove it now. Thus, the conception of real freedom presented above does not merely refuse to confine freedom-restricting obstacles to coercion—whether defined as self-ownership-violation or as right-violation. It also refuses to confine them to obstacles external to the person concerned, or to obstacles that are produced deliberately, indeed produced at all and/or removable by other human beings.[48]

The strongest objection against this broad definition of real freedom is that it fails to capture the important distinction between what I may and what I can, between prohibitions and incapacities. The objection is not only that the language of freedom has more intuitive appeal in the former context than in the latter. While some stretching undoubtedly needs doing, it does not need to reach beyond a recognizably grey area, in which using the word 'free' is still fully intelligible. Even stating that I am not free to travel faster than light is only slightly odd, if at all. More fundamentally, the objection appeals to the observation that what we are concerned with here is the institutional characterization of a free society, and that an institutional set-up is just a way of distributing 'mays', not 'cans'. Hence, stretching the concept of freedom to encompass both the permission dimension and the capacity dimension of the opportunity-set is pointless anyway, since it is only the former that is relevant to our enterprise. Thus formulated, the objection is useful but misguided. It is plainly wrong to assert that because an institutional set-up is a system of permissions, abilities are irrelevant to the task of determining which set-up has the most favourable impact on opportunity-sets. This is so, in part, because what I may is systematically affected by what I can. To illustrate, just think of the warning that appears on a board off Oxford's Magdalen Bridge in the early spring: 'Experienced punters only'. Less trivially, via our earning power, our personal abilities massively affect what we shall be permitted to acquire. Conversely, what I can—over more than the very short term—is systematically affected by what I may. Whether or not I shall stop limping depends on whether or not my wallet or the waiting list will allow me to have the operation I require. Indeed, whether I shall survive at all depends on my entitlements to shelter, food, and drink. Thus, even though only the permission dimension of the opportunity-set is directly affected by the selection of an institutional set-up, the strong two-way causal relation between permissions and abilities makes it altogether impossible to dismiss the ability dimension as irrelevant to the freedom-based choice of such a set-up.[49]

Note, finally, that, though very broad, the characterization of freedom-restricting obstacles that is being proposed is still narrower than some would like it to be. Personal abilities or talents are internal to the person, and it is therefore correct to say that it is possible for freedom, on this conception, to be restricted by internal as well as external obstacles. Moreover, the internal obstacles can take the form of preferences or desires. Addictions or tendencies to burst into fits of anger or to indulge in spiteful behaviour may genuinely reduce a person's ability to do whatever she might want to do, and the inability to resist such tendencies can therefore count as a freedom-restricting obstacle.[50] However, the class of desires that could therefore count as freedom-restricting according to the view of real freedom that is here being proposed does not include all desires that would be regarded as freedom-restricting if one of the 'positive' conceptions of freedom had been adopted (see § 1.5). For a desire to restrict a person's real freedom, it is not sufficient that it should not have been chosen by her. It must also be such that the person could not (sufficiently easily) get rid of it, if only she wanted to. Furthermore, for a desire to be real-freedom-restricting, it is of course not sufficient either (nor indeed necessary) that it should diverge from some normative view about what the person ought to desire. Thus, admitting that there can be internal, and even volitional, obstacles to real freedom as defined does not turn the latter into 'positive freedom' in either of the versions rejected above.[51]

1.8 Real-libertarianism

What is, then, a free society? It is a society whose members are all really free—or rather, as really free as possible. More precisely, it is a society that satisfies the following three conditions:

1. There is some well enforced structure of rights (*security*).
2. This structure is such that each person owns herself (*self-ownership*).
3. This structure is such that each person has the greatest possible opportunity to do whatever she might want to do (*leximin opportunity*).

This third condition is to be understood more precisely as follows: in a free society, the person with least opportunities has opportunities that are no smaller than those enjoyed by the person with least opportunities under any other feasible arrangement; in case there exists another feasible arrangement that is just as good for the person with least opportunities, then the next person up the scale in a free society must have opportunities no smaller than the second person up the scale of opportunities under this arrangement; and so on. I take it for granted that this leximin (or 'lexicographic maximin') formulation is better than either a purely aggregative formula (for example, in terms of the opportunities of society's average member) or a more egalitarian formula (for example, in terms of maximum equal opportunities) to express the idea that the members of a (maximally) free society are *all* as free *as possible*.[52]

A full characterization of this ideal of a free society would require, in addition, a specification of the standards by which conflicts between the three conditions should be settled. If one is to prevent most effectively the violation of rights, for example, one may have to restrict severely the self-ownership of some persons—for example, by arresting those suspected of having violated some rights, by imprisoning or even executing the convict—or to restrict more mildly the self-ownership of all—for example, by limiting the freedom of association in order to forestall terrorism or by imposing conscription in order to ward off external threats. Further, giving all the greatest possible opportunities might also conceivably, though not quite as plausibly, clash with a concern with the full enforcement of property rights. This would be the case if, for example, owing to some causal process (not as a matter of logical necessity), dramatically improving the fate of outcasts led to an erosion of their respect for the property of those remaining wealthier than they. Hence, if one wishes the condition of security to be as fully satisfied as possible, it is at least conceivable that one would have to violate both self-ownership and leximin opportunity.

Furthermore, there is no pre-established harmony between the latter two conditions. Clashes can take very different forms. Some (paternalistic) violations of full self-ownership, such as compulsory primary education, the compulsory wearing of seat-belts, or the prohibition of hard drugs, are meant to expand or protect, be it probabilistically, the opportunity-set of the very person whose self-ownership is being infringed. In other cases, such as compulsory vaccination against infectious diseases, or compulsory recruitment to help prevent a dam from bursting under the pressure of a flood, or the obligation to help a person in danger when the risk to oneself is small, it is the opportunity-set of other people that is being protected or expanded, be it again probabilistically, by the restriction of self-ownership. In other cases again, the conflict appears only under very specific empirical hypotheses. Suppose, for example, that, in the absence of a legal obligation to vote, the proportion of poor people voting is considerably less than if there were such an obligation. Under such circumstances, political platforms will display less concern for the opportunities of the worst off, and the outcome of the political process will systematically diverge from what the leximinning of opportunities would require. Or suppose that, in the absence of a strict prohibition on having more than two children, the population would keep expanding at such a pace that the scarcity of natural resources would make life hardly bearable for the next generation. Under these various circumstances, how can our ideal of a free society arbitrate between the conflicting claims of self-ownership and leximin opportunity?

As they have only little bearing on the argument of the rest of this book—which will concentrate on the opportunity dimension—I shall not discuss these complex issues in any detail. As a rough conjecture, let me just state that a free society should give a priority to security over self-ownership, and to self-ownership over leximin opportunity. But this priority is of a *soft* kind. It does not amount to a rigid lexicographic priority. More specifically, mild disturbances of law and order can be tolerated if getting rid of them would require major restrictions of self-ownership or major departures from leximin opportunity. Thugs and thieves are terrible for freedom, not least of the most vulnerable. But a police state or abysmal poverty is not a price worth paying in order to get rid of every one of them. Further, mild restrictions of self-ownership (which I take to include all those mentioned in the previous two paragraphs) can be incorporated into the institutional framework of a free society if a good case can be made to the effect that a major improvement would result in terms of leximin opportunity. The (rough) metrics which are here being presupposed (what is 'major' and what is 'mild') are clearly in need of further clarification.[53] But there is enough work ahead that does not hinge on the solution of this problem for me to feel free to say no more on the subject and simply to summarize the three conditions and the priority relations among them by means of the following formula.

A free society is one in which people's opportunities are being leximinned *subject to* the protection of their formal freedom, that is, the respect of a structure of rights that incorporates self-ownership. This, in turn, I shall further abbreviate by saying that a free society, as characterized by the three conditions and their articulation, is one that *leximins real freedom* or, more roughly still, one that realizes *real-freedom-for-all* (a phrase I shall often use as a convenient shorthand). And I shall call *real-libertarian* the view that conceives of a just society as a free society in this sense. It does not follow that, for a real-libertarian, the extent to which a society is a good society is determined exactly by the extent to which it is a free society. Justice may be only one of many desirable properties of a society. Perhaps one should depart from strict or maximal justice, for example, if doing so would enable us to make social relations more fraternal. What will be attempted here, however, is to work out and defend a conception of justice while abstracting from the other properties of a society that may be desirable for reasons that do not reduce to their contribution to social justice. And this can only be worthwhile if justice is assumed to be, if not the only property that matters to assessing how good an institutional set-up is, at least one that enjoys some priority over other desirable properties. The real-libertarian conception of justice will be defended here on the background of a view of the good society which ascribes to justice, again, a soft lexicographic priority. I shall argue later that there is generally little to gain, in terms of other desirable objectives, from a departure from maximal real-libertarian justice, but if and when there is a genuine trade off, the priority claim means that it is only when major gains in terms of other properties can be bought with negligible departures from leximin real freedom that injustice is admissible.

We know already, from the discussion of the previous sections, that the real-libertarian position thus characterized does not warrant an a priori case for either pure capitalism (§ 1.3) or pure socialism (§ 1.2). What institutional implications it does have—and in particular whether capitalism or socialism must be a real-libertarian's favourite—is the question I shall address as from the next chapter. However, the general outline of the position is already definite enough to allow us to locate it relative to a number of rival positions. For example, if 'left' is defined by the degree to which a position caters for the interests of the least advantaged, real-libertarianism is well to the left of so-called 'left libertarianism', which insists that an equal distribution of land or of the value of natural resources should constrain voluntary transactions. Although land may be, in some societies, a major determinant of the real freedom that real-libertarianism wants to have leximinned, a real-libertarian demands far more, on behalf on the least advantaged, than an equal access to the value of land. On the other hand, real-libertarianism remains a long distance from straightforward egalitarianism, for three distinct reasons. First, it imposes formal freedom—the respect of a structure of rights that incorporates self-ownership—as a constraint on any equalization exercise. Secondly, it focuses on opportunities, on feasible sets, rather than on the outcomes measured, for example, in terms of income or welfare of people's choices among the options open to them. Finally, it does not demand that the least-advantaged should be given a worst deal for the sake of more equality. Real-libertarianism is not satisfied as long as those with least opportunities can point to another feasible formal-freedom-respecting arrangement in which they would have greater opportunities, while no one would have opportunities as poor as theirs currently are. This indicates in what sense any remaining inequality must be justifiable, on a real-libertarian view, to those who feel they are getting a bad deal. But, however justifiable, undeserved inequalities of opportunities will remain.[54]

Each of these three restrictions describes a major departure from unqualified egalitarianism. At the same time, their conjunction specifies the way in which real-libertarianism interprets the *equal concern* for everyone's interests, which it shares with other so-called left-liberal, or liberal-egalitarian, or, as I shall prefer to call them, *solidaristic* conceptions of justice.[55] As clearly shown by the rejection of various 'positive' interpretations of freedom, real-libertarianism further shares with these conceptions—as well as with standard libertarianism—the general postulate of neutrality or of *equal respect*, that is, the view that what counts as a just society should not be determined on the basis of some particular substantive conception of the good life.[56] This *liberal* or anti-perfectionistic postulate will be taken for granted in most of the arguments to follow. I do not wish to deny that this is a strong normative assumption. But I do not believe that our societies currently meet, nor will ever meet again, the conditions that are required to lend any plausibility to a perfectionistic conception of justice.[57]

In the light of what has just been said, real-libertarianism can be viewed, along with other left-liberal positions, as an attempt to articulate the importance we ascribe to liberty, equality, and efficiency. Liberty comes in through the postulate of neutrality, through the constraint of self-ownership (or fundamental liberties and the like), and through a concern, not directly with people's happiness itself, but with the means required to pursue it. And equality and efficiency are combined in the leximin criterion. Though the latter cannot be correctly described—as it sometimes is—as the most egalitarian criterion compatible with efficiency, it does constitute, among all criteria compatible with efficiency, the one that is most heavily biased in favour of the victims of whatever inequalities are allowed to subsist.[58] Real-libertarianism, thus situated, therefore holds a serious promise of accommodating our twofold point of departure: our capitalist societies are replete with unacceptable inequalities, and freedom is of paramount importance. Indeed, one way of summing up the path that led us to it is by saying: 'If you seriously believe in both these claims, then real-libertarianism is what you should go for.' But is real-libertarianism, on close inspection, consistent with our well-considered judgements? And does it instruct us to resume, on renewed foundations, the old struggle against capitalism, or does it end up justifying (some form) of the latter? Both these questions now require us to turn to a careful examination of its institutional implications.

CHAPTER 2

———

The highest sustainable basic income

PROLOGUE

Δ *To understand what real-freedom-for-all truly means, and to be able to assess what it is worth, it is essential to spell out its specific institutional implications. So, what follows from it?*

Φ Most strikingly, an unconditional income for all. This answer needs to be clarified and qualified in various ways, but the prima-facie argument behind it can be conveyed very simply. If real freedom is a matter of means, not only of rights, people's incomes are obviously of great importance. But the real freedom we are concerned with is not only the freedom to purchase or consume. It is the freedom to live as one might like to live. Hence the importance of granting this purchasing power irrespective of people's work or willingness to work (§ 2.1).

Δ *Does this amount to justifying a basic income, in the sense in which this term has recently been used in Western Europe to refer to a radical reform of the welfare state?*

Φ Not entirely, for 'basic income' usually refers to an income that is unconditional not only relative to people's willingness to work, but also relative to their income from other sources (this is the essential difference with a negative income tax), their place of residence, and their household situation. But real-freedom-for-all can also be shown to generate a presumption in favour of unconditionality along these further dimensions. Consequently, there is, as you are suggesting, a close connection between the conception of justice I am advocating and the demand for the introduction of a basic income (§ 2.2).

Δ *At what level does justice (as you conceive it) require that this basic income be pitched?*

Φ The 'basic' of basic income is only meant to convey the image of a basis to which all other incomes can be added. Basic income is therefore not definitionally tied to some notion of 'basic needs'. How high should it be? Suppose for a moment that people do not significantly differ in their abilities.

If the real freedom of those with least real freedom is to be maximized, then the basic income must be pitched at the highest sustainable level, subject to the protection of everyone's formal freedom. Both incentive and ecological effects must of course be incorporated into the relevant notion of sustainability, and sustainable basic income maximization then provides us with a simple criterion for assessing alternative socio-economic regimes (§ 2.3).

D *You seem to be thinking of this basic income as a cash grant. But surely free access to tools, health care, or public parks also enhances a person's real freedom.*

Φ I am not denying this. With a market economy in place, a concern with maximum individual freedom generates a presumption in favour of cash. But this presumption can be overturned, for example because a particular type of good—say, breathable air or access to streets—is unanimously wanted and cheaper to deliver free of charge. Achieving the greatest possible real freedom for all may therefore require a significant fraction of the basic income to be given in kind (§ 2.4).

Δ *If you are serious about maximizing freedom, should you not give the equal grant each is entitled too 'at the start' as it were, rather than paternalistically—and unfairly to those who happen to die young—spread more or less homogeneously over people's lifetimes? Surely, you cannot just reply that, since people can freely borrow, the two formulas are equivalent. You know how imperfect capital markets are, and you may anyway not want people to mortgage their future stream of basic income.*

Φ I don't have a neat answer—and don't believe there is one. On the one hand, I firmly believe that a society of really free people could not countenance a crowd of elderly destitutes who are paying a heavy price for squandering their one-off basic endowments decades ago. On the other hand, I don't think this reasoning forces us absurdly to assert that ideally people should cash their basic income second by second. Monthly instalments seem a suitable compromise. Arbitrary no doubt, but sensible enough for my taste (§ 2.5).

Δ *Let me now try to spell out a more fundamental worry that has been bothering me from the start about the straight connection you establish between freedom and an income. To keep things simple, suppose people have no other income than their basic income. Assuming they do not have identical tastes, they will choose different bundles of goods. With these bundles, they will be able to do different things. Yet you seem to find it obvious that they all have the* same *real freedom. But how can you be so confident? If the prices were changed, people could buy different amounts of goods with unchanged incomes. The content of some people's bundles would expand, that of others would shrink, and the set of options open to them would correspondingly be affected. Yet you would still have to say, I presume, that they have the same real freedom (§ 2.6).*

Φ Part of the difficulty you rightly stress stems from the fact that 'real-freedom-for-all' is in a way a misnomer—though such a good one that I have decided to keep it. It is not really the size or extent of their real freedom that real-freedom-for-all requires just institutions to maximize for the worst off. It is rather the endowment of means or resources that form the substratum of this real freedom. To be able to say that one of these endowments is larger than or equal to another, one needs a metric, a measuring rod. The most appropriate one is provided by the competitive market prices that emerge from free choices on the basis of equal entitlements.

Δ *Why?*

Φ Because they can plausibly be said to reflect the opportunity cost of the components of each bundle, that is, how precious they are to society or how costly it is to other people not to be able to appropriate them. So, I am not denying that the bundles which an equal basic income gives access to and consequently the 'extent' of the real freedom associated with the basic income vary with the price structure. But the choice of the price structure is not arbitrary. And this fact makes it meaningful to maximize the real freedom of the worst off, understood as the value, using the metric of competitive prices, of the resource basis available to those with least resources (§ 2.7). I realize this is rather abstract, and I suspect I have not found the best way of explaining it. But I trust that if you think this through for yourself, you will see that it goes to the heart of what was rightly bothering you.

Δ *This may solve the problem of comparing (the external-resource basis of) real freedom across individuals in the same society. But it is no less essential, if one wishes to maximize the real freedom of the worst off, to be able to make comparisons across societies.*

Φ Or at least across socio-economic regimes. Our question is not whether one society is better than another in terms of real-freedom-for-all, but only—fortunately—which socio-economic regime would be better from this angle for a given society. The latter question is still a difficult question, but quite a bit easier than the former, and conceptually no more problematic than that of assessing the impact of various courses of action on a country's gross national product, for example (§ 2.8).

2.1 A radical suggestion

What, then, is the best institutional expression of the ideal captured by the slogan 'real-freedom-for-all'? One is really free, as opposed to just formally free, to the extent that one possesses the means, not just the right, to do whatever one might want to do. When arguing against this conception of freedom, Hayek and Buchanan, as we have seen (§ 1.7), were more specific: if one abandons their own, narrower, definition of freedom, one is bound to slip into equating the latter with wealth or the budget-set. This prompts the suggestion that real-freedom-for-all requires us to leximin people's purchasing power, subject of course to respecting everyone's formal freedom. Put bluntly, our ideal requires us to raise the lowest incomes as much as is compatible with a ban on forced labour.

But let us be very careful here. The real freedom we need to be concerned with is not just the real freedom to choose among the various bundles of goods one might wish to consume. It is the real freedom to choose among the various lives one might wish to lead. Stressing this distinction does not deprive income, or the budget-set, of its importance. But it makes it crucially important that the income should be given unconditionally to each citizen, no strings attached, that is, without any constraint other than her budget on not only what she may buy, but also on how she may use her time. Hence the following, far more radical suggestion. If we are serious about pursuing real-freedom-for-all—and if we are willing to abstract for the moment both from dynamic considerations and from interpersonal differences in abilities—what we have to go for is the highest *unconditional* income for all consistent with security and self-ownership.

This is a radical suggestion indeed, not only relative to the libertarians' and their close kin's desperate groping for a narrow concept of freedom, but also relative to the standard social-democratic stance, so concerned with the real freedom to consume as abundantly as one might wish that they lose sight of the real freedom to live as unconventionally as one might fancy. In other quarters, the suggestion may be found more congenial. For example, it can be viewed as reflecting in the most straightforward fashion a key component of the old critique of capitalism by 'scientific' and 'utopian' socialism alike: the revolt against proletarian subjection to the wage relationship, and hence to the capitalists' rule. And it is also in tune with the more recent 'green' and 'alternative' movements' emphasis on quality of life, self-realization, and the preservation of interpersonal relations free of monetary considerations, in contrast to the satisfaction of material desires thanks to a career geared to making as much money as possible. It only encompasses these concerns, however, to the extent compatible with a liberal or anti-perfectionistic standpoint (see § 1.8). What the suggested institutional set-up is intended to do is not to discourage as much as possible waged labour or a career-dominated existence, but to do as much as can be done in order to provide everyone with a genuine opportunity to make different choices.[1] Real-libertarians can side with the old critics of alienation or the new advocates of alternative lifestyles, but only to the extent that their demands require no perfectionistic premiss, no superiority claim on behalf of one particular conception of the good life. If it is true that societies such as ours are heavily biased the other way, this extent can be very large.

As it happens, the suggestion just made converges with a proposal for social policy reform that has recently been gaining ground in a number of European countries.[2] Most of these countries introduced some form of minimum guaranteed income scheme at some point since the Second World War. Such a scheme differs from a social insurance scheme to the extent that its beneficiaries need not have contributed to it out of their past earnings in order to be entitled to benefit from it. But the form of guaranteed income that has been introduced in those countries typically remains conditional in the following respects. (1) To be entitled to the benefit, the beneficiary must, if she is not either working or unable to work, be willing to accept a suitable job, or to undergo suitable training, if offered. (2) She must pass a means test, in the sense that she is only entitled to the benefit if there are good grounds to believe that she has no access to a sufficient income from other sources. (3) Whether she is entitled to a benefit and how high the latter is depends on her household situation—for example, on whether she lives on her own, with a person who has a job, with a jobless person, etc. And finally (4) whether she is entitled to a benefit and how high the latter is depend on her place of residence, on whether she lives, for example, in a metropolitan area, in a provincial town, or in the country.

On the other hand, proposals for what has been variously called a state bonus, a national or social dividend, a citizen's income or wage, a demogrant, a universal grant, a basic income, etc., have typically been proposals for a form of guaranteed minimum income that takes the form of an equal payment to all full members of society, whether or not these four conditions are met. Note that full membership, here, is not meant to involve a restriction to citizens of the country concerned. A sufficient length of legal residence is generally regarded as the key criterion. But full members are supposed to be adults. In most proposals, children either fall under a different scheme or their parents or guardians are entitled on their behalf to reduced amounts. Note, too, that the proponents of such unconditional guaranteed income schemes may but generally do not propose them as full substitutes for existing conditional transfers. For example, most of them want to keep—usually in simplified forms and at reduced levels—state-funded social insurance and disability compensation schemes that supplement the unconditional income in a way that remains conditional in some or all of these senses. Indeed, as long as the unconditional income does not cover what they regard as basic needs, most of its proponents would not want to eliminate even the existing conditional minimum income schemes.

Because it is the expression that is now most widely used, in international discussions at any rate, I shall use the term 'basic income' to refer to a transfer scheme that is unconditional in the four senses mentioned above, whether or not it is meant to be supplemented by conditional schemes. A *basic income*, in other words, is an income paid by the government to each full member of society (1) even if she is not willing to work, (2) irrespective of her being rich or poor, (3) whoever she lives with, and (4) no matter which part of the country she lives in. The choice of the expression is meant to convey the idea that, owing to its unconditional nature, we here have something on which a person can safely count, a material foundation on which a life can firmly rest, and to which any other income, whether in cash or in kind, from work or savings, from the market or the State, can legitimately be added. On the other hand, there is nothing in the definition of basic income, as it is here understood, to connect it to some notion of basic needs. A basic income, as defined, can fall short of or exceed what is regarded as necessary to a decent existence.[3]

2.2 Unconditionality and real freedom

In this light, it is tempting to rephrase the radical suggestion made earlier by stating simply that what a real-libertarian should endorse is the formal-freedom-respecting institutional framework that yields the highest basic income.[4] Before being able to assert this equivalence with any confidence, however, we must check whether a concern with real-freedom-for-all can justify all four of the unconditionalities that define a basic income. So far, only the first of these—the absence of a constraint on the use of one's time in the form of a restriction of the benefit to those willing to accept employment or training—has been explicitly linked to the concern with real-freedom-for-all. What about the other three?

What is involved in the second one—the absence of a means test—is essentially the choice between an (*ex ante*) basic income and an (*ex post*) negative income-tax scheme. At first sight, both approaches may seem equivalent from a real-libertarian standpoint, since exactly the same distributions of post-tax-and-transfer income can in principle be achieved with a basic income scheme and a negative income tax. Or, if there is a difference, it should be to the advantage of the latter, since what it does is simply to avoid the heavy to-and-fro that results from paying a basic income to those with a substantial income and then taxing it back, and this should make a negative income-tax scheme cheaper to run. (The Appendix to this chapter depicts graphically the difference between the two types of scheme, and the difference between both and existing guaranteed income schemes.)

And yet, the absence of a means test gives basic income a decisive advantage in terms of leximin real freedom, for three distinct reasons. First, it is obvious enough, given the time-lag unavoidably involved in any income assessment for tax purposes, that a negative income-tax scheme can only hope to compete with a basic income scheme in terms of leximin real freedom if it is supplemented by a system of advance payments that will at least give people the real freedom not to starve while waiting for the tax administration to calculate their entitlements. But sheer ignorance or confusion is bound to prevent some people from getting access to advance payments they could have claimed. The higher rate of take up that is therefore bound to be associated with a basic income scheme is a difference that matters supremely when prior importance is being given to the real freedom of the least really free.

Secondly, in the case of a negative income tax, the relevant feature of the budget-set takes the form of a contingent promise of corrective transfers rather than of a sum of money on which one can fully bank simply because it is tangibly there. This fact is bound to hamper the confidence needed to actually to make use of the options contained in the (abstractly identical) budget-set. One aspect of this difference relates directly to an important dimension of the 'unemployment trap' to which social workers are usually far more sensitive than economists. What deters people in the poverty trap from looking for a job or taking one is arguably less that they would not have a higher income, or a significantly higher income, at work than out of work, but even more the liquidity gap and the uncertainty involved in renouncing a safe and regular benefit as a result of taking up a job which they may soon prove unable to keep or to bear.[5]

Finally, in an era of computerized transfer payments and pay-as-you-earn tax collection, *and* assuming that there is no need for control on some other grounds (to check work-proneness or household situation, for example), the administrative costs involved in the advance payment scheme that must be coupled to a negative income-tax system make the latter more expensive to run for any given level of income guarantee, and they therefore absorb resources that could otherwise be used to swell this level. Even on its own, this consideration would suffice, given present tax and transfer technologies, to justify the choice for the universal over the means-tested variant of an otherwise unconditional income.[6]

Note that the question of the means test is orthogonal to the question of whether or not the scheme involves an unemployment trap, in the standard economic sense of a strongly dissuasive effective rate of taxation on low earnings. As linear negative income-tax schemes illustrate (see Appendix), a means test does not necessarily involve a higher rate of taxation (or of 'clawback') in the lower ranges of the income distribution. And as some (rather unusual) basic income proposals show, it is perfectly conceivable to have an *ex ante* payment of the minimum income to all with a 100 per cent tax rate on all incomes below some threshold.[7] If one is concerned with the real freedom to work as well as the freedom not to work, would it not be better to exclude this possibility in the very definition of basic income? No, it would not. For factual reasons, it may of course be the case, indeed it is likely to be the case, that a tax schedule which involves the total confiscation of low earnings will not durably secure the highest sustainable yield. But concern with the real freedom to work does not force us to define the maximizing exercise so as to rule this out a priori. The real freedom to accept a low-paid job one would like to take, whether because of its intrinsic appeal or because of the training or experience it provides, is unambiguously increased as the level of the unconditional income goes up. Indeed, the higher the latter, the more one acquires the real freedom to take, be it for a short period, even jobs which pay a negative net wage. Consequently, for basic income adequately to reflect the freedom to work as well as the freedom not to work, no such restriction needs to be made about the way it is funded. Hence, unlike the trap stemming from the means test, the trap stemming from high effective tax rates is not and need not be ruled out by the very definition of basic income.

What does enter the definition of basic income formulated above is the requirement that the right to it and its level should be insensitive to household situation and place of residence. Can this requirement be justified from a real-libertarian perspective? One might think that it can because of the invasions into people's privacy which would be mandated if where and with whom people live were relevant to the determination of their entitlement. But any transfer system demands that one should at least be able to control whether the beneficiary exists and is a resident of the country, and there is arguably no fundamental difference between the obligation to provide this minimal information and the obligation to provide the more detailed information about one's residence that would be required by a more selective or differentiated transfer system. The decisive objection against the latter is rather that there is no positive reason for differentiation consistent with a real-libertarian standpoint. It may, of course, be the case that what one needs when living alone far exceeds what one needs when living in a commune, or that what one needs when living in the capital city far exceeds what one needs when living in a remote hamlet. But from a real-libertarian standpoint, this is irrelevant. What a real-libertarian is concerned to leximin, remember, is not the real freedom to get what a person happens to want, or what she needs in order to maintain her way of life. It is the real freedom to do what she might want to do. It is therefore enough to assume—innocuously enough—that someone living in a commune *might* wish to live alone, or that dwellers of the countryside *might* want to settle in the city, for a uniform, undiscriminating basic income to be the obvious choice.[8]

2.3 Sustainability

So, at least if one still abstracts from interpersonal differences in abilities, one cannot be serious about maximizing real freedom for all without being led to take seriously the idea of a maximal basic income, of the highest unconditional income (in all four senses of 'unconditional' specified above) that could be paid to all full members of the society concerned. If it proves robust, this idea would then offer a simple criterion for the real-libertarian evaluation of competing socio-economic regimes, that is, of the aspects of a society's institutional set-up that regulates the production and distribution of material resources. For any given society, formal-freedom-respecting socio-economic regimes could then simply be ranked according to the level of basic income they would sustainably provide. Sustainability is obviously an essential consideration. If we are concerned with the real freedom of *all*, it is clearly inadmissible to give away society's wealth now, in the form of a lavish basic income, at the expense of economic collapse tomorrow.

This concern with sustainability requires, first of all, that one should pay attention to incentives. The fact that a basic income has been introduced and is expected to remain in place, and the fact that it is being financed, and will keep being financed, in a particular way are bound to have significant effects—since it is required that people should own themselves—on the supply of both labour time and labour effort, and also—to the extent that capital is privately owned—on the supply of savings and investment.[9] This suggests that, for any given type of socio-economic regime, one should select the structure of (explicit or implicit) taxation that can durably generate the highest yield, and that the tax rates should be pitched at a level corresponding to the peak of the associated 'Laffer hyperplane', that is, to the highest tax yield that can be durably generated under this type of regime.[10]

This suggestion takes for granted that, once appropriate deductions are made for the sake of formal freedom, a higher tax yield necessarily means a higher basic income. But what is relevant to leximin real freedom is, of course, the per capita level of basic income, which is affected not just by the total tax yield but also by the number of people between whom it has to be shared. We therefore also need to take demographic effects into account. If an increase in the basic income leads to population expansion, the highest sustainable tax yield may only manage to finance a declining basic income. I have already referred above (§ 2.1) to the possibility that those who are less than full members of the society concerned—children—may get a reduced basic income. One may also wish to introduce the possibility that full members may receive a higher amount as from a certain age, the same for all. This would provide manœuvring room to fine-tune the implementation of our criterion of sustainable basic income maximization without restricting the formal freedom to procreate. In some societies at least, giving a comparatively higher basic income in the form of a universal pension (thus reducing the need for children as a form of old age insurance) and giving a comparatively lower one in the form of universal child benefits (thus increasing the net cost of having children) should not only significantly reduce, but may even offset completely, or reverse, any positive effect a basic income may otherwise have on population growth.[11] A somewhat more nuanced formulation will therefore express more accurately the key idea: under a given type of socio-economic regime, the optimal choice, in terms of tax rates and basic income differentiation, is the one that can durably sustain, as far as one can predict, the highest average basic income.[12] In most of what follows, however, I shall ignore this nuance and keep speaking, more simply, of the highest sustainable basic income.

How high this highest sustainable level can be expected to be is, of course, most likely to be affected by many features of a socio-economic regime apart from the structure and levels of its tax rates or the age differentiation of the basic income. One such feature is the productive potential associated to the regime, that is, the profile of the productivity of human labour once the regime is in place. Other things being equal, if a given level of basic income is to be sustainable, it is essential that this productive potential should not shrink over time. Given the unavoidable depletion of natural resources, this implies that there must be some technological progress and/or net accumulation of physical or human capital, in order to prevent the fall in productivity that would otherwise occur as a result of having to use natural resources that are harder to extract or less convenient to process. This amounts to a criterion of intergenerational justice of a familiar type, which only requires the next generation not to be worse off than the present one, *not* that it should be made better off as a result of the present generation's efforts just as the present generation has been made better off (or so it is generally assumed) as a result of the efforts of previous ones.[13]

On this view, there can, of course, be an expansion of society's productive potential from one generation to the next, and hence an increase in the highest sustainable level of the grant. But this should then be a by-product of the present generation's self-interested activity, or perhaps of its concern with making *sure* enough was left for the next generation, not the direct fulfilment of a requirement of justice. Nor does the criterion require that each member of the present generation should compensate individually for her contribution to the depletion of the natural resources. Its satisfaction is left to the aggregation of people's self-interested individual choices within a framework that creates adequate incentives. Yet, the real-libertarian perspective imposes stricter constraints than the criterion of (aggregate) intergenerational justice it implies. The compensatory contributions must be consistent with everyone in the present generation getting the highest sustainable basic income, and they must benefit everyone in the next generation in the form of a basic income that is at least equal to the present one.

In this light, it is easy to understand that a socio-economic regime which does not take precautions to slow down the depletion of society's natural resources may find itself at a disadvantage compared to one which does. In order to maintain its productive potential once the depletion of natural resources starts biting, it will have to induce a higher rate of accumulation than would otherwise be necessary, at the expense of a higher basic income. Also, we can now see why a socio-economic regime that generates faster technical progress or faster accumulation, with a given rate of depletion of natural resources *and* a given level basic income, can hope to be at an advantage, relative to one which performs less well in this respect. This is not so because growth as such is valued, or because the basic income of later generations is thereby allowed to be higher: the option for a leximin criterion makes such considerations irrelevant. Rather, a superior propensity towards a net increase in productive potential at a given level of basic income makes room for a higher sustainable level of basic income from the present generation onwards.[14]

We thus seem equipped with a simple and handy tool for assessing the merits of competing socio-economic regimes, one that neatly encapsulates the commitments to freedom, equality, and efficiency which real-libertarianism consists in articulating. In particular, it may seem that we now have all or nearly all we need to return to our initial question and have a fresh look at the old contest between capitalism and socialism.

I believe we do. But you may not, because you may have against my simple real-libertarian criterion one or more of the many objections that could be and have been made to it. In the rest of this chapter and in the next two, I shall tackle a number of challenges to the criterion as an adequate operational expression of real-freedom-for-all. In Chapter 5, I shall deal with attacks against the real-libertarian stance itself on the assumption that the criterion expresses it adequately. And it is only in the final chapter that I shall be in a position to return, with the clarity and confidence gained in the course of this long preliminary discussion, to the question of capitalism versus socialism.

2.4 Cash or kind?

A first query that may be and has been raised about the criterion presented above is why it is so obvious that the opportunity dimension of real freedom granted to everyone should be secured through a monetary income, rather than through a grant in kind. The concepts of wealth and income can easily be defined at a level of abstraction sufficient to ensure that they apply to non-monetary and monetary economies alike. Nothing said so far, therefore, entails that the grant should be given as a purchasing power expressed in some currency rather than as an endowment of land or tools or a bundle of goods and services. It is, of course, true that unless exactly identical bundles are given to all, one needs to use some currency in order to value and compare the various bundles and make sure the basic income is (roughly) the same for all. This makes it natural to think of the basic income in monetary terms. But it does not follow that the grant should be given in cash rather than in kind. Should it?

The question is well worth asking, if only because some have forcefully asserted that what a truly free society requires is that each individual should be provided, not with cash, but with (equal, or perhaps leximin, amounts of) means of production.[15] Suppose, then, that in one situation all individuals are given equal amounts of the currency, which they can use as they please, while in another, otherwise identical situation, they are each given a bundle of means of production reckoned to be equal to the cash grant of the first situation. Is there any reason for believing that the second situation may better meet the criterion of leximin real freedom than the first one? It is hard to see what this could be, for *either* the means of production are tradable against other goods or services, and then the second situation is just a clumsy variant of the first one, *or* they are not so tradable, and then, as soon as producing with the means of production they are allotted is not the only thing people 'might want to do', the second situation is bound to be inferior on two grounds. First, assuming the level of the grant to be given, this very restriction on what they can use it for implies a lesser real freedom for the people concerned. Secondly, assuming (plausibly) that not all are equally efficient at managing the means of production they are provided with, a waste is bound to occur, making the highest sustainable level of the grant lower than it could be if purchasing power were distributed instead, thus leaving the keener or more efficient to get hold of a larger share of the means of production. Only a neglect of the wide range of things people might want to do or the granting of a question-begging privilege to the freedom to work with one's own tools can support a real-libertarian case for focusing on productive wealth.[16]

On the other hand, it is important, if a basic income is to be the appropriate embodiment of real freedom to do whatever one might want to do, that it should boost, among other things, the real freedom to acquire and use means of production. And this it can do, in part, precisely because it is given in cash rather than in the form of non-tradable food vouchers or housing grants, for example, and because therefore any part of it that exceeds the barest current needs can be used to build up productive wealth by those keen enough to do so. More importantly, because of its *ex ante* nature, a basic income reduces the personal risk involved in individual or co-operative entrepreneurship—the risk of being unable to feed oneself and one's family in a dignified way as the business is being launched or experiences ups and downs.[17] For this reason, the granting of a substantial basic income is more germane to the access to 'active' property associated with Rawls's ideal of a 'property-owning democracy' than to the *ex post* corrective redistribution which he views as characteristic of the welfare state.[18]

That there is no good reason to give the grant in the form of means of production does not imply that it must be given entirely in cash. It can easily be argued that at least three categories of goods could be given in kind consistently with real-libertarianism. A first category can be derived from the requirements of formal freedom. Police and courts, an effective military or civil defence against external threats, adequate mechanisms for collective decision-making at the various territorial levels, are all services that can legitimately be provided to each member of society, irrespective of whether or not she expresses her willingness to pay for them. Even though they are aiming at protecting her sheer right to live the way she wishes to live, not at providing her with the means for doing so, such services form part of the income that real-libertarianism demands should be unconditionally provided to every full member of society and constitute, therefore, an in-kind portion of their legitimate basic income. In the sequel, however, whenever I shall speak of maximizing the level of basic income, I shall mean the part of the unconditional income that is not justified by this prior concern for formal freedom.[19] Real-freedom-for-all consists in leximinning people's opportunities on the background of a well-enforced structure of self-ownership-protecting rights, and expenditure on the latter cannot be counted as a contribution to the former.

The second category consists of a number of items which are not called forth by the protection of formal freedom but which a real-libertarian perspective requires should be provided free, or at a subsidized rate, because of the positive externalities on everyone's opportunities that can be expected from making them freely or more easily available to all. Some of the funding of education or of infrastructure, for example, can conceivably be justified in this way. The argument is not that everyone wants to consume them at the level provided. Even if only a fraction of society were interested in consuming them assuming they had to pay the full cost, diverting public funds to finance such items (without 'compensation' for those less interested) would none the less be legitimate from a real-libertarian standpoint, to the extent that it would foster productivity to such an extent that the net effect on the highest level of basic income the society could durably afford would be positive.[20] The nature and level of free or subsidized provision that can be justified in this way are debatable. But here is, none the less, another powerful reason why the leximinning of real freedom may require the universal provision of some in-kind income. Once again, however, when later on I shall speak of maximizing the level of basic income, I shall have to mean the part of the unconditional income that is not justified merely by this indirect contribution to everyone's opportunities. An in-kind unconditional income justified exclusively in this way may be part of the optimal socioeconomic regime, but it is not part of the standard by which this optimality is to be assessed.

The same cannot be said of the third category, which consists of items of which it is plausible to assume that no one in her right mind might not want to buy them out of her basic income were she given the whole of it in cash.[21] Not all such items (on a sufficiently coarse-grained classification of items) can be legitimately distributed in kind. For example, although clothes and shelter, drink and food are no doubt indispensable whatever one might wish to do with one's life, there is such variation in both the nature of what the members of a society such as ours actually want in these areas, and in the amounts they are willing to spend on it, that the real-libertarian presumption in favour of cash remains unshaken. However, there are other items with respect to which this presumption has to give way, not because the homogeneity of people's desires resists closer scrutiny, but because of the cost of making individuals pay for the amount each would choose to buy. Typical examples, here, are the provision of clean air through restrictions on pollution, the building, maintenance, and cleaning of streets, or the availability of areas in which one can walk unthreatened by car traffic.

The argument is not that everyone attaches the same importance to clean air, uses streets to the same extent, or finds a safe walk equally essential to her well-being, but that even the least intensive air breathers, street users or walkers can have no less of what they want as a result of in-kind provision: they get cleaner air, or better streets, or quieter footpaths for a cost (in forgone cash grant) that does not exceed what they would have had to pay—administrative costs (in cash and bother) included—for what they would have chosen to consume in the absence of in-kind provision.[22] Once again, the nature and level of in-kind provision justifiable in this way will no doubt often be debatable—how unpolluted should the air be, how well lit the streets, how well kept the public parks? But here lies a further powerful reason why a real-libertarian should not want to monetize people's whole basic income and keep a significant part of it in the form of freely available goods. This time, moreover, the in-kind basic income justified in this way should not be discounted when comparing the levels of basic income attainable under different socio-economic regimes, but constitutes an essential ingredient of the means made available to every member of society in the pursuit of her conception of the good life.[23]

Needless to say, there are countless actual and potential types of government expenditure which fit into none of these three categories.[24] For example, it would be hard to make a real-libertarian case for free, or publicly cheapened, access to degree courses in Etruscan history, to squash facilities, to opera tickets, or to totally unpolluted rivers.[25] What about health care? For real freedom to be leximinned, should health insurance be provided free of charge, or at least heavily subsidized, to all, or should the cash grant rather be correspondingly larger? Some aspects of health care can plausibly be fitted into the second category—for example, vaccination against infectious diseases and any other item whose free provision significantly boosts labour productivity—and into the third one—for example, emergency treatment in the event of an accident unrelated to activities involving special risks. But this does not amount to a comprehensive insurance even for non-cosmetic health care. It would presumably not cover, for example, expensive heart operations or cancer treatments at an advanced age. Leaving out the case in which appeal can be made to productivity considerations (public health) or to the impracticality of discriminating (emergencies), the argument must be that people in their right minds are all sufficiently risk-averse to turn part of their cash grant into an insurance scheme that fully or partly covers a sufficiently similar set of services. But this is not enough, for one could let people opt freely, though unanimously, for such an insurance scheme.[26] To justify turning part of the cash grant into an insurance scheme, one may be able to construct an additional argument to the effect that, under very general conditions, a compulsory basic health insurance is cheaper to run than another, equally universal, where decisions are left to the free choice of each member of society. Alternatively, one may allow some mild form of paternalism in order to prevent some people from failing to use part of their cash grant in order to subscribe to a basic health insurance, which they genuinely want when 'in their right minds'. This appeal to the protection of each member of society against the possibly fatal and irreversible consequences of choices she would herself, under appropriate circumstances, recognize to be misguided not only provides a plausible potential rationale for overriding the presumption in favour of paying the whole basic income in cash. It is also required, as we shall see presently, to justify the payment of a basic *income*, as opposed to a basic initial endowment.

2.5 Initial endowment or regular instalment?

Whether payments are made in kind or in cash, one needs to ask whether real freedom is leximinned through the unconditional granting of a regular income flow or through the unconditional transfer of a stock of wealth at some initial point. Why opt for an indefinite sequence of small payments rather than for a one-off big payment, as was envisaged, for example, in what is probably the earliest formulation of the basic income idea? What Thomas Paine (1796: 612–13) was proposing, apart from a basic pension for anyone over 50, was that out of the national fund to be created 'there shall be paid to every person, when arrived at the age of twenty-one years, the sum of fifteen pounds sterling, as a compensation, in part, for the loss of his or her natural inheritance'. Would this not be better than a monthly or weekly payment if real freedom is our sole concern?

Sure enough, if the whole basic income were given in one go, it may not take long for some to squander all of it and end up destitute. And under many rationales for a minimum income scheme, this would be all we need to justify regular instalments. Take, for example, what may well be the first case for a minimum income, the one uttered by Thomas More's

(1516: 44–5) Raphael: 'Instead of inflicting these horrible punishments, it would be far more to the point to provide everyone with some means of livelihood, so that nobody's under the frightful necessity of becoming first a thief and then a corpse.' What matters here is that no one should at any time be so poor as to be forced to steal, and regular instalments are therefore the obvious choice. Similarly, if the introduction of a minimum income is motivated by the feeling that destitution and the display of destitution jeopardize human dignity or moral worth (see e.g. Fried 1983: 51–2), the payment of a given overall level of income should be spread as thinly as is practical over people's whole lifetimes.

Things are altogether different, however, when the rationale is phrased in terms of real freedom, and even more so when it is phrased in terms of leximin real freedom. First of all, if one discards the unrealistic assumption of perfect capital markets, receiving straight away the discounted value of payments which would otherwise be spread over one's lifetime unambiguously increases one's freedom to allocate a given amount of resources over time. Regular instalments of equal real value, which could be secured through some appropriate sort of investment, correspond to only one of the many time profiles among which one could freely choose if one were given everything at the start. Moreover, if the basic income takes the form of regular instalments of constant magnitude (and even more so if the size of the instalments increases with age), those living to an older age—and thereby enjoying the privilege of being able to use their own life, no doubt their most precious resource, for longer—get a larger total basic income than those dying earlier, and the distribution seems therefore bound to violate the leximin criterion. Hence, a quick reference to the fact that some people may squander the whole of their basic income in a single day if it were given to them in one go is by no means sufficient to justify a basic income flow. It is too easy to retort: 'Too bad, this is what happens in a free society.'

A radical riposte to this argument consists in questioning the assumption that people preserve their identity throughout their existence. If one is willing to assume that, as they grow up and then age, people become 'different persons', one can no longer justify the destitution of an old person by pointing to 'her' frivolous youth. From a real-libertarian standpoint, each of the successive persons the same organism becomes must then be given as high a basic income as one can give to all.[27] The resources of the person I shall be at 50 must be protected against the risk of being given away by that other person I was at 20. No reason either, in this light, to give less per year to an individual who lives longer. For what has been given to 'her' earlier selves has not been given to her. Even apart from practical considerations, solidarity between temporally contiguous selves may well be sufficient for exempting us from making payments second by second. But spacing them out by more than, say, a month, and *a fortiori* lumping them all together into a single payment, would give (some selves of) some people less than is maximally feasible for all.[28]

This radical riposte, however, seems to have strongly counterintuitive implications. Consider the following two schemes. According to the temporally asymmetrical scheme T, you and I are both given an unconditional income of 100 in period 1, and nothing in period 2. According to the personally asymmetrical scheme P, you are given an unconditional income of 10 in both periods, while I am given an unconditional income of 90 in both periods. Following the interpretation just given, a real-libertarian should prefer scheme P to scheme T. Surely, if this is the case, you would be right to complain that this is no way of giving all members of society maximal means for the pursuit of their conception of the good life.[29] Now, part of the counterintuitive character of this implication derives from an unwarranted assumption. If successive selves are really considered as different persons, whatever you and I possess at the end of period 1—what is left of our basic income or whatever wealth we managed to build up in period 1—can be taxed away in order to boost the level of the basic income paid in each period. And this fact, surely, will take away much of scheme T's attraction. Nevertheless, this assumption of strongly discontinuous selves may be found too far-fetched. After all, many of the things we find important to have the freedom to do, and which a basic income would give us the freedom to do, are things which take a long time, sometimes a lifetime, to accomplish. Consequently, the concern with maximum real freedom to do whatever one might wish to do does not sit easily with the assumption of single-period people.

Fortunately, there is an alternative, somewhat looser but less extravagant justification, which simply consists in assuming a universal desire on people's part, when 'in their right minds', to protect their real freedom at older ages against the weakness of their will at younger ages and to do so pretty homogeneously throughout their lifetimes. Remember, moreover, that at this stage of the argument we are still assuming that people's life expectancies are identical, or at least unrelated to differences in 'internal resources' (to be dealt with in Chapter 3), so that one could do nothing to make the level of the regular payment a function of the number of times the payment can be expected to be made. Against this background, a mildly paternalistic concern for people's real freedom throughout their lives, not just 'at the start', makes it sensible to hand out the basic income in the form of a (non-mortgageable) regular stream—just as a mildly paternalistic concern for their formal freedom makes it reasonable to prohibit the permanent alienation of self-ownership, though not the selling of one's labour power for limited periods of time.[30]

This is sufficient to justify understanding the basic income called forth by the real-libertarian approach in the way suggested by the choice of the expression, that is, as an (essentially) pecuniary income stream. There is bound to remain a margin of arbitrariness in determining the rhythm at which payments are to be made (what might be the philosophical justification for choosing seven or thirty days rather than five or twenty?), just as there is some arbitrariness about the length of the notice an employee needs to give when wishing to quit her job. In either case, the shorter the period, the better the real freedom (opportunities in one case, self-ownership in the other) of later stages is protected against irresponsible conduct at earlier stages, but the more restrictions on the time scale of the commitments one is empowered to make. Hence, some pragmatic compromise will have to be struck. But this is definitely not a direction from which the assertion of a strong connection between real-freedom-for-all and a regular unconditional cash payment at the highest sustainable level will come under serious attack.

2.6 *What metric for real freedom?*

Far more serious, it seems, is another problem which can be presented, in its simplest possible form, using the following story. Consider a society in which it turns out that there is no special ground for in-kind universal provision of the sort explored in § 2.4. Hence, its members receive the whole of their basic income in cash. Further, no production is taking place, and we can therefore conveniently assume that each person's income consists exclusively in her basic income, an equal amount of some currency that can be used to buy or rent pre-existing goods. As before, there are no significant differences between people's abilities, and the society's two typical members Funny and Sunny have, moreover, identical tastes, except that Funny loves diving whereas Sunny is dead keen on sunbathing, and that Sunny has, consequently, rented a portion of the beach, whereas Funny has rented a portion of the rocky coast.[31] Subject to formal freedom being respected, the cash grant is pitched as high as possible, which simply means, in this simple case, that all the society's non-human resources (say, beaches, cliffs, and blackberries) are up for rent or sale. Consequently, Funny's and Sunny's and everyone else's real freedom to do whatever they might want to do is, on the view presented so far, as great as possible. So far, it seems, so innocuous.

Suppose, however, that for some reason the price structure changes, and that rents on cliffs fall whereas rents on beaches rise. As a result, Funny's real freedom to do *what she wants* to do increases, whereas Sunny's decreases, since Funny can keep more, and Sunny less, for other purposes (say, for consuming, at an unchanged price, greater quantities of blackberries, with respect to which they are both insatiable) once the rent has been paid. But their real freedom to do *whatever they might want* to do, we seem committed to say, is left unaffected by these price changes. This proposition, however, has disastrous consequences. One of them is that it makes nonsense of the whole discussion of § 2.4, for if any price structure will do, so will, in particular, one which assigns a zero price to some goods, and free provision needs no special reason to be deemed equivalent to cash grants as far as real-freedom-for-all is concerned. The pro-cash presumption, in other words, can only be sustained if the price structure is not purely arbitrary, for what combinations of goods will feature in the opportunity-set associated with a cash basic income is crucially dependent on what prices one decides should prevail.

It will not take long for someone to come up with the suggestion that we should consider adopting the vector of *perfectly competitive equilibrium prices*, that is, in this case, the set of prices that would equalize supply and demand as a result of the atomistic, perfectly informed, and unhindered interaction of Funny, Sunny, and all their fellow citizens, each endowed with an equal basic income.[32] Why should we? One way of focusing on this question consists in noting, first, that the proposal just made amounts to requiring that the heterogeneous bundles of goods (cliffs, beaches, blackberries) different people are endowed with should all have the same competitive value. In other words, the proposal amounts to choosing competitive values as the appropriate metric for judging whether external-resource-based freedom is fairly distributed. As such, it competes with a number of alternative proposals. The problem they all face is that the heterogeneous bundles people are allocated enable them to do different things. Even in a highly commodified economy, they cannot be swiftly exchanged with one another and it cannot therefore be said that two bundles of identical competitive value confer an identical real freedom to do what one might want to do. So, how should our criterion of leximin real freedom apply when people are endowed with bundles of goods which give them different sets of opportunities?

A first possible answer is that one should say that different opportunity-sets are unequal only if one is a proper subset of the other.[33] With such a demanding notion of inequality, however, leximin real freedom would justify—even without any appeal to the contribution of inequalities to the fate of the worst off—such an enormous range of situations intuitively perceived as unequal (say, ten beaches and a castle versus a single blackberry bush) that it is definitely worth looking for something else.

Secondly, one may want to measure opportunity-sets in some physical way, say by counting the options each contains, or perhaps, more subtly, by ascribing each of these options a weight that takes spatio-temporal complexities into account. Relative to the first one, this second approach has the advantage of yielding in principle a complete ordering of opportunity-sets, instead of an extremely partial one, while taking seriously the notion of 'amounts of freedom'.[34] One serious problem with it is that it can only live up to this promise if it can operate with option-sets that can somehow be compared despite their being most naturally interpreted as each containing an infinite number of elements. As one turns from principle to practice, another problem is that the complete ordering quickly degenerates, for lack of relevant data, into an ordering that is hardly less partial than the one offered by the first approach. But even assuming that the mass of relevant data were available, collected, and processed, of what use would be the huge spatio-temporal aggregates of acts we would end up with? True, one could quite conceivably say that these lumps constitute the quantities of freedom associated with various bundles of external resources. But so what? If these quantities turn out to be unequal, does it follow (even leaving aside any argument that pulls apart leximin and equality) that the associated external resources and real freedom have been distributed unfairly? Why should our concern with a fair distribution of external endowments make us care about these complex physical aggregates?

A third approach provides an ethically more appealing way of making different opportunity-sets commensurable. It consists in assessing them in terms of the welfare level which they enable people endowed with the corresponding external resources to achieve. Barring again any argument that pulls leximin away from equality, these resources are fairly distributed when the highest level of preference satisfaction a person can reach with her endowment is the same for all. Here too, refinements and complexities are needed.[35] But they cannot avoid one key difficulty, closely related to the fundamental reason for opting for an approach to justice that focuses on freedom or opportunity rather than on a measure of outcome or achievement. This fundamental reason rests on the notion that, except in special cases of addiction and the like, people must bear the consequences of the preferences or tastes they have on their level of welfare or preference satisfaction. Hence, those with more expensive tastes, with preferences more difficult to satisfy, should not be given greater amounts of resources.[36] True, equalizing people's opportunity for welfare in the sense sketched above is not the same as equalizing their welfare. People remain responsible for the consequences of their actions. Yet, under equal (or leximin) opportunity for welfare, just as under equal (or leximin) welfare, people with more expensive tastes are entitled to extra compensation at the expense of those with more modest aspirations.[37]

2.7 Competitive pricing, opportunity costs, and envy-freeness

On this background, let us return to the proposal that one should assess opportunity-sets by the competitive value of the associated external endowments. Unlike the first approach and like the other two, it potentially provides a complete ordering. But the intuition by which it is guided is no longer that people should get resources that open up possibilities of equal physical magnitude for all. It is not that they should get resources that are equally precious to them in terms of how happy they enable them to be. It is rather that they should get resources that are equally valuable in terms of the potential uses by others that have to be forgone as a result of the allocation that has been made. The more other people care about one particular resource and the less of it there is— shortly, the more precious it is in the society concerned—the higher its competitive price will be. In this sense, it can be said that the metric that is here being proposed for opportunities is one of *opportunity costs*: the weight ascribed to each resource reflects the cost to others of not being able to use it.[38]

A fair distribution of external-resource-based real freedom is then one that is associated with a distribution of external endowments which are equally (or leximinally) valuable in this sense. This fourth approach clearly avoids the indeterminacy of the first one and possesses an ethical appeal the second one lacks. Moreover, while giving people's preferences an essential role, it does not do so in a way that makes it vulnerable to the expensive taste objection, which proved fatal to the third approach, since the role ascribed to each person's preferences is to help determine how valuable each component of each bundle is, not to determine how big her own bundle should be.[39] Just as what counts as a resource is determined by what the members of the community care to bid for, how much a resource weighs in someone's share is determined by how much others care for it (or whatever is needed to provide it), that is, what it 'costs' them not to have it (and the factors its production requires) in their own share. For example, if many happen to prefer cliffs to beaches, those with only beaches in their 'equal' share will have more of them than if it were the other way around.[40] This justifies prima-facie maximal equal cash endowments with the prices of all goods determined by competitive markets. Of course, this presumption in favour of cash and competitive pricing may be overriden by the considerations discussed earlier (§ 2.4), while the presumption in favour of equality may be overriden for the sake of leximin. This will arise in particular, as we shall see (§ 4.4), in situations in which there are structural reasons that hinder competition, or prevent it from clearing the market. In such a situation, those who get the good in short supply appropriate a rent, that is, receive an additional gift, which can be partly—but (for leximin's sake) should not be totally—taxed away, thus generating justified inequalities in endowments.

One further way of putting this proposal into perspective, and thereby providing it with additional support, is by pointing out its close link to the notion of *equity*, as characterized by a number of economists in terms of the conjunction of efficiency and envy-freeness.[41] Suppose for a moment that the relative price of beaches is higher, and that of cliffs lower, than competitive equilibrium prices. By definition, there will then be an oversupply of beaches and an unsatisfied demand for cliffs. The former feature is unattractive because a concern with *maximum* real freedom for all is hardly compatible with leaving some resources unused. And the latter feature is unattractive because it implies that, as a reflection of people's actual opportunity-sets not being fully described by their equal pecuniary endowments, those lucky or quick enough to get hold of the goods in short supply and those not so lucky or so quick will end up with *unequal* opportunities to do what they want. If instead all the available resources are sold at suitable competitive prices, that is, auctioned off to the highest bidder among the perfectly informed and equally endowed Sunnies and Funnies, no usable resource will be left unused and the equality of the budget-sets will be enough to guarantee that no one could achieve more of what she wants with the resources another person has access to than with her own.

These are interesting and attractive properties of equal-endowment competitive equilibria, but they do not provide us with a direct justification of competitive pricing on the basis of real-libertarianism alone, because they appeal to people's freedom to do what they actually want, rather than to their freedom to do what they might want to do (see § 1.5). Departures from competitive equilibrium prices generally create situations in which at least one person could get more of what she actually wants without anyone else getting less, as well as situations in which one person could achieve more of what she actually wants with someone else's bundle than with her own. But this does not imply that the choice of competitive equilibrium prices is mandated, jointly with equal cash endowments, by a concern with equal (which is also, in this simple world, leximin) real freedom to do what one *might* want to do.

None the less, these considerations appeal to an ethically attractive criterion for assessing the fairness of distributions of opportunity-sets which are not proper subsets of one another. It is not enough, if one is to leximin real freedom, to distribute external resources in such a way that no one's opportunity-set (as determined by these resources) is a proper subset of anyone else's. One can further demand *envy-freeness*, that is, require that no one should prefer someone else's opportunity-set to her own—or at least, in leximin fashion, that violation of envy-freeness so defined should only be tolerated to the extent that it serves to improve the position of those who are thereby made envious. In other words, when pursuing leximin real freedom, the egalitarian situation that can serve as a baseline relative to which inequalities in real freedom need to be assessed is one in which all have an 'equal' real freedom, not in the sense that they have identical opportunities, or opportunities of equal spatio-temporal magnitude, or opportunities giving access to the same level of welfare, but in the sense that none of them envies anyone else's.[42]

Once this is agreed, we are a long way towards justifying competitive prices as the appropriate way of measuring external endowments. Two useful theorems establish a close connection between equality as envy-freeness and the use of competitive prices. One states that (assuming internal endowments to be identical) there exists some allocation that is both envy-free and efficient (in the weak sense of Pareto-optimality), and that it can be achieved by a perfectly competitive auction in which all participate with equal purchasing powers—or, equivalently, by perfectly competitive interaction between people initially endowed with an equal share of all external resources. What this first result provides, however, is only a loose justification of competitive prices, because there are, in general, many non-competitive price structures that satisfy the same two conditions. It is not necessary for beaches and cliffs to be priced at their equal-endowment competitive level for the resulting allocation to be both efficient and such that the Funnies have no desire to swap their resources with the Sunnies, nor the Sunnies with the Funnies.[43] Whereas equality of resource bundles as measured by their competitive prices entails equality of opportunity-sets in the weak sense of envy-freeness, the reverse is not true.[44]

But another theorem tightens the connection. In a large economy with tastes widely scattered, it is no longer true that there are many allocations which are not equal-endowment competitive equilibria and yet are both efficient and envy-free. In the extreme case in which there is a continuum of smooth preferences, it can be shown that only a competitive equilibrium allocation with identically endowed traders at the start can both be efficient and satisfy the no-envy test.[45] To the extent that the real world resembles this continuous world rather than the polarized Funny/Sunny one, our problem is solved. If we want to make envy-free-ness at least a necessary condition for equality of external-resource-based real freedom, and if we do not want the allocation to be inefficient, that is, to be such that one could improve on it by giving someone more of what she wants to have without giving anyone else less, then the appropriate valuation must be conducted in terms of those competitive equilibrium prices that would obtain if everyone started with identical endowments. Hence, there is, under the conditions stated, a non-arbitrary price structure that prevents the opportunity-set associated to a given cash income from being left undetermined. True, the sheer notion of equalizing or leximinning people's opportunity to do whatever they might want to do did not suffice to guide the selection. But the close link with envy-freeness provides, I believe, strong backing for the view that the fair way of distributing external-resource-based real freedom is by leximinning people's endowments, valued in terms of competitive prices.[46] We shall return later (§ 4.4) to the question of what should be done in situations of systematic substantial deviation from competitive equilibrium. But assuming, for the time being, the possibility of roughly competitive pricing, the presumption in favour of a maximal universal cash grant with competitive prices is vindicated.

2.8 Comparing real freedom across regimes

We are now in a position to examine another objection to using a cash income as an adequate index of real freedom. There is a serious problem, it seems, as soon as one wants to use it for the sake of comparison across socio-economic regimes, as we definitely need to do if we want to assess the relative merits of different types of regime, such as capitalism and socialism. For suppose, for example, that under socialism level G of the basic income is exhausted by the purchase of some particular bundle of goods g (say, adequate food and accommodation plus the complete works of Marx and a sturdy bicycle), which also exhausts the basic income of those who want to buy it under capitalism. But apart from g, members of a capitalist society could also choose some other bundle g* (say, adequate food and accommodation plus a Nintendo game) unavailable under socialism, which they prefer to g, whereas the opposite is not true. We would then say, presumably, that leximin real freedom is better served by basic income capitalism than by basic income socialism, and perhaps stick to this position even if $g + h$ (say, the same as above plus a Volga car) could be purchased with the grant under socialism, whereas someone confined to the grant could not afford it under capitalism, as long as everyone prefers to $g + h$ at least one of the g^*'s that can be purchased with the basic income under capitalism but are unavailable under socialism. What, however, if some prefer the standard package for which the (highest sustainable) basic income is sufficient under socialism, but insufficient under capitalism, while others prefer at least one of the more varied possibilities accessible with the (highest sustainable) basic income under capitalism? Here we have two opportunity-sets, neither of which is unanimously preferred to, let alone strictly larger than, the other. Which should be deemed superior? [47]

Note, first, that in order to assess the relative merits of capitalism and socialism in terms of our criterion, there is no need to be able to compare, in terms of that criterion, one capitalist society with *another* socialist society. The question is whether, for one particular country with given traditions, tastes, current stock of natural and other resources, etc., socialism or capitalism would perform better in terms of our criterion. Our task is not to provide a meaningful way of comparing the opportunity-set of the least free person in Pharaonic Egypt, Renaissance Tuscany, and Soviet Russia. Nor is it to compare the opportunity-set of the least free in today's Chicago, London, and Hong Kong. It is to evaluate the opportunity-set that can sustainably be provided to the worst off in some given society under alternative socio-economic regimes. This greatly reduces the range of variation in the bundles of goods than can be expected to be available in the two situations to be compared.

Remember, secondly, that under both capitalism and socialism, leximin real freedom will require goods to be priced in a way that reflects their opportunity costs, whether through the operation of actual markets or of institutions that mimic these. There are, it has been conceded (§ 2.4), some categories of goods for which an exception should be made, but the grounds for doing so are the same under capitalism and socialism, and there is therefore no reason to expect their optimal versions to diverge in this respect.[48] Therefore, once it is realized that our attention can legitimately be restricted to the most promising versions of the various types of regime, that is, to forms of socialism or capitalism that have incorporated an adequate protection of formal freedom and adopted price structures that ensure a fair distribution of external-resource-based real freedom, the difficulty of comparing different regimes with regard to leximin real freedom is greatly reduced. It is then not only the range of goods that can be expected to vary little, relative to what is logically possible, from one regime to another, but also the prices at which they are made available.

Thirdly, what has just been said does not rule out that one regime may generate a pattern of demand that will lead to some goods becoming unavailable or available only at a far higher relative price. One could imagine, for example, that one type of regime may foster such a strong taste for single-family housing that high-rise apartment buildings will eventually disappear altogether, or that a more egalitarian type of regime may lead to pricing luxury perfume beyond what one could afford even just once with the highest sustainable basic income, while a less egalitarian regime may, because of economies of scale, keep it more moderately expensive.[49] This is true, but most probably of negligible significance compared to the massive impact, on both the set of goods available and their relative prices, of different rates and types of technical innovation. But the occurrence of technical innovation does not make total nonsense of comparisons of a country's real GNP through time. Indeed, it is precisely one of the main phenomena which such comparisons aim to capture. If anything, comparing lower real incomes through time should be far easier than comparing aggregate incomes. And the comparison, in this respect, of two potential states of the same society is not fundamentally different from the comparison of two successive states.[50]

What if the availability of some goods—for example, the acquisition of means of production in order to set up one's own business—is excluded by the very definition of some type of regime—in this case, socialism—rather than as a result of the development of tastes or technology which it fosters? Even if socialism could offer a higher basic income, would this fact not prevent us from asserting its superiority over capitalism from a real-libertarian standpoint? True, socialism has been defined by the public ownership of the *bulk* of the means of production. Hence, the existence of small private firms is as consistent with it as it is with capitalism. Since only the launching, owning, and running of *small* firms can reasonably be taken to be relevant to *leximin* real freedom, this does not necessarily raise a relevant difficulty. None the less, one cannot rule out a priori that a ban on all private firms, big and small, would make a higher basic income sustainable than under any more permissive form of socialism. But there is no reason why this direct institutional elimination of certain options would need to be treated differently from the indirect elimination through the shaping of tastes or technical progress. If comparisons of real levels of minimum income are meaningful in one case, so they are in the other.

These quick remarks are not sufficient to guarantee that inter-regime comparisons will be a conceptual sinecure for real-libertarians, but only to enable us to proceed until we return to the issue, in the specific context of the comparison of capitalism and socialism, at the start of the final chapter (§ 6.1).

APPENDIX: BASIC INCOME VERSUS NEGATIVE INCOME TAX

The relation between typical basic income and negative income tax proposals can be read from the comparison of Figs. 2.1, 2.2, and 2.3. Both differ from the most common, 'make-up' type of guaranteed minimum income (Fig. 2.1) by making post-tax-and-transfer income (the vertical axis) a monotonically increasing function of pre-tax-and-transfer income (the horizontal axis). But, for a given level of guarantee, and assuming proportional taxation, a negative income tax scheme (Fig. 2.2) achieves the same end result (subject to the crucial qualifications emphasized in § 2.2 above) as a basic income scheme (Fig. 2.3) by only giving to some people the *net* transfer due to them and only taking from the others the *net* taxes owed by them, instead of giving them all the same gross transfer and taxing positively all other income.

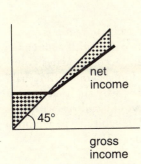

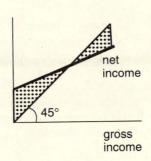

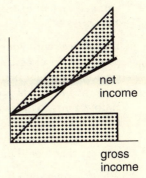

FIG. 2.1. Existing guaranteed minimum income schemes

FIG. 2.2. Linear negative income tax scheme (M. Friedman 1962)

FIG. 2.3. Basic income financed by a linear income tax

CHAPTER 3

Undominated diversity

PROLOGUE

Δ *So far you have reasoned as if there were no significant differences between people's internal endowments: they are identically talented, or at least none of them has a handicap worth mentioning. But surely you cannot say that the highest sustainable uniform basic income will distribute (the resource base of) real freedom in maximin fashion if some people have serious handicaps relative to others. What real-freedom-for-all requires, it would seem, is a highly differentiated system of transfers, not the uniform basic income you simplistically advocate.*

Φ I fully agree with your central premiss—justice, as I conceive it, requires compensation for unequal internal endowments— but only partly with your conclusion. Consider first the simplest possible scheme that accommodates your premiss and yields your conclusion. It consists in adding people's internal endowments to the stock whose value is to be shared fairly by all. Its concrete implication would be that poorly talented people would end up with an enhanced transfer, while highly talented people would be subjected to a lump-sum tax that would more than offset their basic income (§ 3.1).

Δ *What's wrong with that?*

Φ Nothing obvious if people cared about nothing but their purchasing power. But if at least some people also care about leisure or the quality of their work activity, or about success along other dimensions than the earning of money, then the proposal is unacceptably biased. It enslaves people with highly lucrative talents by imposing tough constraints on the use they can make of their time, and it neglects altogether any inequality or handicap that is not reflected in earning power (§ 3.2).

Δ *What's the alternative?*

Φ The most elaborate alternative developed so far—initially by Ronald Dworkin—is one that relies on some notion of insurance behind a veil of ignorance. In its simplest version, it consists in asking people to ignore their own internal endowment, though not the distribution of these endowments in their society, and to decide on this basis how high a premium they would be willing to pay in order to get a correspondingly high compensation in the event of their being poorly endowed.

Δ *Does this approach provide an adequate interpretation of real-freedom-for-all in the presence of unequal talents?*

Φ I don't think so. One interesting objection against this counterfactual insurance scheme is that it leads straight into the equalization of welfare rather than of opportunities, and hence into something very alien to the notion, which I find compelling, that justice is about the distribution of freedom, not about the distribution of happiness. But this objection overlooks the possibility, crucial to this whole approach, of distinguishing two categories of personal characteristics: those for which a person can be held responsible and those for which she cannot (Appendix 1). Dworkin himself also objects to the simplest version of the insurance approach on the ground that it bizarrely asks people to abstract from their talents—for example, musical gifts—while being guided by tastes which have often been shaped by the very possession of these talents. He therefore proposes a more complex scheme, which allows people to know which specific talents they possess, but not the earning power such possession generates (§ 3.3).

Δ *And this is still not good enough?*

Φ I have some specific difficulties with both the simple and this more complex variant of the counterfactual insurance approach. But my most fundamental objection applies to all variants. The very notion of counterfactual insurance opens up the possibility that two people with identical internal endowments but different tastes will be entitled to unequal compensatory external endowments precisely because of these differences in tastes. I have no objection to people ending up with different amounts of compensation as a result of differences in the actual choices they make on the basis of their tastes, but endowing them unequally at the start as a function of their tastes amounts to an unjust rewarding of expensive tastes. The injustice may be milder than if one advocated equality of welfare, but it is basically of the same nature (§ 3.4).

Δ *So, what are you proposing?*

Φ The generalization of a simple idea first formulated, to my knowledge, by Bruce Ackerman. The distribution of endowments is unjust in a society as long as there are two people such that everyone in the society concerned prefers the whole endowment (both internal and external) of one of them to that of the other. It can only be just if this is not the case, that is, if there is undominated diversity (§ 3.5).

Δ *If I understand you correctly, if one weird character finds it better to be crippled than able-bodied, justice will not require any specific transfer to the cripple.*

Φ What is crucial is that the preferences of the weird character should be genuine—she must be fully aware of what life is like when one is crippled and not pretend to prefer being crippled just in order to block redistribution—and also that they should be generally available—not restricted, for example, to members of a small sect whose outlook is totally unknown or unintelligible to the rest of society (§ 3.6). Bearing in mind these two conditions—and also, in the background, the highest sustainable basic income—I do not find it shocking to claim that targeted transfers, whether in cash or in kind, can legitimately stop once undominated diversity is achieved, and I therefore don't find it necessary to move further away from the simple notion of undominated diversity in order to tackle this objection (§ 3.7).

Δ *But can undominated diversity ever be achieved? If we think of some particularly awful handicaps, what we should worry about is probably not that targeted redistribution will stop too quickly if we use your criterion, but rather that it will never stop.*

Φ What we need to tackle this very different objection is a somewhat more qualified version of undominated diversity. It should accommodate some aggregative considerations, for example by stipulating that an 'imperceptible' improvement in a dominated endowment should not be achieved at the expense of a 'massive' shrinking of other endowments (§ 3.8).

Δ *Even so, is it not possible that the need to satisfy your constraint of undominated diversity will drive the maximum sustainable basic income all the way down to zero?*

Φ I am not ruling this out. Indeed, it is quite possible (though by no means obvious) that in many countries of today's world, justice as I conceive it would require the unconditional income to be zero, or to be reduced to a small in-kind component. Adding undominated diversity to the protection of formal freedom as a constraint on sustainable basic income maximization is therefore far from insignificant. But the wealthier, the healthier, and the more diverse a society, the more room there remains for a just unconditional income.

―――――

3.1 The extended auction

For the sake of simplicity, I have most unrealistically assumed so far that people's internal endowments—their talents, their abilities, their capacities[1] in all areas of life—are identical. Once this assumption is lifted, clearly, the simple connection established in the previous chapter between leximin real freedom and maximum basic income cannot be sustained. Take two people with no external resource apart from their identical basic income. If one of them can physically and mentally do everything the other can do and far more, who could possibly claim that they enjoy the same real freedom to do whatever they might want to do? In general, therefore, it seems most implausible to assert that real freedom is leximinned if all one does is give everyone a basic income at the highest sustainable level. Is not a system of differential transfers, in amounts inversely related to people's levels of talent, an obvious and far more plausible alternative? If it is, all the efforts mustered so far in defence of an unconditional basic income will be to no avail. Consistent real-libertarians will have to give it up.

In this chapter, I shall pay close attention to this serious challenge. In the process, I shall be led to discuss the most articulate attempts to perform a task that can be roughly characterized as follows. Is it possible to work out a defensible criterion of distributive justice which at the same time takes us beyond a metric of external goods without taking us all the way to a welfare metric? Somewhat more specifically, is it possible to work out a coherent way of distributing external endowments in a way that accommodates the special needs of a disabled person, for example, without also indulging the expensive tastes some people may possess?[2] For this purpose, it will be convenient to think of Polypolis, a society whose members greatly differ from one another in both their internal endowments or talents—that is, in the capacities they have received from either nature or upbringing—and their tastes—in particular, their income/leisure trade-offs. Suppose that external endowments have just been distributed in the way that would be recommended by a real-libertarian approach if all had identical talents, that is (if the argument of the previous chapter holds water) by giving all (or all those of the same age) an equal basic income at the highest sustainable level. Does real-libertarianism require that one should deviate from this criterion in order to take account of differences in talents—and if so, how?

A first proposal that is worth exploring consists in a straightforward extension of the intellectual device that has been appealed to in the case of external endowments. It was pointed out in the previous chapter (§ 2.6) that a cash grant as such meant nothing for real freedom, except in relation to the bundle of resources it gave access to. The relation between purchasing power and resources is determined by the price structure. It was therefore essential to find a price structure that would not just be arbitrary in terms of maximum real freedom for all. Perfectly competitive prices, it was argued, provide what we need. But then, if we assume—to use Dworkin's (1981*b*) parable—that the immigrants landing on the desert island possess unequal talents, could we not just add these, on a par with fancy pebbles and banana trees, to the aggregate up for bids in the perfectly competitive auction? Each participant in the auction would bid for her own talents (simply to enjoy them, or to put them to some productive use) or other people's talents (to put them to their most productive use and cash in the proceeds), in the same way as they bid for goods. Nothing but the initial cheque—in Dworkin's parable, an equal number of clamshells—can be used to buy all these goods, which the auctioneer allocates to the highest bidder when all cheques have been committed in their owners' best interest.[3] No doubt, a fair amount of intellectual gymnastics is needed to figure out exactly what skills are for sale (only 'talents', i.e. those which have been 'given' to their holder, genetically or otherwise) as well as to imagine how one person's talents could be jointly owned by several people. But the exercise is not fundamentally different from the one that has to be performed in the case of external endowments. What are the implications?

What are now being auctioned off are people's talents, and hence their command over their own time. If people want to retain command over them—which they can be safely assumed to do—they have to outbid anyone else who might be interested in using them.[4] For those without any valuable talent, this is a great advantage. They will be able to appropriate their own time very cheaply, and therefore to gain access to more external resources than was the case when only external resources were being auctioned. For those with highly productive talents, on the other hand, the reverse is the case. They may well have to spend the whole of their cheque buying their own time—indeed, more than their cheque, thereby running a debt which they will have to pay back with the income their talents will enable them to earn. The most straightforward institutional expression of this procedure consists in supplementing whatever follows from a real-libertarian approach to external resources, with a highly differentiated tax-and-transfer system, in sharp contrast to universal systems such as a negative income tax or a basic income. Assuming away, for the moment, any informational problem, such a system consists in identifying the maximum earning power associated with each person's internal endowment, in granting each person with below average talents (measured by the corresponding earning power) a lump-sum subsidy driving her earning power up to the average, and in imposing on each person with above average talents a lump-sum tax driving her earning power down to the average.[5]

The criterion of justice thus proposed for Polypolis, where talents are different, is fully consistent with, indeed a natural generalization of, what is being assumed to be appropriate when talents are identical. The earning power associated with identical internal endowments is, of course, equal for all. Hence, there is then no deviation from the average to be compensated by means of lump-sum transfers or taxes, and the whole procedure reduces to its external-endowment component. In the course of the generalization, however, something has been lost. With identical talents, the auction procedure guaranteed, remember, the satisfaction of a criterion of envy-freeness: the outcome was necessarily such that no one preferred the bundle attributed to anyone else to the one she herself ended up with. In Polypolis, where both tastes and talents diverge, no such guarantee can be given. To understand why, briefly consider the case of Johnson and Jackson, identically talented except for the fact that Johnson is an exceptional runner, whereas Jackson is an amazing singer. If it so happens that there is nothing in life Johnson would like as much as having a great voice, while Jackson's strongest ambition is to win a race, each will envy the other's internal endowment. And no transfer of external endowments—no combination of lump-sum taxes and subsidies—will enable us to get rid of all envy, for any such transfer from Johnson to Jackson will only alleviate Jackson's envy at the expense of aggravating Johnson's, and the other way around.[6] This fact will prove of great importance further on, but it must be acknowledged that equity theorists have, in a sense, managed to get around it by introducing a different criterion of envy-freeness which can be guaranteed to be satisfied by the outcome of the auction even in a Polypolitan context. A distribution is *income-fair* if no one envies the implicit income of any other agent. Johnson's *implicit income* is the competitive value of the consumption bundle accessible to her, including her leisure, evaluated by the maximum competitive wage she could earn, given her abilities. The outcome of the comprehensive auction described above is necessarily income-fair in this sense.[7]

3.2 Working in the peep-show, flirting in the square

There is little doubt that this approach provides a way of performing the task mentioned at the outset. By equalizing maximum earning power or implicit income, it avoids the goods metric's insensitivity to the plight of the handicapped: those with poor abilities will have their earning power propped up to the average. And it does so in a way that avoids the welfare metric's sensitivity to the tastes of the person concerned: true, how much your talents are worth depends on which services are in demand, and hence on everyone's tastes, but whether you possess expensive tastes does not affect in any way what you are entitled to by virtue of the criterion that is being proposed. What someone is owed or owes, if earning power is to be equalized, is determined by her talents and left unaffected by *her* tastes. Thus, the requirements enshrined in the formulation of that task would seem to be satisfied, and we may be tempted to conclude that a system of differentiated taxes and subsidies implied by the equalization of earning power is what justice demands in Polypolis, and also what a consistent real-libertarian should advocate. This would be too rash, however, for the proposal under consideration has two exceedingly unwelcome implications. To understand them, let us turn to Lonely and her sibling Lovely. Regarding taste, both siblings are identical. In particular, they both care comparatively little for a high income, while attaching great importance to the enjoyment of free time. Regarding talent, they are identically mediocre in all respects except one: unlike Lonely, Lovely is truly ravishing.

Let us first suppose that the Polypolitans' tastes (and the available technology) are such that Lovely's gorgeous looks enable her to earn a handsome income by displaying them in a peep-show.[8] Understandably, however, she hates that job—as would her sibling if she were given it. How do the siblings fare under the talent egalitarianism sketched above? Lonely cannot complain. Because of her below-average talents, she is further granted a lump-sum subsidy which raises her earning power to the average level. Given her strong desire for leisure (whether used for sunbathing, praying, or campaigning), she has decided to live off this reasonably high income and forgo any additional income she could earn by renting out her modest talents. Lovely is far less fortunate. Her fabulous earning power means that she is forced to pay as a lump-sum tax an amount of money which she could not possibly earn in any occupation other than daily performance in the peep-show. Far from being able to indulge in the same leisurely life pattern as her sibling, she is forced to devote a large chunk of her time—not all of it, but enough to pay the tax and subsist—doing a job she thoroughly hates. Is this not frightfully unfair to Lovely, indeed a form of slavery that violates self-ownership and constitutes an obvious insult to the ideal of real-freedom-for-all?

Next, suppose that for whatever reason there is no peep-show in Polypolis, nor indeed, more generally, any way of making money out of one's looks. The two siblings are now indistinguishable as far as the auction is concerned, and they will both be entitled (owing to their feebly valued talents) to the same lump-sum subsidy. But Lonely is ugly, while Lovely is gorgeous. And while Lovely has a great time flirting in the square, Lonely sadly sits on a lonely bench and occasionally overhears a bad joke about her spotty face and funny nose. Surely, a procedure which treats them alike does not really equalize the resources they are endowed with in order to pursue whatever they regard as valuable. Good looks may matter a great deal even if they do not add a penny to one's earning power. By reducing the talents to be equalized to those affecting a person's earning power, is the auction approach not unacceptably harsh on Lonely, in this second version of our example, and blatantly at odds with our commitment to give all the greatest real freedom to do whatever they might want to do, and not just to make money?

3.3 *Insurance behind a veil of ignorance*

The two implications thus illustrated by Lonely and Lovely constitute fatal objections to the extended auction. The first of them is closely related to the reason Ronald Dworkin (1981*b*: 312) offers for rejecting the extended auction as an appropriate general interpretation of his principle of equality of resources.[9] That he should be bothered by it is not obvious at once. After all, he is not committed to equalizing Lonely's and Lovely's welfare. And resources, as measured by the (competitively determined) cost to others of one's appropriating them, are distributed in spotlessly egalitarian fashion. True, Lovely has less leisure than Lonely. But then her leisure is far more valuable as an asset for the community as a whole (or at least the subset of it that consists in peep-show customers), though not necessarily as a source of enjoyment for herself. As Roemer (1985*b*: 165) points out, the taste a talented person has for the use of her own leisure can be construed as a form of expensive taste. Moreover, Dworkin (1981*b*: 312) does not want to object to the extended auction on the ground that people such as Lovely are treated like things, or that their self-ownership is violated, for such objections rely 'on the idea of pre-political entitlement based on something other than equality' and is 'inconsistent with the premise of the scheme of equality of resources' under consideration.

The way in which Dworkin articulates his dissatisfaction with this implication of the extended auction is by saying that it fails to meet the envy test relevant to the resource-egalitarian ideal he tries to express. Just as one must 'require that no one have less income simply in consequence of less native talent' (ibid.)—the whole point of the extended auction—one must also require that no one be forced to have less *leisure* in consequence of *more* native talent. Failing to do so would mean an unwarranted bias in the understanding of resources. If it could be assumed that people cared for nothing apart from collecting as high an income as possible, it would be legitimate to conflate resources and earning power, as the auction does. Once leisure-lovers such as our two siblings are brought into the picture, this can no longer be legitimate.[10]

We must, therefore, try to imagine some other device, which would get rid of this bias. One possibility Dworkin invites us to consider is as follows. Ask each person to ignore the particular internal endowment she has, while bearing in mind her particular conception of the good life as well as the distribution of all features of internal endowments in the relevant population, and ask her to say for how much she would insure against the presence or absence of any particular feature. The more important a feature is to her (given her conception of the good life), the greater the compensation she will receive in case she turns out not to have it. But the level of the premium she will have to pay (sensibly at a rate increasing with her earning power) increases as the compensation level goes up and will therefore impose a ceiling on the latter. As we shall see shortly, this is not yet the scheme on which Dworkin settles. But it is worth examining, as it clearly holds a promise of meeting both objections illustrated by Lonely and Lovely. If Lovely wants to make sure she will not be stuck in the peep-show, she will just have to keep the amount for which she insures at a low level. And if being attractive matters a lot to Lonely, regardless of any pecuniary consequences, then she will have to make sure she gets a handsome compensation in case she turns out to be ugly—whether to pay for cosmetic surgery or to enable her to do more of the things for which beauty is unnecessary. Such a scheme obviously raises the practical difficulty of detecting the true importance Lonely and Lovely attach to the talents they do not possess: it is in their interest to peep through the veil and pretend they attach the greatest importance to everything they happen to lack. But we can leave this practical difficulty aside, for the proposal is defective for reasons which would apply—as we shall see—even if its implementation were straightforward.

This hypothetical insurance scheme is worth pondering about,[11] and I shall return to it shortly. But it is important to note that it does not coincide with Dworkin's own proposal. The basic reason why he rejects it is that it relies on the possibility of abstracting from the talents one possesses without also abstracting from tastes one only possesses because of the possession of these very talents. Someone without a musical ear, for example, is unlikely to find music of great importance. This difficulty can be avoided, Dworkin (ibid. 316–18, 324–5) suggests, by adopting a slightly different hypothetical insurance scheme, in which insurance takers know both their tastes and their talents, but not the latter's economic rent, that is, how highly the services of these talents happen to be priced on the market. From behind this somewhat thinner veil of ignorance, each person chooses the height of the earning power which she wants to have guaranteed to herself. If the earning power associated to her talents turns out to be lower, she is given a lump-sum subsidy (the net-of-premium benefit from the insurance is positive). If it turns out to be higher, she has to pay a lump-sum tax (the net-of-premium benefit is negative).

Does this more complex scheme handle the two difficulties illustrated by Lonely and Lovely (§ 3.2)? Let us examine, first of all, whether it gets Lovely out of the peep-show. In a society whose members are exclusively concerned with income, risk-averse people will insure at the highest possible level, and all will end up with average earning power—exactly as they did with the extended auction (§ 3.1). But Polypolis is not such a society. Lonely and Lovely, in particular, are anxious to secure as much leisure as possible, subject to earning a subsistence income. Risk-averse people with tastes for leisure and income similar to theirs will not maximin their potential income, but minimax the number of hours they will have to work in order to gain subsistence. If the grant received as a share of external endowments falls short of subsistence, each sibling will opt for an insurance scheme that distributes lump-sum subsidies and taxes in such a way that she will have to work the same number of hours in order to reach the subsistence level, whatever the maximum earning power her talents happen to be associated with. Instead of Lonely being able to spend all her time on her favourite leisure activities (because of receiving more than subsistence income as a lump-sum subsidy), while Lovely had to work nearly full time at the peep-show (because of the lump-sum tax absorbing, say, 95 per cent of her fabulous earning power), as was the case with the extended auction, both siblings now have to work for, say, fifteen hours a week on their most lucrative activity—say, knitting jumpers in one case, appearing in the peep-show in the other.[12]

Of course, Lovely may still envy her sibling because she would rather knit than strip. But the relevant envy test may be said to be met in the sense that no one has less leisure in consequence of more native talent, any more than 'less income simply in consequence of less native talent'. Moreover, in this modified insurance scheme just as in the previous one, the most defensible decision rule is generally not the maximinning of earning power *or* leisure, but rather the maximinning of utility from both work and income. The extent to which the various available jobs are judged attractive by the people concerned would then automatically be taken into account, and such a scheme would only generate the same outcome as the extended auction, so hard on Lovely, if a person's utility coincided with her income—precisely the assumption under which this outcome would no longer look unfair.

Thus, the thin-veil hypothetical insurance scheme proposed by Dworkin is just as effective as the thick-veil scheme examined before in tackling the first of our two difficulties. But it is hopeless at dealing with the second one. The extended auction was not only unsatisfactory because of its toughness with Lovely stuck in the peep-show, but also because of its toughness with Lonely left alone on the bench. But unlike the first insurance scheme, Dworkin's modified one similarly ignores all talents that are not reflected in a higher potential income, and will therefore be just as callous to Lonely as the extended auction was.[13] This is, no doubt, the underlying reason why Dworkin only proposes this thin-veil insurance scheme for lucrative talents and combines it with a thick-veil scheme for 'ordinary handicaps'. In the case of such handicaps, people are assumed to take an insurance as in the first scheme, knowing what tastes they have, but not whether or not they possess the talents whose absence constitutes a handicap. Thus, if Lonely's ugliness is absolutely horrendous, it will presumably qualify as a handicap, and thereby entitle Lonely to a significant compensation.

3.4 Four objections to Dworkin

This hybrid scheme, Dworkin's final proposal,[14] raises a number of difficulties. He himself mentions as its main defect the fact that envy will persist. After receiving due compensation in accordance with the scheme, an unemployed person is still most likely to envy the circumstances of a film star whose skills are in high demand and therefore command a far higher income, even after the payment of the premium (Dworkin 1981*b*: 329). However, this can only occur if people are not assumed to adopt a maximin criterion in taking their insurance decisions.[15] If they do—as I have argued (§ 3.3) can sensibly be assumed in matters of justice—people will still end up with unequal earning powers (like Lonely and Lovely in the first of our two situations), but the scheme will alter these inequalities in such a way that all possible internal endowments will be equivalent to each person, and hence that any welfare difference that may subsist between people can be ascribed to their tastes, not to their talents.

There are, however, three further objections which apply even to the maximin version of the insurance scheme. First, in the case of inequalities that do not involve handicaps, an arbitrary bias subsists between lucrative and non-lucrative talents. If Lovely's earning power is inferior to Lonely's, while Lonely's flirting power is inferior to Lovely's, Dworkin's scheme legitimates a transfer from Lonely to Lovely to compensate for the latter's inferior earning power, but will do nothing to correct Lonely's symmetric inferiority in flirting power. Why this bias? Why this privilege to those aspects of our internal endowments which are, or can be, marketed, as opposed to those which are not or cannot be, whether for physical or social reasons?[16]

Secondly, the status of the key distinction between ordinary handicaps and the lack of specific talents remains problematic. The plausible intuition behind it is that there are general talents (say, sight) everyone firmly values, whether or not one possesses them. Unlike the desire for specific talents (say, the ability to play the oboe), therefore, the desire for general talents can safely be assumed not to be determined by one's particular internal endowment. Hence, abstracting from this endowment does not force us to abstract from that desire, and the first insurance scheme considered above can make sense: one can meaningfully insure with known tastes against the unknown lack of such general talents—that is, against handicaps. The trouble is that *how much* one cares about the absence of general talents is not independent of the specific tastes one has, nor therefore of the particular talents that may have helped generate these tastes. Having one's left hand paralysed no doubt counts as a handicap, but how much one will want to insure it for behind the veil of ignorance will heavily depend on whether, for example, one has developed, as a consequence of possessing some more specific talents, a powerful passion for playing the piano. Hence if the initial insurance scheme is deemed unsuitable for the lack of specific talents, it must also be deemed unsuitable for handicaps, and consistency requires that the fall-back solution—Dworkin's insurance scheme with known talents but unknown earning power—should apply across the board. Tough luck for Lonely: however ugly she is, as long as her potential income is not affected by her ugliness, no compensation whatever will be forthcoming. No relevant distinction can be made between handicaps and other lacks of talents that would soften the sharp asymmetry between lucrative and non-lucrative talents. The second of our two difficulties remains therefore totally unsolved.

Given the cumulative effect of these two objections, one may well be inclined to re-examine the case for abandoning the thick veil of ignorance in favour of a thinner one. There is little promise in denying that people's preferences, their conceptions of what is important in life, are often deeply affected by the talents they happen to possess. But one could argue that it does not follow—at the level of abstraction at which the whole exercise is pitched—that it is impossible to abstract from the latter without abstracting from the former. The fact that I would not be A had it not been for my being B, does not entail that I could not conceivably know that I am A without also knowing that I am B. However, returning to the thick-veil scheme would not get us out of trouble, because there is a final objection to Dworkin's hybrid scheme that applies just as much to both a pure thin-veil scheme and to a pure thick-veil scheme.

Whatever the variant chosen, the counterfactual insurance scheme can be impugned on the ground that it raises a particular version of the expensive taste problem, and hence fails to accomplish the task that we set ourselves at the start. True, the scheme does not amount, as pointed out earlier (§ 3.3), to equalizing welfare. It does not condone an unfair transfer of endowments from the cheerful to the morose. But it does amount to giving unequal external endowments to people with identical talents, because of their different tastes.[17] Suppose you and I have identical internal endowments, including a pathetic disposition for playing the oboe. I am stubbornly sticking to the ambition of becoming a brilliant oboe player, whether for its own sake or because of the fortune I believe I could earn that way. You instead have wisely shifted your aspirations to table football, which we are both far more gifted for. Under the thin-veil variant of the scheme or under Dworkin's hybrid variant, I shall be entitled to compensation to the extent that being a brilliant oboe player would affect my earning power, whereas you will not. Under the thick-veil variant, I shall be entitled to compensation even if no money whatever can be made by playing the oboe. In all three variants, therefore, we find again the implication it was one of our main objectives to avoid. Compared to you, I have an expensive taste whose cost it is right that I should bear. It is not right that you should be penalized, relatively speaking, for having adjusted your ambitions to your circumstances.

What all three variants of the scheme enable you to do, in effect, is fictitiously to insure against your taste for playing the oboe turning out to be costly, due to the absence of a matching talent. The scheme does not generate equality of welfare because, although it allows you to insure against the lack of talents with given tastes, it does not enable you to insure against your having a taste for doing things requiring a talent that happens to be scarce in the relevant population.[18] Under the proposed scheme, those with a taste for playing the oboe will have access to a level of welfare lower than that accessible to those who have instead (*ceteris paribus*) a taste for another activity—say, whistling—whose exercise requires the use of more widespread talents. Though you will not be worse off because of the *talents* you (do not) possess, you may be worse off because of the *tastes* you have. The scheme, therefore, only generates a limited, taste-sensitive equality of welfare. But this does not prevent it from being vulnerable to the expensive-taste objection, since it gives more or less compensation, as we have seen, depending on people's tastes.[19] It therefore fails to live up to the requirements of the task described at the outset and to provide an adequate interpretation of lex-imin real freedom in the context of unequal talents. By giving more resources to those with expensive tastes, it depresses the real freedom of those with cheaper tastes to do whatever they might want to do.

To this objection—the only one I have mentioned which applies to all three variants of the scheme—one may want to reply that this differential compensation according to tastes is all right, being the outcome of what Dworkin (ibid. 293) calls option luck. An insurance scheme is like a lottery. If you play and lose, you cannot complain that you are unfairly treated compared to your sister who played and won, or to your brother who abstained. Fairness requires equality *ex ante*—which is guaranteed in the scheme by access to the same insurance possibilities and the hiding of actual talents—but not equality *ex post*—the outcome of the insurance scheme may give people with identical internal endowments unequal external endowments. But surely this reply misrepresents the status of the insurance scheme. The taste-sensitive inegalitarian outcome could be characterized and legitimized as option luck only if it were the consequence of insurance choices actually made by the people involved. But of course it is not, the insurance being a purely fictitious thought experiment designed to provide us with a determinate criterion for correcting inequalities of talents. And once it is viewed as such, the taste-sensitiveness of the distribution of external endowments comes out as what it truly is: a blatant departure from the principle that people should be held responsible for their preferences and hence cannot legitimately expect to get more than others identically talented because of the mismatch there happens to be between their talents and their tastes.

It may of course be the case that we are being too fussy, and that, in the context of unequal talents, there simply is no criterion that can meet simultaneously all our desiderata.[20] I do not believe so, and I shall present in the next section an alternative criterion that does seem to do the trick, while preserving—under some conditions—the legitimacy of a basic income. Before doing so, however, one final remark about Dworkin's stimulating approach. We have seen above (§ 3.2) why his criterion for the equality of external endowments could not be generalized into the extended auction to cover internal endowments as well. But should we not ask the converse question? What prevents his criterion for the equality of internal endowments from applying to external endowments as well? In other words, instead of adding people's talents to the goods they have received in order for the whole lot to be evaluated at competitive prices, why do we not add their gifts and bequests to their talents in order for the whole lot to be subjected to the insurance scheme? In the simplest variant, this would mean that people would be asked to retain their tastes—for the intrinsic enjoyment of specific external and internal endowments as well as for the instrumental enjoyment of these endowments through the purchasing power they confer—but to ignore how large their endowments are and what they consist of. They can then take insurance in such a way that their getting the worst external and internal endowment, given their tastes, would give rise to the highest compensation, while their getting their best endowment would make them liable to the heaviest tax. However, this does not really yield a scheme different from the one we have been considering so far. If one opts, as before, for a maximin criterion—and given a number of mild assumptions, such as non-satiation in external endowments—the global insurance scheme thus constructed leads to equalizing the value of external endowments in the special case of identical talents, that is, to the criterion adopted at the first stage of the discussion, at which differences in internal endowments were ignored (§ 2.6). This observation shows the coherence of Dworkin's treatment of external and internal endowments: his treatment of the latter *is* a generalization of his treatment of the former, though not the most obvious one. At the same time, it shows that our negative conclusion about the counterfactual insurance schemes has not been reached at the cost of ignoring their most general version, to which the above discussion is no less relevant.

3.5 Ackerman generalized

Before considering a final proposal, let us first go back a few steps. Both the extended auction, with which we started this discussion (§ 3.1), and, as we have just seen, Dworkin's insurance scheme can be seen as generalizations of the approach adopted in the case of external endowments (§ 2.7). The latter was chosen as the most plausible way of avoiding the ubiquitous indeterminacy that would arise if one restricted oneself to the following formulation: one person is less (really) free than another if the set of options (really) open to the former is a proper subset of the set of options (really) open to the latter. The opportunity cost metric proposed seemed ethically far more meaningful, in particular, than a physicalist metric of spatio-temporal possibilities, and unlike a metric of potential welfare, it does not systematically reward expensive tastes. But now that this metric too has proved inadequate in a context of unequal talents, it is worth going back to the very weak notion of equality as the absence of a strict inclusion of one person's option-set in another person's. Those inclined to discard this suggestion straightaway on the ground of its being excessively inegalitarian should pause to reflect on the following two considerations. First, the criterion of non-inclusion would now operate on the background of a strongly egalitarian distribution of external endowments. Secondly, it could be sensibly improved, and made significantly more demanding, by interpreting options as possibilities of access to some worthwhile existence, or as equipments for some sensible conception of the good life—where what is 'worthwhile' or 'sensible' is decided by its actually being sustained in the society considered.

The latter suggestion amounts to proposing a criterion of justice in matters of internal endowments that can be viewed as a generalization of an idea put forward by Ackerman (1980: 116) in the context of genetic engineering. As Ackerman uses it himself, 'dominated diversity' applies to genetic features only. But the notion generalizes naturally to all talents or aspects of a person's internal endowment, as the latter has been understood so far, including features that are due to accidents (whether ante- or post-natal) or to a person's family or social environment. A's internal endowment (a vector of talents) *dominates* B's internal endowment if and only if every person (given her own conception of the good life) would prefer to have the former than the latter.[21] If there were a boundless variety of conceptions of the good life, such dominance could only occur if A were superior to B in all respects (i.e. in each component of the vector), and hence hardly ever: a blind and deaf spastic may still have nicer hair than some or be better than others at arithmetic, which would be deemed sufficient to make for a more favourable endowment by at least one person, given her conception of the good life. If people's conceptions of life display a convergence on the relative importance given to the various components of the vector, however, what will be required for dominance to obtain will fall far short of superiority for each feature.[22] At the limit, if the only thing people care about is the ability to curl their tongues, superiority along this dimension entails dominance, however poorly one performs in all other dimensions of life.

This criterion is of central importance, according to Ackerman, not only to formulate a consistent liberal position in matters of genetic engineering—which need not detain us here[23]—but also, in case genetic engineering is not used or fails, to determine who owes compensation to whom because of a better internal endowment. Here is Ackerman's (ibid. 132) formula: 'Pick any two people out of the population. Compare their genetic endowments. In principle, two—and only two—conclusions are possible. Either A genetically dominates B and B may properly demand compensatory assistance; or A and B stand in a relation of undominated equality, and B gains no relief—no matter how envious of A's talents he may be.' The precise criterion that emerges roughly coincides with the standard distinction between the 'normal' and the 'handicapped'. For any 'normal' person X, although it will be very easy for *each* member of a large community to name one person she regards as better endowed than X, it is very unlikely that there will be *any single person* which *all* would regard as better endowed than X. For any 'handicapped' person Y, on the other hand, although it will still be possible to find people whom some, indeed all, regard as less well endowed than Y, it will be easy to find people whom all would regard as better endowed.[24] On Ackerman's criterion, therefore, it is very unlikely that any normal person will be entitled to any compensation, while all the 'handicapped' will be entitled to compensation from some other (less) 'handicapped' and from many (not necessarily all) 'normal' persons.

How can this criterion be handled in practice? As Ackerman (ibid. 133) points out, one will have to start by marking out broad categories dominated by a large number of their fellows. But how much compensation is owed by the 'dominators' to the 'dominated'? Minimally, one must make sure that the 'dominated' do not get a worse deal than others in other respects, material wealth or education for example (ibid. 246–7). Beyond that, all Ackerman (ibid. 247–9) says, and claims that can be said, is that in at least one other respect they must be given at least somewhat more than their 'dominators'. However, a more precise suggestion comes up naturally. We have assumed, in our initial characterization of Polypolis, that people had been given the highest sustainable basic income, and that this was what justice required, had they all been equally talented. One could then uniformly reduce this equal amount given to all, and use the amount thus saved as compensation to the 'handicapped' (possibly used to build up the latter's internal resources: money for an eye operation). This procedure comes to a rest as soon as, for each pair of *comprehensive*, that is, internal-cum-external, endowments, there is at least one person who prefers either endowment to the other.[25] Whether this happens before the uniform external endowment given to all is driven down to zero—and hence whether the condition of undominated diversity could be satisfied without violating self-ownership (by introducing lump-sum taxes) is an empirical matter. It depends on the frequency of malformations and accidents, on the wealth of the society concerned, and, last but not least, on the diversity of the conceptions of the good life.[26]

Once again, we seem to have completed our task. Like the extended auction and the various counterfactual insurance schemes considered, the procedure thus sketched recognizes the fact that it would be unfair to distribute external endowments irrespective of people's internal endowment. At the same time, like the extended auction but unlike the counterfactual insurance schemes, it does not give more or less compensation depending on the tastes two identically talented people happen to have. How does it fare with the two difficulties on which the extended auction faltered? Can it simultaneously avoid enslaving the talented (the peep-show) and paying privileged attention to lucrative talents (the bench in the square)?

On the first issue, Lovely and her likes are undoubtedly better protected against any disadvantage they may owe to their talents than was the case with the extended auction. If the society only consisted of people with the same talents as Lonely and Lovely and if the external resources made available to each of them from the outside (say, from nature) were sufficient to cover subsistence, there would be no redistribution whatever from leisure-loving Lovelies to equally leisure-loving Lonelies, however high the former's earning power. If instead some work is needed to reach subsistence, some redistribution from those with access to quicker ways of earning the required income will be in order—unless working in a peep-show is regarded by all as lexicographically worse (i.e. worse no matter how well paid) than earning one's living by knitting. But this will never reach the point where the Lovelies would prefer the Lonelies' fate to their own, since it is only as long as everyone prefers Lovely's situation to Lonely's that redistribution is warranted.

It is, however, important to recognize that the pattern of transfers that maximizes basic income subject to the constraint of undominated diversity is generally not the only one (if there is one) that satisfies the latter. Instead of diminishing everyone's basic income in favour of those with dominated internal endowments, up to the point where no comprehensive endowment is dominated any longer, one could carry on up to, for example, the far more distant point where distributing any further to those with dominated internal endowments would begin to involve dominance of the others' comprehensive endowments. Stopping the process *as soon as at least one* person starts preferring the fate of the handicapped is no more legitimate than stopping it *just before everyone* prefers it, or indeed anywhere in between. The second extreme possibility is just as consistent as the first one with equality of endowments, conceived as undominated diversity. If it were adopted, we would of course be stuck with the slavery of the talented. Assuming there is at least one person in Lovely's society who has no other concern than earning as much money as possible, Lovely would then be faced with a heavy lump-sum tax that will force her to work for long hours in the peep-show, no matter how much she loathes the job.[27] Undominated diversity, however, is not proposed here as a full characterization of the ideal of real-freedom-for-all, but as a component of such a characterization that enters as a constraint on the maximization of everyone's basic income.

Secondly, does the scheme grant any privilege to inequalities in lucrative talents? Clearly not. Whether for lucrative or non-lucrative talents, only 'handicaps', that is, unanimously recognized overall disadvantages, are allowed compensation. As far as lucrative talents are concerned, these disadvantages need not take the form of one or more major identifiable defects, such as blindness or paraplegia. They can simply consist in the inability to make ends meet, owing to a modest endowment for those features whose services happen to be in demand on the market.[28] In a rich society with a substantial (highest sustainable) basic income, this case may never occur. But in a poor society, where both the wage rate for the unskilled and the highest sustainable level of basic income are low, this case will often occur. In order to fund the required transfers, one may then have to drive the basic income down to zero. Indeed, one would have to drive it into negative figures (in the form of a lump-sum tax) if this were not pre-empted by the constraint of self-ownership. This is the case in which concern with real-freedom-for-all recommends a conditional type of guaranteed minimum income, for if the most effective way of identifying most of those whose endowments do not enable them to earn a living, is by restricting transfers to those who give evidence that they are unable to find an adequate job, then it makes sense to propose that the minimum guaranteed income scheme should be conditional, in the sense of involving a willingness-to-work requirement. Moreover, once there is a need for a requirement of this sort, an *ex ante* transfer system is no longer necessarily cheaper to run, even with computerized payments, than an *ex post* one. Hence there are conditions under which it is right, from a real-libertarian perspective, that the minimum guaranteed income should be work-tested and means-tested.[29] Beyond the unanimously recognized necessities, however, the fact that someone is bad at earning money does not justify any transfer at all on the basis of our criterion of undominated diversity, providing of course (as is likely in a heterogeneous society) that all those better than her at making money are worse than her in at least one other respect that is judged decisive by at least one person.

Before considering some objections, it may be illuminating to relate the present approach to the notion of envy-freeness closely related to our criterion for the fair distribution of external endowments. What is required by the Dworkin–Varian criterion of envy-freeness over external endowments is that there be no pair of people such that one prefers the other person's endowment to her own. What undominated diversity requires is only that there be no pair of people such that *all* prefer one person's endowment to the other's.[30] As mentioned earlier (§ 3.1), the first criterion is generally impossible to satisfy, as soon as endowments are understood to include internal features: someone with Lonely's endowment and an overwhelming drive for income will envy Lovely's endowment as long as they have the same external endowment, but Lovely will envy that person's comprehensive endowment as soon as one tries (however inadequately) to reduce this envy with some compensating transfer of external resources. The second criterion—undominated diversity—can be viewed against this background as replacing envy-freeness by *potential envy-freeness* and thereby avoiding the general impossibility just mentioned. For comprehensive endowments to be distributed in a fair fashion, it is no longer required that no one should envy anyone else's endowment, but only that no one should envy anyone else's endowment under at least one available preference schedule (that can vary for each pair-wise comparison). In other words, the partial ordering given by the intersection of all the individual orderings of the various comprehensive endowments is taken to provide a characterization of unfairness.[31]

3.6 Not enough redistribution?

In this light, let us first consider the objection that our criterion justifies far too little redistribution. It is enough for one queer fellow to consider blindness a blessing for compensation to the blind to cease to be required. To tackle this challenge, one should begin by stressing that the relevant preference schedules must be genuine and somehow available to the people concerned. For redistribution from the A-endowed to the B-endowed to stop, it is not enough for someone to declare, or even to believe, that B is just as good as A. It can only stop when it is true that at least one person who knows and understands all the consequences of having B rather than A judges in the light of her conception of a good life that B is no worse than A. Some of the queer fellows one may have in mind can no doubt be disqualified on the ground that they do not understand what they are talking about. If any are left, they are likely to belong to isolated subsocieties, whose cultural world is unavailable to others (this is precisely why these regard them as queer), and hence whose preference schedules cannot be viewed as generally available.[32] If these two conditions are met, that is, if there is no problem with either understanding or availability—and if, therefore, there is no 'queerness' left—there is nothing shocking, it seems to me, in discontinuing redistribution.

Cannot one then object, secondly, that the proposed solution, even if it is acceptable in general, does not fit the case in which the only person whose tastes prevent dominance from occurring is precisely the person whose endowment is found worse by everyone else, typically a person afflicted by a handicap and attempting to come to terms with her situation by adjusting her preferences. Along with welfare egalitarianism, undominated diversity seems to have the unwelcome consequence of penalizing people with adaptive tastes. One amendment worth contemplating is to exclude a person's own preferences from the pair-wise comparisons that are relevant to the criterion. But this would clearly be a bad move. To start with, it would allow people with identical handicaps to be entitled to different levels of compensation—an implication that was decisive in the rejection of Dworkin's scheme. For a particularly perverse illustration of this implication, imagine two people, one of them the single atheist in her community, who lacks a feature—say, comfortable knees—that is required to perform some essential religious practice—say, spending hours praying. The suggested amendment bizarrely implies that the atheist, who does not care a little bit about the lack of this feature, would receive compensation, while the believer, who is made bitterly miserable by this incapacity, would receive nothing.[33] Furthermore, the suggested amendment would generally fail to block the penalization of adaptive tastes, for the simple reason that one can usually expect a number of similarly situated people to have developed similar tastes. Hence, the adaptive tastes of some others would prevent redistribution to each of them.

One might wish to deal with both objections to the suggested amendment by requiring that one should discount not only the preferences of the person who risks losing her entitlement to compensation because of adaptive tastes, but those of all the people who share her objective situation. However, the hopelessness of this strategy becomes blatant as soon as one realizes the difficulty of meaningfully characterizing 'similar situations' when comparisons need to range over comprehensive endowments that are points in multidimensional continua. Hence the following suggestion. Why not stick to the simple criterion of undominated diversity without either the original or the modified amendment? Having an unusual pattern of preferences that happens to be (or has become) well suited to one's particular set of capacities and handicaps can then legitimately disqualify someone for compensation she would otherwise be entitled to. But what is wrong with this? One must, of course, make sure that the preferences are genuine, that they do not rest on delusion, and are consistent with full information and understanding. This should take care of the cases in which 'penalizing' adaptive preferences is uncontroversially counterintuitive. Beyond this, ignoring some people's preferences would amount to not giving them the equal respect they deserve.

Another objection to the effect that undominated diversity does not justify enough redistribution stresses the relevance of features of a person's situation that do not belong to her comprehensive endowment. To illustrate, suppose, first, that people have identical talents, equally valuable external endowments, and the same preferences, including a strong attachment to the place where they grew up, but that the cost of living happens to be far higher (for reasons that are of no intrinsic value to the people concerned) in some places than others and hence that some people can satisfy their desire to keep living in their homeland only at the expense of a lower standard of living. Secondly, suppose that people have identical talents, equally valuable external endowments, and the same preferences, including a strong sense of duty towards their elderly relatives that imposes strong constraints on what they can do with their lives, but that some of them have elderly relatives and others not. In either example, there is no dominated diversity among comprehensive endowments. Yet, one cannot say: it is up to the people who feel hard up to adopt another preference schedule available in the community. There is none, since all preferences are assumed identical. This suggests that envy-freeness and undominated diversity should rather be defined over 'situations' (in a sense that encompasses but reaches beyond external and internal endowments), as suggested in fact by Tinbergen (1946: 59–60) in the first known formulation of the concept of envy-freeness. In both our examples, undominated diversity would then justify granting unequally valuable external endowments to identically talented people as a way of compensating disadvantages in objective situations more broadly construed. But here again, preference diversity will soon block the need for compensation: it is enough that one of the community's members should not give a damn about living close to her birthplace or about assisting her elderly relatives, for the ground for special compensation to disappear.[34]

3.7 Alternative strategies

Thus, my general strategy for tackling the objection that undominated diversity does not require enough redistribution consists in stressing that the preferences involved must be both genuine and available. It is worth stressing that in so doing I am rejecting at least three alternative strategies one might think of. One consists in viewing endowments not as means for pursuing what it is *possible* for people to *believe* to be a good life, but rather as means for pursuing what we *know* to be a good life. The latter may not be conceived in a very homogeneous way and may therefore also fall short of providing a complete ordering.[35] Yet it could be restrictive enough to allow for redistribution despite the presence of odd preference profiles that would block it if the criterion of undominated diversity were adopted. Adopting this first strategy, however, would amount to 'thickening' one's conception of the good beyond the equal respect assumption, one of the core presuppositions of real-libertarianism (§ 1.8).

The second strategy upholds this assumption, but weakens the requirement that redistribution is only warranted when there is unanimous agreement that one endowment is superior to another. Why not be content with, say, a two-thirds majority? In most cases, this suggestion too would get rid of the difficulty presented for undominated diversity by the possibility of queer or adaptive preferences. But it raises fatal difficulties of its own. First, it opens the possibility of cycles closely analogous to those exemplified by Condorcet's paradox: there may be a majority preferring A's endowment to B's , another majority preferring B's to C's, and yet another preferring C's to A's. In that case, one would need to redistribute from A to B, and also from B to C, thereby making the majority preference of C over A even stronger than it was. With unrestricted preference profiles, only unanimity guarantees that such cycles, which make the criterion useless, do not occur. Secondly and more fundamentally, the sheer number of people holding a particular conception of the good cannot really be relevant. What matters, as explained above, is whether people could feasibly adopt—and hence could fairly be held responsible for failing to adopt—a view by reference to which their endowment would be no worse than the one to which it is being compared. This is what availability (in any number) in the person's community is meant to provide a (roughly) sufficient condition for.

The third strategy consists in turning to the variant of the welfarist approach that comes closest to the approach that is being proposed here. It is presented and defended under the heading of equal opportunity for welfare in various papers by Richard Arneson (1989, 1990*a*, 1991, 1992*a*) and has already been briefly discussed in connection with the just distribution of external endowments (§ 2.6). The key question to ask, when considering this alternative criterion, is whether tastes are supposed to be malleable or given. If they are supposed to be fully malleable, everyone can be blissful with any endowment, and all endowments become equivalent. If instead tastes are given, the untalented with a taste for playing the oboe will have a lesser opportunity for welfare, and will therefore be entitled to a compensation to which an identically talented person with no such taste will not be entitled. In order to avoid the dilemma between bliss in all cases and the rewarding of expensive tastes, one can sensibly restrict malleability to 'accessible' preference schedules, that is, to tastes one has the capacity, though not necessarily the desire, to acquire. Equality of opportunity for welfare is then achieved if the expected level of welfare under the best suited of accessible preference schedules is equal for all (presumably taking the cost of taste alteration into account). The dilemma is avoided, since (1) owing to the limits on accessibility, not all endowments yield the same opportunity for welfare, and (2) if two people have the same talents, including the same grip on their tastes, equal opportunity for welfare treats them identically, irrespective of their current tastes.

This comes quite close to undominated diversity as clarified above—so close that one may wonder whether any difference is left.[36] Since the criteria of accessibility (as used to reinterpret equal opportunity for welfare) and of availability (as used to clarify undominated diversity) are practically equivalent, where can the difference be? Consider a society with two categories of people: some with a taste for a quiet, undemanding life—call them hippies—and others with great ambitions—call them yuppies. The hippies have talents slightly better adapted to a quiet life than the yuppies, and the yuppies possess talents far better suited to their own ambitions than the hippies. Yet, with given tastes, the hippies' opportunity for welfare or preference satisfaction (on any non-tautological interpretation) is far superior to the yuppies', precisely because of their lesser 'ambitions'. Neither category, however, would like to swap its situation (talents plus tastes) with that of the other if it could: in a hippie's view, a yuppy's life is sheer nonsense, while, in a yuppy's view, a hippie's life is pure mediocrity. Against the background of this story, let us contrast the implications of undominated diversity and equal opportunity for welfare under two different factual assumptions.

Suppose first that tastes are not malleable: people are stuck with them, and the inability to change them is therefore a feature of their internal endowment. As we have assumed that there was no envy—and hence *a fortiori* no dominated diversity—in terms of overall situations, undominated diversity does not require any transfer. But as we have assumed differences in the expected levels of preference satisfaction, equal opportunity for welfare does require a large compensatory transfer, curiously perhaps from the less talented hippies to the more talented yuppies, to enable these to satisfy their tastes to the same extent as the hippies satisfy theirs. (This would hold even if the yuppies had talents better suited not just to their own, but also to the hippies' lifestyle). There is nothing counterintuitive about the latter implication, one might argue, if one thinks about it as compensation for an addiction. But the notion of an addiction conflates two things: an addiction is a taste one cannot (easily) get rid of, and it is a taste one does not identify with, one that can be an obstacle to the pursuit of one's fundamental aims. In our example, however, only the first feature was assumed. If the second feature were too, envy-freeness may no longer obtain and, if it does not, undominated diversity is likely to join equal opportunity for welfare in justifying a transfer to the addicted yuppies. If the second feature is not present, however, that is, if the yuppies are stuck with their ambitious tastes, but would not want to get rid of them anyway, all things considered, if they were not, then what is it that justifies a transfer from the less talented hippies to the more talented yuppies, as equal opportunity for welfare, unlike undominated diversity, would recommend? It can only be the (illiberal) view that there is only one thing that matters or should matter to people, or to the distribution of resources among them, namely (opportunity for) welfare or preference satisfaction.

Let us now suppose, secondly, that each category could adopt (at negligible cost) the other category's tastes. People's particular tastes (or their inability to change them) could then no longer be regarded as a fixed feature of their internal endowment. Undominated diversity will again, though for a distinct reason—the absence of envy, with current preferences, over the bundles of talents (not over the overall situations)—fail to require any transfer. Equal opportunity for welfare, on the other hand, will again justify a transfer from those less well equipped for an ambitious life (the hippies) to those better equipped for it (the yuppies), though this time only to the extent required to equip the latter as well as the former for an undemanding life, and thereby giving them the same opportunity for welfare under the most favourable set of tastes. (In this case, unlike the first one, the transfer would go the other way if the yuppies were better equipped for both types of life.) Such a transfer would be justified, from the standpoint of equal opportunity for welfare, even if the yuppies looked down upon the mediocre life of the hippies and would never avail themselves of this possibility of pursuing happiness. Why? The answer, once again, can only be that all that matters or should matter, whatever people think about it, is (opportunity for) welfare or preference satisfaction. If this monistic view of the good is abandoned, undominated diversity is the obvious alternative.[37]

3.8 Too much redistribution?

Let us now turn to the symmetric objection. Far from implying too little redistribution, is it not the case that undominated diversity justifies too much of it? One reason may be that, in recommending redistribution when it does, it is being inconsistent with the expensive-taste argument used against Dworkin's (§ 3.4) and other proposals (§ 2.6). If we say, as we have done, that those with a taste but no gift for playing the oboe must not make others bear the cost of this unfortunate taste, should we not also say that the blind with a taste for seeing, or the deaf with a taste for hearing, must similarly be made to bear the full cost of the tastes they happen to have? The formulation just given highlights the intuition behind the criterion that is being offered. Compensation between two people stops when potential envy-freeness starts, when the repertoire of available preference schedules is such that neither endowment is unanimously preferred to the other. The fact that everyone prefers endowment A to endowment B provides highly plausible ground for considering that the person endowed with B must not be held responsible for persistently preferring A to B. She cannot reasonably be expected to adopt a preference no one has. This is why the blind or the deaf can safely count on significant levels of compensation.[38] But if this is the underlying intuition, we must, of course, be careful to pick an adequate definition of the relevant community. The inability to make an effective use of one's fists, to afford a pilgrimage to Mecca, or to match the colours of one's clothes may count as 'handicaps' to be compensated if a pretty homogeneous cultural group is taken as the relevant community, but not if a large, diverse, pluralist society is selected instead. The nature of customs, and the degree to which they are shared, thus enter the determination of what counts as adequate compensation according to the criterion that is here being offered.[39] In a society such as ours, with real exit possibilities from homogeneous groups and ubiquitous mass media spreading the awareness of diverse conceptions of the good life, the relevant universe of preference schedules is very large.[40]

There is a second reason why a consistent real-libertarian may be led to think that the proposed criterion leads to an excessive level of redistribution. Is the strict satisfaction of undominated diversity not likely to require the unreasonable sacrifice of much real freedom on the part of most members of the community?[41] True, in a society with a wide diversity of conceptions of the good life, the level of redistribution required to meet undominated diversity is far less than the level that would be required to achieve equality of welfare, for example, or equality of resources in the sense of the extended auction. As soon as one person genuinely finds an initially dominated endowment at least as good as that of the contributors to the redistribution scheme, redistribution can stop. But clearly, some people may be so badly handicapped that even massive transfers from the rest of society would hardly make their situation more attractive, and would therefore still fail to meet the criterion.

In order to deal adequately with this objection, undominated diversity must be qualified in two ways. First, once sustainability is brought into the picture, it is not the simple version of the criterion that provides a legitimate constraint from a real-libertarian standpoint, but a leximin variant of it. If the impact of the taxes and transfers required to sustainably maintain undominated diversity is such that everyone would gain from keeping some pattern of dominance in place, concern with the greatest real freedom for all will obviously recommend that the latter be tolerated.[42] Secondly, like the priority of formal freedom, the priority of undominated diversity must not be understood in rigid fashion. 'Mild' violations of it can be admitted if they prevent 'considerable' losses for the rest of society. Hence, before reaching the point where further redistribution to the badly handicapped becomes counterproductive in absolute terms (taking dynamic effects into account), it may be legitimate to stop it because very large further transfers would only produce a hardly noticeable improvement in the beneficiary's situation. These two qualifications should go a long way towards meeting Sen's (1990*b*: 462–3) concern that 'aggregative considerations' including—but not reducing to—Pareto-optimality, should be brought into the picture and soften undominated diversity's exclusively distributive concern, or Arneson's (1992*a*: § 5) objection that there are significant non-egalitarian values by which egalitarian concerns should sometimes be overridden.[43]

Thus clarified and qualified, the requirement of undominated diversity remains an important constraint. In all circumstances, it will reduce significantly the highest sustainable level of basic income, and in some circumstances, it will drive this level down to zero.[44] But it does not seem unreasonable to believe, bearing in mind the qualifications that have just been made, that under the conditions that now prevail in advanced industrial societies, the highest sustainable basic income consistent with both formal freedom and undominated diversity can confidently be expected to be quite substantial, indeed to exceed what is there unanimously considered as belonging to the bare necessities. In a society that is not only sufficiently diverse (which makes dominance less frequent for 'subjective' reasons), but also sufficiently healthy (which makes dominance less frequent for 'objective' reasons) and sufficiently affluent (which drives up the average external endowment), a small minority of 'handicapped' people will be entitled to differentiated transfers, but the majority consisting of 'normal' people will remain entitled to a substantial basic income.[45]

APPENDIX 1: ROEMER VERSUS DWORKIN

In one of the most thorough discussions of Dworkin's approach, John Roemer (1985*b*, 1986) considers and rejects the simple insurance scheme sketched in § 3.3. To start with, the latter has a number of embarrassing implications. For example, like the extended auction (§ 3.1), it 'appears to overcompensate those whose bad luck we wished to repair': the talented become worse off than the untalented.

Moreover, though introduced in order to soften the fate of the talented (relative to the extended auction), the insurance scheme makes the talented worse off than under the extended auction scheme (Roemer 1985*b*: 173). However, these claims crucially depend on the assumption that each agent 'agrees to make payments to or to receive payments from others, depending on which state of the world occurs, in such a way as *to maximize his expected utility* over the various states of the world'. Roemer (ibid. 159) recognizes that 'the expected-utility model of behavior, and therefore in particular of insurance-taking behavior, has been challenged in recent years'. And he further concedes that 'Dworkin does not propose this kind of insurance (which economists consider to be rational insurance), but rather a minimum floor insurance policy where a person insures himself not to maximize expected utility, but to guarantee some minimum income. Dworkin does not describe in a sufficiently precise way how his catastrophe insurance is defined [. . .].' (Roemer, ibid. 175)

The obvious alternative conjecture, which Roemer does not consider, is that Dworkin's agents want to maximize not expected utility but minimum utility. Maximin makes a lot of sense when what is at issue is not one of the many decisions which you have to take in the course of your life, but the one big decision which determines how much will be put at your disposal to conduct the whole of your life. The case for expected-utility maximization is compelling when there is a long run to think about. But it falls apart when the coin is tossed only once.[46] In the first-best world considered here, such maximin welfare insurance (with known tastes but unknown talents) yields equal welfare in all circumstances with given tastes.[47] Both of Roemer's embarrassing specific implications mentioned above are then avoided: when this criterion is used instead of utility maximization, the talented cannot become worse off than the untalented (with the same tastes), nor worse off than under the tough deal they got out of the extended auction. When interpreted in this more charitable way, the insurance scheme is immune to the fire of Roemer's muskets.

But it does not seem capable of escaping his heavy artillery, for Roemer does not rest content with pointing out embarrassing implications. He also establishes a general impossibility claim to the effect that 'there is no mechanism which distributes transferable resources in a way which resource egalitarianism requires, except one: the mechanism that allocates resources to equalize welfare' (see Roemer 1985*b*: 175–6; and 1986). If this claim is valid, and actually says what it seems to say, then there is no way in which our task, as characterized in §3.1, can ever be completed, and the insurance scheme, like any other scheme that does not end up equalizing welfare, is bound to violate at least one of the plausible desiderata that make up the requirements of resource egalitarianism. One of these, the axiom of consistency, stipulates that as one extends equalization to a new type of resource, those who have few of these resources are not made worse off as a result. Innocuous though it seems, this requirement is question-begging. If resources are defined as anything that may affect one's welfare, including the 'tastes' which, jointly with a person's objective situation, determine a person's level of welfare, then this axiom directly entails the demand that people with expensive tastes should not be penalized. If instead one makes a sharp distinction between people's endowments—what is given to them, without their bearing any responsibility for having or lacking them—and their tastes or ambitions—which they can legitimately be held responsible for, then this axiom no longer does such a thorough job. As Roemer (ibid. 179–80) recognizes *in fine*, one can avoid the reduction of equality of resources to equality of welfare, even at a first-best level of analysis, if one succeeds in 'formulat[ing] criteria for differentiating those aspects of a person which constitute his resources from those which constitute his preferences'.[48]

However, once this conceptual distinction is made, it is not impossible in principle (though not easy in practice) to draw a meaningful boundary—at least for anyone who does not hold a determinist position.[49] Factors which do not qualify as endowments can then prevent equality of resources from collapsing into equality of welfare, thereby blocking the compensation of expensive tastes. Once the relevant boundary is drawn, the hypothetical insurance scheme described above no longer has the consequence that one should tax the cheerful and subsidize the morose up to the point where they will all be equally (un)happy. Given the background assumptions—including the interpersonal comparability of welfare levels—people with identical tastes will, whatever their talents, end up with the same welfare. But people with different tastes will not.

APPENDIX 2: AFFLUENCE, OPULENCE, ABUNDANCE, AND MINIMUM INCOME GUARANTEES

Because of the constraint of undominated diversity, there are situations in which a real-libertarian conception of justice requires that the minimum income guarantee should take the form of a work-tested and/or means-tested scheme, rather than that of a genuine basic income. These situations can be characterized as follows. Define an *affluent* society as a society which can sustainably guarantee all its members, without violating their self ownership, access to an income at least sufficient to cover what they unanimously regard as the bare necessities. Define an *opulent* society as a society which can sustainably grant all its members, without violating their self-ownership, a *basic income* (as defined in § 2.1) at least sufficient to cover what they unanimously regard as the bare necessities. Except under the unrealistic assumption that the highest sustainable guaranteed income is unconditional in the four senses that define a basic income, real-libertarianism requires the minimum guaranteed income to have no basic income component in a society that is not affluent, to have some basic income component in a society that is affluent but not opulent, and to consist entirely of a basic income in an opulent society.

In a language suggested by Nove (1983) and used in Van Parijs (1993a: ch. 10), opulence coincides with abundance in the relatively weak sense of uncompelled supply sustainably covering subsistence demand. Stronger senses of abundance include the sustainability of zero-price supply covering subsistence demand and the sustainability of zero-price supply covering zero-price demand. If P means sustainability, while G refers to the level of the unconditional basic income and N_i, W_i, and X_i refer to the needs, wants, and overall income of individual i, these three notions can be characterized, respectively, as

$$P \ (\forall \ i, G \geq N_i) \ (\text{opulence}) \tag{1}$$
$$P \ (\forall \ i, G = X_i \geq N_i) \ (\text{strong abundance}) \tag{2}$$
$$P \ (\forall \ i, G = X_i \geq W_i) \ (\text{absolute abundance}). \tag{3}$$

Affluence, which is much weaker than even the weakest of these three abundance concepts, can in turn be characterized as the sustainability of generating and distributing income in such a way that everyone's needs are covered, i.e.

$$P \ (\forall \ i, X_i \geq N_i) \ (\text{affluence}). \tag{4}$$

But being a matter of distributive sufficiency, affluence is still far more demanding than *aggregate sufficiency*, or the sustainability of generating an aggregate income covering aggregate needs, i.e.

$$P \ (\Sigma \ X_i \geq \Sigma \ N_i). \tag{5}$$

APPENDIX 3: UNDOMINATED DIVERSITY AND ENVY-FREENESS

The proposed criterion of undominated diversity (or potential envy-freeness) can be formally characterized as follows, with E_i standing for individual i's comprehensive endowment, and with $\geq_k$ (resp. $>_k$) standing for 'strictly preferred to or judged equivalent by individual k' (resp. strictly preferred by k):

$$(\forall i)(\forall j)(\exists k) \ (E_i \geq_k E_j) \ (\text{undominated diversity}). \tag{1}$$

It is obviously far weaker than envy-freeness, or

$$(\forall i)(\forall j) \ (E_i \geq_i E_j) \ (\text{envy-freeness}). \tag{2}$$

It is also far easier to satisfy than 'potential envy-freeness' (see Fleurbaey 1994) understood as the existence, for each person, of some existing preference schedule (possibly, but not necessarily, her own) which would, if she adopted it, make her prefer her own endowment to that of all the others, i.e.

$$(\forall i)(\exists k)(\forall j) \ (E_i \geq_k E_j) \ (\text{'potential envy-freeness'}). \tag{3}$$

But it is far stronger than two other construals of the expression 'undominated diversity' (see Fleurbaey 1991). One only requires that there be no person whose endowment is preferred by all to all other endowments, i.e.

$$\neg(\exists \ i)(\forall j) \ (\forall k) \ (E_i >_k E_j) \ (\text{no unanimous best choice}). \tag{4}$$

The other requires that there be no person whose endowment is found strictly worse by all than all other endowments, i.e.

$$\neg(\exists\, i)(\forall j)\,(\forall k)\,(E_i <_k E_j)\ \text{(no unanimous worst choice)}. \tag{5}$$

An interesting strong variant of undominated diversity is suggested by Iturbe and Nieto (1992), as modified by Fleurbaey (1994): Choose the size ($\leq n$) of group K (including i) as small as possible and require

$$(\forall i)(\forall j)(\neg\exists\, K)(\forall k \in K)\,(E_i <_k E_j). \tag{6}$$

When envy-freeness is possible, this criterion selects an envy-free allocation. When it is not, the criterion does not jump all the way, as does undominated diversity, to requiring only that i's endowments should not be recognized as inferior to j's by all n members of society. More demandingly, it requires its not being recognized as inferior by some subset K of members of society. This refinement of the criterion of selection has the advantage of ordering, in the spirit of the approach I am proposing, large sets of allocations which the latter leaves unordered. It is therefore better equipped to face the objection of not being redistributive enough (§ 3.6). However, given the adjustments that need to be made, whichever variant is chosen, in order to accommodate the objection of being too redistributive (§ 3.8), I do not believe the guidance given by the stronger variant would differ noticeably from that given by my simpler variant.

CHAPTER 4

Jobs as assets

PROLOGUE

Δ *Perhaps you have done enough, by bringing in your constraint of undominated diversity, to assuage my feeling that your interpretation of real-freedom-for-all was biased against the poorly talented. But I feel even more strongly that this interpretation—basic income maximization subject to some constraints—is biased in favour of the lazy, of those who choose to spend their days surfing, at the expense of the hard workers.*

Φ Would you mind calling these the crazy? It is all too easy to let moral preferences between different conceptions of the good life creep into the argument and pervert its conclusions.

Δ *Fair enough. I realize that your conception of justice as real-freedom-for-all is committed to an equal respect towards the various moral outlooks that coexist in our pluralistic societies. But my point is precisely that your interpretation is discriminatory. To make things simple, suppose Crazy and Lazy are identically talented. With the highest sustainable basic income in place, you may wish to tell Crazy that she should not complain about Lazy's cushy situation, since she could have made exactly the same choice. But if there were no basic income at all, I could similarly tell Lazy that he should not complain about Crazy's lavish income, since he could also have made exactly the same choice. By opting for a maximum basic income, you arbitrarily make things as good as possible for Lazy, but as bad as possible for Crazy. Do you call that fair? (§ 4.1).*

Φ Not—I agree—if your story about Crazy and Lazy were the full story.

Δ *Actually, your bias is the same as the one contained in Rawls's initial formulation of his Difference Principle. As was pointed out to him over twenty years ago, maximizing the income and wealth of the worst off is optimal for leisure lovers. He accepted this criticism and has since suggested that his Difference Principle should be modified so as to get rid of this bias, by adding leisure to the list of social primary goods.*

Φ I like Rawls a lot and often have the feeling that, deep down, he's got it all right. But in this case I believe he is demonstrably wrong. If you look at his suggestion carefully (see Appendix), you will notice that he swings all the way and introduces the opposite bias. And yet I believe that there is a non-arbitrary, 'neutral' point. To enable you to see why, let me fill in your simple story. Crazy wants a higher income and is therefore prepared to work more. If for this purpose she uses no more than an equal share of society's scarce resources—say, land—she should not be taxed one penny to help feed Lazy. But she may also want to use more than her share. In that case, those who get less than their share will be entitled to the competitive value of what they give up. If you accept this—to do so for the right reason, you need to remember what I said two chapters ago about the metric of real freedom—and if you think through this example, you will realize that you have accepted the justice of a basic income at the level of the per capita value of society's external endowments (§ 4.2).

Δ *What's this supposed to mean in the real world?*

Φ At first sight, that the total of what is donated or bequeathed in a society should be taxed at 100 per cent and distributed equally among all. But this must be immediately qualified, above all to recognize that if this basic income is to be sustainably maximized, a far lower tax rate is likely to be appropriate.

Δ *Even a very brief look at the relevant figures should tell you that the basic income you have justified in this way is pathetically low.*

Φ I know, and this puzzled me for a while. For it does not square easily with the strong intuition that we are jointly inheriting a tremendous amount of wealth from past generations, mainly in the form of technology in the broadest sense. Moreover, no attempt to spot and seize more subtle forms of wealth transfer seems to yield anything substantial (§ 4.3).

Δ *Consequently, your 'neutral' solution forces you to content yourself with the highest basic income that can be financed by taxing wealth transfers.*

Φ I did not say that—and won't. In fact, if I had to, this whole book would not be worth the trouble I took to write it.

Δ *So, where do you find a way of legitimately boosting your basic income?*

Φ The crucial fact to notice is that, owing to the way in which our economies are organized, the most significant category of assets consists in jobs people are endowed with. Jobs are packages of tasks and benefits. Of course, for jobs to count as assets, they must be in scarce supply. Even if people all had identical skills and even under perfectly competitive conditions, job scarcity is systematically generated for reasons neatly brought out by some recent developments in the microeconomics of unemployment, such as several variants of the so-called efficiency-wage approach. As long as jobs are scarce, those who hold them appropriate a rent which can be legitimately taxed away, so as substantially to boost the legitimate level of basic income (§ 4.4).

Δ *But why are you taking the shortage of jobs as a fact of life? Even if you believe, as most people seem to do now, that aggregate demand boosting won't durably do the trick, you should at least consider alternative microeconomic policies such as working time reduction, employment subsidies, or transfers targeted to the involuntarily unemployed. If any combination of such policies is successful, then you are left with no rent to seize and redistribute.*

Φ There are strong reasons to doubt that any such combination can ever get near to full success, especially if you bring in the fact that jobs are highly differentiated and hence that, even if no one is involuntarily jobless, there can still be plenty of rents distributed in very unequal fashion. But my objection against such policies is more fundamental: they all amount to using scarce resources in a discriminatory way, with a bias towards those with a stronger preference for being employed. If you wish to favour one particular conception of the good life, say so. But you cannot do so consistently with the neutrality requirement that is an essential component of real-freedom-for-all (§ 4.5).

Δ *Even in a world of identically skilled people, it seems tricky, to put it mildly, to assess and capture all employment rents. Are you thinking of organizing job auctions?*

Φ Theoretically, yes. But as far as practical implementation is concerned, one should simply think of a wage tax whose level and pattern is determined so as durably to maximize the tax yield. Because the value of a job is not exhausted by the level of its wage, you will not catch all rents in this way. But you will not catch more than the rents, as long as one can assume that there is no forced employment (jobs can always be given up) and that people are given time to adjust to the tax structure (hence the importance of the durability condition).

Δ *Does this mean that, in addition to wealth transfers, only wage income can legitimately be taxed? Are you leaving the self-employed alone? And what about capital income?*

Φ I confess that I would be embarrassed had this been an implication of my interpretation. Fortunately, it is not. Analogous reasonings apply to these other categories of income. What we end up with is rather a basic income at the highest level that can be sustainably financed by taxing all forms of income in predictable fashion, possibly at highly differentiated rates (§ 4.6).

Δ *You mentioned earlier that you were assuming, for the sake of simplicity I suppose, that all workers had identical skills, or perhaps identical capacities to acquire skills. What happens if you drop this assumption?*

Φ I believe the consistent extension to this general case consists in asserting that skilled workers appropriate employment rents—and hence that their wages can legitimately be taxed—as soon as some other people would want to do their jobs at the current conditions, even if these other people do not possess (the ability to acquire) the required skills. And if this is the correct extension, then income taxation at the sustainable yield-maximizing rate (or pattern of rates) remains the best practical implementation, bearing in mind, of course, that skill acquisition may be discouraged by the expectation of low post-tax returns.

Δ *This seems to imply a very generous compensation for inequalities of talents. Is this not contradictory to the comparatively stingier compensation justified by your criterion of undominated diversity?*

Φ Jobs, which talents help give access to, are part of the external endowments whose value real-freedom-for-all wants distributed so as to maximize the endowment of the worst off. This is what a maximum sustainable basic income achieves. In the case of internal endowments, the possibility of enslaving the more talented forced us to be more cautious and to restrain more tightly our egalitarian impulses. But the two aspects are perfectly consistent. Indeed it is only because I treat skilled jobs the way I have just indicated that I feel comfortable when faced with the charge that undominated diversity is too stingy with the poorly talented (§ 4.7).

Δ *I can see the analogy, crucial to your argument, between jobs and external assets of the standard kind. But where do you stop? Can't you view a person's partner, for example, as part of her endowment? What about a differentiated tax on scarce partners to boost your basic income even more?*

Φ I found no decisive way of breaking this further analogy. But perhaps there is nothing troubling about it. What do you think? (§ 4.8)

4.1 The Crazy–Lazy challenge

Leximin real freedom, according to my initial claim (§ 2.1), requires that the level of the unconditional income be maximized, subject to everyone's formal freedom being adequately protected. Taking differences in talents seriously, as was done in the previous chapter, forced us to introduce a major qualification, in the form of an additional constraint on basic income maximization. The latter provides a defensible interpretation of leximin real freedom only if one ensures that no one's comprehensive endowment is strictly dominated by anyone else's. This qualification, however, does nothing to alleviate another, very serious objection, that can be, and has been, levelled against the initial claim, and that applies no less when there is no difference whatever between people's talents.

To understand the nature of this objection, consider Crazy and Lazy, two identically talented but rather differently disposed characters. Crazy is keen to earn a high income and works a lot for that purpose. Lazy is far less excited by the prospect of a high income and has decided to take it easy. With the basic income at the highest feasible level, as our criterion recommends, Crazy is rather miserable, because her net income falls far short of the income she would like to have. Lazy, instead, is blissful. When added to the small income he earns, the grant he receives is more than sufficient to cover what he regards as his material needs. Does not the high grant justified by our criterion illegitimately discriminate against Crazy in favour of Lazy? Should one not, from a real-libertarian point of view, lower the grant all the way to the point at which Crazy (who would pay less in tax) would be no less happy, no less successful in the pursuit of her conception of the good life, than Lazy (who would then be receiving a smaller grant)?

Underneath this phrasing of the objection, however, is the supposition that it is welfare, not some index of real freedom, that needs to be lex-iminned. But this is emphatically rejected by real-libertarians, on the (by now familiar) ground that it would involve discrimination in favour of those with more expensive tastes.[1] The less happy Crazy is with the money she earns—which is already quite a bit more than what Lazy gets—the more money she should be allowed to have according to the criterion implicit in the objection. But if one assumes, as real-libertarians insist one must, that people can be held responsible for their tastes, letting Crazy get a higher income because she is less happy than others is illegitimate. It amounts to giving her more means than others have for the pursuit of her conception of the good life, *whatever this may be*, even though it does not make her better equipped for the pursuit of her conception of the good life *as it is* than others are for the pursuit of *their* conceptions of the good life. From a real-libertarian standpoint, Crazy can certainly be left with more income than Lazy if this helps increase the level of the grant, but not, as would here be the case, at the expense of a decrease in that level, and hence a worsening of the fate of the least-advantaged. So far, our claim is safe.

Yet, it cannot survive the challenge presented by Crazy and Lazy. For Crazy's complaint can be backed in a distinct and far more effective way.[2] Instead of saying 'Given my aims in life, I am less happy than you are under this maximum feasible basic income and the implied tax rate, and I should therefore receive more', Crazy can say: 'You and I have identical talents. So why on Earth do we need a basic income at all?' Lazy cannot reply that in the absence of a grant he would be totally unable to indulge in the kind of life he enjoys, or that he would then be far less happy than Crazy would be, or that he would even be less happy than Crazy is with the grant at its maximum level. He cannot give any of these replies, because they are all vulnerable to the very same expensive-taste objection that smashed the first formulation of Crazy's plight. Further, he cannot usefully point out that it is up to Crazy to adopt the same easy-going lifestyle as himself and hence that she cannot claim to be treated unfairly at any level of the grant.[3] For under the assumption of equal talents, Crazy can use exactly the same argument to defend a zero, indeed a negative level of the grant. Nor can he insist that what matters is sovereignty over one's time, that is, the real freedom to work and not to work associated with one's basic income, rather than the real freedom to consume and accumulate associated with one's potential income. He would then need to rely on perfectionistic premises fundamentally alien to a real-libertarian approach.[4]

As a last resort, Lazy will perhaps want to argue that, just as it may not be in his own interest, under some plausible conditions, to have income taxed at 100 per cent (the maximum sustainable tax yield may be reached at a lower rate, because of a sharp fall in Crazy's level of effort), similarly it may not be in Crazy's interest to have income taxed at 0 per cent. For a number of reasons, her highest sustainable net income may correspond to a higher rate. This may be due, for example, to the fact that Lazies, when deprived of any significant right to income, will develop a strong propensity to acquire their means of subsistence by theft, and that the cost of effectively enforcing Crazy's property rights over her legitimate belongings will accordingly swell significantly. More interestingly, the same situation could arise even under the assumption of strict compliance because of a 'tragedy of the commons' phenomenon.[5] Externalities of production may be such that the higher aggregate level of effort induced by the absence of taxation will generate a significantly smaller total product, and hence a smaller income even for the Crazies, than if the level of effort had been depressed by a positive tax rate and a positive grant. What can be expected from this sort of argument, however, is at most some narrowing of the wide range that separates the basic-income maximizing rate from the one that is most favourable to Crazy's interests, but not a criterion that would enable the real-libertarian approach to select from this wide range a non-arbitrary 'neutral' point, against which neither Crazy nor Lazy would have a valid complaint. Should we give up? Not yet. Let us first examine how the position expressed in Rawls's *Theory of Justice* faces a closely related problem, and how Rawls has attempted to solve it.

In its original formulation, Rawls's Difference Principle is the requirement that socio-economic advantages (income and wealth, powers and prerogatives, the social bases of self-respect) should be maximinned, that is, distributed in such a way that the least-advantaged end up with at least as many such advantages as the least-advantaged would end up with under any alternative arrangement. What sort of transfer policy does this principle justify? As long as no precise index of socio-economic advantages is being put forward, no rigorous derivation is possible. But a quick look at Rawls's list of types of socio-economic advantages arguably establishes a strong presumption in favour of a basic income. First of all, as soon as the highest sustainable basic income exceeds what the Lazies regard as the subsistence level, the maximinning of income demands a basic income at maximum level. If the minimum income guarantee were restricted to those willing to work full-time and pitched at a higher level still, this would not prevent Lazies (of average productivity) from working part-time and earning less than the minimum income guarantee. In a sufficiently opulent society, in other words, the Difference Principle would recommend a basic income even if it were exclusively concerned with income.[6] True, the income guarantee, understood as the income accessible to anyone willing and able to work full-time, may well generally be higher under some sort of conditional scheme than under a basic income scheme. But it is income, and not potential income, that appears in the Difference Principle. Rawls, moreover, also mentions wealth, and the receiving of wealth may precisely be interpreted as differing from the receiving of an income by virtue of its unconditional nature, of the lack of any counterpart in the form of (labour or capital) services. Further, Rawls mentions the powers and prerogatives attached to social positions, and there is no doubt that an unconditional income confers upon the weakest more bargaining power in their dealings with both potential employers and the State, and hence a greater potential for availing themselves of powers and prerogatives, than a transfer contingent upon the beneficiary's availability for work and/or the satisfaction of a means test. Finally, Rawls mentions the social bases of self-respect, and there is again little doubt that a transfer system that is not targeted at those who have shown themselves 'inadequate' and involves less administrative control over its beneficiaries is far less likely to stigmatize them, humiliate them, make them ashamed of themselves, or undermine their self-respect.[7]

In this light, Rawls's position and in particular his Difference Principle appear to recommend—subject to the respect of fundamental liberties and of fair equality of opportunity—that one should introduce a wealth-distributing, power-conferring, self-respect-preserving unconditional basic income, indeed that one should introduce such an income at the highest sustainable level. The Difference Principle is a maximin criterion, and the level of the basic income determines the bundle of socio-economic advantages available to the worst off, to those who have nothing but that basic income. Thus, it seems that Rawls should fully endorse, in the Lazy–Crazy case, the scheme that maximizes the level of basic income, and hence favours as much as possible Lazy's interests. Indeed, this scheme arguably spells out, in this simple test case, what Rawls must mean (at least if he is to remain true to his liberal stance), when rejecting welfare-state capitalism on the ground that it aims at 'the redistribution of income to those with less *at the end* of each period, so to speak', and not at 'the widespread ownership of productive assets and human capital at the *beginning* of each period' which is mandated by the Difference Principle.[8]

4.2 *Rawls versus Dworkin*

Yet this is clearly not the response to the Crazy–Lazy challenge for which Rawls himself opted. Richard Musgrave (1974: 632) had confronted him long ago with a variant of Crazy's plight : 'Implementation of maximin thus leads to a redistributive system that, among individuals with equal earnings ability, favors those with a high preference for leisure. It is to the advantage of recluses, saints, and (nonconsulting) scholars who earn but little and hence will not have to contribute greatly to redistribution.' Musgrave's own alternative proposal was that one should stick to a welfarist approach: lump-sum taxation must be used to equalize (or maximin) 'goods and leisure potentials', understood as 'potential welfare'.[9] This proposal was unambiguously rejected by Rawls (1974: 654–5). The appropriate response, in his view, consisted instead in a major alteration of his Difference Principle along lines which he then hardly sketched, but which he has since spelled out somewhat. This alteration consists of adding leisure to the list of socio-economic advantages governed by the Difference Principle. More specifically, 'twenty-four hours less a standard working day might be included in the index as leisure. Those who are unwilling to work would have a standard working day of extra leisure, and this extra leisure itself would be stipulated as equivalent to the index of primary goods of the least advantaged. So those who surf all day off Malibu must find a way to support themselves and would not be entitled to public funds.'[10] When applied to our Crazy–Lazy story, it can easily be shown that this formula necessarily yields a basic income equal to zero.

Rawls's proposal has the advantage of getting rid of the (pro-Lazy) bias generated by the standard Difference Principle's focus on income (at the expense of leisure), while avoiding the expensive-tastes problem intrinsic to Musgrave's proposal and any other welfarist approach. But it has a fatal defect. To identify the latter in its simplest form, let us start from a situation in which the Difference Principle (leisure included) is satisfied, and assume some exogenous change (say, the random discovery of another reserve of natural resources) which makes it possible to redistribute more to the least-advantaged. What form should this redistribution take? Leaving incentive issues aside for a moment, the consistent implementation of Rawls's proposal requires that the funds thus becoming available be used as a subsidy proportional to the number of hours worked. For if the subsidy were more than proportional, the primary goods index of full-time workers would grow faster than that of part-time workers. And if it were less than proportional, the index of part-time workers would grow faster than that of full-time workers.[11] What would be wrong with such a proportional subsidy?

One old objection to distribution in proportion to work is that it conflicts with efficiency even in the weak sense of Pareto-optimality, by providing *excessive* incentives to work. It is, for example, precisely after being confronted with a similar objection by Abba Lerner that Oskar Lange, in his famous discussion of market socialism, required the 'social dividend' on publicly owned capital to be distributed among citizens as a basic income, irrespective of their work effort, rather than, as he initially proposed, as a function of their competitive wages.[12] This objection, however, need not worry Rawls unduly. To start with, Pareto-suboptimality in welfare terms—the fact that everyone's utility could be increased—does not necessarily mean that everyone's index of primary goods could be increased, and only the latter would create a problem from his point of view. Further, if it were the case that distributing part of the available funds irrespective of work performance would increase even the income of full-time workers—for example, because of the 'tragedy of the commons' effect mentioned earlier (§ 4.1)—maximin considerations would allow Rawls to depart from strict proportionality.

Far more serious are the tricky conceptual difficulties unavoidably raised by any approach that gives a key role to the notions of work and leisure. What shall we count as work? (Cleaning one's clients' shoes, cleaning one's children's shoes, cleaning one's own shoes, cleaning one's doll's shoes?) How should hours of work be made comparable? (Should one hour of effort-intensive work be equivalent to one hour of relaxed work, one hour of dangerous work to one hour of safe work, one hour of useless work to one hour of useful work, one hour of pathetically inefficient work to one hour of highly productive work, and, if not, what conversion coefficients should be used?) And if, besides actual work, involuntary leisure is also recognized as giving rise to some legitimate claim, what is the appropriate metric? (Could, for example, an unfulfilled strong or permanent desire to work a little be deemed equivalent to an unsatisfied mild or intermittent willingness to work a lot?) Although some believe that difficulties of this sort provide an overwhelming pragmatic case for an unconditional income support system, there is no need for me to press them here for the following reason.[13]

There is another objection which is, in my view, decisive and challenges the very consistency of Rawls's proposal with a liberal perspective. His proposal involves an unjustifiable bias against some of those who are, using Rawls's own standards, among the least-advantaged. For simplicity's sake, just consider the extreme case of those who do not work at all. If they have no income, their primary goods index is set equal, we have seen, to that of the least-advantaged full-time workers. If we were to put Rawls's proportional subsidy proposal into practice, this index would go up as a result of the conjectured exogenous change. But clearly, this improvement in the measured condition of this fraction of the least-advantaged is purely fictional. It hides a stagnation of their situation in absolute terms and a worsening of their relative position, and simply reflects the fact that their leisure is postulated to be equivalent, at any particular time, to the income enjoyed at that same time by the least-advantaged full-time workers. Why could this subcategory of the least-advantaged not claim a real share in the exogenously generated benefit, instead of being treated to a sheer semantic trick? What the proposal (and beyond it the whole idea of adding leisure to the list of primary goods) amounts to is a prescription to share out among the sole workers, and as a function of their working time (somehow measured), the whole of the production surplus—that is, of whatever is left of the product after taking away what is needed to feed and motivate the workers—whatever the sources of this surplus.[14] No such proposal could possibly be justified by a non-discriminatory concern with the real freedom of the least-advantaged. From a pro-Lazy bias, we have swung all the way to a pro-Crazy bias, that could be vindicated only on perfectionistic premisses. All three difficulties are inherent in the strategy suggested by Rawls, and the third one constitutes, in my view, a decisive defect which can only be remedied by turning to an alternative strategy.[15]

This strategy is in fact a direct corollary of the option adopted earlier as regards the metric of external endowments (§ 2.6). Like Rawls's and unlike Musgrave's, this strategy, inspired by Dworkin's (1981*b*) conception of equal external resources, does not lead back to welfarism. Unlike both, it is consistent with the (first-best) justification of an unconditional income. In order to understand how it solves our problem, let us return once again to Lazy and Crazy. In order to generate the level of income she wants to reach, it is safe to assume and crucial to notice, Crazy needs certain assets external to her talents, say a plot of land. Endowing (identically talented) Crazy and Lazy with equal plots of land certainly constitutes one non-discriminatory allocation of real freedom between them. But if this endowment is not tradable, if they are both stuck with it, this allocation cannot be optimal from a real-libertarian standpoint. It will not give either Crazy or Lazy the highest attainable level of real freedom. Crazy may be desperate to use more than her plot of land, while Lazy would not mind being deprived of some or even all of his in exchange for part of what Crazy would produce with it. This directly yields the following suggestion. There is a non-arbitrary and generally positive legitimate level of basic income that is determined by the per capita value of society's external assets and must be entirely financed by those who appropriate these assets. If Lazy gives up the whole of his plot of land, he is entitled to an unconditional grant at a level that corresponds to the value of that plot. Crazy, on the other hand, can be viewed as receiving this same grant, but as owing twice its amount because of appropriating both Lazy's share of land and her own. Thus, in our society of Crazies and Lazies, the legitimate level of basic income is just the endogenously determined value of their equal tradable right to land.[16]

But how is the value of the external assets to be assessed? Consider again our example. Crazy is interested in acquiring Lazy's plot, but not at any price. Lazy is not opposed to giving up his plot, but again not at any price. Between the highest price Crazy is willing to pay for it (which may conceivably come close to average income in our two-person society) and the lowest price Lazy is willing to accept for it (which may conceivably come close to zero), there may exist an extremely wide range of possible settlements. Which of these is picked out as expressing the 'genuine value' of the land is of paramount importance, since it determines whether nearly the whole social product or practically nothing is up for leximin redistribution. It determines, in other words, whether in practice the level of basic income picked by the Dworkinian criterion will be nearly indistinguishable from its highest sustainable level, or whether it will reduce the grant to a sheer trickle. Suppose there are many Crazies and many Lazies who attempt to make the best possible separate deals with one another, under the guidance of an auctioneer who keeps them fully informed about all offers made. Could not the (uniform) terms on which a plot of land will tend to be exchanged under such circumstances—its competitive equilibrium price—provide a meaningful notion of value? This is at any rate the proposal that flows directly from the solution offered earlier (§ 2.6) to the analogous Funny–Sunny problem in the context of a world without production, and hence with no room for income-leisure trade-offs.[17]

Here again, of course, the outcome—and hence the degree to which each person will be able to satisfy her tastes—will depend on the distribution of tastes in the population. How much the land will go for—how much milk and muesli Lazy will be entitled to in exchange for giving up his claim to his share of the land—will depend on supply and demand, more specifically on the balance of Lazies and Crazies and on how keen members of either group are to hold part of the land. But a work-independent income is unambiguously justified. Those who have appropriated no more and no less than their per capita share of land then pay a rent exactly equal to their basic income. Those who have appropriated less pay less—possibly nothing at all. Those who have appropriated more pay more—and can do so, precisely because the assets they have appropriated can be used productively. Without lifting a finger—beyond what is needed to press his right to an equal share at the auction—Lazy is thus entitled, in the form of a basic income, to some share—possibly quite substantial—of what may look like the product of nothing but Crazy's labour.[18]

How can this counterfactual competitive assessment be justified? As in the Funny–Sunny case, by its connection with the absence of envy. However, in the Crazy–Lazy world, where production is present, envy-freeness does not imply that Lazy does not prefer Crazy's final bundle of goods to his own: he does. Nor does it imply that the welfare he derives from his idleness is greater than the welfare Crazy derives from her productive activity: Crazy may well enjoy her work even more than Lazy enjoys his leisure.[19] What *is* implied, however, is that Lazy, *keeping his own current preferences*, does not prefer Crazy's vector of consumption *and activities* to his own. And this, assuming a perfect market, is guaranteed, since Lazy and Crazy have identical talents and are given an equal entitlement to land. The converse proposition, on the other hand, remains invalid. Nearly whatever the value ascribed to land—that is, nearly whatever the level of the basic income, from zero to the per capita social product—Lazy and Crazy will not envy one another. Yet only one value matches the criterion of equal endowments. As in the Funny–Sunny case, a second step is required to tighten the link: in a society that differs from the dichotomic Crazy–Lazy world by virtue of having a large number of members whose tastes form a continuum (and satisfy some additional conditions), only competitive equilibria can guarantee the satisfaction of envy-freeness and Pareto-optimality.

What is, then, the relevant pool of external assets? Our Crazy–Lazy story may suggest that the external assets whose value a real-libertarian should endeavour to distribute in leximin fashion coincide with natural resources. But this is not the case.[20] What is relevant, from a real-libertarian standpoint, in this situation in which internal endowments are assumed to be equally distributed, is of course the whole set of external means that affect people's capacity to pursue their conceptions of the good life, irrespective of whether they are natural or produced. External endowments, in other words, include whatever usable external object in the broadest sense individuals receive access to. Such material objects as factories and stamp collections, private houses and public bridges, such immaterial objects as nursery rhymes and computer pro-grammes, the work ethic and nuclear technology constitute external assets on a par with beaches, pumpkins, and parrots. The relevant pool coincides with the external wealth with which people are endowed.[21] An equal distribution of their value therefore amounts to taxing the value of all gifts and bequests at 100 per cent and distributing the proceeds in the form of a uniform basic income.[22]

It does not follow, however, that real-libertarianism should endorse this confiscatory tax scheme. A first objection against the latter consists in complaining that a 100 per cent rate conflicts with the real-libertarian concern for neutrality as between life plans.[23] For such a tax scheme amounts to discriminating in favour of the selfish person, whose desire to consume all her income is left unhindered, whereas the altruist's inten-tions are thwarted by the systematic confiscation of whatever she gives. There is, of course, no doubt that the real freedom to lead an altruistic sort of life is reduced by a 100 per cent taxation of gifts. But the *minimum* real freedom to lead such a life—which is what matters from a leximin perspective—is not. Or at least it is not as long as the basic income does not exceed the subsistence level. If it did, an amount corresponding to the positive difference should be exempted from gift taxes, in order to guar-antee that those with the smallest endowments could use them as much as possible (i.e. consistently with their subsistence) in an altruistic as well as in a selfish way. But this refinement of the legitimate tax base is sufficiently mild for it to be ignored in the sequel.[24]

This cannot be said for another amendment prompted by a second and more obvious real-libertarian objection to the proposed confiscatory tax scheme. As the total amount that gets saved, invested, or preserved may well be adversely affected by high rates of taxation, 100 per cent is not likely to be the choice that maximizes the tax yield, nor therefore the level of the grant. Knowing that at least part of the endowments will not be distributed in egalitarian fashion, but rather left, say, from parents to their children, may induce the previous generation to take more trouble in looking after the assets they have themselves inherited (less depletion, less deterioration), as well as to display more enthusiasm in creating new assets (through harder work and more extensive savings). Consequently, real-libertarianism's concern with leximin real freedom will recommend that one should diverge from strict equality of endowments, not to favour Crazy over Lazy or the other way around, but to allow Crazies and Lazies born to rich parents to keep, in view of 'retroactive' incentive effects, more than their share of external endowments.[25] If one is concerned with people's leximin real freedom, the optimal choice is then the one that maximizes the yield of such a tax on gifts and bequests. The difference between the criterion involved here—which could be called the Dworkinian criterion—and our initial criterion—which we saw could not withstand the Crazy–Lazy challenge—is then not more nor less than the restriction on the tax base. Subtracting from Crazy's income more than the value of the external endowment she has somehow received, as allowed by our initial criterion but not by the Dworkinian one, would amount to giving her a smaller endowment than to Lazy, and is therefore inconsistent with our real-libertarian perspective, duly specified so as to rule out discrimination.

As long as one abstracts from the constraint of undominated diversity (see § 3.8), the level of basic income thus justified is bound to be strictly positive. It could only fall to zero under the far-fetched assumption that no one attached any value to inherited external endowments and/or if a positive rate of taxation on these endowments, once anticipated, made them vanish altogether. Would it be high? In a country like France, for example, the total value of what gets officially bequeathed or donated every year amounts to less than 3 per cent of GNP, while the total yield from gift and inheritance taxes is about 0.25 per cent of GNP.[26] This gives us an idea of both the upper and lower bounds of what can be expected from such taxation. Clearly, the corresponding estimates for the legitimate level of basic income go from the pathetically low to the frankly negligible.

4.3 Can our inheritance be boosted ?

Is there any reason why such figures should significantly underestimate the legitimate tax base? To start with an extreme suggestion, let us remember the argument mentioned above (§ 2.5) as one conceivable way of justifying that basic income should take the form of regular instalments rather than of one initial endowment. If the person 'I' am now is distinct from the person 'I' shall be tomorrow, whatever the former person leaves to the other must be assimilated to a gift or a bequest. What I save this month is part of the endowment with which the person I shall be next month starts life and must therefore be added to the pool on which it is legitimate to draw in order to finance the grant. If this view were accepted, the size of this pool would no doubt be greatly enhanced. But even leaving aside the tight limits on tapping this pool that would be imposed, on leximin grounds, by incentive considerations, it would obviously be very odd simply to assimilate all forms of saving, all benefits one derives from one's past efforts, to pure manna. In the present context, such assimilation is bound to generate strong challenges, which are even more likely to leave us sceptical about the strongly discontinuous conception of the person than when we first met it. The question is no longer (as it was in § 2.5) whether a gift will be made in one go or in many, but whether what you would like to keep for tomorrow can be taken from you tonight.

Secondly and less fancifully, one might want to point out that the figures that have been mentioned are bound to take no account of a very large number of small (interpersonal) gifts (from pints in the pub to Mother's Day presents). But it would no doubt be silly to try to seize such gifts in order to finance a higher basic income, partly because many of them cancel each other out—no human individual could reach adulthood in the absence of innumerable goods and services she is treated to throughout her childhood—but above all because the administrative cost of monitoring them would be prohibitive. More significant private gifts, skilfully hidden in order to evade taxation, are no doubt also ignored, but it is unlikely that what could be gained from identifying them and adding them to the tax base would be, all costs considered, very significant.

Thirdly, one might suggest that the value of some publicly owned goods be added to the value of privately owned assets. This does not make sense in the case of goods that are genuinely available to all (say, sunlight or breathable air) and therefore constitute a universal grant in kind which it would be pointless to monetize. But what about public parks stuck in the middle of exclusive residential areas, for example? Here again, I do not believe that there is much room for raising the legitimate tax base, both because we must check to what extent the receivers are not also the givers (as they are if, for example, the park amenities, if not the land on which they rest, are financed by a local tax) and because most, if not all, of the value of such a public good may be incorporated in the increased value of the surrounding land and buildings, whose value is already up for redistribution. In the case of other public goods, such as a toll-free bridge, one must be careful not to focus exclusively on direct beneficiaries. You may never have crossed the bridge, but the tomatoes you eat are cheaper or fresher or both because the bridge exists. Here again, it is most unlikely that a detailed accounting would swell significantly what is up for distribution.[27]

There is, however, a fourth possibility, which deserves more thorough discussion. From rudimentary cooking recipes to sophisticated industrial software, it is obvious enough that much of our material standard of living, much of our wealth, can be ascribed to our technology.[28] If we could add the value of all inherited technology to the value of all inherited capital, would the amount available for financing everyone's basic income not be greatly increased? To the extent that technologies are protected by patents, and hence privately appropriated, they do not raise any specific problem: their value can and must be assessed in exactly the same way as that of material goods, and their transfer has already been subjected to the yield-maximizing taxation discussed earlier. But this applies only to fairly recent innovations. Many of the technologies we use are incorporated in an age-old wisdom that has become common knowledge (making fire, using the wheel) or are available at a cost that may well approximate the competitive value of the medium that carries their description (say, an engineering handbook) but that is, no doubt, negligible relative to what would be the competitive value of the technology itself, if it were privately appropriated. But precisely because these technologies are, as such, freely available, are they not part of a basic income in kind, along with the air we breathe or the streets we use? It would then be pointless to embark on the arduous task of estimating their (counterfactual) competitive value, since they are already given equally to all.

To clarify this issue, it is helpful to return to our world of Crazies and Lazies. We concluded earlier that, if the Crazies appropriated all the land, a non-discriminatory concern with real freedom required Lazies to be given an equal (or leximin) share of the competitive value of the land, even if the Crazies did all the work. Suppose now that the Crazies do not need any land to do their work, but only an inherited, freely available technology. Might it not be said that here, unlike in the case of land-using production, the Crazies do not owe the Lazies any part of the product, because the Lazies do not 'give up' their share of technology as they did with their share of land? The technology is just as available to the Lazies after the Crazies have started using it as before. Why should the Crazies have to pay anything to the Lazies just because only they have bothered to pick up what everyone is and remains equally free, though unequally keen, to pick up?

In a way, this rhetorical question is misleading, because it does not sufficiently distinguish between a payment that is demanded by way of compensation for some harm done and one that is demanded as a charge matching the fair value of what is being taken. Remember that what justified the payment in the case of land was not *compensation* for some damage or welfare loss. Some Lazies may not mind at all giving up their share of land—their reservation price may be zero—and yet they remain entitled to a share of what the Crazies produce, as long as the competitive price is positive. What justifies the payment is a concern to equalize the assets each is endowed with for pursuing her conception of the good life, where assets are evaluated by their opportunity cost, that is, by how precious (at least some) others find them. True, the fewer people are interested in some asset and the less keen they are to acquire it, the lower its value. In particular, if those interested in it are fully satiated with less than the total amount available, that is, if there is no scarcity, the value of the asset would be zero. But the fact that some people (here, the Lazies) show no interest in that asset does not imply that it should count for nothing in the relevant asset accounting, nor that taxing those who derive benefit from it is illegitimate. One may then consider proceeding by letting the auctioneer sell each technique to the highest bidder, or rather, since the use of techniques, unlike that of machinery or land, is not exclusive, by selling it (at a uniform price) to as many bidders as will maximize the proceeds. There may be cases in which the technique is so universally useful that everyone will buy it—which is distributionally equivalent, in our scenario, to making it freely available to all. But in most cases, only some people—typically, the Crazies—will bother to pay the price that is being asked, and—contrary to what was implied in the rhetorical question—an unambiguous increase in the legitimate level of the grant would seem to result.

Unfortunately for those who would like to boost the legitimate level of basic income, this interpretation of the auction cannot be sustained. For what the auction should reveal, as just recalled, is the opportunity cost of appropriating what is on offer. And precisely because of the non-exclusive nature of technology, this opportunity cost is zero. It is of course true that the production of techniques involves an opportunity cost. It mobilizes time and material resources for the sake of research and development. But what we are talking about is the technology we have inherited, along with natural resources and physical capital. Hence, even if it is legitimate that its value, measured by its opportunity cost, should be added to the tax base out of which the basic income can be financed, this is of precious little help. Since this value is zero, the level of the basic income that can be justified on real-libertarian grounds gains nothing whatsoever from the inclusion of inherited technology in the common pool.

At this stage, only a minor qualification must be added to soften this sobering conclusion—and reduce its counterintuitive appearance.[29] There is an important indirect way in which technologies affect what is available for unconditional distribution. Even in a world of equal talents, legally unprotected technologies are not equally available to all. Many technologies can be used only by those who possess the amount and the type of physical capital on which they can be used. Whenever there is such a restriction, the technologies enhance the competitive value of the material goods that confer upon their possessors the ability to use them. And the leximinning of external endowments, as construed in the previous section, automatically takes this into account. Hence, the basic point remains unshaken: no independent valuation of technology can help us beyond the basic income level justified by the argument of the previous section.

4.4 Equal endowments in a non-Walrasian world

This conclusion sounds like very bad news, especially if one bears in mind that in order to satisfy the prior principle of undominated diversity (§ 3.5), one will have to reduce further, possibly even exhaust altogether, the amount that is legitimately available for universal redistribution. Is it not obviously the case, in the light of our reasoning so far, that the level of basic income that can be justified from a real-libertarian standpoint is so low that it is hardly worth talking about? No, it is not. My claim is that, under contemporary conditions in the advanced capitalist world, a very substantial basic income is warranted from such a standpoint. This conclusion can only be reached, however, if it is realized that a crucial aspect of our endowments has been completely overlooked so far.[30]

To see this, let us stick for the moment to a situation in which all people are identically talented, and suppose that the value of all bequeathed and donated wealth has been distributed as a real-libertarian wants it to be. In a very simple society of independent producers, there is indeed nothing, or hardly anything, to add. First, it may no doubt be the case that some people will use this wealth, whether for consumption or production purposes, in a way that improves or worsens the situation of others through mechanisms that involve neither exchange nor gift, that is, by generating positive or negative externalities (say, beautiful trees and dirty smoke). In this society as in any other, some (unavoidably imperfect) shadow pricing of externalities will be required if an equal (or leximin) distribution of endowments is to be approximated. If Jon and Ben are identically endowed, except for the fact that Jon has a splendid view over Ben's garden, while Ben has to put up with Jon's smoke, equality (or leximin) of endowments will require that some appropriate correction be made for Ben's benefit.[31]

Secondly, it may also be the case, in such a society, that owing to some stroke of luck, one independent producer will manage to benefit, in the context of exchange relations with others, from some particularly favourable deal. This benefit must then be treated in the same way as an unexpected inheritance, and accordingly added to the tax base. But to the (possibly small) extent that such benefits are genuine strokes of luck, they tend to cancel each other out in the long run and require no special correction. If instead they are the reflection of superior (buying or selling) talent, they have already been catered for, in so far as they must, by the constraint of undominated diversity.

Let us now shift from this society of independent producers to a society in which production is mostly organized through the employment relation. In such a *job society*, it may be the case that received material wealth is distributed in leximin fashion and that talents are identical, while some people have a job and others (who would like to have one) do not. If this is only a temporary situation, which briefly affects people between jobs or as they first arrive on to the labour market, there is again not much for a real-libertarian to worry about, as it does not significantly affect the distribution of real freedom. This fits in nicely with the customary 'Walrasian' assumption that the labour market, like any other market, tends to clear, that in the absence of institutional constraints (such as a statutory minimum wage) anyone who wants a job and is qualified for it will get one at the standard rate for a given type of skill.

But suppose now that we are in a *non-Walrasian economy*, that is, that for some reason the labour market does not tend to clear. This may be because of obstacles to perfect competition, such as minimum wage legislation or union monopolies. But it may also be due to mechanisms that are consistent with perfect competition, such as those highlighted by the so-called insider–outsider and efficiency-wage theories of involuntary unemployment. Both sets of theories generate the conclusion that even in a competitive context, firms will pay their employees higher wages than those they could get away with by hiring equally skilled unemployed workers. According to the insider–outsider approach, even in the absence of collective organization, workers can durably claim a wage that significantly exceeds the market-clearing level because of the bargaining power they derive from the existence of hiring, training, and firing costs. According to the efficiency-wage approach, it is in the firm's interest to pay its workers more than the market-clearing wage, because of a positive causal link between wages and labour productivity. In most variants, this rests on the assumption that workers shirk less if the cost to them of losing their job is higher. In other variants, it rests on the alternative assumption that workers will be motivated to perform better by the feeling that their employer is paying them more than was strictly necessary. Thus, if any variant of either of these two approaches is correct, even a perfectly competitive economy could be non-Walrasian in the sense indicated.[32]

Suppose further that, in the context of such an economy, wealth has been distributed in impeccably equal fashion. Given the momentous implications of protracted unemployment both for current earnings and for future prospects, this departure from the market-clearing ideal can no longer be dismissed as a marginal phenomenon, and it is therefore clearly untenable to say that the employed and the (identically skilled) unemployed enjoy equal access to the means required for the pursuit of their conception of the good life. In a non-Walrasian economy, in other words, people's endowment is not exhaustively described by their wealth (in the usual sense) and their skills: the holding of a job constitutes a third type of asset.[33] How can equality of endowments be conceived in this modified context? One obvious suggestion is to proceed in exactly the same way as with external wealth, that is, to conceive of jobs as assets, the value of which needs to be distributed equally among all. In the case of scarce land, we gave each member of the society concerned a tradable entitlement to an equal share of that land, and the endowment-equalizing level of the basic income was given by the per capita competitive value of the available land (see § 4.2 above). Similarly, in the case of scarce jobs, let us give each member of the society concerned a tradable entitlement to an equal share of those jobs.[34] The endowment-equalizing level of the (additional) basic income will then similarly be given by the per capita competitive value of the available jobs. If involuntary unemployment is high, the corresponding basic income will be high. If all unemployment is voluntary, no additional basic income is justified by this procedure.

If this is indeed the correct procedure, room is made for a sizable increase in the level of basic income that is warranted on real-libertarian grounds. It amounts to sharing among all the *employment rents* otherwise monopolized by those in employment. These rents are given by the difference between the income (and other advantages) the employed derive from their job, and the (lower) income they would need to get if the market were to clear.[35] In a situation of persistent massive unemployment, there is no doubt that the sum total of these rents would greatly swell the amount available for financing the grant. And it is then no longer ludicrous to suggest that the non-discriminatory concern with people's access to the means for the pursuit of their conceptions of the good life, the leximinning of real freedom, should demand that people be given an adequate basic income. Not, of course, under any circumstance, but *inter alia* under those circumstances—affluent societies with high rates of unemployment—in which a popular demand for basic income has been taking shape, under the pressure of a deep feeling of injustice. I say *inter alia*, because, as soon as there are several types of jobs, the existence of employment rents no longer needs to be coextensive with involuntary unemployment: there may be huge employment rents even if everyone has a job, because many people with lousy jobs may be willing and able to do other existing jobs far more attractive (financially or intrinsically) than theirs at the going wage. What is crucial to my argument is the existence of large employment rents, as manifested by the presence of envy over job endowments, and not the fact that many people are without a job at all. The conclusion, therefore, fully applies to affluent countries, such as the United States, in which the rate of unemployment is comparatively low, just as much as to Western Europe.

4.5 Sharing, bribing and the elimination of job scarcity

In order to clarify further the position that has just been presented and spell out its implications in a world that is more complex than the one assumed so far, let me now consider a number of instructive objections.

Consider, first, the following anomaly. Jobs constitute assets whose value is to be shared because some people are involuntarily unemployed. If there were no such people, those who choose not to work, the voluntarily unemployed, would receive no basic income in addition to their share of external assets of the standard kind, as discussed in the previous chapter. By using employment rents to swell the basic income, does one not provide unnecessary benefits to people who are already 'happy' with the present situation? Should one not instead restrict the benefits of rent sharing to the involuntarily unemployed, those who are really affected by the scarcity of jobs? No, one should not, at any rate as long as one wishes to stick to the liberal ban on discrimination between conceptions of the good life, for adopting a policy that focuses on the involuntarily unemployed amounts to awarding a privilege to people with an expensive taste for a scarce asset. Those who, for whatever reason, give up their share of that asset and thereby leave more of it for others, should not therefore be deprived of a fair share of its value.

This provides the most fundamental reason, though not the only reason, why any *job-sharing* strategy, say through a compulsory reduction in maximum working time, is bound to perform worse than basic income as a strategy against unemployment, from a real-libertarian standpoint. To start with, job sharing raises the obvious problem of commensurability. Given that no two jobs are identical, how can we make even abstract sense of an equal distribution of jobs—as opposed to an equal distribution of their value along the lines of the previous section?

Secondly, if jobs were meant to be equally distributed to literally all—including the voluntarily unemployed—it is obvious at once that the resulting situation would be dramatically inferior in terms of real freedom to one in which it is instead an equal tradable right to a job that is distributed equally to all. Both those who want to get more and those who want to get less than their equal share of jobs enjoy more real freedom to pursue their life plans in the latter situation than in the former. Both a higher income and greater leisure are accessible to (though not enjoyed by) each person in the latter situation than in the former. If, instead, job sharing through compulsory working-time reduction is meant to be restricted to the involuntary unemployed, it constitutes an unfair discrimination in the distribution of assets at the expense of the voluntarily unemployed, that is, people who, for whatever reason (repulsion to being bossed around, care for an elderly relative, lack of a valued skill, etc.), do not seek employment. This is the case for two distinct reasons. First, the very fact that firms choose not to spread employment more evenly among those wanting to work strongly suggests that doing so would run against their concern with maximizing their profits.[36] Compulsory working-time reduction can, therefore, be expected to have a negative impact on profits, and hence on the value of assets and on the maximum level of basic income that can be financed by taxing the transfer of standard wealth (along the lines of § 4.2). It would, therefore, diminish the endowment of some of the least privileged, those who, even after jobs have been shared, would have nothing to live on but a basic income. Secondly, even if there were no negative impact on profits, restricting redistribution to the involuntarily unemployed would amount to giving more assets to some than to others because of their 'expensive' taste for these assets. The argument is exactly analogous to the one used in § 4.2 to handle the conflict between Crazy and Lazy in the context of standard external assets. Both, say, land and jobs are scarce assets that must be distributed in non-discriminatory fashion. There is no reason whatever, from this standpoint, why those who do not insist on having a physical share of it and therefore leave more for others, should receive nothing at all, letting the land-greedy or job-greedy appropriate the whole value of these assets.

Both these last two points are directly relevant to assessing those strategies which attempt to get rid of job scarcity instead of administering it, by *bribing* either the (potential) employees or the (potential) employer. The 'employee-bribing' strategy consists in paying unemployment benefits to the involuntarily unemployed and to no one else. It works on the labour supply side and aims at turning involuntary unemployment into voluntary unemployment.[37] Ideally, it consists in handing out carefully targeted benefits just sufficient to make some people give up their job and others their desire to get a job. The 'employer-bribing' strategy, on the other hand, consists in paying subsidies to employers as a function of the number of workers they employ. It works on the labour demand side, by reducing the net cost to the employers of hiring additional workers, or at least additional workers belonging to those categories which are currently affected by involuntary unemployment. The level of bribing required to achieve full employment (if achievable at all) using these strategies will vary greatly depending on the context, in one case mainly as a function of how keen the involuntarily unemployed are to work, in the other mainly as a function of how unprofitable the newly created jobs would be in the absence of subsidies.

In order to discard these strategies, I do not need to argue that they are bound to be unsuccessful, or that the price for success is not worth paying. Both bribing strategies are vulnerable to the objection that they involve unjustified discrimination against the voluntarily unemployed, for precisely the same two reasons just mentioned in connection with the sharing strategy. First, unless some powerful externality is involved—say, if keeping people busy on subsidized jobs strongly boosts the value of real estate by keeping criminality under check—the taxation required to finance the bribes to either the employees (benefits) or the employers (subsidies) can safely be conjectured to have a negative net impact on profitability, and hence on the highest sustainable level of basic income that can be financed with wealth transfer taxes. It can, therefore, be expected to reduce the resources made available to the voluntary unemployed. Secondly, even if this were not the case, bribing strategies would still be unfair to the latter, since they amount to allocating more assets to those with an 'expensive' taste for scarce jobs than to others. To put the matter differently, let us admit that full employment can be reached through both selective bribes (of either kind) and basic income, and that one needs to take less assets away from the employed in order to reach it through the former than through the latter.[38] It is then true, *ceteris paribus*, that *everyone's* real freedom *to earn* is greater under a bribing regime than under a basic income regime. But it does not follow that either bribing strategy is superior to the basic income strategy in terms of real freedom. This would amount to giving an unjustified privilege to the freedom to earn at the expense of the freedom to enjoy free time. Here again, a meaningful neutral perspective can only be achieved by looking at the endowments that underlie real freedom. Both bribing strategies then appear to allocate unequal endowments to otherwise identical people just because they have different tastes, that is, they appear to generate an inequality of endowments that cannot conceivably be justified by a favourable impact on the size of the endowment available to the worse off.

The unfairness of such discrimination is clearly perceived and sometimes bitterly resented, for example, when women looking after their children at home receive an income of their own or fail to do so, depending on whether or not they are supposed to be willing to accept a job. In the case of wage subsidies, the unfairness is obscured by the fact that it seems plausible enough to say that the joint labour force, subsidizing and subsidized alike, produces all the real income that is distributed as either wages or transfers. But a worker hired thanks to a subsidy that serves no other purpose than to offer her a job (and no other subsidy is concerned by the present discussion) is of course, in that capacity, a net consumer of assets. The key point, here, is that this allocation of extra assets is unfair to people who only differ from these workers through their tastes. It is fully consistent with the notion that workers should be adequately rewarded, in the sense that they should earn an additional income that at least compensates the effort they devote to working. This constraint is no less respected under the basic income strategy than under the alternatives. It does not justify any pro-worker bias in the redistribution of rents.

Suppose, however, that one can get rid of (more than 'frictional') involuntary unemployment, not through a (discriminatory) policy of job sharing, selective benefits, or wage subsidies, but by some other means, say the substitution of a share economy for a wage economy or the dismantling of all the rigidities that hinder wage flexibility. Once full employment has been achieved in this way, can it not be said that the second type of scarce external assets has disappeared, that there are no employment rents to be collected in order to fund a more generous basic income? It must first be conceded that, if there is only one type of job, the elimination of involuntary unemployment does indeed have this implication. There are then no employment rents or, if you prefer, the employment rents have been appropriated by the employer instead of the employee. But if other things could be kept equal—if one could assume away, in particular, any negative effect on labour productivity or the stability of effective demand—then this fall in wages would result in higher returns on physical and financial assets, and hence in a significant increase in the value of society's capital. As a consequence, people's per capita share of external assets in the standard sense would be greater, and the maximum level of basic income that could be financed by taxing these assets could therefore be expected to be significantly higher than it is with wages as they stand.

It is reasonable to suppose, however, that there will be overwhelming real-libertarian grounds for discarding such a market-clearing strategy.

First, keeping wages above the market clearing level is most likely to have a positive effect on profits, for example for efficiency-wage or effective-demand reasons. And secondly, rents incorporated in wages may be far easier to tax—mainly, but not only, because of labour being less mobile than capital, than if they were appropriated by capital owners. Thus, leximin real freedom is unlikely to recommend equalizing employment rents by forcing market clearing. Thinking about the latter strategy can be illuminating, though, in so far as it enables us to understand better the nature of employment rents: the latter can also be viewed as a way in which workers manage to tap—whether because of capitalist self-interest or owing to their own individual or collective power—part of the value of society's productive potential, that is, of its accumulated material means of production, of its production technology, and also, more broadly, of its economic and social organizational know-how. This explains why the taxation of inherited capital and technology could only lead to a counterintuitively low level of basic income (§ 4.3), and also how the taxation of current wages can be a way of capturing part of what has been left to us by previous generations.[39]

Suppose next that we have several types of job, while still assuming that people all have the same skills. It is then no longer true that, if all those looking for a job actually find one, there are no employment rents to be shared. Such rents exist whenever some people would like to do someone else's job at the going wage. And if jobs vary in both their pecuniary and non-pecuniary features, this may happen on a massive scale even if there is full employment of all those wishing to work. Involuntary joblessness is not essential. It only makes employment rents particularly conspicuous. Hence, whatever strategy is used against full employment, even full success would not undermine the justification for an additional basic income stemming from the existence of a type of asset that had been overlooked so far.

4.6 *From job auctions to income tax*

While still abstracting from differences in skills, let us now ask how one could implement in practice the demand that this further aspect of people's endowments should be distributed in leximin fashion. Ideally, there should be simultaneous auctions for each type of job, which will determine the competitive price for each of them. Let us first suppose that this set of auctions can be held, and hence the employment rents associated to each type of job precisely assessed. The emerging price will correspond to a large proportion of the wage for jobs which are intrinsically attractive to many. It will correspond to a smaller proportion for jobs which are hard, dull, or hazardous, and done only for the material rewards attached to them. For full equality to be achieved, this price must then be subtracted from the corresponding wage, while the proceeds will swell the basic income. But here again, and even assuming the rent component of wages can be exactly identified, taking the dynamic effects of redistribution into account forces one to recognize that the leximin solution is most likely to diverge substantially from full equality. The very suppression of the rent may have a significant cost in terms of profitability, and hence on the basic income that can be sustainably financed by taxing the transfer of external wealth (as discussed in § 4.2). How high this cost would be can be expected to be very sensitive to the nature of the mechanism that generated the rents.

In the gift-countergift variant of the efficiency-wage model, for example, the cost to the employer of the latter's gesture of offering more than the market-clearing wage matters arguably more to the workers' effort than the money that ends up in their pockets. In which case a very large proportion of the rent could be taxed away without much effect on work effort or profitability. In the labour-discipline (or shirking) variant, on the contrary, it is the size of the sanction, and hence the level of the net wage that is supposed to affect the workers' effort. None the less, one could in principle capture all rents at no cost in work effort by selling the access to each job for a given period at its competitive price and stipulating that the price paid is lost if the worker is caught shirking and dismissed in the course of the period.[40] However, let us not forget that what is being taxed away must be redistributed to all, with the consequence of improving the fall-back situation, reducing the cost of being dismissed and hence, according to this approach, reducing effort and profits.[41] Suppose next that the rents are appropriated as the result of tough individual or collective bargaining. Surely, the workers who managed to reap such rents in the first place can be expected to react to attempts to redistribute them by successfully bargaining for a compensatory wage increase. Only a tough and permanent statutory incomes policy could prevent this, and such a policy would throw overboard all the efficiency advantages of a responsive labour market. Thus, even assuming that the rent component can be precisely assessed through a set of auctions, there will generally be at least some loss in profitability from suppressing the rent, and hence a fall in the basic income that can be financed out of external assets of the standard kind. It does not follow, of course, that the basic income-maximizing rate of taxation on employment rents is zero, for what is being taxed is also used to feed a higher basic income. Taking both effects into account, the rate of tax on (perfectly identified) employment rents that maximizes the sustainable level of basic income (not the rate of profit) may therefore be quite high.[42]

In practical terms, however, the idea of organizing a large independent set of auctions, each matched to a particular type of job, does not make much sense. Indeed, jobs differ along so many dimensions and their value can be dramatically affected by so many changes (from the mood of the supervisor to the schedules of the public transport network) that the very notion of a 'type of job' is rather problematic. It does not follow that employment rents cannot be redistributed. But this will have to happen in a grosser way, through tax schemes that focus, unoriginally, on the incomes jobs give access to. One consequence is that it will no longer be possible to tax differently two jobs yielding the same wage but very unequal in terms of non-pecuniary advantages. This amounts to taxing the rent on the more pleasant job at a lower rate than the rent associated to the less pleasant one. Why should this bother us? As the uniform—that is, job-type-insensitive, but not necessarily proportional—taxation on wages increases, it will soon reach a point at which the whole of the rent of some intrinsically most unattractive sort of job has been seized: for the corresponding net wage, no one envies those who hold that sort of job. Are we stuck here, if we do not want to subtract from the wages of those who hold such jobs more than the corresponding rent? Are we forced, for this reason, to let all other workers get away with the rent they have appropriated? No, we can keep going, protected as we are against the risk of taking away more than is legitimate by the absence of involuntary *employment*: no one is stuck with a job with a negative rent. If one bears in mind the crucial fact that every worker gets a basic income *and* would still get it if she voluntarily gave up her job, one can safely assert that every worker will appropriate a share of the employment rents that is at least equal to that appropriated by those who do not work.

But we must be aware of the erosion of the tax base that is being triggered by any further increase in the level of taxation, as a result of two complementary processes. One is simply that some jobs, and the corresponding wages, will disappear. As employers do not find any candidates for some jobs at the going net wage, they will have to leave the jobs vacant or, if these are too precious to them, raise wages, but then generally at a level of labour demand that is lower than before. In either case, some jobs have disappeared. The other process is the substitution of non-pecuniary for pecuniary aspects of the rent. Non-pecuniary advantages can take many forms: Christmas parties and business dinners, free private phone calls and the use of sports facilities, thick carpets and relaxed coffee breaks, training, contacts, and participation in the firm's decision-making process. Since these advantages are not taxed, or hardly so when they are, it is increasingly in the mutual interest of employers and employees to swell them relative to the wage, as the rate at which the latter is taxed increases. As a result of these two processes, maximin considerations—the concern with maximizing the minimum share in these rents, that is, the level of the basic income financed by their redistribution—will have to halt the rise in the rate of taxation long before it could hope to capture 100 per cent of the rent, even if one were to abstract from the impact on profitability mentioned earlier.

After a long detour, it is now clear that we are back to a criterion that is not that different from the simple criterion which we seemed forced to give up under Crazy–Lazy pressure at the beginning of this chapter (§ 4.1). At least in a context in which no account is taken of differences in skills, the maximin or leximin version of our generalized Dworkinian criterion recommends that wages should be taxed up to the point at which the tax yield, and hence the basic income financed by it, is maximized. No bias against hard workers is involved, only an attempt to redistribute as much as is not counterproductive of the rents which would otherwise be monopolized by, and very unequally distributed among, the employed. Those with lousy, unattractive, negligible-rent jobs will benefit from such redistribution no less than the unemployed. How far short of full rent equalization the yield-maximizing point will lie and to what level of basic income it will correspond are of course contingent matters, which depend on many factors, including for example the extent to which some of the most tangible non-pecuniary advantages (car firms, business trips to exotic locations) can be assimilated to monetary income for tax purposes. Let me just mention two less obvious factors, which I believe to be of central importance.

First of all, it is important to bring in at this juncture the various efficiency arguments that have been made in favour of a basic income, compared to conditional transfer systems of the sort that currently exists in developed welfare states. Whether the introduction of a basic income in the latter context would involve any significant increase in relevant marginal tax rates and, if so, whether this would have a noticeable impact on the supply of labour and capital, are issues that have frequently been discussed. But according to those who advocate a basic income on economic grounds, these are issues of secondary importance compared to the significant contribution an unconditional basic income could make, as part of a new 'social contract', to a functioning of the labour market far better suited to current technological conditions.[43] If they are right, the redistribution of employment rents in the form of a basic income (subject to the constraint of undominated diversity) could go a long way before reaching the yield-maximizing point.

The second factor I want to stress relates more specifically to the redistribution of employment rents appropriated or protected by collective bargaining. It is quite possible that resolute collective resistance by organized workers could defeat, through a strategy of retaliatory moves, any attempt substantially to redistribute the assets they control. But the resoluteness and hence the chances of success of this resistance are crucially affected, in a democratic society, by whether or not the organizations involved can make a plausible public claim to the effect that their demands are fair demands, that what they are asking for is no more than what is owed them by virtue of their work. This is one reason why the sort of inquiry to which I am here trying to contribute is of far more than sheer speculative interest.

But precisely, are not waged workers bound to find what is here being proposed most unfair, to the extent that it is their wages, rather than just any income, that will have to finance a universal transfer enjoyed not only by themselves, but also—in a capitalist society—by employers and the self-employed? Does the assimilation of jobs to assets not lead to a stunning class bias against waged workers? Properly understood and extended, it does not. To see this, note, first of all, that jobs are not only held by waged workers in the strict sense, that is, people who get from the owners of the firm which employs them a payment whose absolute amount is prearranged. They are also held by workers who get from their employer a fixed percentage of the firm's profits or value added as in Martin Weitzman's (1984) or James Meade's (1989) share economy, or by workers who get a fixed percentage of the value added of a firm they jointly own themselves as in an economy consisting in co-operatives.

In all these cases, however, access to employment depends on being accepted by someone else, and hence it is easy to understand the possibility of shortages of positions, and hence of envy for someone else's position. But what about self-employment, including self-employment of a sort that involves the hiring of others? How could there be envy for someone else's self-employed job, and hence employment rents, since by definition no one else's approval is needed to get such a job? To start with, there are some self-employed jobs—taxi driver, pharmacist, retailer for some brands—for which there is often no administratively free access. And to the extent that the price of the licence remains below the latter's competitive value, self-employment rents are obviously present in such cases. But they can also be present in the absence of such institutional restrictions. When the job consists of providing services—from house cleaning to computer repairs—to some regular customers, the latter will be willing to pay more than the market-clearing fee in order to secure compliance and efficiency on the part of self-employed providers of services they cannot fully monitor, for reasons strictly analogous to the efficiency-wage mechanism.

More generally, practically all self-employed jobs consist in occupying a slot in the market which most other people cannot enter at will. Probably the main restrictive factor, and hence the most pervasive source for the possibility of envy, is the lack of the required skills. This is, of course, the case for most waged jobs too. But at this stage, to allow an orderly analysis, I am still assuming, that everyone is equally talented and skilled. How this approach generalizes in the presence of unequal skill levels is a question I am leaving for the next section, where this simplifying assumption will be lifted. Another restrictive factor is, of course, the unequal access to capital. True, this capital need not be owned by the self-employed person since capital markets make it possible to borrow. Capital markets, however, display tendencies towards rationing for reasons closely analogous to those analysed by efficiency-wage theories in the case of labour markets. Borrowers need to be kept in line by the fear of a costly 'contract termination', just as workers do. There is therefore a systematic shortage of credit at the equilibrium interest rate, just as there is a systematic shortage of jobs at the equilibrium wage.[44] Even if all were equally wealthy, access to credit would therefore be monopolized by some who do not pay its full price, and the income from credit-dependent self-employment would include a rent component which could be legitimately taxed away. Moreover, even if all gifts and bequests were justly taxed (see § 4.2), different people would still have unequal capital endowments. And this inequality results in an unequal ability to acquire the means of production required by various sorts of self-employment, both directly and indirectly, that is, via the advantage conferred, in the competition for scarce credit, by the possibility of using one's wealth as a collateral. This is yet another reason why the income from self-employment can be subjected to taxation along with wage income.

So there is no reason why the latter should carry the whole burden of legitimate taxation. It may be true, however, that the income of a self-employed worker or of a worker employed in a profit-sharing or co-operative firm, is generally less certain, less cushioned against risks, than that of a wage-earner in the strict sense, and that the size of the rent embodied in the corresponding jobs is accordingly lower, other things remaining equal. But in the sustainable-yield-maximizing income tax scheme that is being proposed, this will have to be taken into account and may lead to some differentiation between the taxation of fixed wage income and other forms of labour income. But this differentiation, if any is needed, is unlikely to be of such nature and significance that waged workers could take offence at it.

What about pure capital income? If (identically talented) people started off with equal material endowments and there were no systematic appropriation of rents along the way, there would be no justification to tax away the benefits deriving from their decision not to consume some of their income and invest it instead. But given that even an optimal taxation of material gifts and labour income would leave people's external endowments highly unequal, interests and dividends too can legitimately be subjected to maximum-yield taxation, at least providing that no forced saving occurs and—one should add—that the tax scheme can be adequately anticipated. The yield-maximizing taxation of people's income from savings can only guarantee—so far as possible—the leximinning of external endowments if no one incurs negative rents, which could easily happen if tax schemes took people by surprise. But here again the requirement of sustainability should suffice to ensure this. The sustainable-yield-maximizing scheme may quite possibly differentiate the rates on labour income and capital income (even when assessed net of inflation) and, within the latter, between rates on safe interest income and on risky dividends. But from our job auctions, it is now clear that we have moved back to a pretty comprehensive tax scheme. However, before being able to conclude that the initial simple claim (§ 2.1) is vindicated after all, we must first face yet another challenge, one that arises as soon as we recognize that one massively important determinant of people's very unequal access to jobs is their very unequal level of qualification.

4.7 An inconsistent proposal? Employment rents with unequal talents

It is now time to bring in a complication that was at the very core of the previous chapter but has been ignored ever since we considered the Crazy–Lazy challenge at the beginning of this one. How does the approach developed here in response to this challenge apply to situations in which it is acknowledged that people have different internal endowments and, partly as a result of this, unequal productive skills? In particular, is the rather generous redistribution of employment rents implied by the approach presented in this chapter not inconsistent with the rather stingy redistribution from the talented to the less-talented endorsed in Chapter 3? I shall first examine this question under the simplifying assumption that people's skills, that is, their current productive abilities, are simply talents, that is, abilities they have received as part of their internal endowments. Towards the end of this section I shall make room for the acquisition of skills, thereby lifting this simplifying assumption.

There is, no doubt, some significant interaction between the leximin distribution of employment rents and the satisfaction of undominated diversity. It is conceivable, for example, that someone whose comprehensive endowment would not be dominated if employment rents were not redistributed (owing to a high earning power) would be entitled to a targeted transfer after redistribution (owing to some handicap in another dimension) as a result of a reduction in the market return on her productive talents. However, by far the most significant impact that can be expected in this respect from the redistribution of employment rents is that, as the level of basic income increases, fewer and fewer people will be unable to earn a living (at a level unanimously considered indispensable) prior to the targeted transfers called for by a concern with undominated diversity. Consequently, fewer and fewer people will need to claim membership of a special category (of 'handicapped') in order to get an undominated comprehensive endowment. Taking job assets into account does not lead one to be less generous with the 'handicapped'—their overall income will be at least as high as if job assets were overlooked. But it does lead one to be less discriminating, to give lesser amounts in targeted fashion, thereby reducing the humiliation associated with the need for some special treatment, the trap created for the 'handicapped' by the conditional nature of the specific benefits to which they are entitled, and the size of the control apparatus required to administer selective schemes. There is a crucial interdependency here: how high the basic income can be lifted will depend on how much we need to set aside in order to satisfy the prior requirement of undominated diversity, but how much we shall need in order to satisfy this requirement depends on the level of basic income. But no vicious circle is involved. However tricky this may all be in practice, it is unproblematic in principle.

There is, however, something else that looks far more worrying. Consider a situation in which there is a limited number of identical jobs which people with different levels of talents would like to hold. Dumb is denied a job because he lacks the talent to do it, while Clever is denied the same job because of a shortage of jobs. The approach developed in the present chapter implies that Clever is entitled to redistribution up to the point at which no one wanting to work is left without a job. But the approach developed in Chapter 3 in order to deal with differences in talents would seem to imply, it seems, that redistribution to Dumb should stop as soon as anyone prefers Dumb's situation to that of the job holders. This is just a reflection of the fact that the potential envy-freeness associated to our criterion of undominated diversity will be achieved with less redistribution from the job holders than the actual envy-freeness associated with our criterion of job asset equalization. Is there not a deep inconsistency here between a rather stingy treatment of the untalented and a rather generous treatment of the rationed? Does consistency with Chapter 3 not entail that we have done all that needs doing for the jobless as soon as voluntary unemployment appears, and not at the much more ambitious point at which involuntary unemployment disappears, with the consequence that no increase in the level of basic income will have been justified as a result of drawing job scarcity into the picture?[45]

A first answer to this challenge is that unlike talents, job assets belong to people's external, not internal endowments, and hence that the reason behind the departure from the comparatively strong criterion of envy-freeness in the case of talents (§ 3.2) does not apply to the case of job assets. This reason was that as soon as we have both different talents and different tastes there is generally no way of achieving envy-freeness. But this is not the case with inequalities in access to jobs, and we have seen that the competitive auction for job assets provides a way of meeting the criterion of envy-freeness, in exactly the same way as Dworkin's auction does in the case of standard external assets. What consistency requires is not an extension of the ungenerous approach we had to resort to in the case of talents, but an extension of the generous one that commended itself in the case of external assets of the standard sort. Because jobs do not stick to people in the way talents do, there is no problem involved in making job holders, unlike talent holders, pay the full price of the assets they appropriate. It is up to them to divest themselves of these jobs once the price of keeping them is such that they envy the jobless, just as they can and should give up under analogous circumstances a piece of land which they are not that keen to work on.

It may be objected that the failure to get access to a job, with given productive talents, should be assimilated to the lack of a talent to sell oneself to an employer. Our ungenerous, basic-income-depressing criterion for internal-endowment equalization (undominated diversity) would then apply, and nothing would be gathered for the financing of a basic income. Accepting this objection, however, would have unacceptable implications. If it is applied to job assets, the strategy it suggests should also be applied to standard external assets. The failure to get access to a significant amount of wealth must then be interpreted as the lack of the ability to prompt donations or bequests—at any rate in societies such as ours, in which people are not forced to leave all their belongings to their legitimate children—and the very notion of equalizing external endowments would fall apart completely. Even though it cannot be denied that talents play a role in securing access to external assets of all sorts, the fact that minute variations in these talents, or differences in the context with identical talents, can lead to tremendous differences in the amount of assets controlled by a person makes it obvious that one should firmly resist this reduction of all inequalities in external endowments—both wealth and jobs—to differences in internal endowments.

But we are not out of trouble yet. As soon as there are several types of jobs, with different talent requirements, the question arises of who is supposed to take part in the auction that will determine the value of job assets. One respectable answer is that for any type of job, only those who are adequately qualified for it are allowed to make bids. Of course, qualification for a job is often a matter of degree, and those who are comparatively less well qualified must accordingly make bids that include a compensation for their lower productivity. The level of the rent is then reached when, for that type of job, nobody is involuntarily unemployed in the usual technical sense, that is, none of those appropriately qualified and willing to do the job at the going rate is left jobless.[46] As pointed out earlier (§ 4.4), this does not mean that the rent associated with a particular job is zero as soon as all the people who could do it have some job: some of them may just have settled for a less desirable job of another sort.[47] But if this is the right way to proceed, jobs requiring high levels of talent will have few people bidding for them and will therefore end up being valued far less, other things being equal, than jobs requiring low levels of talent. Moreover, since they could not do the job anyway, those who are not suitably qualified cannot claim any share in the rent associated with those jobs. The rent associated with low-talent jobs, on the other hand, should be distributed to all, since even the highly talented workers who are voluntarily staying away from such jobs in order to take high-talent ones have a legitimate claim on a share in the rent on the ground that they are giving up their own share of such jobs. If this is the correct interpretation of how the auction should be extended to this more complex situation, then instead of justifying a higher basic income for all, we end up justifying a differentiated grant whose level rises with the number and value of jobs one is talented enough to occupy. To illustrate, suppose that Dumb and Clever do the same unskilled job for the same wage and with equal efficiency. They will be taxed in the same way for the job they occupy, but Clever will receive a higher transfer because there are more jobs she could have occupied. This amounts to an ethically absurd redistribution from the poorly talented to the highly talented, which will generally not be offset by the transfers required to satisfy the criterion of undominated diversity.

Is there another consistent and general interpretation of the auction that does not have this unwelcome implication? The idea developed in the previous sections is, after all, that of sharing among all a type of asset that would otherwise be appropriated, very unequally, by some. But then if, in the absence of redistribution, some people are prevented by their lack of talents from getting access to any part of these assets, this should not affect their claim to a share in the value of these assets any more than if they had been denied such access by the sheer shortage of jobs. If the wealth stocked on top of a cupboard is to be shared among all, it makes no sense to restrict it to those tall enough to reach it. Consistency, this suggests, requires that one should determine the rent associated with each type of job by letting both those suitably qualified and the others bid for them. But could such a procedure not lead to many jobs being held by people who like them a lot but are utterly incompetent at them? Of course, it could. But there is, fortunately, no need to turn the auction idea into a practical device that could conceivably work even in the presence of many types of job and levels of talent. In the presence of different types of jobs, pragmatic considerations have already led us earlier (§ 4.6) to dispense with a scheme of simultaneous auctions and achieve a leximin distribution of employment rents by simply taxing jobs as a function of their wages only, up to the point at which the sustainable yield starts declining, and next distributing the proceeds equally among all. There is no reason why this procedure could not be extended to the case in which, in addition to several types of job, we also have different levels of talent. The ban on involuntary *employment* still protects us against imposing negative rents on some workers, and the fact that the basic income financed by the tax is distributed to all makes it an appropriate index of the minimum share in the value of employment rents. What is novel is only that the tax on some (highly skilled) job might quite possibly have exceeded the rent associated with it, *if* the latter had been legitimately determined by an auction among those who are actually capable of doing the job. (In the extreme case in which there is just one such person, the rent so determined would be zero.) Part of what is being taxed, in other words, is a return to talents. It corresponds to that part of the employment rent in the broader sense proposed here (that is, as assessed by everyone participating in the auction for highly skilled jobs) which some workers can appropriate because of the talents they possess.

Here again, the taxation of the income associated with the job is a handy but imperfect tool, relative to what would be possible if the rent component of each job could be neatly identified. This is particularly true once room is made for skill acquisition. Two types of job may command the same high wage because of the high skills they require. But in one case, the needed skills may just be raw talents, whereas in the other they can only be acquired at the cost of lengthy and tedious training. Yield-maximizing job-insensitive wage taxation will fail to capture much of the rent associated with the first type of job because it cannot tax the second job at a lower rate. It is true, of course, that the acquisition of a skill is a sunk cost, and that people who have made this human capital investment will keep working even if they are taxed at such a rate that the rent associated with their job becomes negative: had the workers known the terms in advance, the supply of labour for this job would have fallen short of the demand. But precisely, this would be unfair. The leximin distribution of external endowments requires the predictability of the tax rates. If some jobs give rise to negative net rents, those who hold them will have a smaller external endowment than those who hold no job. To prevent this, the ban on involuntary employment and the unconditionality of the basic income are essential but insufficient. It is also indispensable that taxation should not take them by surprise. But bearing in mind that sustainability should also cover the impact on skill acquisition, this should be guaranteed by the requirement that the tax schedule should *sustainably* maximize the yield. Our initial criterion of sustainable (and constrained) basic income maximization (§§ 2.1, 4.1) is thus pretty much vindicated after all.

In this light, let us return to the question of whether this implicit taxation of talents is consistent with our criterion of undominated diversity. We have seen that those who are better paid because their talents give them access to more highly skilled jobs will pay higher taxes than those restricted by their lack of talents to poorly paid jobs. This is clearly more than is demanded by our criterion of undominated diversity, since the latter requires no transfer from those with highly skilled jobs to those with unskilled jobs, as long as the latter provide a wage sufficient to cover what is unanimously regarded as indispensable. But it is definitely consistent with undominated diversity, since the very fact that the incumbents of highly skilled jobs choose them and hold on to them shows that despite the (expected) higher taxation, they would not like to swap positions with the net beneficiaries of this taxation. Hence the latter does not threaten the satisfaction of envy-freeness, let alone of potential envy-freeness. We can now see how taking seriously the idea that jobs constitute a category of external assets enables us to substantially attenuate the ungenerous implications of undominated diversity as a criterion of talent 'equality'. This is not only the case because better-paid jobs contribute more in taxes, but above all because the less valuable one's talents, the more one will gain, in terms of opportunities for fulfilling occupations, from an increased basic income. If your earning power is low, there may be only very few occupations that will give you a subsistence income with no basic income or a low one. With a substantial basic income, your choice will be far greater because you then need less income, if any, to reach subsistence.

4.8 A slippery slope ? From the right to work to the right to marry

This last remark is directly relevant to a frequent objection to the introduction of a basic income. Going for the latter, it is often claimed, amounts to a sell-out. By responding in this way to the monopolization or the very unequal distribution of valuable employment, one is giving up the equal right to work and settling for an equal right to income, by no means a perfect substitute. Paid work offers opportunities for social contacts, satisfying activities, social recognition, and social power which pay without work does not supply. Surely, access to these must be a component of the real freedom one is concerned to leximin, and is totally ignored by the approach adopted here.

This objection raises an important issue, but is profoundly mistaken. First of all, the non-pecuniary aspects of a job are an essential part of the rents we have been concerned to capture. They are fully taken into account in the hypothetical auction device: the fact that bids need to be formulated in money obviously does not imply that the bidders are blind to the non-monetary aspects of what they are bidding for. And in our second-best income tax scheme, they play a crucial role in keeping the yield-maximizing tax rate above what it would be if all there was to a job were the money it gave. If people find having a job very important for any of the other reasons just mentioned, this will accordingly swell the value of aggregate job assets as revealed by the auction and raise the level of the basic income that can be achieved by taxing wages. It is, therefore, unfair to say that the approach presented here reduces the importance of jobs to the incomes they give access to.

Secondly, it must of course be recognized that even if employment rents were fully equalized, not everyone would have a job. But everyone wishing to have one would. And as far as jobs are concerned, this possibility of getting one is all a real-libertarian standpoint requires. What matters from that standpoint is not that people should work, but that they should have the right to work, in the strong sense of a real opportunity. Whether or not it is actually exercised, this right to work is everyone's privilege and has by no means been displaced by a right to income. What real-libertarianism recommends, however, is not strict equality but leximin. And when leximin diverges from equality, what has just been said is no longer true. Leximin considerations can legitimize the persistence of some involuntary unemployment. Should it not be conceded that for those affected by such unemployment, the right to work has been swapped for a right to income? No, it should not. For one must bear in mind that, unlike minimum guaranteed systems of the standard type, basic income is an income one is allowed to keep when earning additional income from waged labour or self employment. Hence, the higher the level of one's unconditional income, the higher not only one's consumption power, but also one's ability to get access to jobs with desirable non-pecuniary features. For the higher the grant, the easier it is to create one's own job by becoming self-employed, to work part-time or to accept a lower wage *in order to* get a job that has a non-pecuniary feature (including training opportunities that improve future pecuniary prospects) to which one attaches particular importance. The involuntary unemployment that is countenanced by the application of our principle, is therefore most unlikely to take the form of forced inactivity. With a high basic income, it can safely be predicted that all those who wish to perform paid work will actually do so (abstracting from search periods), whether as waged or self-employed workers. But among all those workers, some will unavoidably get jobs which others would prefer to their own. This is the form the persistence of employment rents would take. Such persistence implies, of course, that real freedom in general and the real freedom to work in particular are not equal for all. But if the leximin criterion has been met, any attempt to reduce this inequality in an unbiased way would reduce someone's real freedom below the level currently enjoyed by the least advantaged.

By asserting that the basic income strategy caters adequately for the right to work, I do not mean to imply that there is no better way of looking after this dimension of freedom. One could devise policies that provide jobs with good pay and comfortable working conditions to anyone wishing to perform paid work. But this would again amount to redistributing employment rents in a discriminatory fashion, as was the case with straight wage subsidies (see § 4.5). It would amount to giving a liberally unjustified privilege to those who have a stronger preference for waged labour. The approach presented here, therefore, does not require that the right to work should be swapped for a right to income, nor that priorities should be shifted from the former to the latter. All it requires is that no special privilege be given to one dimension of freedom over another, or that people with different tastes should not be treated in discriminatory fashion.

Thus, it is not the case that we have unduly neglected the right to work. But should we not rather be wary of having given it an undue privilege?

Could we not go—are we not forced to go—even further than we have gone? I have mentioned earlier (§ 4.4) that, besides labour power, there may be other commodities that often fail to fetch a market-clearing price. The rationing they are subjected to, however, does not appear to be so significant as to require special attention. But does the logic of our approach not take us beyond the realm of what is usually regarded as commodities? Suppose, for example, that there is a shortage of marital partners, whether for a purely demographic or a cultural reason. More women, say, wish to have a husband than there are men wishing to have a wife, for reasons unrelated to the material advantages associated with partnership, which we assume to have been dealt with in accordance with the principles that apply to any gift (see § 4.2). How should a real-libertarian handle this situation?

Leaving things as they are is prima facie unfair because some people monopolize a scarce asset. Sharing men equally among all women would be suboptimal in terms of real freedom, because some women want a man by their side all the time, while some others could not care less. Sharing men exclusively among those women who care for a man would give an unfair advantage to people with an expensive taste for the asset in scarce supply. So the ideal solution must consist in giving all women an equal tradable right to men, and let them then trade in perfectly competitive fashion until the market-clearing price of partnership is reached. Those who end up with a man after the auction and would have had one without it will, of course, be made worse off by the procedure: they now have to pay for their privilege. Those without a man both after the auction and without it will instead become better off: they are given an equal share in the value of the scarce asset. This procedure consistently implements, it seems, the notion that everyone has an equal right to marry—just as everyone has an equal right to work—while being compatible with not everyone choosing to marry—just as not everyone need choose to work. Is this further extension of our approach not so obviously absurd that it casts serious doubts on the real-libertarian perspective as a whole? Or is there a way of protecting the latter against such doubts by pointing to a crucial disanalogy that would block the suggested extension? Tackling these questions, as we shall see, will further clarify the presuppositions of the approach adopted in this chapter.[48]

At first sight, this looks easy enough. For a start, it does not seem to make much sense to speak of men as *one* asset and of setting up an auction to determine *the* value of this asset. But this does not point to a relevant difference. Jobs too form a very heterogeneous pool, and nothing in our approach implies that the desirability, or the scarcity, of all elements in this pool should be equal, nor therefore that the value of each type of job should be the same. Partners and jobs are not fundamentally different in this respect. In neither case can the heterogeneity of the scarce asset exempt us from sharing its value.

Secondly, one may be tempted to emphasize that the 'asset' which is now being considered consists of *people*. We therefore hit against the constraint of self-ownership, for which there is no equivalent in the case of jobs. But this will not do either. True, if marital partners belonged to another species—say, plants—they would presumably count as external assets of the standard kind and would have been treated in exactly the same way as any other such asset (§ 4.2). But this does not establish a disanalogy with the non-standard case of jobs. Suppose the jobs in short supply are all in two-person firms (the employer and the employee). The auction for jobs will then determine who is going to work with whom, just as the auction for partners determines who is going to live with whom. If men themselves should be allowed to determine whom they are going to accept as a partner and on what terms, then why should not employers be allowed to determine whom they are going to accept as a collaborator and on what terms?[49] It is our concern with equalizing people's real freedom that leads us in the latter case to alter the terms of the transactions that would spontaneously take place. In so far as the possibility of living with someone—and who one lives with—is no less important a component of real freedom than the possibility of having a job—and what job it is—interference with the terms of voluntary agreements in order to equalize real freedom is just as much required when there is a shortage of partners (or, more generally, envy over partnership endowments) as when there is a shortage of employers (or, more generally, envy over job endowments).

Nor is it relevant to point out, thirdly, that the preferences and choices of the men being chosen play a crucial role, and that therefore the allocation determined by a unilateral auction is unacceptable. In the case of jobs, we had to take differences in talents into account, with the consequence that an auction in which all could take part would allocate jobs to people lacking the required skills. This had and was to be avoided, by adopting the maximum-yield tax scheme. But the fact that talents are so distributed that people have very different chances of obtaining desirable jobs or partners does not affect the need to try and distribute the value of scarce assets in leximin fashion.

A fourth potentially decisive difference stems from the fact that jobs are for production, whereas marital partnerships are not. But once again, this cannot be an adequate response to the challenge posed by the analogy. This is not only the case because households are often production partnerships in the usual sense or because one may, moreover, want to extend the concept of production, following Gary Becker (1981), to cover household production. More fundamentally, even if marital partnerships were for consumption only, this would not constitute a relevant difference. As we have seen earlier (§ 2.7), standard assets which can only be used for consumption purposes, say, a beach, are to be shared among all in essentially the same way as productive assets.

What is crucial in the case of jobs, however, may not be the fact that we are dealing with productive assets, but more specifically—and fifthly— the fact that we are dealing, via jobs, with external means of production (capital and technology) that should be distributed equally to all. Unlike couples, jobs are not just associations with other people. As argued earlier (§ 4.5), they can be viewed as taps fitted on to a pool of external assets to which all have an equal claim. What is crucial, in other words, is not the link between jobs and production, but the link between jobs and means of production. But there is nothing essential about the relation between jobs and means of production. To present the matter as sharply as possible, suppose available technology is such that in order to produce anything at all, one needs no capital whatever (goods are sung into existence) but one hundred workers (forming a choir), with strongly diminishing returns beyond that level. Teams are formed, and some people are left behind. Incomes and other advantages (prestige, etc.) associated to membership in one of the teams are distributed equally among the members of each team. There is here no connection whatever with material means of production, and yet we feel that our concern with leximin real freedom is not consistent with leaving those left behind uncompensated. Indeed, it seems pretty obvious that if the auction for scarce jobs is a plausible mechanism for equalizing assets, there is no reason for not applying it to this case as well. It may be the case here that other people are the condition of access to some immaterial external asset, namely the use of some inherited technology. But this is not necessarily the case. Collaboration with a number of other people as such may be the key asset that makes production possible. And there is then no crucial difference left with the case of scarce partners.[50]

Finally, it may be pointed out that, in the case of partnerships, there is (generally) no equivalent to a wage, and hence no base for a taxation scheme to get off the ground—and a taxation scheme, as we have seen (§ 4.7), is strictly required if we want to make concrete sense of leximin rent distribution in a situation in which talents vary. But is this a fundamental difference? Imagine a situation with a high basic income in which various types of jobs are offered and taken for no pay. Huge rents could then still be appropriated by some, because of the intrinsically more attractive nature of their jobs. Is there no way of further redistributing this rent in the form of a higher basic income? There may be, for example by taxing gross wages at more than 100 per cent or, more sensibly perhaps, by leaving labour unpaid and imposing a uniform tax on each job holder (to be paid out of her basic income). In this society in which working has become consumption, the level of the tax has made jobs so costly that any further increase would induce so many workers to quit that the tax yield would fall. If the forming of partnerships constitutes another major way in which unequal opportunities get appropriated, could not an analogous procedure be conceived? Since, be it only for the same reasons as in the case of jobs, an auction is not appropriate, could one not tax partnerships at a yield-maximizing level? One may, of course, quickly reach this point, owing to partnerships being discouraged or going underground, and it is therefore most likely that it would not be worth bothering. But the difference is then only of a pragmatic nature. Wages do offer a convenient basis for taxing the appropriation of jobs: they generally make it possible to collect more than if all jobs were taxed at the same level. But they are not essential either to jobs or to taxation. Once again, no fundamental disanalogy emerges.

This sequence of failures prompts the following tentative conclusion. It is not partners but partnerships—which are, like jobs, a more or less codified bundle of rights and legitimate expectations—that are on offer in the hypothetical auction. Once this is made clear, the consequences of the 'equal right to marry' are not obviously less acceptable intuitively, than those of the 'equal right to work'. Whenever there is rationing, a gift is objectively being made to those who get hold of the scarce asset. The value of what is thus being given has to be redistributed in leximin fashion. This is what is being achieved by financing a basic income out of whatever scarcity rent is sufficiently sizable and seizable to be worth chasing—a condition unlikely to be met in the case of partnerships. This is, perhaps, not strong enough a safeguard against such invasion of privacy on grounds of real freedom. I am not ruling out that there may be a better one. But I doubt that one could be found which does not throw overboard an overarching concern with a fair distribution of life chances in order to protect spheres of life which fall outside the reach of distributive justice.

Even the embarrassment of this analogy, therefore, should not shatter our confidence in the claim that real-libertarianism, as characterized, commands the introduction of a basic income at the highest sustainable level consistent with formal freedom and undominated diversity.

APPENDIX : CRAZY, LAZY, AND RAWLS'S
REVISED DIFFERENCE PRINCIPLE

According to Rawls (1988: 257), 'twenty-four hours less a standard working day might be included in the index as leisure. Those who are unwilling to work would have a standard working day of extra leisure, and this extra leisure itself would be stipulated as equivalent to the index of primary goods of the least advantaged.' What does this imply for the legitimate level of basic income in the Crazy–Lazy story (§4.1)? Suppose Crazy's working time (n hours) defines standard working time, while W represents the corresponding post-tax wage, m ($< n$) the number of hours worked by Lazy, and G the level of the grant given to all. Crazy's index of primary goods is then given simply by her total income:

$$PG_{Cr} = W + G \quad \text{(Crazy's index)}.$$

Lazy's index, under Rawls's expanded account, is given by his net wage (a fraction m/n of Crazy's) plus his basic income (G) plus the value of his leisure when assessed by reference to 'the index of primary goods of the least advantaged [full-time worker]' (a fraction $(n - m)/n$ of Crazy's index):

$$PG_L = (m/n) \cdot W + G + ((n - m)/n) \cdot (W + G)) \quad \text{(Lazy's index)}.$$

For maximin to be satisfied, it is necessary that Lazy's index should not exceed Crazy's index, which reduces, after simplifications, to the requirement that:

$$((n - m)/n) \cdot G < 0.$$

Since Crazy works more than Lazy ($n > m$), it is obvious that this condition can be satisfied only if there is no basic income (G = 0).

It is worth noting that once we drop the (Crazy–Lazy) assumption of identical talents, this conclusion remains valid, but a new consequence emerges. The revised Difference Principle will now require a differentiation of the rate of taxation depending on how much people work. In the absence of such differentiation, the highly skilled who work short hours will enjoy a level of primary goods that far exceeds, owing to a higher hourly wage, that of unskilled people who earn more but need to work far longer in order to do so. The revised Difference Principle must demand that at least part of this excess be taxed away. To illustrate, suppose Clever, by working 1 hour a day, earns half what Dumb earns in a full 8-hour day. Part of Clever's income must then be redistributed to Dumb, despite Clever's income being half that of Dumb's. Why? Dumb's index of primary goods is simply given by his wage, since he is assumed to have no leisure:

$$PG_D = W \quad \text{(Dumb's index)}.$$

Clever's index is obtained by adding her income to the value of her leisure, as assessed by reference to the income of the least-advantaged full-time worker (namely Dumb):

$$PG_{Cl} = (1/2) \cdot W + (7/8) \cdot W = (11/8) \cdot W \quad \text{(Clever's index)}.$$

The simplest implementation of the underlying criterion consists in taxing income at a proportional rate and distributing the yield as a subsidy proportional to the number of hours worked, which amounts to a progressive tax on hourly wages. Full equality of primary goods indexes will then be reached only when the tax rate is 100 per cent and all income is distributed in the form of proportional work subsidies. The Rawlsian solution to the Crazy–Lazy problem (§4.2) is just a special case. Given that Crazy and Lazy are equally gifted for the only existing type of work, there is only one rate of pay. Distributing the whole product according to the length of people's labour is then strictly equivalent to leaving untouched the pre-tax distribution of income.

CHAPTER 5

Exploitation versus real freedom

PROLOGUE

Δ *So far, I have been testing your claim that basic income maximization (subject to some constraints) provided the best interpretation of your conception of justice as real-freedom-for-all. I cannot say I am 100 per cent convinced, but you had obviously thought about the various questions I asked (in fact, I suspect I would not have been allowed to ask them otherwise), and I must admit that some of the objections I thought might be fatal have been successfully rebutted.*

Φ I am sure you have not exhausted your stock of objections, though.

Δ *It would be silly to try to go through all possible objections. But I would really like to formulate better than I have done so far what bothers me most fundamentally with your proposal. Basically, I still find you too soft on the surfers. Do you remember the story of the Little Red Hen? Well, I really feel that the Little Red Hen was right in turning down the animals who wanted to share the bread she made after having ignored all her requests for help in making it. And it seems to me that basic income maximization does not accommodate this strong intuition. But the best way of formulating my objection is probably not by claiming, as I did before, that you are giving surfers a privilege that is inconsistent with real-freedom-for-all, but rather by arguing that real-freedom-for-all fails to incorporate an important aspect of social justice, crucially relevant in the context of a discussion of socialism versus capitalism, namely the condemnation of exploitation.*

Φ What do you call exploitation?

Δ *What about something like 'taking unfair advantage of someone else's work'?*

Φ Fine with me (§ 5.1). I suppose that 'taking' must be understood as excluding genuine gifts, while covering both the case in which the advantage is appropriated through the exercise of some form of power and the case in which the existence of some positive externality makes free-riding possible. In any event, the crucial question, for our purposes, is to spell out what it is for an advantage to be 'unfairly'—and hence exploitatively—taken (§ 5.2).

Δ *Right. If we find an appealing criterion of unfairness that cannot be accommodated by real-freedom-for-all, I shall have a foundation for my exploitation-based challenge against your proposal.*

Φ The most convenient way to proceed may be to consider a number of common characterizations of exploitation and spell out the underlying criterion of unfairness. About one of them, I think we shall quickly agree that it does not provide the right track. Exploitation is frequently conceived as the appropriation of part of a worker's (net) product by virtue of something else than one's labour—owning some means of production for example. This conception could be called 'Lockean' because the notion of fairness to which it appeals involves a right of the worker to the entire fruit of her labour (§ 5.3).

Δ *Why did you say that this cannot be the right track?*

Φ First, because the proposition that workers are the creators of the whole product, on which their right to the entire product is usually supposed to rest, is either tautological and irrelevant or plainly false. And secondly because—contrary to my firm intuition and, I should hope, yours—the recognition of such a right would justify inequalities, however large, that stem, for example, from the fact that unequally fertile soil makes workers unequally productive (§ 5.4).

Δ *What's the alternative?*

Φ Take, secondly, the classic characterization of exploitation as the unequal exchange of labour value: someone is exploited if she contributes more socially necessary labour than she appropriates through her income, and she is an exploiter in the converse situation. I call this the Lutheran conception of exploitation because the underlying criterion of fairness is one of fair exchange, clearly stated in a striking passage from Luther quoted by Marx in this connection. The problem with this second conception is not only that the concept of labour value raises some notorious difficulties. More fundamentally, you will need little reflection to realize that, except under extremely restrictive factual conditions, assessing people's contributions and their rewards in terms of how much labour value they contain makes no normative sense whatever (§ 5.5).

Δ *Labour value may not be the most adequate metric for either people's contributions or their rewards. But, surely, recognizing this does not make nonsense of the more general idea that justice requires contributions and rewards to be closely related. Disproportionality between work performed and income earned may not be an acceptable definition of exploitation because it does not entail that one person is taking advantage of someone else's work. But the discussion of the Lutheran conception naturally leads to it and it constitutes, moreover, a plausible criterion of unfairness which is clearly alien to real-*

freedom-for-all and may well provide a foundation for the moral indictment of basic income.

Φ Fair enough. But please, let's not confuse proportionality and positive relation. That income should be *strictly proportional to* work effort is blatantly incompatible with a basic income. But it is hardly an intuitively obvious requirement of justice. That someone's income level should be *positively affected by* her work, I find on the contrary intuitively compelling. But it is perfectly consistent with a basic income. Indeed, the latter is part of a set-up that aims to equalize (or at least to maximin) people's opportunities or endowments—rather than their achievements or their incomes—and thereby unavoidably gives differences in effort a far stronger hold on outcomes, relatively speaking, than if inequalities of opportunities were left alone. So, the strong justice-based appeal of increasing the grip of differential effort on differential reward (not of achieving proportionality between them) is perfectly at home in a basic income society (§ 5.6).

Δ *I am not sure this does full justice to the hard-working Little Red Hen. Is there any further conception of exploitation that could enable me better to articulate my objection?*

Φ I doubt it. The only other significant (and significantly different) approach to exploitation is the one developed by John Roemer. According to his characterization, someone is capitalistically exploited, roughly, if she would become better off as a result of an equalization of people's current capital endowments, and someone is a capitalist exploiter if she would become worse off as a result of such equalization. Further types of Roemerian exploitation are generated by varying the category of assets concerned: not only capital, but also skills, feudal bonds, etc. (§ 5.7). The underlying criterion of fairness is that some people should not be better off, and others worse off, as a consequence of an unequal distribution of assets. Once you start spelling out the associated notion of justice—equality of assets—and modifying it so as to meet powerful objections—responsibility for the consequences of one's choices, no equalization at the expense of the worst off, no enslavement of the talented—you will soon be back to something very close to real-freedom-for-all and hence to basic income maximization (§ 5.8).

Δ *Too bad for the Little Red Hen.*

Φ Not really. If she uses no resource in scarce supply, she can legitimately keep the whole of her product. If she does—as all her kin do in the real world—then she cannot fairly complain about a scheme that distributes maximally among all the value of the scarce assets very unequally appropriated by some.

5.1 Deriving an advantage from someone's work

As announced at the start (§ 2.3), the many challenges considered in the previous three chapters all consisted in questioning the link between a conception of social justice as real-freedom-for-all and the (constrained) maximization of an unconditional basic income. They all took it for granted that social justice was appropriately conceived as leximin real freedom. But are there no powerful reasons for doubting the adequacy of this real-libertarian conception of justice? Indeed, is its inadequacy not exposed by the very fact that the various challenges considered so far could be defeated and hence that the justification of a possibly substantial income even for those who choose not to work could plausibly be regarded as one of its consequences?

By spelling out the lethal defects of standard libertarianism, Chapter 1 led us step by step to real-libertarianism as an attractive way of articulating the importance we attach to freedom, equality, and efficiency. But it made no systematic attempt to seek out, let alone to tackle, the main objections that could be made to the claim that real-freedom-for-all is all there is to social justice. Nor is it part of the purpose of this book to provide a comprehensive discussion of these objections, most of which apply more broadly to the whole family of liberal-solidaristic conceptions of justice, or indeed to all liberal theories in the sense indicated (§ 1.8). However, there is one such objection which I cannot hope to evade in the context of this book. Whereas appeals to freedom have provided the simplest and most frequent ethical case for capitalism, the simplest and most common ethical argument for socialism is to be found in the indictment of *exploitation*, described by Friedrich Engels (1873: 214) as 'the basic evil which the socialist revolution wants to abolish by abolishing the capitalist mode of production'. By itself, this already strongly suggests that the assessment of the relative merits of capitalism and socialism will remain seriously incomplete, and suspiciously biased in favour of the former, as long as the issue of exploitation is not explicitly brought into the picture. Moreover, the very fact that real-libertarianism ends up justifying an income for the voluntarily idle further suggests that, far from providing foundations for the critique of exploitation, it unashamedly legitimizes the latter on an unprecedented scale. For those who believe that exploitation is an evil, introducing an unconditional basic income, whether under capitalist or socialist conditions, seems bound to make things far worse, not better. And if this is what real-libertarianism recommends, too bad for real-libertarianism.

In order to assess these suggestions carefully, let us first make sure we use a precise definition of exploitation which at the same time captures at least roughly the sense in which the term has been used from the Saint-Simonians onwards in the critique of capitalism and promises to provide us with an ethical standard for the assessment of socio-economic regimes that cannot be accommodated by a real-libertarian conception of justice.[1] *Exploiting* someone, I submit, consists in taking unfair advantage of someone else's work.[2] According to this definition, it makes no sense to ask whether there is anything wrong with exploitation. Exploitation is, by definition, unfair. Such a stipulation does not make us beg any important question, providing one realizes that the criterion of unfairness can be elaborated in different ways. We shall later examine various conceptions of exploitation which differ precisely according to the way in which this criterion is specified. But let us first sharpen the other components of the proposed definition of exploitation, by asking, against the background of a very simple economy in which the exploiter is entirely idle, what it means that, for exploitation to be present, some *advantage* must be *taken* from *someone's work*. In the process, I shall point out a number of ambiguities and difficulties that surround the concept of exploitation, and also identify a number of dimensions along which existing definitions of exploitation vary. Along each dimension, I shall make a choice suited to the purpose which the concept is here meant to serve, even though, in several cases, another choice could have been made without damaging consequences.

First, I shall suppose that the exploitee, the 'someone' whose work is being taken advantage of is a *human being* or a set of human beings. Hence, it makes sense to speak of the exploitation of one particular worker, not just of the working class as a whole. But the concept does not cover the exploitation of a non-human animal or species.[3]

Secondly, a human being can only be exploited if she performs some *work*. Letting one's husband live off one's dowry or being photographed in the street (without having had to pose) do not qualify as activities and cannot, therefore, I shall further suppose, give rise to exploitation, however large—and possibly unfair—the benefit derived by the husband or the photographer. Not all activities constitute work. Yet I shall not suppose that work needs to be toil or drudgery. It can also consist of activities performed for their own sake. In other words, work does not need to be prompted by a threat or an extrinsic reward. If you thoroughly enjoy fiddling about on my computer the way I tell you to and would do so even for no pay, you do not toil but play. None the less, it is quite conceivable that you may be exploited if I make handsome profits out of the softwares you produce. For an activity to qualify as work, I shall rather suppose, it must be one that is geared to the production (whether pleasurable or not) of a benefit that is external to the performance of the activity itself—and is, therefore, also capable of being enjoyed by others. This benefit need not be a material object. It can consist of the songs one sings no less than in the potatoes one grows. And it can also consist of both consumption and production goods. But pure play cannot be work: one can only work when playing football if one does so, or trains for doing so, in front of an audience. Nor can pure consumption be work, even though consumers are occasionally said to be 'exploited'.[4] One implication of this characterization is that a paid activity can generally be presumed to be work in the relevant sense. This is not because the payment indicates that the activity would not have been performed without external reward: it might well have been, and in any case it is work, and not toil, that is required for there to be exploitation. The ground for the presumption is rather that if the activity had not been expected to produce some benefit of some use to others, no one would bother to pay for it. 'Expected' is important here, because it is the expectation of the benefit, rather than its actual production, that turns an activity into work in the relevant sense: a worker is working even if the goods she produces end up remaining unsold—or harming their purchasers. To be paid, on the other hand, is by no means a necessary condition for an activity to qualify as work and hence to be liable to exploitation. Work can also be rewarded by some income in kind, by prestige gains, by gratitude, or not be rewarded at all. It is only in the very broad sense so clarified that I shall here be supposing, as is usually done, that only workers can be exploited.

Thirdly, in order to be an exploiter, one needs to derive an *advantage* from someone else's work.[5] To clarify this notion—and by the same token a family of related notions commonly used in connection with exploitation—suppose there are just the two of us on an isolated plot of land. I do nothing. You grow potatoes. For a benefit to accrue to me, it is not sufficient that I should appropriate part of your total product, that is, some of the potatoes you have grown in the period considered, for these may just refund me for the potatoes I put at your disposal at the beginning of the period. But it *is* sufficient that I should appropriate part of your *net product*, that is, what is left of your total product when the material means of production used up in the process of bringing it about have been replaced. It is, on the other hand, not sufficient that you should produce some *surplus*, that is, what (if anything) is left of the net product once whatever is needed to reproduce your labour power has been subtracted. But it is sufficient (as well as necessary) that you should produce a *surplus product*, i.e what (if anything) is left of the net product after subtraction of all the potatoes you keep for yourself, whether or not they are required for the reproduction of your labour power. The labour expended in producing the surplus product is often called *surplus labour.*[6] Thus, in our example, your producing a surplus product or, equivalently, your performing surplus labour is a necessary and sufficient condition for me to exploit you, that is, to take advantage of your work. The *production* of a surplus or, more weakly, that of a net product are not sufficient conditions, but they are—beyond the very short term— necessary ones.[7] *Appropriation* by me of part of the surplus or of the net product, on the other hand, is both a necessary and a sufficient condition of my taking advantage of your work. But my appropriating part of the total product, though necessary, is generally not sufficient. It is only if I have not provided you with any of your (destructible) means of production—for example, if the reason why you let me benefit from your work is not that you need my tools but that you fear my fists—that appropriating part of your product is just as much a sufficient condition for exploitation as is my appropriating part of your net product.

This characterization of the 'advantage' component of exploitation is pretty unproblematic, at least in the simple sort of situation considered here. (The 'taking' or 'appropriation' component, loosely used so far, remains to be clarified in the next section.) Some of its implications, however, are worth spelling out more fully. First, for me to exploit you, it is not necessary that I should *consume* part of what you produce. Consumption by me is only a necessary condition for your being exploited, in the above example, if the economy is stationary, that is, if the number of potatoes that are being planted does not increase from year to year. But if, instead of being consumed, the part of your net product I appropriate is entirely accumulated—I eat none of the potatoes I take but use them all to increase the number of potatoes planted next year—I am still deriving a relevant advantage according to the above characterization, even if—whether in intention, in actual fact, or both—this accumulation serves to swell your consumption, and not mine, at a later stage.[8] And so I am if I donate the part of your product I appropriate to my grandmother or send it off to the Third World.[9] The underlying idea, in all these cases, is that, however honourable the use I make of your surplus product, I am still depriving you of the choice to decide what to do with it.[10] Thus, consumption by the exploiter is not a necessary condition for exploitation. Nor is it necessary, by definition that the exploiter's *welfare* should be increased as a consequence of exploitation. If I get some of the potatoes you grow in exchange for letting you use a piece of land I own, this will constitute exploitation irrespective of whether I would prefer you to keep your potatoes and leave my land alone. Of course, if I am out to maximize my welfare and entitled to decide what happens to my land, I shall not remain such a begrudging landlord for long. But this does not refute the proposition that I do not need to gain welfare, any more than

I need to consume, in order to derive an advantage in the sense relevant to exploitation.

5.2 *Power, gifts, free rides*

While not necessary, is it sufficient for exploitation to occur that I should consume part of your product or increase my welfare thanks to your work? No, it is not. To see why, let us now focus on what is conveyed by the proposition that exploitation consists in *taking* advantage, in *appropriating* part of the product, in *extracting* a benefit, not just in deriving a benefit or enjoying an advantage.[11] In this respect, the first and most obvious point to note is that I can derive a benefit from your work without taking advantage of it, if the potatoes you give up in my favour are a *genuine gift*, an entirely voluntary transfer of part of your net product. This holds whether I am your infant child, your crippled grandmother, your vicar, your landlord, or the Princess of Wales.[12] But let us beware of excluding too much.

First of all, the fact that you voluntarily engage in an agreement that enables me to derive a benefit from your work does not imply that this constitutes an entirely voluntary and hence non-exploitative transfer of part of your product. In other words, the absence of any coercion does not turn the provision of a benefit into a genuine gift, and hence coercive exploitation is not the only type of exploitation.[13] Let me spell this out. You are *coerced* by me into doing something if you are led to do so as a result of my suppressing some of the options you could legitimately expect to have open to you. You are coerced into giving up some of your potatoes to me if you have grown them on land you legitimately own and I take them by force or credibly threaten to beat you up or burn your house if you do not give them. Coercive exploitation, in this light, covers both the appropriation of benefits through the violation of self-ownership—for example, the feudal corvée—and through the violation of legitimate ownership over external objects—systematic plundering, for example. It does not matter, for our present purposes, where exactly the line is drawn between coerced and voluntary transfers.[14] The key point here is simply that exploitation reaches far beyond coercive exploitation into the area of voluntary transactions. It is not necessary that the exploitee be forced into the exploitative deal. She can also be lured into it.

In the case of market exploitation, on the other hand, the exploiter does not suppress some options that would otherwise be open to the exploitee, but offers a new one which the exploitee prefers to those she previously had available to her. If you let me have some of the potatoes you grow, you can use my land. Accepting this offer may not simply make you better off than under the status quo ante. If you do not own any land yourself and there is no other fertile land around, it may even save you from starvation and thus dramatically increase your welfare level. Exploitation is thus consistent with the exploitee being extremely (and rightly) keen about the exploitative deal and the exploiter far less, indeed possibly (as illustrated in passing in the previous section) not at all.[15] Of course, when the exploitative deal is what saves you from starvation, it may be said that you are still, if not coerced into accepting it, perhaps *compelled* to accept it, owing to the lack of any tolerable alternative. But the disjunction of coercion and compulsion in this sense is no more necessary to exploitation than is coercion alone. If you had your own plot of land on which you could grow enough for subsistence and only worked on mine in order to increase your consumption beyond the subsistence level or in order to gain some leisure (my plot is far more fertile), this would not put an end to exploitation as we need to understand it here.[16] One implication of deciding otherwise would, of course, be that a capitalist society with a substantial basic income would be free of exploitation—which would amount to dodging, not meeting, the challenge which we are here preparing to consider.[17]

What is, then, the key distinction between ('involuntary') exploitation and ('voluntary') gift? Whether coerced or not, whether compelled or not, the cases of exploitation we have just been looking at involve a transfer of (at least) part of the product which is, *ceteris paribus*, involuntary. The exploitative deal as a whole may be voluntary—in the sense of uncoerced or uncompelled or both—but the transfer part is not, whereas it is in the case of a gift. One way in which one can try to clarify this distinction is by pointing out that exploitation, unlike gift-giving, involves the exercise of *power* by the recipient of the benefit over its producer.[18] Power is here understood, roughly, as the ability to make someone do something she would not otherwise have done by affecting the pay-offs of her actions, rather than by, for example, providing her with some information.[19] Coercion is just one form taken by the exercise of power in this sense. The control over some asset that is precious to the producer of the benefit is another. Of course, the ownership of the means of production is the category of asset that has been central in the exploitation-based critique of capitalism.[20] But it must be noted that Proudhon, for example, saw the root of exploitation in the advantage the employer could take from the 'enormous force that results from the workers' unity and harmony, from the convergence and simultaneity of their efforts'. Without either providing material means of production or using coercion, some 'non-worker' can appropriate part of the workers' product, simply because she *knows* how to organize the co-operation of workers and is thereby enabled to cash in on the benefits yielded by economies of scale.[21] Thus the possession of knowledge is another, possibly more fragile, power base for taking advantage of someone else's work.[22]

Let us further note that there is no reason to presume that power-based benefit extraction is restricted to the economic sphere. It may also permeate private, intimate relationships. Suppose for a moment that I fall in love with you. Being loved confers power. Because I love you, I watch and mind your whims, frowns and smiles. You can, therefore, use them as carrots and sticks to make me do things for you which I would otherwise never have dreamt of doing. And even if you do not *use* them as carrots or sticks, they can *function* as such to your advantage. Given the account of power proposed above, no more is needed for there to be power-based benefit extraction. For if I grow your potatoes (or sew your socks) because I love you, whether or not power is involved depends on what goes on in my mind, not in yours. If I am working hard on your potatoes (or on your socks) because I am afraid that otherwise you might slam the door or burst into tears, or because I hope you will grow fonder of me as a result, or agree to join me for a walk up the hill—and I care about all these things because of my love for you—then you owe your ability to consume part of the product of my work to the power my love for you bestows upon you. If you accept my present, therefore, you take advantage of my work, whether or not you have intentionally done anything to prompt it—just as you take advantage of my work when just passively accepting the potatoes I give you by way of rent on the land you inherited and I cultivate.[23] Though voluntary when taken as a whole (no coercion is involved), the provision of a benefit is, here again, involuntary *ceteris paribus*: it would not have taken place in the absence of the sanctions—the slammed door, the walk on the hill—whose effectiveness reflects the fact that you are holding something precious to me. Can you, as a non-worker, then ever derive a benefit from my work without relying on some form of power? Yes you can, if my gift is inspired by a pure sense of duty or by altruistic feelings of gratitude, solidarity, pity, etc. which, unlike love, do not confer power on to their objects.[24]

However, this is not the sole possibility. It is also possible for me to derive benefit from your work as a *free-rider*, that is, as a result of your activity generating positive externalities, or benefits which, given the structure of property rights, you cannot prevent me (at a reasonable cost) from enjoying. To see what is involved, take first the case of standard joint products, with no externalities involved. When growing potatoes, you unavoidably produce leaves. Suppose you keep all the potatoes and eat them, while I take the leaves, for which you have no use. Although I consume part of the product of your work, you do not work more than is necessary in order to produce what you consume yourself. Yet, unless you altruistically give the leaves to me, some exercise of power must be involved—whether in the form of coercion or of control over something precious to you—if I am to get hold of the by-product of your work. In contrast, suppose now that in addition to potatoes you grow tulips, in order to enjoy their sight. Here again, your work generates as a by-product a benefit to me, though this time one that has the character of an externality, of an effect which cannot adequately be protected by your property rights. This benefit can be either similar to the benefit you derive yourself—I too enjoy the sight of the tulips—or of an altogether different nature—because my bees buttress your flowers, I can eat more honey. But in order to enjoy that benefit, I need not rely on either your altruism or my power. It is enough for me to pick what you cannot (affordably) prevent from flowing to me.

Free-riding, thus characterized, is no doubt a very pervasive phenomenon. It encompasses, for example, what Mancur Olson (1965: 22–36) calls the 'exploitation of the great by the small', as illustrated by the case of a large firm in whose interest it is to finance infrastructural investments which smaller firms are then able to use at no cost to themselves, or by the case of a superpower which develops, in its own interest, costly defence systems which also 'protect' free of charge neutral or allied countries. The 'exploited' party need not be bigger or wealthier, however, for the phenomenon to occur. When both parties could afford to contribute to the benefit to exactly the same extent, one may still produce it on its own because it attaches greater importance to it. If we both use the same photocopying machine, while its use is far more essential to you than to me, I am unlikely to go through the time-consuming business of getting it repaired if I find it bust one day, and am likely to discover that you have dealt with it (out of self-interest, not out of public spirit) when I return some time later. This is not free-riding of the small on the great, but of the light (users) on the heavy.

One area is which free-riding is arguably present on a massive scale is household interaction, where benefits enjoyed by both partners keep being produced by the one who cares most about them. Tidying up the mess is a simple example.[25] In the absence of an explicit agreement, the job will keep being done by the partner who cares most about having a tidy house. There will be free-riding as soon as the less tidy partner cares to any extent about the difference between the current state of the house and the state in which it would have been had no one done anything. Whether she has contributed to creating the mess is immaterial, even though one may want to reserve a special term—say, parasitism—to the situations of free-riding in which this is the case.[26] Also, the latter term applies, whether the partner who does the job does so out of sheer self-interest or because of some belief about how someone in her position should behave. For example, you may clean the floor, buy the kids' Christmas presents, get the luggage ready for the family holiday, not simply because you enjoy doing these things—or having these things done—more than I do, but because you happen to be a mother and to believe that this is all part of a mother's role. In either case, free-riding is involved.[27]

So, free-riding is pervasive. Along with power-based benefit extraction and in contrast to genuine gifts, it provides us with a type of mechanism for *taking* advantage of someone else's work.[28] This second type of mechanism is arguably just as relevant to our inquiry, because of a close analogy between free-riding on the self-interested (or possibly role-conscious) cleaning activity of one's flatmate and free-riding on the self-interested (or possibly work-ethic-guided) economic activity of all those who make a net contribution to the unconditional basic income. In either case, the benefit is enjoyed by some, not because of some voluntary donation on the part of the others, nor because the latter are subjected to the power of the beneficiaries, but because the physical or institutional environment is framed in such a way that the producers cannot help provide a free ride to those who, because of different preferences, opt for idleness. It must, of course, be conceded that the externality involved in the basic income case is of a peculiarly artificial nature, and one, moreover, that essentially involves the exercise of power by the tax authority over the net contributors. One may, therefore, prefer to read this situation as one in which power-based benefit extraction is at work, though with the benefit extractor—the taxing authority—distinct from the beneficiaries. Between these two readings, however, I do not need to choose here. Whichever is chosen, the (prima-facie) crucial question is: 'Is it always *unfair* to take advantage of other people's work?' In other words, does one *exploit* someone as soon as one takes advantage of her work whether through the exercise of power or through free-riding? If the answer is positive, it is obvious at once that the approach developed in the first four chapters is seriously defective.

Let us not panic too quickly, however. As soon as we lift one simplifying assumption that has been with us since the beginning of this chapter—the assumption that the beneficiary is not working herself—it appears very quickly that the answer to the above question can only be negative. Why? Suppose you and I are two independent, equally wealthy, equally productive farmers, who exchange with one another part of our respective products (say, beans for carrots). Each of us works. Each of us derives a benefit from the other's work, thanks to the advantages flowing from the division of labour. And each of us exercises power over the other: I control assets—my labour power and my land—to which (or to whose product) you attach some value, and I use this fact to make you do something—give up some of the carrots you have produced—which you would not otherwise have done, and the other way around. In this situation, therefore, there is power-based benefit extraction from someone else's work, though of a reciprocal sort. If, instead, co-operation between us took the form of joint work in a single production unit, rather than that of trade between separate units, the power I owe to my labour power would no longer materialize in an identifiable product. But, assuming both parties are motivated by self-interest, there would again be (mutual) power-based benefit extraction. In either case, however, it obviously make no sense to call the interaction unfair, nor, therefore, to speak of exploitation.

So, if the notion of exploitation is to fulfil the critical function ascribed to it, it needs to be given a more restrictive definition. One straightforward way of getting rid of the counterexamples just given would be to require the exploiter to be idle, that is, to perform no work. But surely the notion of work used (negatively) in the definition of the exploiter must be the same as the one used (positively) in the definition of the exploitee. And this notion, we have seen (§ 5.1) needs to be very broad—so broad, for example that all capitalists are most likely to do some work, whether by being involved in the management of their firms, by occasionally clipping a few coupons, or by getting a spoon from the kitchen in order to eat their pudding. Consequently, if exploitation could only be exploitation by non-workers, it would apply so seldom that it would, again, fail to fulfil the critical function ascribed to it. An alternative, more promising strategy consists in looking for a suitable definition of exploitation by asking directly when taking advantage of someone else's work would be unfair. Different answers to this question offer as many definitions of exploitation, each inspired by a particular ethical stance. If one of these answers proves defensible enough—and at the same time irreducible to the real-libertarian approach—we shall have found a way of articulating precisely the challenge which this chapter aims to consider.

5.3 Lockean exploitation

A first proposal consists in stipulating that there is *exploitation* if anyone appropriates, or jointly controls, part of the net product by virtue of something other than her labour contribution to it.[29] In other words, one can only appropriate, or participate in control, *qua* worker, and any departure from this norm constitutes exploitation. This is actually the notion of exploitation that underlies the familiar definition of the rate of capitalist exploitation understood as the ratio of profits (including rents and interests) to wages (both direct and indirect): it is the ratio of what is appropriated in the formal economy (coercion-based or love-based exploitation are left out of the picture) by virtue of something else than one's work, to what is appropriated by virtue of one's work, including contributory pensions, unemployment benefits, or health insurance.

To prevent unnecessary confusion, it is of some importance to emphasize that this definition of exploitation makes no use of the concept of labour value.[30] Indeed, even the assessment of the *extent* of exploitation so conceived need not appeal to such a concept. This is obvious if the net product were to consist of a single good—say, corn—or if the structure of the average bundle appropriated by virtue of one's work were the same as the average bundle appropriated by virtue of something else (say, both bundles consist of beer and corn, with half as many bushels of corn as bottles of beer): the ratio of physical quantities provides all we need. If, as is likely, this condition is not met, some common measuring rod must be found. This is where the concept of *value* usually comes in. One way in which different types of goods can be made commensurate is by selecting one particular basic good (that is, one that enters the production of all other goods), whether produced (corn) or natural (oil) and asking how much of that good is used on average, whether directly or indirectly (e.g. via workers' consumption), to produce one unit of each type of good. Labour is, of course, the numeraire usually thought of in this context. But nothing in the approach considered in this chapter forces us to measure the rate of exploitation in terms of labour value. Any other basic good will do and, contrary to what Marx (1867: 51–2) himself suggested in his own justification for the choice of labour, there are many such goods.[31] Indeed, nothing forces us to measure it in terms of values, rather than in terms of market prices. In particular, measuring the rate of exploitation in terms of prices partly shaped by capital inputs is perfectly consistent with decreeing that there is exploitation as soon as any part of the net product is appropriated by virtue of capital ownership—not just when capital owners are rewarded in excess of the marginal product of capital.[32] The definition of the surplus product involves an essential reference to labour—it is what is left of the net product when labour has been rewarded—but by no means does it follow that labour must be chosen as the measuring rod. As soon as the 'law of value' does not hold, that is, as soon as equilibrium prices diverge from labour values—for example, because of unequal requirements in natural resources or unequal capital intensities in the various sectors—prices better reflect how precious, in terms of resource requirements, the various parts of the net product are. And there is then every reason to choose prices, rather than labour values, in order to measure the extent to which workers are exploited.

Other characterizations of exploitation, apparently very different from this one, turn out to be closely related. Take, for example, the one suggested by Lawrence Crocker (1972), which shares with the one offered above the advantage of side-stepping any reference to labour values: A *exploits* B if at least part of the surplus product (what remains of the net product, once workers have had their rewards) to which B contributes is under the control of an individual or group A which does not include all the (labour) contributors to the surplus product and only them.[33] Barring far-fetched coincidences, whenever there is exploitation in the earlier sense of appropriation *qua* non-worker, there is also exploitation according to Crocker's characterization.[34] On the other hand, it is easy to think of situations in which there is exploitation in Crocker's sense, yet no appropriation *qua* non-worker: all claims to the net product may be strictly restricted to those who contribute to it through their labour, while some whose wage exceeds the value of their contribution, and whose contribution to the surplus product is therefore negative, are none the less participating in the joint control of the surplus product. Hence, Crocker's definition can be regarded as strictly broader than the other one.

Both the latter and Crocker's variant, however, satisfy the minimal conditions for providing a definition of exploitation, as spelt out in the previous sections: they select a proper subset in the set of situations in which someone is taking advantage of someone else's work. Moreover, whichever definition is chosen, it is obvious at once that the appropriation of profits by capitalists—whether or not they happen to do any work—constitutes exploitation, and that so does the citizenship-based appropriation of part of the surplus product which an unconditional basic income would institutionalize.[35] Before granting this twofold conclusion, it is essential to scrutinize the ethical underpinnings of this sort of definition: why is it necessarily unfair to take advantage of someone else's work in a way that satisfies the stipulated conditions? The obvious answer is that *workers are entitled to the whole fruit of their labour*. And it is because this entitlement principle is commonly associated with Locke's view of original appropriation that I shall be speaking of a Lockean conception of exploitation to describe the approach illustrated by the above two definitions. Before examining this principle (see § 5.4), however, I want to briefly review a number of conceptual difficulties that beset the definition of exploitation as appropriation *qua* non-worker—as well as variants of it such as Crocker's.

First of all, take the case of owner-managers who get paid, as residual claimants, an income which rewards jointly their capital and labour inputs. Could it not be said that an entrepreneurial form of capitalism, where all capitalists are owners-managers, could be altogether exploitation-free?[36] To avoid this implication—it is obviously unacceptable to say that there cannot be exploitation, however high the owner-manager's income or however low her labour input—without generating the equally unpalatable symmetric implication—it is obviously unacceptable to say that there always is exploitation, however low the manager's income and however high her labour input—one cannot avoid appealing to some evaluation of the owner-manager's work. An obvious suggestion is that one should consider at least part of her income as a wage—plausibly, what she would have earned, had she brought no capital along with her labour—and the remainder (if any) as the surplus product, whose exclusive appropriation by just one of the people who contributed to producing it constitutes exploitation as defined.

This leads, however, to a second and more general difficulty. According to our definition, there is exploitation as soon as anyone appropriates any part of the net product by virtue of something other than her labour. Who is exploited? Surely all those who contributed to the surplus product that is being appropriated. Who are they exactly? Perhaps all the workers in the firm under consideration and only them? This *local* interpretation of the surplus product is clearly inadequate, however. For suppose a capitalist turns a division of her profitable company into an independent subcontracting firm which pays low wages and makes no profits, but enables the company it supplies at low prices to make huger profits than before. Surely, the workers of the new firm have not stopped contributing to the surplus product appropriated by the capitalist, and hence being exploited by her. What is the alternative? If workers in the subcontracting firm must be regarded as contributing to the capitalist's surplus product, as they certainly should be, why not the capitalist's software consultant or the workers in the co-operative that provides the latter with recycled paper, or those who built the machines used in this co-operative, etc.? This suggests that the only coherent alternative is a *global* interpretation of the surplus product. Earning profits, or more generally an income that exceeds one's imputed wage, amounts to appropriating a chunk of it, thereby becoming the exploiter of workers who may be waged or self-employed. Can one then even conceive of an exploitation-free regime? Yes, but only an autarkic form of socialism in which the whole global surplus product is jointly controlled by all the workers who contribute to it and only by them.

The room thus left for exploitation-free economic regimes is pretty narrow, but sufficient, it seems, to defeat the objection that exploitation characterizes 'any society in which investment takes place for a greater future product (perhaps because of population growth)' and 'any society in which those unable to work, or to work productively, are subsidized by the labour of others'.[37] However, this narrow room is also threatened once it is realized that even if participation in the democratic process is restricted to contributors to the surplus product and if all of these are perfectly informed, it is still possible for decisions on how to allocate the surplus product to go against the will of the majority of those who contributed to it. This can happen, for example, because the pragmatic limits of large-scale direct democracy make it unavoidable to lump together many issues into a small spectrum of electoral platforms: whether voters are assumed to support the platform they agree with on the issue closest to their heart, or on the greatest number of issues, it will standardly happen that the stand adopted on an issue in the winning platform will contradict the position of the majority.[38] Furthermore, even if the majority of workers does get its way in such a regime, can one really be sure that no one is taking unfair advantage of other people's work? What, for example, if a minority of those who contributed to the surplus product—conceivably a minority that produced most of the surplus product—is consistently outvoted by the majority? If control over one's surplus product is what counts, why should the losing minority not be considered exploited by the majority in this socialist context, just as workers are exploited by capitalists in a capitalist context?[39]

Thus, by adopting the global interpretation, it is possible to make the notion of surplus product coherent, but at the expense of making very problematic even the sheer conceptual possibility of an exploitation-free socio-economic regime. But there is a third and even more awkward conceptual difficulty. Whether under the local or global interpretation, contributing through one's work to the net product does not amount to contributing to the surplus product. This is obvious enough when labour payments exhaust the net product, thus leaving no surplus product. But this can also happen to individual workers when there is a positive aggregate surplus product. Below some level of efficiency and/or beyond some level of pay, a worker is bound to make a contribution that falls short of her wage. This does not turn her into an exploiter according to our definition, but it should certainly prevent her from being exploited, since she makes no contribution to what the exploiters appropriate.[40] How can this be assessed? One obvious suggestion is that one should compare what the firm or the economy produces (somehow measured) with and without the worker's contribution, and compare the difference to her wage. But as is well known, using this method leads to great embarrassment. Consider a firm or an economy which operates under decreasing returns and hires identical workers up to the point where the marginal product is equal to the wage. Take any of the identical workers away, and the profits will shrink, which establishes, according to our criterion, that each of them contributes to the surplus product. But suppose one extra worker is hired. Taking any of the workers away then swells profits, and none of them (nor anyone else) could then be said, using our criterion, to contribute to the (still very real) surplus product.

This difficulty may not be insuperable. One could for example assess the ratio of the surplus product to the net product for the relevant unit as a whole and stipulate that those who contribute to the surplus product are those whose wages do not exceed the average wage for a particular type of job (with given productivity), or whose productivity does not fall short of average productivity (with a given wage) by more than that ratio. There are no doubt subtleties that could not be handled in this way.[41] But this would avoid the embarrassment both of a positive surplus product to which no one contributes (as can happen under marginal product accounting) and of a positive contribution to the surplus product with pathetically inefficient work and huge wages (as can happen under average product accounting), though admittedly at the cost of bringing in a framework for evaluating contributions and retributions that is not that different from the value accounting which this approach offered the prospect of avoiding.

5.4 Creators keepers

Instead of pursuing these conceptual difficulties, however, I now want to turn to the ethical basis of the criterion of unfairness that the proposed definition of exploitation consists in articulating. As a preliminary step, note that exploitation, as characterized by this definition and its variants, cannot be understood—as both injustice and exploitation often are—as a subspecies of inequality. To see this, just imagine an economy in which everyone performs exactly the same amount and type of work, with no difference in enjoyment and productivity, and in which everyone gets exactly the same income, part of it as a wage and the other part as capital income. (All agents happen to own bonds which yield exactly the same interest payments to each of them.) This is exploitation in the sense of appropriation *qua* non-worker: interest on bonds is not cashed by virtue of one's labour contribution. Yet, it cannot be viewed as a type of inequality, nor as a departure from a principle of justice of the form 'To each according to . . .', since the agents are identical and are treated identically in all relevant respects. This does not show that the underlying principle of justice is indefensible, but it makes clear that this principle cannot be of the standard, 'patterned' type.

The principle that workers are entitled to the whole fruit of their labour, briefly suggested above as the most suitable ethical basis for the proposed definition of exploitation, is precisely an unpatterned principle. Along with libertarian principles of the sort discussed and rejected earlier (§ 1.3), it belongs to the family of *entitlement principles of justice*, in a strong sense which views individual entitlements, not as an expression of the just institutional framework but as a constraint on it.[42] Clearly formulated by Ricardian socialist Thomas Hodgskin (1825) and by Joseph Proudhon (1840),[43] it later found its way into the Gotha Programme, the first programme of a social democratic party, in which it was detected and firmly criticized by Karl Marx (1885). According to this particular entitlement principle, the only basis for entitlement to the net product is labour performed in the current period. The performer of such labour is given a right to the whole of her net product, and any violation of this right is an injustice.

How can such a right be vindicated? The most straightforward and common way is by invoking a 'creators keepers' principle, in conjunction with a minor premiss to the effect that labour, and labour alone, creates the net product.[44] But whether or not one accepts the ethical principle, this argument is threatened by an obvious objection which the minor premiss cannot hope to escape. Capital enables labour to produce more (or better) than it would without capital, just as labour enables the Earth to produce more (or better) than it would without labour. If the latter fact is sufficient ground for declaring that labour contributes to the production of the product (what else could be?), then the former fact is sufficient ground for declaring that capital too contributes to production.[45]

Can the argument be salvaged? Two main strategies have been proposed. First, one can point out that, after all, capital is just congealed labour, that the tools and factories were made by workers—possibly with the help of other tools and factories, themselves made by other workers, etc.—and that, therefore, recognizing the productive nature of capital does not undermine the claim that labour (as an intergenerational whole), and labour only, creates the product.[46] But this misses the key point. As advocates of capitalism such as David Friedman (1973: 61–2) are quick to point out, 'the trouble with this argument is that it does not recognize that paying for tools today and waiting for years to get the money back is itself a productive activity, and that the interest earned by capital is the corresponding payment'. The point is that current production is boosted not, as such, by labour performed in the past, but as a result of the fact that someone who could have consumed part of the product of that labour decided not to consume it, but to invest it instead, by buying or making tools rather than consumer goods.[47] The argument does not require this 'waiting' to involve any 'abstinence', any hardship, or anything else that may pass as 'deserving'. Non-consumption may be due to sheer satiation or inertia. All that matters is that such 'waiting' is productive, contributes to the creation of the product—just as the right to the full product of one's labour that is being invoked does not depend on labour being arduous.[48] Thus, whether it is stemming from past wages (saved by workers) or past profits (saved by capitalists), capital makes an irreducible contribution to the product of the current period. Bringing in past workers, therefore, fails to salvage the workers' claim to the full product, even if one could leave aside the productive role of natural resources.

A second strategy, suggested by G. A. Cohen, focuses precisely on the key importance of natural resources. It accepts that capital is productive in the relevant sense but denies that, as a result, the 'creators keepers' principle grants capitalists a legitimate claim on part of the net product.[49] Capitalists, Cohen argues, are not the legitimate owners of the capital they provide and they cannot make a legitimate claim on the product that is based on their contributing to production something they do not legitimately own, something they have (ethically speaking) stolen. True, the product would be less if the capitalists had consumed what they have invested. But so it would if the brigands had burned the field, and this does not give the brigands a legitimate claim on any part of the product. Why should one hold the view that capital is stolen by its very nature, not just in those particular cases (however frequent) in which capitalists owe their wealth to some recent or ancient fraud or theft? Because the means of production, Cohen replies, are ultimately made up of natural resources, which are not up for grabs but the joint property of society— or mankind—as a whole.

But if this is indeed the case, there is a disaster in store. True, the claim that natural resources are jointly owned by all challenges the capitalists' ownership of their capital without challenging the workers' ownership of their labour power. But it challenges just as powerfully the right to the fruit of one's labour as the right to the fruit of one's capital. Consider a worker who adds her labour to natural resources in order to produce carrots and tools. If joint ownership of the world shatters her title to the tools thus produced, and hence to the income she may earn, say, from lending them to others, then there is no reason why it should not also shatter her title to the carrots she produces, or to the income earned by selling them. There are, of course, other views about legitimate entitlements to natural resources: everything up for grabs (*à la* Rothbard or Kirzner), everything up for grabs under the constraint of a proviso (*à la* Locke or Nozick) or equal division (*à la* Paine or Steiner). But if one adopts any of these views, it is no longer possible to claim that the ownership of capital is always illegitimate. For this claim to be valid, joint ownership needs to be assumed. And if it is, the workers' right to the entire product of their labour is radically undermined. What would prevent capital from claiming any part of the product would also prevent labour from claiming the whole of it.

In this light, there appears to be precious little hope of managing to justify the worker's right to the entire product on the basis of a creators keepers principle. Might an alternative foundation be found? I very much doubt it, because of the most unpalatable implications of such an unqualified right. Recognizing that right would force us to endorse massive inequalities between the rewards of workers (or countries) operating under different conditions. Those who happen to produce far more than others because of the greater fertility of the soil or the superior efficiency of the tools put at their disposal would be entitled to a far greater share of the total product than those who have access only to inferior means of production. And any redistribution from the 'great creators' to the 'poor creators' would consequently be either theft or charity, not a demand of justice.[50]

5.5 Lutheran exploitation

In our search for a suitable characterization of someone taking *unfair* advantage of someone else's work, the difficulties just reviewed are not fatal. But they prompt us to redirect our hopes away from the entitlement approach to justice. What other approach to justice could provide us with a better basis for articulating the exploitation-based critique of both capitalism and basic income? A first step along an alternative route can be found in the common definition according to which there is *exploitation* if some (the exploited) contribute more labour value, or more socially necessary labour, to production through their direct labour than they appropriate through their income, while others (the exploiters) contribute less than they appropriate. Or, more briefly, there is exploitation if there is net appropriation of labour value, or *surplus value appropriation*.[51] In the simple case (taken for granted in §§ 5.1–2) in which there is a set of homogeneous workers on one side and a set of non-workers on the other, surplus value is being generated if and only if surplus labour is being performed or a surplus product produced. (Remember that the surplus product is defined as the part of the net product appropriated by non-workers and surplus labour as the labour performed in producing it.) In this simple case, therefore, taking advantage of someone else's work (by appropriating part of the surplus product) always constitutes exploitation. In the general case in which everyone works to some extent, however, the definition of exploitation as surplus value appropriation— just as the definition in terms of appropriation *qua* non-worker explored in the previous two sections—provides a way of distinguishing fair from unfair ways of taking advantage of other people's work.

Unlike the previous one, however, the definition considered here uses explicitly the notion of labour value, which has been the subject of much controversy. The labour value of a product is usually defined as the amount of labour that is socially necessary for its production. More precisely, the labour value of one unit of a product is the amount of unskilled labour that enters on average, given the existing equipment and technology, whether directly or indirectly, the production of that unit. Contrary to what is sometimes done, I am here interpreting necessary labour as an average amount, not as a minimum (or optimal) amount.[52] The former choice has the advantage that it postulates a state of affairs that is certainly possible—since it actually obtains—whereas the technique singled out by the latter choice may be so capital-intensive that it could not possibly be used throughout the economy, given the current capital stock.[53] Further, and also contrary to what is sometimes done, I am here postulating that value is created as soon as the goods are produced, whether or not that value is subsequently 'realized', that is, whether or not the goods are sold on a market.[54] Indeed, and contrary to what is generally done, following Marx himself, I am not restricting the relevance of the concept of labour value to market economies. There may be a point in doing so for some purposes. But there is none in the context of our normative enquiry. Since we want exploitation to make sense under feudal or household conditions, our criterion of unfairness must apply under these conditions too. And there is no reason why it should be a priori absurd to determine average labour requirements for the performance of tasks or the production of goods in the absence of markets.[55]

The choices just made get rid of some common objections to the surplus value definition of exploitation. Before examining how the latter can be used in our enquiry, however, it is fair at least to mention three nagging and widely discussed conceptual difficulties that threaten the very possibility of a meaningful definition of labour value. First, how do we ascribe labour values in case of joint products, goods that are produced together by the same production process? Low fat milk and cream provide the standard illustration, but all externalities—central to the free-riding variety of exploitation—give rise to the same difficulty. Computing the average amounts of labour required for the production of each of the joint products amounts to double (or multiple) counting. On the other hand, partitioning the labour involved in joint production among the joint products is bound to rest on an arbitrary weighting of the two products.[56]

Secondly, as soon as one wants to measure the labour-value contribution of any subset of the total working population—as one must if one wishes to determine whether a worker, or the workforce of a firm, or the working class of some open economy is exploited—one cannot simply postulate that the labour value produced is equal to the total labour performed. One must weight the amount of labour performed by some coefficient reflecting labour productivity. If, for whatever reason—obsolete technology, inferior raw materials, poorer skills—I am less efficient at producing steel sheets than the average steelworker in my firm, or in my country, or in the world at large, the amount of value I contribute per hour is less than an hour. But the productivity of my labour can only be assessed in a compelling way if I produce on my own a clearly identifiable product, and even so only relative to other workers producing the same outputs with the same inputs. How could my productivity as a manager be measured, for example, if the job pattern of the firm I manage is unique among firms producing the same sort of product? And yet, without some sensible assessment of such productivity, it is impossible to say how much labour value I contribute to production, nor, therefore, whether it falls short or exceeds the labour value I appropriate through my income.[57]

Thirdly, labour is, of course, a very heterogeneous good, which cannot provide an adequate currency. In the definition of labour value offered above, reference is made to simple labour. Simple labour must certainly be unskilled labour. Skilled labour cannot be aggregated with unskilled labour, on an equal footing, to provide an overall measure of labour expended. But it can in principle be converted into unskilled labour, by using conversion ratios which express the amount of unskilled labour which is required on average, whether directly or indirectly (via the production of means of production or of skilled labour power) to turn one unit of unskilled labour into one unit of a specific type of skilled labour.[58] The fundamental problem, however, is that unskilled labour itself is heterogeneous. The source of the problem is not the existence of unequal innate talents or the coexistence of different ways of using labour to produce the same things. Since labour value has been defined by reference to average amounts, there is no need for homogeneity at either of these levels. The really hard problem arises from the need to aggregate amounts of unskilled labour expended on different tasks. What enables us to say, for example, that one hour spent conscientiously dusting a piano is worth the same as one hour spent heaving it up to the third floor? Should one use physical effort as a common rod, or mental attention, or some weighted sum of these attributes, and if so, with what weights, and with the attributes measured in what way? Marx's own solution to the problem—as suggested by his elliptic utterances on the matter and as required by his assumption of equal rates of exploitation across branches—is to ascribe to each type of labour a weight proportional to the wage rate it fetches.[59] Such a move would be consistent with refusing similarly to give other factors of production a weight proportional to their rewards—which would undermine the whole enterprise. But it would hardly make sense in a normative perspective. How much a person contributes in labour value, and hence how large a share of the product she could appropriate without this giving rise to exploitation, would then be partly determined by what her wage, and hence her share of the product, happens to be in actual fact.

These are three serious difficulties, which cannot be written off as sheer hair-splitting. Indeed, some may wish to declare the whole approach a non-starter because of the absence of any prospect of solving them in anything like a satisfactory way. But let us be broad-minded. Let us suppose that all the conceptual difficulties can be solved or bypassed, and hence that contributions and rewards can be meaningfully and accurately measured in terms of labour value, as defined. The surplus value definition of exploitation offered above then seems very promising for our purposes. To start with, like the Lockean definition, it fulfils the minimal conditions for exploitation spelt out at the start (§§ 5.1–2): the appropriator of surplus value is necessarily taking advantage of someone else's work.[60] Next, it is obvious at once that, even if capitalists all do some amount of work, capitalist economies will be characterized by massive unbalances of labour value accounts, with some appropriating far more labour-value, and others far less, than they contribute. By contrast, a socialist regime could match contributions and retributions so as to get far closer to an equal exchange of labour value.[61] Moreover, giving everyone an equal unconditional basic income is most likely to create further pressure away from equal exchange. At the same time, the new definition appeals to an intuitively attractive notion of fairness as equal exchange that is sufficiently different from the entitlement conception of fairness appealed to in the previous chapter, to hold the promise of escaping the fatal difficulties which the latter raised. I shall call *Lutheran* the approach to exploitation illustrated by this definition, by reference to Marx's (1867: 207 n. 15) quotation from Martin Luther in his discussion of the allegedly equal exchange between workers and capitalists: 'Whoever takes more or better than he gives, this is usury and is not service but wrong done to his neighbour, as in the case of theft and plunder.'[62] Once labour value is unambiguously chosen as the metric of fair exchange, this ethical principle provides a clear criterion for deciding when advantage is unfairly taken from someone else's labour.[63]

Can this principle be defended? Let us start by emphasizing that unequal exchange in this sense is not only compatible with its victim (the exploited) gaining from exchange, that is, increasing her welfare as a result of it, but even with its victim gaining more from it than its beneficiary (the exploiter). If, for example, some capitalist is the only potential employer around in some particular area, the capitalist's failure to hire some particular worker is likely to be far costlier, in terms of welfare, to the latter than to the former. Even though the worker would contribute more labour value—and the capitalist less—than she gets back, the worker would obtain far more welfare from the transaction than the capitalist would. Further, unequal exchange in the sense considered does not require that any monopoly power be exercised by the beneficiary at the victim's expense.[64] Even if a highly centralized trade union faces a large number of independent capitalists and gets far higher wages for its members than they would earn under perfect competition, there will still be unequal exchange, in the sense specified, at the workers' expense. Fairness, here, is neither a matter of how much welfare is being derived from the transaction by either party, nor a feature of the background conditions under which the transaction takes place.[65] It depends exclusively on the balance of contributions to and benefits from co-operation, as measured in some objective way. But can labour values defensibly be used for this purpose? It will not take me long to show that they cannot.

Let us look at the benefit side first. Even assuming that the labour value of each good can be assessed in a perfectly accurate way, it is not possible to determine the labour value of the benefit a worker derives from social co-operation through the income she earns, as soon as part of her income is not consumed by her but saved and invested, say through the mediation of a bank, and hence ceases to be physically identifiable. Moreover, even in the absence of saving, whenever the workers' pay takes the form of a money income which they are able to spend on various baskets of goods, the labour value of what workers appropriate becomes dependent upon the vagaries of consumer choice. As soon as prices are not proportional to labour values, workers with identical incomes and contributions may conceivably end up as victims or beneficiaries of unequal exchange, depending on whether they happen to spend their incomes on goods which require a comparatively large amount of capital or natural resources to be produced, or purchase instead the products of comparatively labour-intensive processes.[66]

Both difficulties can be solved in one stroke, however, if one replaces the proposed definition of exploitation as net labour-value appropriation by the modal definition of exploitation as *necessary* net value appropriation suggested by Roemer (1982*a*: 121–3), and if one modifies the underlying criteria of unequal exchange accordingly. According to this alternative definition, there is *exploitation* if some (the exploited) necessarily contribute more labour value to production through their direct labour than they appropriate through their income, however the latter is spent, and also if others (the exploiters) necessarily contribute less labour value than they appropriate through their income, again no matter what bundle of goods the latter is used to buy. In other words, an *exploited* person is now one who would have a labour-value deficit even if she were to spend all her income on those goods which, for a given price, embody most socially necessary labour. And an *exploiter* is someone who would have a labour-value surplus even if she were to spend all her income on those goods which, for a given price, have the lowest labour content.

It must be conceded at once that this modal definition creates a possibly quite large grey area of people who are neither exploited nor exploiters. The closer the correlation between people's labour-value contribution and their overall income and the looser the correlation between prices and labour values, the larger the grey area can be expected to be.[67] One can even imagine situations—for example, one in which all do the same work and earn the same income, while spending the latter on goods with different labour contents—in which everyone is either exploited or an exploiter according to our earlier definition, whereas, according to the modal definition, no one is. Moreover, there are conceivable situations in which there is exploitation—because there are exploiters—according to the modal definition, yet in which no one is exploited; and other, symmetric situations in which there is exploitation—because some are exploited—but there are no exploiters. Yet the toleration of such a grey area is a price worth paying if it makes it possible to define exploitation even when the part of the product that is being appropriated by workers cannot be identified, and if it frees a person's exploitation status from its absurd dependence on consumer choice.

Another apparent weakness of this modal definition is that it unavoidably refers to money incomes and prices, whereas the initial definition was formulated purely in labour-value terms. But this should not be a problem, since labour values themselves are not independent of incomes and prices. Outside the special case of constant returns to scale, how much labour is socially necessary per unit of each good crucially depends on the scale of production for that good, and hence on the pattern of demand, itself directly affected by the price structure. This prompts the suggestion that perhaps one should go all the way and adopt income rather than labour-value content (whether actual or maximum and minimum) as the appropriate metric on the benefit side. Indeed, a little reflection soon reveals that this is exactly what needs to be done, not just for the sake of simplicity, but because using (monetary) incomes to assess benefits is clearly superior from a normative point of view.

To see this, imagine a society all of whose members work equally hard, long, and productively, even though pay discrimination has the result that some—call them Whites—earn wages that substantially exceed those earned by the others—call them Reds. Society's net product over the period considered consists exclusively of houses that have all cost the same quantity and quality of labour time (with Reds and Whites working together), some of them on the hillside with a lovely view of the bay, the others in the mosquito-ridden swamps that lie along the coast. It so happens that the market-determined rent of a house on the hillside matches exactly a White's income, while the far lower rent of a house on the coast matches exactly a Red's income. All Whites and Reds spend their incomes accordingly. If labour values were the appropriate standard for measuring the benefits received by the co-operating parties, no unfairness whatsoever would be involved in this situation. Each White and each Red would appropriate exactly the same amount of labour value, which is also equal to what each of them has contributed. There is, therefore, no net labour-value appropriation, nor *a fortiori* necessary net-value appropriation. (The Reds could not have used their incomes to acquire more labour value than they appropriated, but they were none the less not forced to acquire less. And the Whites could not have acquired, by spending all their incomes, less value than they contributed, but they were not compelled to acquire more.) And yet, this is surely a case of unfair co-operation, the unfairness of which is perfectly transparent if incomes are used to assess benefits or rewards, but badly obscured if labour values are used instead, whether in accordance with the original surplus-value definition or with its modal variant. As this example shows in an extreme form, when relative prices deviate from relative values, it is clearly income that matters to the fairness of co-operation, with labour-value content only an awkward and unnecessary proxy.[68]

On the contribution side, labour value does not fare any better—even abstracting once again from all conceptual difficulties. To see this, we can keep basically the same illustration, while substituting uniformity for diversity along the benefit dimension, and diversity for uniformity along the contribution dimension. Less elliptically, suppose that all the houses which constitute the net product of the present period have not only cost identical amounts of labour but also occupy equally valuable positions, and that each of society's members gets an identical income, which she spends on one of these houses. On the other hand, while they all work equally long and hard, some—call them Blacks—are more productive than the others—call them Greens—for example, because they happen to operate more powerful tools. Hence, the Blacks contribute more labour value, that is, more socially necessary labour, than the Greens in any given time span, and also more than they appropriate or than they can appropriate with the incomes they get. Whether under the initial or the modal net-value-appropriation definition, the (more productive) Blacks are exploited and the (less productive) Greens are exploiters, even though they all work just as hard and get exactly the same reward for their work. This embarrassing implication is strictly parallel to the one that I argued counted decisively against the right to the whole product of one's labour (§ 5.4). If we do not want to make it a demand of justice that the lucky Blacks should be paid more than the less lucky Greens, we must abandon labour value not just as the ethically appropriate metric for assessing benefits, but also as the ethically apt metric of contributions. As this example shows in an extreme form, when work effort deviates from socially necessary labour, it is clearly work effort that matters to the fairness of co-operation, with socially necessary labour only a cumbersome and redundant proxy.[69]

It thus turns out that, even leaving aside all the conceptual difficulties attaching to the concept of labour value, the conception of exploitation as net value appropriation (or as necessary net value appropriation) is indefensible, because the principle of equal or fair exchange to which it appeals is unacceptable. It does not follow that exploring this 'Lutheran' approach to exploitation has taken us to a dead end. It is worth pursuing the evident suggestion that emerges from the discussion of the previous section, namely that the criterion of fairness to which we need appeal is one that requires income to be distributed according to work effort.[70]

5.6 *To each according to her efforts*

The normative principle that is thus being suggested is quite familiar. Its underlying the exploitation-based critique of capitalism gains further plausibility from the fact that Marx (1875: 20–1) proposes something closely akin to it as the principle of distribution that would be appropriate at the lower (later called 'socialist') stage of the communist society: 'To each according to her labour'.[71] Contrary to appropriation *qua* non-worker (§ 5.3) or unequal exchange of labour value (§ 5.5), disproportionality between income and labour cannot claim to provide an acceptable definition of exploitation, that is, of taking unfair advantage of someone else's work. It is easy to conceive of the principle 'To each according to her labour' being violated, without those treated worse than required providing any benefit to those treated better than required. If you and I (the only two members in our society) work equally hard on our respective plots of land, but you grow four times as many Brussels sprouts as I do, whether because of the strength of your arms, the fervour of your prayers or the make of your tractor, then I am unfairly treated according to our criterion, even if we do not have anything to do with one another—and hence you cannot benefit from my work. Indeed, I could be unfairly treated even if *I* benefited from *your* work—say, through your transferring to me one out of every four sprouts you grow.[72] However, the recognition of this fact does not jeopardize the relevance of the ethical principle to which we have been led. The latter may well put us in a position to articulate the twofold challenge to the approach of the previous chapters in no less sharp a form than would have been possible if some principle of equal exchange had made sense. Under capitalism, the very existence of private profits generates a massive departure from proportionality between income and labour, and the introduction of an unconditional basic income is most likely to make things even worse.

Rather than rushing to conclusions, however, let us first look somewhat more closely at the proposed principle of fair distribution. Labour being heterogeneous, it is crucial to the application of this principle that labour contributions should be made commensurable. Marx himself, in this context, only mentions the length and intensity of labour. But surely, if intensity matters, so must irksomeness, risk, boredom, etc. If one is looking for a fair pattern of distribution, safe, easy, or enjoyable work should not be reckoned equivalent, other things being equal, to dangerous, taxing, or tedious toil. What common currency could we use to make the principle applicable? Perhaps the most promising candidate, from a normative standpoint, is the level of *disutility*—that is, the negative effect on a person's welfare, relative to some baseline situation, and other things remaining equal—associated with the various types of labour.[73] For disutility to fulfil this function, it needs to be interpersonally comparable—a controversial assumption which I shall here take for granted. No less obviously, the disutility caused by a given activity to the people who perform it may vary significantly, as preferences may differ widely from one individual to another. And just reward, as defined by the principle under consideration, may accordingly imply unequal pay for identical jobs. Furthermore, a given type of activity performed by a given individual may also generate very different levels of disutility depending on how long she has been performing it. Thus, not only could you find it more or less unpleasant to rub my back than I would find it to rub yours, but I am also likely to derive less disutility from rubbing your back when I start doing it (I may even enjoy it) than if I have been doing it for a whole day.[74] These various implications may make the principle rather hard to handle in practice, indeed so hard that the use of a very rough approximation is likely to be the best we can afford. But they do not make the principle inconsistent, nor useless for our purposes.

Let us go further. If disutility is the currency in which labour contributions to the product need to be measured in order for their just claim to the total product to be determined, does consistency not force us to reward in accordance to the same principle non-labour contributions to production which involve some disutility? Take, again, an extreme example, which brings out what is at issue in the simplest possible form. Suppose you and I arrive on a desert island which we divide equally between ourselves. In the course of the first year, you use all the wood on your half of the island, whereas I keep enough of it for the wood to reproduce itself from one year to the next. As a result, I suffered from the cold the first year more than you did: the fact that I abstained from consuming as much as you was a source of disutility. At the same time, my saving some of my wood in the first year contributed to overall production, by preserving self-regenerating capacities. If labour contributions to the product are rewarded according to the disutility incurred, surely my disutility-generating saving should also give rise to a legitimate claim to part of the product—not, of course, to the part of the product it 'created' (we are no longer in a Lockean perspective), but a proportion of the total product that matches the disutility of saving. In the case of saving, no less than in the case of labour, the amount of disutility will, of course, depend on the preferences and situation of the individuals concerned. In one case, it is determined by how much they value the most valued alternative use of the time they spent working, and in the other by how much they value the most valued consumption bundle they gave up in order to save. In some cases, in which the saver is indifferent between present and future consumption and in which no risk is involved, there may be no disutility whatever incurred, and hence no legitimate claim generated—just as particularly pleasant work fails to command any reward according to our principle. Let us express as 'To each according to her productive efforts' the generalization of the principle 'To each according to her labour' to which this discussion has led us.[75]

With this modified principle of proportionality, it is, of course, even less true than with the initial one that unfairness necessarily takes the form of exploitation, that is, consists in taking unfair advantage of someone else's work. For a saver who is not rewarded in proportion to the disutility she incurs in saving is not exploited, since it is her saving effort, not her work effort, that is being taken unfair advantage of.[76] But again this is not a problem for our purposes. For even when unfairness is characterized as a lack of proportionality between income and productive effort broadly conceived, it is obvious at once that capitalism fails badly to achieve anything like a fair distribution of incomes. True, any saving or investment that involves some disutility would legitimately command some reward—this could be viewed as the grain of truth in one of the most common justifications of profits.[77] Moreover, competitive forces generate a tendency for factors of production to be rewarded according to the marginal disutility of providing them: if the income you would earn by working or saving one more unit exceeds the sacrifice this would involve, you will want to work or save more, up to the point where the sacrifice is just compensated by the additional income. None the less, even at a perfectly competitive equilibrium where rate of pay and marginal disutility are strictly equal, the distribution of incomes generated by capitalism will massively and systematically diverge from what proportionality between total disutility and total reward would require, if only because of the highly variable extent to which people are endowed with the various factors of production that command a reward.[78] If disequilibrium and monopolistic situations are brought into the picture, things get even worse, as the mechanism which enables disutility to shape rewards has had no time to operate or is more or less completely switched off. True, under socialism, there is no guarantee either that a better match will be achieved between reward and effort, and, if only for informational reasons, a perfect correspondence is anyway out of reach. But the public ownership of the bulk of the means of production undoubtedly puts society in a position to shape far more precisely the distribution of income and hence perform far better according to the proposed principle.[79] Finally, the introduction of a basic income, of an income granted to all irrespective of their productive effort, does not exactly look any more promising with the broader than with the narrower version of the proportionality principle.

So, if fairness is a matter of proportionality between income and productive effort, the approach developed in the previous chapters is bound to be badly defective. But why should incomes be distributed in proportion to effort? A first line of argument is directly suggested by the place Marx (1875: 21) himself assigns to the principle 'To each according to his labour' in his Critique of the Gotha Programme. It consists in viewing such a principle as no more than a second best that is 'unavoidable' at the first stage of the communist society, 'as it developed, after protracted birth pangs, out of capitalist society'. As soon as the conditions for the higher stage of communism are fulfilled, it should be replaced by a principle of distribution according to needs. To put it differently: as long as the state of abundance—in which all the labour required will be forthcoming spontaneously—is not achieved, the egalitarian ideal of distribution according to needs is out of reach. For the sake of efficiency, one will then have to stick to a system that provides adequate incentives by distributing the product in proportion to productive efforts.

Phrased in this way, the argument is untenable. As already mentioned (§ 4.2), distribution in proportion to effort generally fares badly in terms of efficiency, because it systematically provides incentives to overperform, to make efforts involving more disutility than efficiency requires—under some assumptions even to the point of making proportionality worse, in terms of efficiency, than strict income equality. This is the case even if the amount of useful things generated by a person's activity (her productivity) is a simple strictly increasing function of the disutility incurred in the process of performing it (her effort). In the absence of such a simple relationship, proportionality between income and effort contains a further source of inefficiency, as it fails to provide workers with incentives for specializing in what they are good at. Moreover, even this further consideration remains in a static framework and, therefore, ignores the dynamic inefficiency that results from the removal of any incentive for individual workers to improve work organization and tools in such a way as to reduce the effort required. To all this, it may be retorted that over- or ill-directed performance may be avoided by telling workers exactly what activity they should choose and for how long. But if this were possible, we might as well dispense with 'To each according to her labour' altogether, and go straight for 'To each according to her needs'. Since it is not, those committed to this ideal should opt for a distribution scheme that provides adequate incentives without losing sight of the objective. In the light of what has just been said, this scheme will certainly not distribute income in proportion to effort. It will consist, far more plausibly, in distributing as large a share of total income as possible according to needs (and hence irrespective of productive contributions), subject to the constraint that everyone achieves some minimum standard of living. Under a defensible interpretation of 'needs', this amounts to something very close to maximizing the sustainable *relative* level of basic income, subject to a constraint of undominated diversity, and hence—in particular—of securing everyone's subsistence (see § 3.8). We are then back to a close variant of the real-libertarian criterion proposed in the previous chapters, and hence very far from anything that could feed a radical challenge to the latter by articulating the exploitation-based critique of both capitalism and basic income.[80]

Let us, therefore, turn to a second strategy. Could distribution in proportion to productive effort not be viewed as a principle of adequate compensation that would follow from some egalitarian theory? The choice of disutility as the metric of productive effort suggests a connection with welfare egalitarianism,[81] which, for reasons presented earlier— essentially, the overcompensation of people with expensive tastes (see §§ 2.6, 3.7, 4.1)—cannot provide an acceptable conception of justice. But one can think of a different sort of egalitarianism, for example, one which requires that everyone should receive the same income, except that those with special needs would receive an additional income in accordance with undominated diversity or some similar criterion and that anyone who makes a productive contribution would get an additional income matching her level of effort. True, if the latter is measured by disutility (relative to the no-work situation), some mild version of the expensive-taste problem still arises: of two people doing the same job, the one who is fussier about doing it would be rewarded more than the other. But it can be avoided—and in the same stroke the formidable practical difficulty of administering a system that rewards the same job differently depending on who performs it—by adopting some 'objective' evaluation of the irksomeness of each task, for example by working out the disutility the members of the particular society considered would derive *on average* from performing the task.[82] Once protected in this way against earlier objections, does this second strategy not lead us to a plausible conception that would clearly demand, this time as a matter of justice and not of expediency, that income be distributed as a function of productive effort?

Perhaps, but precisely 'as a function of' and not 'in proportion to' productive effort. Even leaving aside the treatment of special needs, the proposed egalitarianism does not demand that the net product be entirely distributed in proportion to productive effort. As soon as the economy produces more than is required to compensate the burden of productive work, distributing everything in proportion to productive effort would amount to overcompensating it. Adequate effort compensation is, therefore, perfectly consistent with an unconditional basic income. Indeed, the latter provides the most natural way of distributing the surplus once adequate compensation has been secured, at least on the background assumption of free occupational choice. And since the egalitarianism that is here being appealed to is bound to rank equality at a higher level of income for all above equality at a lower level, we are then back to a criterion of constrained basic income maximization that can again hardly provide a firm basis for a radical challenge to our real-libertarian criterion. Fair enough, the two criteria will not coincide: the (income-cum-burden) egalitarian constraints are strictly tighter than the real-libertarian ones. Under the (principled or pragmatically motivated) assumption of free occupational choice, it follows from this difference both that the legitimate level of basic income will generally be higher in the real-libertarian than in the egalitarian perspective and that the latter is more likely than the former to favour socialism. But does the tightening of the constraints make any ethical sense? Barring forced labour, the egalitarian constraints prevent, for example, using the labour of those who incur *more* than average disutility from performing a particular task, however good they are at performing it, since the pay they would get would less than compensate the trouble they took. Why should this sort of loss be imposed on everyone, including the worst off? Not even in order to guarantee the equalization of production-related welfare, since those who suffer *less* than average disutility from performing socially useful tasks keep enjoying a higher level of welfare than their fellows. If some are thus allowed to extract a sizeable welfare surplus, why should others not be allowed to do the same, especially if by doing so one induces them to swell a social surplus that can be shared among all? Why not let maximin prevail over Pareto-inferior equality, thus giving up any patterned restriction on the rewarding of productive contributions and admitting any reward structure that will at least compensate the contributors—an outcome guaranteed by the ban on involuntary employment and the predictability of the tax structure—providing the fate of the worst off, appropriately measured, is thereby made as good as it can be? In the absence of any persuasive rebuttal—and I cannot think of any—it is not just that this second strategy supports no radical challenge to real-libertarianism. It supports no serious challenge whatever.

The first two strategies were rather convoluted. Why not proceed more directly by defending proportionality between effort and reward for its own sake, as a direct expression of an appealing conception of justice as desert? Such a conception is often traced back to book 5 of Aristotle's *Nicomachean Ethics*. Social psychologists have discussed it extensively under the heading of 'equity'. And surveys have repeatedly shown that it plays a major role in everyday ethical judgements about distributive matters.[83] If 'To each according to her efforts' commands direct allegiance as a plausible interpretation of justice as desert, there is no need to discuss problematic connections with an ideal of distribution according to needs for which it would provide a provisional substitute or with an egalitarianism of income-burden bundles of which it would constitute one facet. We then get directly from the principle itself the support we are seeking for the twofold challenge to the approach of the previous chapters: if this is what justice means, an unconditional basic income could hardly feature in the criterion for assessing alternative regimes, and room would be made for a strong case for socialism which real-libertarianism could not conceivably accommodate.[84]

To avoid fatal confusion, let us start off by distinguishing carefully the proposition that the whole product should be distributed in proportion to effort from the far weaker proposition that income should be an increasing function of effort or—weaker still—that there should be a positive correlation between effort and income. Whereas there is little doubt that the weakest formulations would, on due reflection, command wide adhesion, it is far less certain that the strongest one would, especially as one moves from the distribution of rewards in limited co-operative ventures—to which social-psychological experiments and survey results are usually restricted—to the distribution of income in society as a whole.[85] But if only the weakest version of the principle needs to be accommodated, it becomes redundant in the context of a fair distribution of opportunities, as specified by our real-libertarian criterion. In such a context, there are several good reasons for expecting a strong positive correlation between income and productive effort.

First, if there is no involuntary employment (no forced labour), the income and other advantages associated to each job must more than compensate the subjective burden involved in performing it. The tendency thus generated towards some correlation between reward and effort is significantly strengthened as a basic income is introduced and increased, since this makes it harder to find incumbents for high-disutility low-pay jobs, and at the same time easier to find incumbents for low-disutility low-pay jobs: the availability of a basic income makes it less costly both to turn down a low-paid job if it is intrinsically unattractive and to accept it if it is intrinsically attractive. Secondly, the correlation between income and productive effort is likely to be improved, relative to the present situation, even by the fact that an income would henceforth be granted to many people who have chosen to have no paid job for at least part of their adult lives—for most of these people are housewives who perform crucially important (re)productive activities without any formal income. A closer fit could no doubt be achieved, but at the (arguably prohibitive) cost of transforming household activities into waged labour. Thirdly and more generally, a state of affairs that realizes the real-libertarian criterion will boost the correlation between effort and reward because the distributive measures it involves effect a significant equalization of wealth in the broadest sense (including claims on differential returns to internal endowments) and thereby attack straight on one of the most powerful sources of discrepancy between effort and reward. Finally, as mentioned earlier, social psychologists have documented that proportionality between reward and effort often provides a compelling criterion of fairness in micro-social interaction and that serious departure from such proportionality breeds resentment, and hence disruption and inefficiency. If this is the case, one can safely expect that the institutions endorsed by the real-libertarian criterion, owing to the concern with efficiency incorporated in the latter's maximin formulation, will allow micro-social distributions to be affected, be it only very roughly, by a tendency towards such proportionality, thus contributing further to the overall correlation between income and productive effort.

It does not follow, of course, that the realization of stronger versions of the principle 'To each according to her efforts' would be guaranteed in a regime that satisfies the real-libertarian criterion. Because of its maximin nature, the latter would tolerate, for example, that some people who happen to be more ingenious or to have specialized in a more useful line of activity would be rewarded more than others who make more effort than they but are less ingenious or happen to produce useless things in a wasteful way. In particular, as soon as risk is allowed—as it doubtless needs to be in an efficient economy—the shaping of the income distribution by effort levels is constantly disrupted.[86] One may take a gamble at some utility cost and lose it, thus becoming worse off than before. This may happen in all sorts of ways: by investing one's money in the wrong type of business, by chasing a client to no avail, by taking a course that unexpectedly fails to improve one's job prospects. All this, however, is fully consistent with a strong positive correlation between effort and reward, while kept in check by the real-libertarian requirement that a contribution should thereby be made to the opportunities of all. Is the equalization of opportunities (up to the point where it becomes counterproductive) that follows from this requirement not more than sufficient to accommodate the extent to which we believe income should be sensitive to effort, at least at the level of society as a whole?[87]

On the other hand, the principle of proportionality between income and effort loses all plausibility in a situation in which there are arbitrary inequalities in the opportunity to engage in productive effort. If I have no land on which I could work or if I am involuntarily unemployed, it is obviously unfair to invoke such a principle in order to deny me any income, or even to give me less income than someone else who has been given the opportunity to work and uses it in exactly the same way as I would have used it had I been given it. Proportionality between income and effort is, therefore, fundamentally incomplete as a specification of distributive justice. It needs to be supplemented with a fair distribution of opportunities—as characterized by the real-libertarian criterion or its cognates. And if a fair distribution of opportunities is necessary anyway, why should we not find it sufficient to accommodate the desert dimension which the proportionality principle wants to introduce? After all, the (sometimes tricky) distinction between opportunities, endowments, or real freedom versus outcomes, achievements, or welfare, and the option for the former against the latter, were precisely motivated by ethical convictions which the advocates of desert should find quite congenial: the belief that people should be held responsible for their choices (and indeed for their preferences), that justice is about equal (or leximin) possibilities, and that the mess or wonders people make of these possibilities do not need to be corrected. Are the claims of 'desert' not sufficiently—if tacitly—honoured in this way?[88]

A negative answer to this question, an insistence on a closer fit between effort and income than the one that flows from a comprehensive equalization of opportunities, can only stem from an illiberal, discriminatory privilege given to a life of productive effort. Some, no doubt, may want to reward effort, or labour, beyond what is countenanced by equal respect (in the sense of § 1.8), because of the intrinsic value they attach to it, because it constitutes a central component of what they regard as a good life. But in our pluralistic societies, departure from the distribution of income that would most favour one particular conception of what virtue or perfection consists in can no longer provide a plausible interpretation of what unfairness means. Consequently, an insistence on what effort deserves that is not satisfied by the equalization of opportunities cannot vindicate the claim that, through a basic income or through capitalist relations, some people are taking *unfair* advantage of other people's work.[89]

5.7 Roemerian exploitation

Let us now turn to a third and very different characterization of exploitation, to be found in John Roemer's (1982a, 1988) so-called game-theoretical or property-relations approach. Considering the latter is all the less avoidable as ethical superiority is one of the key advantages Roemer invokes on its behalf.[90] The usual approach, Roemer complains, 'fails to locate the source of exploitation in the unequal *and unfair* distribution of the productive assets'. While Marx himself repeatedly emphasized the relevance of the distribution of the means of production to his analysis of capitalist exploitation, the originality of Roemer's approach consists in *defining* capitalist exploitation in terms of this connection and then generating by analogy a whole family of exploitation concepts.[91] In this section, I shall present this approach, and also to some extent reconstruct it to make it as suitable and robust as possible for our purposes. In the next section, I shall examine whether it makes it possible to articulate a stronger exploitation-based challenge against real-libertarianism than the more conventional Lockean and Lutheran approaches.

In his initial formulations, Roemer (1982*a*: 202–11; 1982*b*: 94–7) defines capitalist exploitation using variants of the following 'game-theoretical' condition, which I shall call the withdrawal definition. A coalition is *capitalistically exploited* (*exploits capitalistically*) if it could do better (would do worse) for its members by withdrawing with a per capita share of the means of production and organizing optimally, while its complement would do worse (could do better) as a result. The underlying intuition is that capitalists would lose out if they left with no more than an average share of society's capital, whereas the workers would gain. Clearly, for this criterion to be operational, the means of production must be measurable in such a way that it is possible to determine when everyone gets a 'per capita share' of them. This is achieved by assimilating heterogeneous amounts of means of production to quantities of wealth assessed at their competitive prices. Further, it must also be possible to compare the situation of the members of the withdrawing coalition before and after withdrawal. In his more careful formulations, Roemer indicates that this comparison must be conducted, not in terms of incomes, but in terms of 'full incomes'—that is, the incomes agents would earn if they maximized their incomes (thus giving no value to leisure or work quality)—or of 'material welfare'—that is, some increasing function of income, leisure, and the quality of work. The distribution of income which is relevant to the present discussion must always be understood as relating to material welfare or full income in these senses.

Even so, there are a number of implications which show that the withdrawal definition originally proposed by Roemer provides a rather cumbersome way of expressing the underlying intuition. First of all, as soon as there are significant economies of scale, the above definition may yield the consequence that the workers are not exploited even if capital owners appropriate an enormous share of society's income. In particular, an individual worker or a small group of workers can practically never be exploited according to this definition, because what they would gain by being allotted more capital would be more than offset by losing the benefits of large-scale co-operation. Symmetrically, though less realistically, under sharply decreasing returns to scale, capital owners would benefit from withdrawing despite the sharing out of their capital, thus preventing the withdrawing workers (who gain both from the increase in their share of capital and from the decrease in scale) from being exploited according to the proposed definition.[92] A similar problem arises, secondly, from the existence of complementarities. Consider, for example, the situation of a group of workers with very specialized skills, which they are currently able to market against a decent income (think of dwarves employed as clowns). If they withdrew with their per capita share of the means of production, they would certainly become worse off, however small their current share of the means of production. Under no circumstance, therefore, could such a category be labelled capitalistically exploited by virtue of the proposed definition, however huge the profits their employers owe to their labour. More generally, if those who are better endowed with means of production also have skills whose use greatly benefits those with less material endowments, the latter's withdrawal with a per capita share of the means of production would not improve but worsen their position. Hence, they are not exploited according to the proposed definition, however little they are paid for the work they currently do.[93] Thirdly, consider situations where some group appropriates part of the product through some mechanism other than the market. For example, a king taxes the landowners. If it is the case that the latter would be better off (and the king worse off) after withdrawal with their per capita share of the means of production, they are capitalistically exploited according to the proposed definition, even though their becoming better off has no connection with capital ownership.[94]

One could attempt to solve each of these difficulties separately, in more or less *ad hoc* fashion.[95] But it is also possible to observe that all of them derive from the fact that the withdrawal definition combines two operations which should be carefully dissociated: it divides society into two parts, and it equalizes capital among its members. What the definition is intended to capture is the effect of the latter operation only, while each of the difficulties mentioned points to one way in which it also captures the effects of the former operation.[96] This immediately suggests a modification of Roemer's initial formulation. Instead of working out what would happen to some group's income if it withdrew with its per capita share of the means of production, why not simply ask what would happen to that group's income, or indeed to any particular individual's income, if ownership of the means of production were equalized within society as it is? This yields the following counterfactual condition, which

I shall call the equal-distribution definition: A is *capitalistically exploited* (*capitalistically exploits*) if she would be better (worse) off, while her complement would be worse (better) off if society's means of production were equally distributed, everything else remaining unchanged.[97] Since no slicing of society is involved in the counterfactual exercise which this formulation supposes, economies of scale and complementarities are no longer a problem. And since everything apart from the distribution of capital is assumed to remain unchanged, non-market interaction no longer poses a problem either.

However, this reformulation raises difficulties of its own. First, think of *efficiency effects.* Suppose that an unequal distribution of the means of production has a strong positive influence on efficiency, whether because of the incentives it provides for capital accumulation or because it makes it possible to allocate more means of production to those likely to make a more productive use of them because of having proved able to do so in the past. By getting rid of the unequal distribution of capital, one is also getting rid of the (putative) positive effects of such distribution. It follows that, on an appropriate time-scale and assuming sufficiently strong effects, someone who does nothing at all and lives off other people's work thanks to the capital she owns may not be an exploiter according to this definition. The withdrawal definition had the advantage of avoiding this difficulty by allowing the withdrawing coalition to organize optimally—including by distributing capital unequally among its members if efficiency could thereby be boosted.[98] Secondly, consider so-called *price effects.* Reallocating wealth does not only affect income and material welfare directly, by generating so-called *income effects*, that is, by giving wealth to some and taking it from others. It also affects them indirectly, by generating *price effects*, that is, by inducing changes in relative prices and hence in income possibilities for the various agents. Using such a general equilibrium model, it is possible to show that the 'beneficiaries' of the reallocation may conceivably become worse off, and its 'victims' better off as a result of it, even in a perfectly competitive economy with standard preferences and a unique and stable equilibrium.[99] Consequently, wealth equalization may increase the welfare of agents whose wealth is being decreased and decrease the welfare of agents whose wealth is being increased, even abstracting from all efficiency effects. But surely it makes little sense to say that I am capitalistically exploited if I have *more* than average wealth (and hence would own less wealth after equalization) but would become better off as a result of equalization because of the induced price effects. And it makes equally little sense to say that I am a capitalist exploiter if I have *less* than average wealth and would be made worse off by wealth equalization, due to perverse price effects.[100] This difficulty too was avoided by the withdrawal definition, which simply stipulated that each member of the withdrawing group *could* be made better off, not that she *would* through the operation of a price mechanism. Thirdly, even under the standard assumptions of perfect competition, general equilibrium models do not generally yield unique solutions. There may be several equilibria with an identical distribution of endowments, and depending on which equilibrium is selected, agents end up with more or less income as a result of capital equalization. Given the previous difficulty mentioned—the transfer paradox and related phenomena—this opens up the possibility that some agents are exploited or exploiters depending on which of the counterfactual equilibria is chosen as a baseline for comparison. Again, the withdrawal formulation avoids this difficulty by asking whether there exists at least one feasible allocation which improves the fate of every member of the withdrawing group.[101]

The appropriate response to these difficulties is neither to return to the withdrawal formulation nor to abandon counterfactual formulations altogether.[102] It is rather to introduce additional strictures in the characterization of the counterfactual exercise, so as to capture exclusively that aspect of the causal link between the distribution of wealth and the distribution of income which matches our intuitive notion of capitalist exploitation. I suggest the following formulation: A is *capitalistically exploited (capitalistically exploits)* if she would be better (worse) off, while her complement would be worse (better) off if society's means of production were equally distributed, everything else remaining unchanged *and abstracting from both efficiency effects and price effects*. It must be conceded that this move deprives the counterfactual exercise of any substantive interest.[103] With efficiency and price effects neutralized and assuming standard preferences, one can safely expect more wealth to be associated with strictly greater material welfare. We are, therefore, left, in a capitalist economy, with the handy though trivial conclusion that an agent capitalistically exploits (is capitalistically exploited) if and only if she owns more (less) than the average amount of means of production. Note, however, that this conclusion only holds under specific institutional conditions. Capitalist exploitation, as here defined, consists in wealth-based income inequality.[104] The handy conclusion just stated expresses the equivalence, in a particular institutional context, between this capitalist exploitation and wealth inequality. In a different context, for example in a society in which income is entirely distributed according to one's caste or by a lottery, there can be any degree of wealth inequality without any capitalist exploitation.

One of the most attractive features of Roemer's conception of exploitation is that it easily lends itself to generalization, beyond the case of capitalist exploitation. Roemer distinguishes three additional types of exploitation, which he contrasts with capitalist exploitation. The withdrawal definitions which he gives for each of them raise difficulties strictly analogous to those discussed above in connection with capitalist exploitation. I shall, therefore, define them instead using the corresponding equal-distribution formulations. To start with, what Roemer (1982*a*: 199–200) calls feudal exploitation refers to situations in which some people's material welfare would go up as a result of cutting their ties with their society even if they took along nothing but their own material belongings.[105] What is thus captured is the impact of the unequal ownership of people. More formally, A *is feudally exploited* (*feudally exploits*) if she would be better (worse) off if everyone enjoyed full formal freedom, everything else remaining unchanged and abstracting from possible efficiency and price effects. Under plausible empirical assumptions, the proposed definition leads to a handy though trivial criterion for assessing the presence of exploitation: an agent is feudally exploited if she does not fully own herself, and feudally exploits if she owns (at least partly) more people than just herself.[106] Feudal exploitation, so conceived, is not confined to feudalism or slavery. It is also meant by Roemer (1982*a*: 243–4; 1982*b*: 102–3) to encompass, for example, compulsory redistribution in favour of a bureaucratic élite in a socialist country, in which all have an equal share of the means of production. More generally, any coercive payment (in the sense of § 1.6), whether in labour, in kind, or in cash, and whether democratically decided or not, might be construed in an analogous way.

The counterfactual equalization can also be modified in two further ways so as to define what Roemer calls socialist exploitation and needs exploitation.[107] A *is socialistically exploited* (*socialistically exploits*) if she would be better (worse) off if all assets, both alienable (wealth) and inalienable (skills) were equally distributed, everything remaining unchanged and abstracting from possible efficiency and price effects. And A *is needs exploited* (is a *needs exploiter*) if she would be better (worse) off if all assets and needs were equally distributed, everything remaining unchanged and abstracting from possible efficiency and price effects. Needs must here be understood as independent of skills: think of the amount of food and drugs one requires to stay in good health. And material welfare, the variable in terms of which one is judged better or worse off, must now be allowed to be affected by objectively assessable needs, not just by the amount of income and leisure one can enjoy. The type of situation Roemer has in mind is one in which neither skills nor wealth are differentially rewarded—think, for example, of an income-egalitarian society—but in which material welfare is unequally distributed due to uncompensated inequalities in needs.

To make Roemer's typology convenient for our purposes, some further tidying up is required. His four types of exploitation are defined by decreasingly demanding conditions. Barring flukes, the presence of feudal exploitation implies the presence of capitalist exploitation, which in turn implies the presence of socialist exploitation, which in turn implies the presence of needs exploitation.[108] This has the unwelcome implication that someone can be, for example, a capitalist, socialist, and needs exploiter despite having less wealth, less skills, and more needs than the average member of society, simply by virtue of the extent to which she benefits from feudal rights over others. Such counterintuitive implications prompt the following reformulation of Roemer's typology, which establishes symmetry and logical independence between the four notions. Let us introduce the labels *wealth exploitation, skills exploitation*, and *health exploitation* to refer to the impact on the distribution of material welfare of the unequal distribution of wealth, skills, and needs, respectively. Feudal, wealth, skills, and health exploitation then constitute four elementary types of Roemerian exploitation, associated to the unequal distribution of formal freedom, of alienable means of production, of inalienable means of production, and of the capacity to turn income into material welfare (as determined largely, though not exclusively, by one's physical and mental 'health'), respectively. This eliminates the counterintuitive implications mentioned above: unlike Roemer's needs exploiter, a health exploiter, for example, must owe at least some of the material advantages she enjoys to her superior health, and cannot owe them all to her feudal rights, wealth, or skills.[109]

Is this inventory exhaustive, or are the elementary types of exploitation it lists arbitrarily picked from a large, possibly infinite pool of exploitation types? In standard neo-classical models of a perfectly competitive economy, income is distributed entirely to owners of capital and labour power according to their marginal productivity. Wealth and skills, therefore, constitute the only types of assets in which income inequalities can be rooted. Material welfare, however, is not just affected by income, but also by health (or needs)—which gives us three and only three elementary types of exploitation compatible with such models. In economies different from those such models aim to describe, of course, Roemer agrees that there is room for something else, namely feudal exploitation. But the latter can be pulled in two directions. *Either* feudal exploitation is defined strictly as inequality of material welfare stemming from unequal ownership over people—in which case it can be construed, along, say, with land exploitation, as a species of wealth exploitation, though one which it may make sense to set apart to the extent that ownership over human wealth is not easily tradable against material wealth. This type of exploitation disappears once the (perfectly enforced) abolition of slavery and feudal bondage has made every person the full owner of herself. *Alternatively*, feudal exploitation can be defined more loosely—as Roemer (1982*a*: 243) slips into doing when proposing to relabel it 'status exploitation' and analysing under this heading exploitation in existing socialist countries—as any inequality of material welfare that stems from the unequal distribution of assets other than wealth and skills. In addition to feudal exploitation in the narrow sense, the fact that Party members in socialist countries have access to more goods, shorter queues, or to a better service for the same price provides a typical instance of status exploitation in this broad sense. Whereas the narrow interpretation only covers the sort of exploitation that cannot be present in a free market economy—that is, exploitation resting on the negation of formal freedom—the broad interpretation covers all those sorts of exploitation which cannot be present in a free market economy *as portrayed by standard neo-classical models*—that is, any inequality in material welfare (with given needs) that cannot be ascribed to the unequal ownership of productive assets. By looking at market economies through the glasses of such models, one risks overlooking this distinction and presuming, therefore, that the only types of exploitation which cannot be seen through these glasses are those excluded by the very notion of a free market economy. Such a presumption is plainly wrong. In real-life market economies, income is substantially influenced by age, race, gender, confession, citizenship, and many other variables which are not reducible to either wealth or skills. These constitute the many dimensions of the heterogeneous notion of status exploitation, as defined above in purely negative fashion, each of which provides a further item on the list of elementary types of exploitation.

Could this list not be shrunk, either through the reduction of some dimension to others or through the selection of a privileged subset of dimensions? For example, gender-based wage inequalities may simply reflect different probabilities of absenteeism and career interruption. Similarly, race-based inequalities may stem from the fact that black shop assistants may put some customers off and be less 'productive' for this reason. Some amount of reduction to inequalities in skills (broadly interpreted) is no doubt possible, but I trust that being female or black often means a lower wage *without* a lower productivity, for example, because of a pure discrimination element on the part of 'irrational' employers, or because of systematically unequal access to information on the labour market. The impact of age on material welfare can also partly be reduced to the impact of age-dependent skills—a positive impact as long as age is associated with greater experience and reliability, but a negative impact once it starts being associated with outdated training and lack of flexibility. It can also partly be dissolved by substituting a life-cycle perspective to a snapshot one. But the age cohort one belongs to may nevertheless have a significant irreducible effect on one's expected material welfare, for example because it affects the probability of having to join the dole queue as a school-leaver (with long-term consequences on employability and career length), because it determines the extent to which one will have to suffer ecological damage, or pay the (net) cost of it, and because it strongly influences, in contemporary welfare states, the proportion of one's earnings that will have to be taxed away to pay for the education of the young and, above all, the pensions and health care of the elderly.

Alternatively, one might wish to shrink the list by restricting exploitation to inequalities of material welfare stemming from differences along *some* of the dimensions mentioned—for example, Roemer's initial list. One possible argument is that the dimensions not included in this short list only exert a negligible or transient influence on the distribution of income. But this is plain nonsense. Even leaving aside gender, racial, and generational inequalities, it is evident enough, in today's world, that whether or not one holds a proper job and what citizenship one possesses are factors that shape the distribution of income to at least the same extent as do wealth and skills.[110] Another possible argument is that a restriction is required because of the specific explanatory use for which the concept of exploitation is meant. If the purpose is to explain changes in the mode of production, it may make sense to focus on those inequalities which are rooted in the distribution of the property rights which define the mode of production, that is, on inequalities stemming from the unequal distribution of 'productive assets'. But quite apart from failing to yield a justification of Roemer's short list—why should needs exploitation be included ?—this argument is irrelevant anyway. Our purposes are of a normative nature, and it is hard to see why 'productive' assets should have a privilege in this respect. Why should inequalities systematically related to gender, race, or citizenship be any less objectionable than inequalities rooted in wealth or skills? If Roemer's notion of exploitation is intended to be ethically defensible, I believe there is no way of cogently resisting an open-ended extension of the list of elementary types of exploitation.[111]

5.8 Asset-based inequality

Like the approaches considered in previous sections, this approach to exploitation as asset-based inequality of material welfare clearly enables us to avoid saying that there is exploitation as soon as anyone takes advantage of someone else's work, without thereby forcing us to restrict exploitation to cases where the exploiter is totally idle. But unlike the other approaches—the Lockean definition of exploitation as appropriation *qua* non-worker and the Lutheran definition of exploitation as unequal exchange of value—it does not provide a defensible definition of exploitation, because it does not entail that someone's work is being taken advantage of, and hence does not satisfy the minimal conditions spelt out at the beginning of this chapter (§§ 5.1–2). This is obvious at once for Roemerian exploitation, defined most broadly as the disjunction of an unlimited number of elementary types of asset-based inequalities. For example, it is easy to imagine an unhealthy and disabled person with some wealth, who is health-exploited or skills-exploited and even exploited overall—she would be better off if all assets were equalized, or their influence on material welfare neutralized—while doing no work at all. Further, for Roemerian exploitation to obtain, it is not even necessary for the exploiter to derive any benefit from the exploitee, whether through a power or externality mechanism: the exploiter and the exploitee could live on two isolated islands and still potentially lose and gain, respectively, from the equalization of the relevant type of asset. This holds in particular for wealth exploitation, or capitalist exploitation, which can occur in the two-island example, notwithstanding the fact that no benefit is derived nor any power exercised nor any externality produced. Nor do the wealth-exploited need to work: an unemployed rentier who gets by with the meagre interests on her below-average savings could see her lot improved if wealth were equally distributed.[112]

Roemer is well aware of this discrepancy between his approach and the minimal conditions for a definition of exploitation to be intuitively acceptable, and in an attempt to reduce this discrepancy he suggested a number of additional conditions for exploitation, rather than just 'unfair treatment', to be present.[113] For our purposes, however, there is no need to discuss such conditions. We can simply take asset-based inequality as a characterization of the 'unfairness' component of exploitation, or of what makes it exploitative to take advantage of someone else's work when it is exploitative. There is then no problem about recognizing that a full definition can only be obtained by combining the characterization of so-called Roemerian exploitation with the other components spelt out earlier (§§ 5.1–2) or that the unfairness identified as Roemerian exploitation can be no less, and no less objectionably, present in situations that fail to be exploitative because they lack the other features which a full definition requires. Recognizing all this does not undermine, in principle, the potential of Roemer's criterion of unfairness (which I shall keep referring to as Roemerian exploitation) from articulating an exploitation-based challenge to the real-libertarian approach presented in previous chapters.

To scrutinize this potential, let us start by asking what the abolition of Roemerian exploitation would amount to. First of all, a society without asset-based inequality need not be an egalitarian society, whether in terms of assets or in terms of material welfare. Assets can remain unequally distributed—indeed, in many cases (talents, gender, age, and so on) there is no real option—because all the abolition of Roemerian exploitation requires is the absence of inequalities in material welfare generated by the unequal distribution of assets. And this can be achieved either by equalizing the asset concerned, or by neutralizing the impact of its unequal distribution on the distribution of material welfare. Incomes too can remain unequally distributed, not only because the abolition of health exploitation requires by itself differences in incomes to match differences in needs, but above all because any inequality in material welfare stemming from choice rather than from the unequal distribution of assets is perfectly consistent with the abolition of Roemerian exploitation. (The fact that choice may significantly affect the distribution of wealth, health, skills, etc. does not invalidate the distinction, given a period of reference, between income inequalities deriving from the constraints imposed by the distribution of assets and those deriving from differences in preferences and actions on this background.) More generally, the Roemerian conception of unfairness—unlike the Lutheran one—does not specify a pattern to which the distribution of income has to conform.[114] 'To each according to her labour' is one of the distributions of material welfare which may result from the abolition of Roemerian exploitation, but only one out of infinitely many. Distribution by lottery is another. Equal distribution of half of the national income and distribution of the rest according to labour performed is another again. All the Roemerian approach does is specify a list of factors which are not allowed to causally affect the way in which income is distributed. Hence, to determine whether indeed Roemerian exploitation has been abolished, one cannot content oneself with looking at the observable distribution of incomes. One has to investigate its causal history, check how it came about. In this respect, Roemer's approach is closer to the Lockean approach or even to libertarian entitlement conceptions of justice than to the Lutheran approach or other patterned conceptions.[115]

In this light, it is clear that the abolition of Roemerian exploitation is not incompatible with the institution of an unconditional income. Indeed the granting to all of an equal unconditional income that would exhaust the total net product, after subtraction of the additional allowances for people with special needs, would be one way of guaranteeing—as much as institutions can—the total eradication of all forms of Roemerian exploitation. Hence, the Roemerian challenge to the real-libertarian approach could not rest on a principled condemnation of basic income. But concern with the elimination of Roemerian exploitation might nevertheless confer on socialism some significant advantages to which real-libertarianism is blind. True, socialism, defined by self-ownership and the public ownership of the bulk of the means of production (§ 1.1), does not entail the abolition of all dimensions of Roemerian exploitation. Indeed, we have seen that skills-based exploitation is at the core of what Roemer himself calls socialist exploitation. But thanks to the public ownership of a large proportion of society's means of production, socialism greatly reduces wealth exploitation.[116] Moreover, owing to the better grip on the distribution of income this public ownership gives society, it also provides a potential for the reduction of other forms of Roemerian exploitation—for example skills-based, gender-based, or jobs-based— which the more decentralized income determination mechanism associated with capitalism is lacking.

The strength of this sort of argument obviously depends on the plausibility of the underlying criterion of unfairness. What then is wrong with Roemerian exploitation or more specifically, for a start, with the type of Roemerian exploitation that is central to capitalism, wealth exploitation? Roemer's own answer is that there are cases in which there is nothing wrong at all with it. For there can be a 'clean path to exploitation', and we must accordingly make a distinction between just and unjust wealth exploitation depending on whether or not *initial* assets are equally distributed.[117] Starting with equal amounts of capital, some people can work harder and/or consume less while others are lazier and/or greedier. As a result, capital will soon be unequally distributed, and some will earn less than others for this reason. Inequalities of income are then generated by the unequal ownership of capital assets. But since the latter is itself the outcome of choice in an earlier period, what could possibly make such a situation ethically objectionable except a morally arbitrary distinction between the outcome of choice (as opposed to asset distribution) in the 'current' period and the outcome of choice in the 'past'?

It may no doubt be the case that the outcome of past choices with equal initial assets is objectionable for some other reason. For example, the preferences underlying the choices made by the lazy/greedy may have been manipulated or the information guiding them distorted by people who have an interest in leaving the lazy/greedy no other choice than working for them. Or, even with unmanipulated preferences and undistorted information, such choices may have led to consequences unwanted by those who made them. For example, the individually rational choices made by the lazy/greedy may give the industrious/thrifty a power position which they would certainly have refrained from giving them had they been able to take a collective decision. There may be quite a bit of dirt on the clean path after all.[118] Conceding this, however, does not affect the point the clean path example is meant to make. For dirt, in the sense just illustrated, can also be found in choice-based (or non-exploitative), as opposed to asset-based (or exploitative) inequalities in the current period. Condemning some situations as wealth-exploitative does not imply that all situations which are not wealth-exploitative are all right. But if they are not, this is not because they are wealth-exploitative. The fact that the situation at the end of the perhaps-not-so-clean path may not be all right, therefore, does not make it wealth-exploitative. And we are still without a good ethical reason for condemning any inequality resulting from the unequal distribution of assets in the current period, rather than just those resulting from asset inequalities 'at the start'. If none can be found, the criterion of fairness that enters Roemerian wealth exploitation must be rephrased to refer to initial, rather than current assets. As Roemer (1985a: 44) puts it himself: 'the most consistent Marxian ethical position is against inequality in the initial distribution of productive assets.'

One implication of this shift is that the discrepancy between Roemerian wealth exploitation and exploitation as conceived in the Lockean or Lutheran approach further widens: if I 'start' with less than average wealth, I can never be a wealth-exploiter, on this modified account, however huge an amount of wealth I manage to (cleanly) accumulate over the years and however high the profits I derive from this wealth. Another implication is that we are now getting quite close to the notion of external endowment that plays a central role in the formulation of the real-libertarian approach (see § 4.2). Clearly, the assets people are endowed with 'at the start' must be understood as whatever assets they receive, whether at the beginning or in the course of their lives. Further, the alienable assets which are Roemer's concern must be understood as including all external assets, whether or not they are used, or even usable, for productive purposes. Not only can productive and non-productive assets be exchanged against each other, but possession of both types of assets clearly affects material welfare. Finally, the way in which Roemer makes bundles of alienable assets commensurable is by assessing them at their competitive value, and there seems, therefore, to be no significant difference left between equalizing external endowments and abolishing Roemerian wealth exploitation in the modified sense we are now exploring.

Strictly speaking, there are, however, three ways in which the equality of external endowments is more demanding than the elimination of Roemerian wealth exploitation. First, Roemerian wealth exploitation does not only require than an inequality in alienable assets should exist, but also that it should affect the distribution of material welfare. So it could in principle be eliminated by preventing endowments from affecting material welfare, rather than by equalizing them. However, endowments deprived of any impact on material welfare would presumably cease to count as endowments, and this first difference is, therefore, insignificant. Secondly, Roemerian wealth exploitation can in principle be abolished, according to Roemer, through the public ownership of alienable assets, not only through their equal division. From Roemer's own perspective, however, it is very doubtful that public ownership could be judged equivalent to equal division on grounds of fairness. As pointed out earlier (§ 5.3), equal—and *a fortiori* unequal—participation in democratic—and *a fortiori* undemocratic—decision-making over jointly owned assets is fully compatible with an actual control over these assets by a majority and a use of this control to enhance the welfare of its members at the expense of other members of the community. There may be sound instrumental reasons—to which we shall return at length in the next chapter—for favouring the public ownership of productive assets. But the fairness considerations that underlie Roemer's approach are bound to favour equal division over public ownership.[119] Thirdly, we have seen that a defensible notion of external endowment had to cover job assets (§ 4.4), a category which Roemer obviously does not mean to subsume under his notion of wealth. However, the same arguments that led to the broadening of the notion of external endowment should similarly lead to introducing a notion of jobs-based exploitation and an associated notion of fairness which should treat job assets as just a component of external wealth.

So, none of these three differences points to a genuine discrepancy between the ethics that underlies the demand that Roemerian wealth exploitation be abolished and the real-libertarian concern with external endowments. Does this mean that the two perspectives coincide? Certainly not. Let us bear in mind that the situation from which Roemerian exploitation has been *abolished* (the actual equalization or neutralization of assets) need not be the situation by contrast to which Roemerian exploitation is being (negatively) *defined* (the *ceteris paribus* counterfactual equalization or neutralization of assets). If only because the counterfactual thought experiment explicitly abstracts from any efficiency and price effect, the latter situation is generally impossible to bring about. When asking whether an agent would be better or worse off if wealth had been equally distributed or had no influence on income, one deliberately ignores the fact that such equalization or neutralization could depress aggregate income and, therefore, also the income of some at least of those who are said to gain from the static counterfactual exercise. That this counterfactual situation should generally be unachievable does not entail that Roemerian exploitation cannot be abolished. But it does entail that such abolition generally involves a cost which is deleted from the counterfactual exercise, but must be taken into account when assessing the desirability of an exploitation-free society. And in a way, this is exactly what the real-libertarian approach does when proposing that external endowments should not be equalized but leximinned. Rather than abolishing Roemerian wealth exploitation at all costs, it proposes to reduce it up to the point at which a less exploitative situation starts becoming worse for the exploited. This is a true disagreement, though one which, once clearly formulated, should easily give way to a strong consensus around the real-libertarian side.[120] Thus, once leximin has replaced strict equality in order to rule out absurdly counterproductive egalitarianism, and once job assets are paid the attention they deserve in advanced economies, Roemer's approach to wealth exploitation effortlessly converges with the real-libertarian treatment of external endowments and should find the idea of introducing the highest sustainable basic income most congenial.[121]

But even though wealth exploitation is the aspect of exploitation to which Roemer has paid by far the greatest attention, it is not the only one. And the implications of Roemer's approach taken as a whole may diverge from those of the the real-libertarian approach far more significantly than our focus on wealth exploitation suggests. No such divergence is to be expected on the side of feudal exploitation, since the ban on feudal exploitation has been explicitly characterized as the respect of formal freedom, a central component of the real-libertarian framework. Moreover, there is nothing in what Roemer says about the relationship between feudal and capitalist exploitation to indicate that he would not go along with the sort of priority that is being given (in § 1.8) to the respect of formal freedom. More complex is the relationship with skills exploitation, health exploitation, and welfare inequalities rooted in the distribution of other types of inalienable assets (race, gender, etc.). Like inequalities based on the distribution of alienable wealth, inequalities based on the distribution of inalienable assets are arguably objectionable only if they derive from unequal *initial* endowments, understood as whatever features people are given, whether by nature or by their social origins. The problem with inalienable assets is, by definition, that they stick too much to the person to lend themselves to redistribution. Rather than trying to equalize ownership of the relevant (initial) assets, we shall, therefore, have to go for a neutralization of the effect of their unequal ownership on the distribution of material welfare. Such neutralization can partly be achieved by preventing discrimination (or organizing reverse discrimination) in access to education, housing, or jobs, for example. But such a strategy is either absurdly costly or simply irrelevant when used to neutralize the impact of unequal talents or needs on the distribution of welfare. In these cases, neutralization can only use compensatory transfers of alienable assets. But what is the criterion that should guide compensation? Equality of welfare or of opportunity for welfare would obviously neutralize the impact of the distribution of any type of asset on the distribution of welfare. But it is open to objections that have been mentioned before (see §§ 2.6 and 3.7), and would anyway be inconsistent with the requirement that external wealth should be equalized (rather than distributed so as to equalize welfare) spelt out above in connection with Roemerian wealth exploitation. What is the alternative? I have offered one in Chapter 3. There are no doubt many others, including several I have discussed in the process of explaining my reasons for preferring my own favourite criterion: undominated diversity. But these reasons are just as relevant to the selection of the ethical principle that underlies the condemnation of (duly modified) Roemerian skills or health exploitation as they are to the formulation of the real-libertarian approach. If they were regarded as decisive in the latter context, they should also be regarded as decisive in the present one, and the demand for the neutralization of inalienable assets should, therefore, be reconstructed along the following lines: alienable assets should be transferred so that all could achieve, *not* the same level of preference satisfaction, but a quality of life that would not be unanimously considered as worse (in terms of what is thought to matter ultimately, whether preference satisfaction or something else) than that achievable by others.

This principle, I believe, expresses the ethical concern encapsulated in Roemer's notions of socialist and needs exploitation (tidied up into skills and health exploitation). Of course, it calls for differentiated transfers of alienable assets, and, therefore, does not strengthen, but qualifies, the justification of an unconditional basic income stemming from the ethical concern encapsulated in Roemer's concept of capitalist exploitation (tidied up into wealth exploitation). At least when formulated in such a way that efficiency considerations are taken on board, however, the constraint it imposes should leave plenty of room, under contemporary conditions, for the justification of an unconditional basic income (see § 3.8). It thus turns out that the conception of justice that underpins Roemer's original and illuminating approach to exploitation is far from creating a threat to the real-libertarian approach. Hence, the task of this section was not to undermine or circumscribe the plausibility of an alien moral intuition, but rather to clarify, unfold, and gently massage the underlying ethics so as to bring into full light its surprising proximity to the ethical vision developed in previous chapters. Once a few sensible amendments have been made—the most significant of which consists of substituting leximin for equality at any price—both are arguably just different phrasings of the same conception. Concern with asset-based inequality and the pursuit of real-freedom-for-all direct us to the same sort of criterion for assessing socio-economic regimes. In particular, both recommend that the respective ethical merits of capitalism and socialism be judged in terms of the maximum basic income they can be expected to sustain subject to the protection of formal freedom and undominated diversity or to some similar constraints.

CHAPTER 6

Capitalism justified?

PROLOGUE

Δ *I am sure that I could come up with some further objections, but what I am really interested in at this stage is what the implication of all this is for the debate about capitalism versus socialism. Let us accept that real-freedom-for-all is what social justice is all about, and that it has to be understood as requiring the maximization of an unconditional income subject to formal freedom being protected and to no one's endowment being unanimously found worse than someone else's. Is capitalism then to be preferred to socialism, or the other way around?*

Φ This is a question no one could answer. Not just because the relevant factual questions are tremendously complex, nor just because the answer may vary according to historical circumstances, but above all because the private or public ownership of the bulk of the means of production, which distinguishes capitalism from socialism, is only one of the many relevant dimensions along which socio-economic regimes may differ. So, the appropriate formulation of the question is whether there is any strong reason to believe that the optimal variant of capitalism would perform better in terms of our criterion—constrained basic income maximization—than the optimal variant of socialism, where 'optimal' is of course defined by reference to this very criterion.

Δ *This is hardly an easier question.*

Φ Here is how I think we can most conveniently approach it. How well a regime performs in terms of our criterion is bound to be strongly affected by its economic efficiency. Now, compare Eastern and Western Europe before the fall of the Berlin wall. How can you resist the presumption that, as far as economic efficiency is concerned, optimal capitalism is bound to have the upper hand? This is not more than a presumption, but one that is strong enough to locate the burden of proof firmly on the side of socialism (§ 6.1). And so the next question to ask is whether there is anything in the large arsenal of arguments for socialism that may still be relevant and powerful enough to shake this efficiency-based presumption in favour of capitalism.

Δ *Is it not wrong—and biased in favour of capitalism—to focus exclusively, as you seem to be doing, on economic efficiency? Might it not be the case that for some reason—less competition or less consumerism, for example—socialism makes it easier to satisfy the constraints of formal freedom and undominated diversity? And if this were the case, optimal socialism could be inferior to optimal capitalism in terms of economic efficiency, and yet afford a higher legitimate basic income.*

Φ I agree that this is an interesting possibility. But when scanning the literature for arguments of this sort, I could not spot anything that was not either circular or very feeble (§ 6.2). I am more impressed by arguments to the effect that socialism, though possibly worse at generating a large product, is better at seizing it for the sake of unconditional redistribution.

Δ *You seem already to be taking for granted that optimal socialism is worse than optimal capitalism at generating a large product. Aren't you letting the advocates of capitalism get away with what may be sheer media-fed prejudice?*

Φ As you know, there is a massive theoretical literature on the economic advantages of socialism over capitalism. I spent thousands of hours going through it. Most of the arguments I traced relate to capitalism's static inefficiency, its systematic wastage of existing resources. They conform to two main patterns: either they focus on significant departures from the blueprint of a perfectly competitive economy, or they emphasize economic activities that could be dispensed with under socialism.

Δ *How weighty do you find such arguments?*

Φ Arguments of the first sort—those relating to so-called market failures—I find devastating when directed against those who base grand claims about the efficiency of existing capitalism on the pathetically neat proof of the optimality of perfectly competitive market equilibria. But I find them practically irrelevant when comparing optimal feasible capitalism and optimal feasible socialism.

Δ *Why?*

Φ Take, for example, the market failures that stem from environmental externalities. Optimal capitalism will administratively correct prices so as to take these into account, be it very imperfectly, as would no doubt optimal socialism. How vigorously this can and will be done under a particular socioeconomic regime, however, seems to depend far more on the exact design of its political institutions than on whether it involves the private or public ownership of the means of production.

Δ *What about arguments of the second sort, those relating to dispensable activities?*

Φ The paradigmatic example is advertising: how much more cheaply could many goods be produced if advertising budgets were scrapped! But as soon as you realize how crucial a role advertising (true and false) plays in the efficient working of a market economy—competition is not just a matter of competitors being there, but of their being perceived by potential customers—I doubt you will still believe, if you have ever done so, that there is much of a danger for the pro-capitalist presumption from this side (§ 6.3).

Δ *Isn't all this peanuts compared to what I have always thought was by far the most ruinous form of resource wastage under capitalism: mass unemployment?*

Φ Take the case of cyclical unemployment first. It is clear that optimal capitalism should come equipped with countercyclical policies that will significantly dampen cyclical fluctuations. And the effect of remaining fluctuations on unemployment might be further reduced, as argued by Meade or Weitzman for example, if workers were paid at least partly in fixed-percentage shares of the profits rather than in fixed absolute wages. Why couldn't optimal capitalism be a share economy?

Δ *Some have argued, however, that the length and depth of capitalism's cyclical crises were due to profits being durably squeezed by the pressure of the organized working class. And I cannot see how demand management or a share system could tackle this.*

Φ What about other institutional devices such as corporatist incomes policies centrally decided by trade unions and employers' organizations? Or, if this proves either infeasible or insufficient, what about turning all firms above a certain size into worker-owned co-operatives? If protracted cyclical unemployment is a serious problem for capitalism's efficiency, there is a wide range of existing and possible institutional devices that can be incorporated into optimal capitalism as ways of alleviating it—all the more easily, in several cases, if one can count on the presence of a substantial basic income (§ 6.4).

Δ *What you are saying is that cyclical unemployment can be handled through the fine-tuning of optimal capitalism. But what about the permanent 'reserve army of the unemployed'? You don't need to buy silly functionalist claims about the 'needs of capitalism' in order to believe that, irrespective of cyclical fluctuations, involuntary unemployment is a permanent feature of capitalism. Even with a substantial basic income, the efficiency-wage approach, for example, would still predict equilibrium unemployment. Moreover, a well-organized workers' movement might successfully keep the wage level above the equilibrium level that would prevail in an atomistic economy.*

Φ Efficiency-wage arguments are hardly relevant here. According to such arguments, involuntary unemployment is just the by-product of what is required to make workers optimally productive, namely paying them more than the market-clearing wage, and optimal socialism should, therefore, accommodate it too. As to the second possibility you mention— privileged job holders organizing to boost their wages at the cost of permanently swelling unemployment above what market-clearing or efficiency requires—my response is not that formal-freedom-respecting socialism could experience this too, which is true but insufficient. It is rather that, under both optimal capitalism and optimal socialism, there is nothing sacrosanct about the organized jobholders' main weapon: the right to strike. If—I emphasize the 'if'—the problem you mention is serious enough, the right to strike of privileged categories of workers should be curtailed or even scrapped under both optimal capitalism and optimal socialism (§ 6.5).

Δ   *Thus, you are unimpressed by the various static-efficiency arguments we have been talking about: the presumption in favour of optimal capitalism remains unshaken, either because the inefficiency pointed out by the critics of capitalism can be removed through an appropriate designing of optimal capitalism's institutions, or because it is a comparatively minor side-effect of a factor that contributes to capitalism's efficiency. But the decisive economic advantage boasted by many advocates of socialism—Marx and orthodox Marxists included—is not a matter of statically efficient resource use, but of dynamically efficient resource generation.*

Φ   This is true, but we must bear in mind that it is probably capitalism's conspicuous superiority in this respect—both historical and theoretically grounded—that has done most to incorporate the pro-capitalist presumption into the common wisdom of our time. The imperative to innovate or perish, which accounts for much of capitalism's historical performance, lies at the very core of any capitalist regime. And although it is easy to understand how appropriate reforms could help close the gap between socialism and capitalism in this respect, it is hard to see how they could turn a serious handicap into a decisive advantage. To be sure, Marx's feeble argument about the 'fettering' of productivity growth under capitalism will not achieve this. Nor can I see much promise in the subtle variants of this argument developed more recently (§ 6.6).

Δ   *Hence, you conclude that there is little hope for the pro-socialist side to regain the upper hand in terms of either static or dynamic efficiency. And yet you mentioned earlier the possibility that a socio-economic regime might be less efficient economically, no better at meeting the constraints of formal freedom and undominated diversity, and still able to sustainably generate a higher basic income.*

Φ   Yes, optimal socialism might still enjoy a crucial advantage in terms of popular sovereignty, understood roughly as a political community's ability to steer the use of its resources according to its democratically determined will. The ownership of the means of production by the political community protects a socialist society against its redistributive policies being thwarted by the private capital owners' decisions to stop investing or invest abroad. There are conceivable historical circumstances in which this may be a decisive advantage for optimal socialism, as far as the sustainable maximization of basic income is concerned. But I very much doubt that these circumstances currently obtain or will ever obtain again. For both capitalist and socialist countries are immersed in the world market and are, therefore, subjected, particularly as far as income distribution is concerned, to the tight constraint of competitiveness.

Δ   *But could a socialist society not cut itself off from the world market? True, it would have to bear the cost of forgoing its share in the benefits of a worldwide division of labour and technical progress, and this needs to be taken into account when assessing its potential for funding a substantial basic income. But its distribution policies would no longer be constrained by the need to mind its competitiveness.*

Φ   Remember that the socialist countries we are talking about would be constrained by the protection of formal freedom. The lower average standard of living and the higher potential for egalitarian policies that can be expected from disconnection from the world market will jointly mean that the highly-skilled will have generally much to gain from leaving the country. And to retain its precious human capital, a formal-freedom-respecting country can neither censor information nor prohibit emigration. In today's world, therefore, and bearing formal freedom in mind, even optimal autarkic socialism cannot reasonably be expected to topple the efficiency-based presumption in favour of optimal capitalism (§ 6.7).

Δ   *By emphasizing competitiveness the way you just did in order to vindicate your negative conclusion about socialism, are you not seriously undermining your own belief in the possibility of a high basic income in capitalist countries? It is not enough to argue that a transfer system with a basic income at its core would be better, in terms of economic efficiency, than the welfare state as currently organized. What is under pressure now, for reasons you hinted at, is any sort of generous transfer system. Bearing sustainability in mind, shouldn't real-freedom-for-all recommend something like the dismantling of the welfare state rather than its replacement by something more ambitious?*

Φ   This risk is great if we don't simultaneously struggle to redesign our institutions in two directions. One is democratic scale-lifting: we must urgently, and in all sorts of ways, establish and strengthen supranational democratic institutions which determine the rules under which the transnational market operates—including as regards income distribution—instead of being governed by them, as national democracies increasingly are. The other direction is solidaristic patriotism: we must also urgently, and in all sorts of ways, preserve and develop institutions that nurture strong feelings of allegiance towards generous distributive institutions at whatever level they exist, and thereby reduce the pressure against redistribution that stems from opportunistic behaviour by the holders of precious factors.

Δ   *Surely, there must be a tension between the cosmopolitanism of the first strategy and the patriotism of the second.*

Φ To some extent there is, and we must, therefore, be all the more thoughtful when selecting the institutional means for the pursuit of either (§ 6.8). But we should not be too fussy. If we are to preserve and regain the leeway required to go forward, or even simply to prevent the world-wide collapse of social solidarity, both strategies are essential. Careful thought and resolute action are urgently needed in this area. No time should be wasted.

Δ *Get on with it then!*

—————

6.1 Optimal capitalism versus optimal socialism

We can now return to where we took off (§ 2.3), prompted by a sequence of powerful challenges, for an unexpectedly lengthy detour. The criterion initially suggested in order to evaluate socio-economic regimes—basic income maximization subject to the protection of formal freedom—has now passed the test of these challenges, but has also been clarified and qualified along the way. I can of course not claim to have examined all conceivable ethical challenges to this criterion, nor to have said enough in reply to those I did examine for everyone to feel fully comfortable with it. But it is now time to stop searching our moral intuitions and turn, at least from a distance, to the real—or really feasible—world, in order to ask the following question. Supposing all relevant ethical considerations are encapsulated in our (duly qualified) criterion, do we have any strong reason to believe that capitalism should be preferred to socialism or the other way around? In other words, should a real-libertarian embrace capitalism or socialism?

As emphasized earlier (§ 2.3), socio-economic regimes vary along many dimensions, only one of which refers to the nature of the ownership of the means of production, that is, to the distinction between capitalism and socialism. Now, the formulation of the above question presupposes that this dimension matters to the satisfaction of the real-libertarian criterion, but not that it is the only dimension that matters, nor the dimension that matters most. There may well be a greater difference in performance, as measured by our criterion, between various forms of capitalism or between various forms of socialism than between some forms of capitalism and the forms of socialism that match them in all respects except the ownership of the means of production. Indeed, the fact that both capitalism and socialism are compatible with both the presence and the absence of a basic income provides an obvious illustration of this possibility. Moreover, it is easy to imagine that one form of capitalism—say, with a basic income but without compulsory labour management—may perform better than the matching form of socialism, while another form of socialism—say, with a basic income and with compulsory labour management—may perform better than the matching form of capitalism. Consequently, the question asked in this chapter cannot be whether capitalism is always better or always worse than socialism according to our criterion—the answer in either case is trivially negative—nor even whether capitalism is better or worse than socialism, other things remaining equal—this would not be one but an endless set of questions admitting of contradictory answers. The question must rather be whether the best feasible form of capitalism according to our criterion—for short, *optimal capitalism*—performs better or worse than the best feasible form of socialism according to our criterion—for short, *optimal socialism*.

This is a complex and tricky question, and one which it is particularly easy to handle unfairly, if only because no one knows where exactly the limits of the feasible are beyond what came into existence and lasted for more than a short while. It is, therefore, all too easy to camouflage one's prejudices in favour of either type of regime behind peremptory claims about the limits of what is feasible under the other, so that one ends up with on one side a flattering ideal version of one type of regime and on the other side (a close variant of) the unattractive historical realization of the other type of regime. Moreover, the wealth of empirical and theoretical arguments that are relevant if one is to determine which variants of either type of regime are feasible and how each would perform in terms of our criterion would hardly fit into a multi-volume summa, let alone into a single chapter. It includes, in particular, the countless arguments that have been offered to establish or refute the superior economic efficiency of either capitalism or socialism.

My task, however, has been greatly facilitated by Eastern European history of the late twentieth century, out of which capitalism has emerged, whether one likes it or not, with the benefit of a strong presumption of superiority in terms of economic efficiency, productive potential, wealth-generating capacity. It does not follow of course that we must henceforth consider as established that the best feasible version of capitalism is more efficient than the best feasible version of socialism, let alone that the former is superior to the latter by real-libertarian standards. But at least it is clear on which side the burden of proof lies. Even though superior economic efficiency does not guarantee a higher sustainable basic income, it certainly constitutes a strong prima-facie advantage in this respect. If some variant of socialism is to win out all the same, one will have to pull out of the vast store of arguments deployed over the years against capitalism those which have somehow passed the test of both history and theory, while at the same time remaining—or becoming—relevant when what is at stake is not economic efficiency as such, but real-freedom-for-all. In this light, the modest ambition of this chapter should be clear: not a grand synthesis of the many facets of the political-economic debate between capitalism and socialism, but a selective review of some of the most important among them in order to sketch what I believe to be the state of the question once real-freedom-for-all is chosen as the guiding principle.

Before embarking on this task, let me clear some more rubble out of the way. Now that the focus is directly on a comparison of capitalism and socialism, one may start doubting again that sustainable basic income maximization, subject to the constraints of formal freedom and undominated diversity, is truly all there is to real-freedom-for-all. How should we take into account, for example, the fact that the members of a socialist society jointly own the bulk of the means of production, or the fact that consumption patterns and hence accessible bundles of goods may diverge significantly depending on whether capitalism or socialism prevails? Several of these doubts have already been dealt with before (see esp. §§ 1.2, 2.8). I want, however, to pick three of them at this stage in order to illustrate further and to clarify what a comparison between optimal socialism and optimal capitalism is supposed to mean.

First, is it not relevant to point out that socialist societies are able to, and have actually tended to, guarantee an effective right to a job, thus disqualifying the great emphasis in Chapter 4 on the redistribution of job assets in the form of a basic income? The answer cannot just be that a capitalist society could in principle do precisely the same by making the State the employer of last resort (at sufficiently low wages), while maintaining the bulk of the means of production in private hands. More fundamentally, as explained earlier (§§ 4.4, 4.7), the fact that everyone has a job does not mean that employment rents have disappeared. Whether because of efficiency-wage considerations, bargaining power, bureaucratic interference, differences in talents, etc., many jobs are bound to be envied, in a socialist society too, by people who are deprived of access to them. Moreover, again as argued above (§ 4.5), attempts to get rid of this job scarcity through more targeted policies than a uniform job-independent income are vulnerable to the objection that they are discriminatory, hence at odds with the ideal of leximin real freedom and, therefore, out of place in the characterization of optimal socialism.[1]

Secondly, does the fact that socialist economies tend to be characterized by shortages on commodity markets not affect the relevance of a basic income as the key basis for assessment? It would if the presence of these shortages did not make one suspect that such socialist societies have not achieved the socialist optimum in terms of leximin real freedom. If the rationing takes the form of an unorganized shortage, with some people having access to the good and others not at all, we find ourselves in a situation analogous to involuntary unemployment: if there are deep-rooted reasons for not trying to get rid of the shortages altogether, one should tax the rent appropriated by the lucky (or wily) and redistribute it in the form of a higher basic income. There may, of course, be special reasons for an organized rationing in some areas, either because of its contribution to boosting the highest sustainable level of basic income (for example, the restriction of higher education not to the highest bidder but to the ablest pupils) or because of its contribution to satisfying the condition of undominated diversity in the most effective way (for example, under conceivable circumstances, by providing food and shelter to everyone). But under similar circumstances, such rationing would be justified under both socialism and capitalism (see § 2.4). The presence of goods shortages beyond such cases generates the presumption that real freedom is not being leximinned as much as the public ownership of the means of production allows. It does not show that the constrained maximization of basic income is not what a real-libertarian assessment of capitalism and socialism should be concerned with.

Finally, consider the frequent claim that socialism is bound to perform worse than capitalism in terms of freedom, because of the ominous black-listing power it confers upon the State by virtue of the latter's monopoly of employment.[2] Because it owns the (bulk of) the means of production, the State can implement Trotsky's famous motto, 'Who does not obey shall not eat', and it cannot be taken for granted that the tendency to do so will be diminished by democratic control, as the holders of state power will then have strong incentives to use state appointments as a way of securing their electoral support. This sort of consideration is not captured by the concern with formal freedom—as it would be if the motto were 'Who does not obey shall be imprisoned'—nor by the concern with undominated diversity—as it might have been if ethnicity, for example, or some other feature of a person's internal endowment, had been the sole criterion of discrimination. But should not a real-libertarian nevertheless condemn a regime which systematically generates such blacklisting *even if* it durably provided a higher basic income than is possible under capitalism? No, she should not, for the higher the basic income, the less truth there can be in the statement 'Who does not obey shall not eat', not only as regards obedience to state officials, but also as regards obedience to one's boss or to one's spouse. And if greater real freedom for all in this multidimensional sense can only be achieved at the cost of ideological (in addition to talent and, possibly, kinship) discrimination for access to desired jobs, so be it. Of course, such discrimination is not something a real-libertarian will be enthused by: it is bound to be a drag on economic efficiency and, more fundamentally, it is likely to bias the political process so as to undermine the long-term viability of a truly unconditional basic income—why would blacklisting for access to jobs not spread to blacklisting for access to income? But such effects are automatically taken into account by our criterion of sustainable basic income maximization, and it is, therefore, most implausible that a regime that countenances state blacklisting to any significant extent will perform best according to this criterion. Is optimal socialism such a regime? Asserting this would require one to argue that no feasible regime could durably combine public ownership (however organized) of the bulk of the means of production with an articulation of political institutions, the judiciary, and the media that would preclude the ideologically deviant from being denied a job. Who could provide such an argument?

6.2 *The capitalist shaping of preferences*

Having thus clarified what it means to assess the relative merits of optimal capitalism and optimal socialism from a real-libertarian standpoint, let us start our critical review of potential grounds for overturning the presumption that exists in favour of the former, by asking whether there is any reason to expect the constraint of undominated diversity to be more easily satisfied under socialism than under capitalism. If this were the case, less funds would need to be diverted away from basic income into differentiated transfers for the compensation of handicaps, and optimal socialism may, therefore, be preferable to optimal capitalism on real-libertarian grounds despite its lesser economic efficiency. Why might this be the case? Not because objective circumstances, such as the health condition of the population, can be expected to be affected by a difference in the ownership regime. Under both types of regime, public health, work safety, and environmental measures can be taken, and part of the basic income can be given in the form of a free health insurance (see § 2.4), on grounds consistent with real-libertarianism and unaffected by the nature of the ownership of the means of production.

However, the ease with which undominated diversity can be satisfied does not depend only on the objective features of the internal endowments of society's members. It also crucially depends on the prevailing pattern of preferences (see § 3.5). And this pattern, arguably, is at least partly shaped by the nature of the socio-economic regime.[3] Let us just examine the relevance of one argument of this sort, which is interesting both in its own right and as an illustration of the difficulties associated with this line of argument. One major defect of capitalism, according to G. A. Cohen (1978: 297–307), is that it 'tends to promote one of the options [for using the fruits of the technological improvements it generates], output expansion, since the other, toil reduction, threatens a sacrifice of the profit associated with increased output and sales, and hence a loss of competitive strength'. This tendency accounts for the fact that the secular rise of output has been substantially higher than the increase in free time, especially if one pays attention to the growth of what Illich (1981) calls shadow work, the work required to take one's labour power to the office or one's purchasing power to the supermarket shelves and back.[4] Under contemporary capitalism, profit maximization drives firms to advertise the advantages of consuming their products, not of enjoying leisure. This leads to a discrepancy between the workers' 'pursuit schedule' and their 'satisfaction schedule', between their behavioural disposition to seek more consumer goods and the actual satisfaction gained from possessing them. The resulting bias in favour of income and against leisure implies that a capitalist society systematically allocates its resources in a way that fails to maximize its member's satisfaction.

From a real-libertarian perspective, the argument, as presented so far, is simply irrelevant. What matters from such a perspective is not whether the use made of resources could be improved in terms of aggregate welfare, but whether it could be improved in terms of leximin real freedom. But it is easy to rephrase the argument so as to make it relevant from a real-libertarian perspective, via its impact on the satisfaction of undominated diversity. Compared to socialism, what the bias in advertising generates under capitalism, is a greater consensus on the importance of income not just at the level of the pursuit schedule, but also—let us admit *contra* Cohen—at the level of the preference schedule. But if there is a consensus on the overwhelming importance of income, our criterion of undominated diversity will require us to spend large amounts to compensate in a differentiated way those with talents that confer a comparatively low earning power. And little—if anything—will then be left to feed an unconditional basic income. If the level of the latter is a good index of the real freedom enjoyed by those with least real freedom, it follows that the argument provides a reason for favouring (unbiased) socialism over (biased) capitalism on real-libertarian grounds.

Against this argument, one may first deny the reality of the bias. For example, one may point to the perfect symmetry between the capitalists' interest in low wages and their interest in long working time, and infer that there is every reason to believe that they will try just as hard to keep the former down as to keep the latter up.[5] The point, however, is not that capitalists are keener to concede higher wages than shorter hours, but that they are systematically induced to boast of how great it would be to earn a lot, not how great it would be to work little. And it is the induced effect on workers' tastes that underlies the alleged bias. Alternatively, one may object that consumption takes time and hence that boasting of the importance of consumption goods amounts, *ipso facto*, to boasting of the importance of free time.[6] This objection would be fatal if the goods advertised were on average of such a nature that the *additional* time one would need to take off in order to consume them would at least match the working time required to earn what is needed to buy them (think of international footpath maps). In most cases, however, no additional leisure is required (it takes no more time to swallow a mouthful of Pepsi than a mouthful of water). And one can, therefore, safely maintain that the bias persists even if the implied promotion of leisure is fully taken into account. Finally, it might be argued that the bias can hardly be ascribed to capitalism as such, since its paradigmatic version is totally free of it. Under perfect competition, prices are parameters for individual firms, which simply select their level of output in such a way that their marginal product equals the given price. Firms are then essentially indifferent about gaining or losing a customer, and will not waste resources on advertising. However, both existing and feasible capitalism, it is easy to respond, is characterized by less than perfect information and/or less than perfectly free entry. Unlike perfect competition, such monopolistic competition, in Martin Weitzman's (1984: 35) words, 'exerts steady pressure on output markets, in good times and bad, because at any given moment firms are actively seeking to expand production and sales'. Monopolistic firms are, to a varying extent, price makers, and will generally find it in their (profit-maximizing) interest to set the price higher than the marginal cost. At this price, firms will continually want to sell more than buyers are willing to purchase, for unlike what happens under perfect competition any extra customer brings in extra profits. Lavish showrooms and enticing adverts are the consequence.[7] Though absent from sufficiently abstract models, the bias can, therefore, safely be ascribed to feasible capitalism.

But so what? Does it really follow that socialist societies will find it easier to achieve undominated diversity? First, is it not possible to argue that optimal socialism displays a similar bias? It has no doubt been a central characteristic of Soviet-type economies—to use again Weitzman's (ibid. 36–7) formulation—that keen buyers are there trying to overcome the resistance of coy sellers, rather than keen sellers trying to overcome the resistance of coy buyers. In such a context, there cannot be the same kind of pressure for a greater weight given to income as against leisure. But this systematic shortage of goods is precisely a feature which, I have just argued (§ 6.1), socialism should get rid of, if it is to compete with capitalism in terms of leximin real freedom. As more autonomy is given to publicly owned firms in order to achieve this outcome, is one not bound to witness the appearance of exactly the same type of bias as under monopolistic capitalism? But suppose, secondly, that the bias does remain stronger under optimal capitalism than under optimal socialism. It should not be taken for granted that the net effect of this stronger bias on the highest sustainable level of basic income is bound to be negative, even if the funds needed for compensating those with a 'handicap' in earning power have to increase as a result of greater taste homogeneity. Not only may it be the case that advertising, the immediate cause of the bias, plays an essential role in making competition effective and hence in generating the benefits associated with competition (see § 6.3 below). Above all, the bias itself seems bound systematically to boost the supply of formal labour and the level of taxable output, and therefore to shift upward the highest level of basic income that can be durably sustained. This appears especially likely, as soon as one realizes that unlike the positive effect on the supply of labour, and hence on the redistributive potential, the negative effect (via reduced taste diversity) on the ease with which undominated diversity can be satisfied will remain very limited as long as even only a small minority in the society concerned remains unaffected by advertising and keeps giving great weight to free time as against income.[8] To put it roughly, a low earning power does not provide a ground for compensation as long as someone in the society concerned does not mind earning so little. The labour supply, instead, will increase as soon as anyone starts giving increased importance to income. It is, therefore, by no means certain that the net effect of the bias on the maximum basic income consistent with undominated diversity, if there is one, should be negative.[9]

Thus, the real-libertarian version of the taste-induction argument in favour of socialism hinges on risky empirical conjectures and may easily turn into a pro-capitalist argument. If we are to shatter the presumption—that capitalism makes it possible to sustainably yield (consistently with undominated diversity) a higher basic income—we shall have to look in a different direction. Henceforth, I shall simply assume that the impact of socio-economic regimes on preference patterns is either negligible or irrelevant, and hence that all we need to be concerned with from a real-libertarian point of view is the total amount sustainably available for transfers, whether differentiated (in order to achieve undominated diversity) or not (as a basic income). This forces us to tackle head-on the issue of economic efficiency, even though, as we shall see (§ 6.7), this is not the only relevant dimension left. Economic efficiency breaks down, according to a useful distinction, into *static efficiency*, or efficiency in the allocation of productive resources, and *dynamic efficiency*, or efficiency in the generation of these resources. On both counts, the common wisdom captured in our initial presumption is that capitalism is bound to perform far better than socialism. Yet, both aspects of efficiency have been the focus of a wide spectrum of irrationality-based critiques of capitalism. I shall now proceed to a selective screening of these critiques in an attempt to identify those, if any, which offer some promise of overturning the pro-capitalist presumption.[10] I shall first consider, from a real-libertarian standpoint, a number of aspects of static inefficiency that have played a prominent role in the economic critique of capitalism (§§ 6.3–5) and next turn to the key dimension of dynamic inefficiency (§ 6.6).

6.3 *Market failures and dispensable activities*

Standard accusations to the effect that capitalism systematically allocates productive resources in an inefficient way rest on the one hand on the massive presence of so-called *market failures*, wasteful departures from the allocation a perfectly competitive market is supposed to guarantee, and on the other hand on the massive presence of *unproductive* activities, which alternative socio-economic regimes could dispense with. I shall devote the following two sections to the crucially important phenomenon of unemployment, the (cyclical or permanent) waste of productive human resources, a particular type of market failure which is of special interest because of the closeness and complexity of its relation to both economic efficiency and real-freedom-for-all. In the present section, I shall briefly assess the real-libertarian potential of anti-capitalist arguments relating, first, to the other main categories of market failures— monopolies or, more generally, the ability of economic agents to affect market prices, and externalities, that is, benefits and costs that are not reflected in the price system—and next to the two categories of (putatively) wasteful activities most often invoked in this context—policing and advertising.

The monopoly-based argument against capitalism can be briefly stated as follows.[11] With a given cost structure, profit maximizing monopolists or oligopolists select a lower level of output and a higher price than would have been the case under perfect competition. This does not only constitute a Pareto-suboptimal situation in itself, but the higher prices also distort the whole signal system that enables a perfectly competitive economy to minimize costs. The strength of this argument has been notoriously qualified by Joseph Schumpeter. To start with, he points out, 'competition of the kind we now have in mind acts not only when in being but also when it is merely an ever-present threat. It disciplines before it attacks. The businessman feels himself to be in a competitive situation even if he is alone in the field [. . .]. In many cases, though not all, this will in the long run enforce behaviour very similar to the perfectly competitive pattern.' (Schumpeter 1943: 85) This qualification has now been refined and developed by the so-called theory of contestable markets. A perfectly contestable market is a market into which entry is absolutely free, and from which exit is entirely costless. If such a market has at least two firms, equilibrium prices and output levels will be exactly equal to what they would be under perfect competition.[12] Thus, even a highly concentrated market structure is consistent with the achievement of static efficiency. Of course, the condition of perfect contestability is still very demanding, and since investment involves *sunk costs*, that is, costs which are irreversibly wasted if the firm moves out of the market, real-world capitalism is often very far from meeting it. Nevertheless, the monopoly-based argument loses much of its sharpness as a result of this first qualification. But Schumpeter's main—and most famous—reply is of a different nature. It consists in conjecturing that the static inefficiency associated with monopolistic capitalism is a necessary condition of—and a light cost to pay for—its tremendous dynamic efficiency. The truth of this conjecture would not imply the pointlessness of well-designed anti-trust policies, nor that the removal of obstacles to competition can often increase economic efficiency—and the conception of optimal capitalism will have to take this into account. But it would imply that the distance of actual or feasible capitalism from the mutually equivalent blueprints of perfectly competitive capitalism and rationally planned socialism, despite its cost in static efficiency, may none the less involve a significant gain in terms of overall economic efficiency, and hence also, presumably, in terms of leximin real freedom. I shall return to this conjecture in due course (§ 6.6).

Secondly, consider the static inefficiency associated with environmental externalities. It is sometimes claimed that it is capitalism, rather than industrialism, that is at the root of the environmental crisis, or at any rate that socialism is better equipped to tackle the latter. As Oskar Lange (1937*a*: 126) puts it: 'A socialist economy would be able to put all the alternatives into its economic accounting. Thus it would evaluate all the services rendered by production and take into the cost account all the alternatives sacrificed [. . .]. By doing so it would avoid much of the social waste connected with private enterprise.'[13] But, as Lange is well aware, it is in principle possible, in a capitalist context, to introduce, for example, so-called Pigouvian taxes and subsidies in order to bring private costs and benefits at least roughly in line with social costs and benefits. Indeed, this is precisely the way one should proceed in a socialist economy, if for some other reason a significant degree of decentralization in decision-making proved essential (see § 6.6). Thus the difference in the potential for internalizing external costs is not exactly sharp.[14] Moreover, the economic agents' regime-dependent incentives to make use of this potential need to be brought into the picture. It has been argued, for example, that since, under private ownership, the value of individual people's assets is affected by externalities, they will be more strongly motivated to mobilize and put pressure on political authorities in order to stop nuisances or encourage the production of positive externalities.[15] This is, of course, just one example. Much will depend on the detailed design of political institutions under either capitalism or socialism. The point is that even if the 'potential' for internalization were significantly greater under socialism, this would not *ipso facto* warrant ascribing to the latter a more powerful tendency to avoid static inefficiency of this sort. The historical record of socialism in this area does not settle the issue, but it hardly makes the attempt to establish such a tendency very promising.

However, the static inefficiency ascribed to capitalism is often of an altogether different nature. Even if they were perfectly competitive and hence, by definition, free of any market failure, capitalist economies would still be wasteful, it is argued, because they call into existence a number of activities that contribute nothing to people's welfare and can, therefore, be viewed as a drag on overall labour productivity, while being dispensable under socialism.[16] One prima-facie plausible example of such activities is the enforcement of capitalist property rights. In Orwell's (1945: 45) post-revolutionary farm, 'since no animal now stole, it was unnecessary to fence off pasture from arable land, which saved a lot of labour on the upkeep of hedges and gates'. Somewhat less metaphorically, capitalism requires courts, police, lawyer services, night-watchmen, and barbed wire if it is to effectively protect private property—a costly set of *faux frais* which a socialist society should be able to do away with. But why should it? Obviously not because no property claims exist in a socialist society. Not only would any regime with any chance of qualifying as optimal socialism in this context retain extensive private property rights over means of consumption (my fellow-citizens would not be allowed to take my pipe off my lips, nor to move into my flat in my absence) but public ownership too gives rise to property claims (if a park or a factory is publicly owned, this does not mean that anyone, or any-one sharing its ownership, can use it as she pleases). The answer must rather be that whatever property claims exist under socialism are less in need of protection than those existing in a capitalist society. Why should this be the case?

We cannot reply that less people will dwell in a state of deprivation and hence have no option but to infringe property rights in order to survive. For this would beg the question: by scrutinizing the possible sources of capitalism's static inefficiency, we are precisely trying to find out whether there is any hope of establishing that its potential for financing a high basic income is less than socialism's—a conclusion that cannot be used as a premiss. We cannot reply either that the structure of property rights that characterize socialism would enjoy such a degree of legitimacy that spontaneous compliance would be far more widespread than under a sys-tem, such as capitalism, that is based on 'non-generalizable interests'. Again, this would be question-begging, for if capitalism's claim to be able to guarantee more real freedom for all were established, its legitimacy would be as firmly rooted in 'generalizable interests' as one might wish.[17] We may want to reply, finally, that the development of market relations leads to a rapid erosion of religious and moral codes of conduct, whose discreet but effective operation, both within and between firms, used to make the cost of enforcing property rights tolerably low. This does not beg the question, but raises another problem. Taking for granted that such moral erosion is an established fact, it is by no means obvious that it is specifically related to capitalist relations, rather than to the increased occupational and geographical mobility, the growing anonymity and independence that are associated with industrialism, whatever the prop-erty regime. It is, therefore, a price to be paid by any society that does not want to do away with the efficiency gains made possible by industrial production, and one that offers no prospect of being reduced through the public appropriation of the means of production. (Here again, the histor-ical record of socialism is not exactly heartening.) Might the process reach a point at which the cost of the repression required to step in for dwin-dling moralities exceeds the long-term gains from industrial develop-ment? Who can tell? But this ominous prospect, if real, would be a problem for optimal socialism and optimal capitalism alike.[18]

Advertising offers another typical example of waste through dispens-able activities commonly attributed to capitalism. Much advertising looks like a ludicrously expensive way in which competing capitalist firms attempt to grab from one another a roughly given total demand. It is expensive because, even though capitalists will only advertise so long as it pays them to do so, they are often driven into mobilizing large funds for no other end than the preservation of their market shares. It is ludicrously expensive because what consumers gain in information about the products is out of proportion with the advertising bill which, in the end, they have to foot. One may feel tempted to reply that optimal capitalism will, therefore, have to include a highly restrictive regulation of advertising. But this would probably be mistaken, for the argument sketched above completely overlooks the main role of advertising in a capitalist economy. Even if advertising gave no information, or only misleading information, about the properties of the product that is being advertised, it would still perform the crucial function of making consumers aware of the existence of alternatives to the product or brand they are currently buying. Competition is a matter of perception, not just of existence, of such alternatives. Advertising is the powerful force that constantly breaks the 'cognitive' monopolies firms tend to enjoy with their regular consumers. In its absence, capitalist firms would not be driven to innovate to anything like the extent they actually are, because their customers would not know, or would take a very long time to learn, about the new products developed by their competitors or about the low prices the latter can offer owing to technical progress. As in the case of monopolies, a shortsighted obsession with static wastage should not obscure the central part played by advertising in the dynamics of capitalism.[19]

6.4 Crises

Thus, neither the unproductive activities nor the market failures briefly discussed in the previous section offer a promising basis for overturning the presumed superiority of optimal capitalism over optimal socialism. However, by far the most serious and credible attack against capitalism on grounds of static inefficiency has focused on another type of market failure not considered so far: capitalism systematically generates massive involuntary unemployment and thereby wastes huge amounts of society's most precious type of productive resource, human labour power. The root of the problem is not, as such, the *anarchic* nature of the capitalist mode of production.[20] In a system without a central co-ordination of economic decisions, and hence with only an *ex post* validation of production, there are, of course, going to be mismatches between supply and demand, and in particular disproportionalities between the wage-goods sector and the capital-goods sector. As moderate fluctuations in the demand for various consumption goods are systematically amplified into major fluctuations in the demand for capital goods, firms find themselves stuck with products they cannot sell, capacity they cannot use, and workers they have to lay off.[21] However, as long as aggregate demand does not shrink, this mechanism only generates ephemeral unemployment, while the economy adjusts to the shifting pattern of demand by gradually moving labour and capital from one branch to another.[22] The theme only becomes relevant if it can be asserted that, beyond such swift adjustments, capitalism generates, for deep-rooted reasons, protracted crises of a cyclical kind or indeed a permanent 'reserve army'. Whether protracted unemployment is cyclical or persists from cycle to cycle, it obviously constitutes a waste of resources which, if significant and deep-rooted enough, may well cast doubt on the presumptive real-libertarian credentials of optimal capitalism.

Theories that claim to establish that protracted crises are inherent in the functioning of capitalism come in two main varieties.[23] So-called *underconsumptionist* theories locate the root of these crises in the fact that workers tend to receive an insufficient share of the product. The central idea is that a lack of aggregate demand generates a cumulative process of overproduction, unemployment, and excess capacity—on the 'Keynesian' pattern—and that the chance of this occurring on a massive scale is the greater, the smaller the share of total production absorbed by workers' consumption.[24] The key point is that whereas the demand for consumption goods is fairly predictable in both size and content because it stems from the needs of the working population, the demand for capital goods is determined by capitalists' expectations about profitability, and hence far more volatile. While it is in principle possible for investment demand to systematically fill any 'demand gap' between total output and demand for consumption goods, its volatility makes this unlikely, and increasingly so as the gap widens.[25]

For the underconsumptionist argument to be relevant in the present context, it is, of course, not sufficient to show that the tendencies it describes have been present in some historically realized forms of capitalism. One must be able to argue that even optimal capitalism must display them to a significant extent. But the actual development of capitalism has already shown that the demand gap can be prevented from widening through an institutional coupling of rises in productivity and in the workers' standard of living, while the debt- or deficit-financing of transfer systems and other public expenditures in downturn periods can function, whether deliberately or not, as a 'built-in stabilizer', as an effective instrument for softening cyclical fluctuations.[26] Now, optimal capitalism is not only bound to involve a systematic boosting of the workers' purchasing power as a direct consequence of the transfers commanded by undominated diversity and basic income maximization. Over and above this, some institutionalized linkage between wages and productivity or some institutionalized braking of downturns through public investment programmes or earnings-related unemployment benefits may well prove useful to forestall protracted crises, or greatly reduce the probability of their occurrence, and thus to avoid wasting the labour of all the workers who would have been jobless had no such measures been taken. If some analysis along these lines is correct, the level of output and hence of basic income that can be durably secured will be higher in a type of capitalism that incorporates such demand-management institutions. Optimal capitalism, therefore, will be a capitalism of this type, thus making itself far less vulnerable to the underconsumptionist attack than the type of capitalism that yielded the heavy historical record of tragic periodic slumps. But even so, underconsumptionists could still say, the very fact that investment decisions are largely in the hands of the private owners of capital maintains the possibility of unemployment through lack of effective demand, cyclically actualized to an extent that may have been reduced but remains significant.

Could it not be argued, however, that even this weaker version of the underconsumptionist argument is misguided? In his plea for a 'share economy', Martin Weitzman's (1984) central thesis is precisely that adjustment through unemployment is not a necessary feature of capitalism, but only of a version of capitalism in which the workers' pay takes the form of fixed wages. If instead the workers' pay took the form of a share corresponding to a fixed proportion of the firm's profits or revenues, Weitzman argues, adjustment would not take the form of lay-offs but of fluctuations in the workers' pay level. Of course, just as the 'fixed' wage levels have to be negotiated at regular intervals, so do the 'fixed' share ratios, and the long-term equilibrium level of pay is the same in both cases. But the fact that a firm's poorer performance (e.g. due to a fall in demand) is reflected in an accordingly lower pay means that firms will want to hang on to their workers for longer than under fixed-wage capitalism, and that workers will retain their employment with the firm as long as doing so does not become so unattractive that they can find a better prospect elsewhere. Excess demand for labour will have become a permanent feature of the economy. Because the benefit that would follow from introducing a share system is at least in part an externality (the benefit of increased job security does not generally offset the cost of decreased income security, unless job prospects in other firms are improved through the generalization of the system), capitalist economies will not spontaneously converge to a generalized share system. But if the institutional framework of capitalism were suitably modified—whether through the differential taxation or the straight prohibition of fixed wages—so as to bring about such a system, cyclical unemployment could be eradicated. Is the price to be paid for this eradication not too high for the share system to have a chance of featuring in optimal capitalism? Under a share system, after all, workers are constantly at the mercy of market conditions driving their wages, be it temporarily, below the subsistence level. But Weitzman's reasoning still applies (though with diminished strength) if workers are allowed to keep part of their pay in the form of a fixed wage and, above all, let us bear in mind that, under optimal capitalism, the share system should be combined, as in James Meade's (1989, 1990) Agathotopia, with a substantial basic income. The latter would arguably make the former acceptable to the workers and thereby workable, while the former would contribute to durably raising the level of the latter by getting rid of the cyclical unemployment emphasized by underconsumptionist theories.[27]

On the other hand, neither demand management nor Weitzman's strategy enables us to handle so easily the second type of crisis-based critique of capitalism. Quite unlike underconsumptionist theories, *profit-squeeze* theories locate the root of protracted cyclical crises in the fact that workers tend to get too much, not too little, of the product. The main idea can be briefly summarized as follows. As capitalist economies expand in periods of boom, they unavoidably reach a point where labour is in short supply and workers, therefore, in a position to get rapid increases in their direct or indirect wages, as firms attempt to retain their current workers (the greater probability of finding another job increase the propensity to quit) and to attract new ones (both from other firms and from the non-capitalist sector). Despite the benefits associated with economies of scale, full capacity utilization, and technical progress, rising wages gradually lead to a fall in the rate of profit, as their negative impact is exacerbated by decreasing work discipline and growing absenteeism (the prospect of being dismissed is no longer frightening), by the fact that firms are increasingly forced to resort to less-qualified and -experienced workers, and by increased pressures on imported raw materials and capital goods as well as on the credit market. This fall in profitability eventually erodes business confidence, and a crisis of overproduction sets in.[28]

It is easy to understand why the reflationary demand-management policies a government could meaningfully use when the downturn stems from some other cause do not make much sense when the problem is a profit squeeze. If successful in maintaining full employment, they simply perpetuate and exacerbate the very source of the trouble, a debilitating pressure on profitability whose effects must be counteracted through more and more deficit spending, with runaway inflation as a consequence. If this is to be avoided, there is no option for the governments of capitalist countries but to refrain from such damaging full-employment policies, and passively accept the recessionary consequences of the profit squeeze. There is, on this view, an unescapable dilemma between a profit squeeze and runaway inflation. And, at least on the assumption of free collective bargaining, the crisis will have to be long if the ultimate source of the trouble is to be, if only temporarily, removed. Profits can only be restored when the ratchet effects of working-class power have been smothered, and explosive inflationary expectations killed, by a protracted recession.[29] Nor would a shift to Weitzmanian capitalism be of much help according to this analysis. Like reflationary demand-management, it would perpetuate the cause of the trouble instead of removing it. Boldened by the absence of unemployment, workers would successfully bargain for such high share ratios that capitalists would stop investing, waiting for the climate to improve. Surely, if even optimal capitalism is necessarily plagued with the massive wastage of long cooling periods of this sort, this should go some way to rehabilitating the chances of optimal socialism.

It may be objected that the situation would be no better under genuine socialism as I have defined it (§ 1.1), that is, when the public ownership of the means of production is combined, as it is not under Soviet-type socialism, with the protection of formal freedom, including the workers' right to engage in free collective bargaining. Sustained full employment will then feed distributional struggles that cannot be expected to be any less acute than under capitalism. Note, however, that to the extent that the surplus is now publicly owned, these distributional struggles need not affect the extent to which it is invested, let alone the extent to which labour resources are fully used. Moreover, the very fact that the surplus is collectively controlled should dispel, or at least mellow, the suspicion that it may be used for purposes other than domestic investment (capitalist consumption, hoarding, foreign investment) and thereby reduce the workers' incentive to make maximum use of their bargaining power for the sake of raising their current wages.[30] So, even though distributional struggle under free-collective-bargaining socialism may have a bad impact on efficiency in other ways, there cannot be a socialist analogue of recurrent profit-squeeze-generated unemployment. Can optimal capitalism be shaped so as to alleviate this disadvantage? Two tracks are worth exploring.

First, what would prevent a capitalist country from introducing a democratically accepted incomes policy, with the wage and price controls this involves, in order to prevent a damaging profit squeeze? There is, after all, some empirical evidence to the effect that in countries in which centralized unions and social-democratic rule make such an agreement possible, economic performance, as measured in terms of investment or employment, is better than elsewhere.[31] True, this type of solution has aroused principled objections, most interestingly within the framework of the so-called theory of the legitimacy crisis. Incomes policies constitute the clearest and most extreme instance of the politicization of class relations characteristic of advanced capitalist countries. As long as the State's intervention in the economy remains marginal, the key economic decisions are taken implicitly, anonymously, and their outcomes, for example, as regards the distribution of income, are perceived as 'natural' by those affected. But as soon as the government's decisions profoundly and visibly affect the working of the economy and thereby the material welfare of individuals and groups within it—most conspicuously in the case of incomes policies—the 'naturalness' disappears and the need for legitimacy arises. As capitalism is based on 'non-generalizable' interests, the intrusion of a 'visible hand' that leaves the capitalist nature of the system untouched is, therefore, bound to lead to a 'legitimacy crisis'.[32] No voluntary wage restraint, no willing subjection to an incomes policy, so the argument goes, can be expected from the organized working class, because it would serve the capitalists' illegitimate interests. Arguing in this way, however, would again amount to begging the very question we are trying to answer. If real-freedom-for-all represents a plausible conception of justice and if some form of capitalism can be shown to achieve it best by securing, durably and consistently with the usual constraints, a higher basic income than any feasible alternative, then capitalism's intrinsic lack of legitimacy cannot be taken for granted in the course of challenging its presumptive superior economic efficiency. As soon as some maximin criterion has been judged more meaningful than equality at any cost, it is no longer enough to say that a capitalist society is a 'class society', that its reproduction rests on the 'privileged appropriation of socially produced wealth', to be able to infer that its organization principle imposes 'non-generalizable interests' (see Habermas 1973: 132–3, 148–9) and hence that workers will never voluntarily agree to a wage restraint that would prevent a profit squeeze and the resulting protracted recession. Why could some form of capitalism not be viewed as a fair socio-economic regime, irrespective of the great inequalities it countenances, if its powerful dynamics is used to feed a basic income at a level that exceeds anything achievable under socialism?[33] And if democratically self-imposed incomes policies would further contribute to this performance, why should they be ruled out on this ground as being impossible? I am not asserting here that optimal capitalism must be a corporatist regime in this sense, but only that, if profit-squeeze-induced recessions are a major source of inefficiency, corporatism is an (at least locally feasible) option that is well worth considering.

In some places, however, the culture or deeply ingrained organization of the working class may make this option unavailable. But there may be alternative solutions. Consider, secondly, Peter Jay's (1977) proposal of a 'workers' co-operative economy', which was prompted by the same problem in the acute form it had been taking in Britain in the mid-1970s. Decentralized collective bargaining, Jay argues, drives capitalism to the wall. But why would the workers not agree to preserve the benefits of a competitive market and keep rewarding capital at market prices, while defusing the risk of explosive collective bargaining by being turned into the owners of their firms? What he proposes is to make any firm that employs over a hundred workers the property of its employees on a one-man-one-vote basis. Capital would be available on capital markets both in the form of fixed-interest loans and in the form of risk-bearing shares that do not convey any power. Capital of the latter kind would be forthcoming, Jay argues, because worker-owned firms would themselves impose the discipline required for them to be able to keep raising outside capital on favourable terms. They would appoint efficient managers and restrain their own wages in such a way that profits would remain high for both distribution and reinvestment. In this capitalism in which workers hire their bosses, collective bargaining has no place. The workers' incomes are directly determined by the anonymous constraints they face on their product and factor markets—at least providing they do not form cartels to enable themselves to raise prices at the expense of workers in other industries, a possibility that can be dealt with using anti-trust policies of a sort analogous to those introduced under more standard variants of capitalism. Though some may want to label it 'market socialism', this co-operative economy, in which capital owners would keep collecting returns on their investments, while firms would still be privately owned and driven by the profit motive, is still well within the boundaries of capitalism. But by turning workers into residual earners, it is meant to make workers more 'responsible', to make them less prone to demand pay levels that squeeze profits and thereby seriously disturb the smooth functioning of a market economy. As usual, one must pay attention to net effects. In particular, one must beware of avoiding recessions at the cost of bringing in the structural unemployment that is specific to an economic system in which hiring decisions are taken by those currently employed: as they are concerned with value added per capita, worker-owned firms of the standard type will tend to hire less than standard capitalist firms, and *a fortiori* than Weitzmanian partnerships, without the creation of new firms taking up the slack.[34] But there are various ways in which this difficulty can be overcome, or at least significantly reduced. Jay himself proposes that capitalist firms employing less than a certain number of workers should be allowed to persist side by side with co-operatives. Moreover, it is important to bear in mind once again that, assuming affluence,[35] optimal capitalism must incorporate a basic income, whose very presence makes it systematically easier to start new businesses, whether on one's own, with partners, or with waged workers (see § 2.4).

Thus, if it is true that capitalism's claim to greater economic efficiency is seriously challenged by the systematic occurrence of profit-squeeze-induced recessions, optimal capitalism can in principle opt for either a corporatist or a co-operative guise, depending on whether working-class traditions and modes of organization make centralized bargaining or decentralized co-operatives a more accessible strategy. Both modifications would be moves towards the grey area, but still quite a distance from the public ownership of the means of production constitutive of socialism. Admittedly, a pure corporatist or co-operative economy cannot at the same time be a pure share economy *à la* Weitzman, and the best strategy for systematically blocking demand-induced recessions may, therefore, clash with the best strategy for warding off profit-squeeze-induced recessions. But impure variants of the various strategies can to some extent be combined, and my purpose is not, in any case, to provide a full institutional characterization of optimal capitalism. To what extent corporatism, co-operatives, and/or partnerships should be encouraged or imposed in order viably to maximize the economic efficiency of a form of capitalism that incorporates a basic income, supplementary targeted transfers, predictable taxation, and environmental protection, depends to a significant extent on the particular history and circumstances of the country concerned. The purpose of this discussion is not to provide the analysis needed to single out the optimal combination. It is, more modestly, to illustrate how wide a spectrum of resources is available to optimal capitalism in this context. The existing stock of capitalist institutions does not exhaust the arsenal that can be mobilized. The very introduction of an unconditional income would facilitate further institutional changes, for example, towards a share economy *à la* Weitzman or towards a co-operative economy *à la* Jay. And this potential provides further ammunition against the claim that capitalism's ability to yield a sustainably high basic income is badly affected by the static inefficiency it owes to massive and inevitable cyclical unemployment.

6.5 *The reserve army of the unemployed*

We cannot leave the topic of unemployment yet. Even if one admits that capitalism can equip itself with institutions that prevent or minimize unwelcome cyclical unemployment, it may still massively underuse the available labour power due to the permanent presence, in good times and bad, of a 'reserve army' of unemployed workers. Why should this reserve army be an intrinsic feature of capitalism? We cannot be satisfied with the answer that it is in the capitalists' interest that there should be one, or that it is a requisite of the smooth functioning of the capitalist system. Although it is in each individual capitalist's interest that there should be a large number of unemployed people wanting to work at the going wage, it should also be in each capitalist's interest to offer jobs to some members of this reserve army for less than the wage she is currently paying her own workers. Since capitalists do not act as a class but as so many self-interested individuals, the functionalist argument gives no sound reason for expecting them to stop bidding against one another for potential workers before reaching the point at which no one with the right skills is left involuntarily unemployed at the going wage.[36]

Thus, owing to faulty microfoundations, the functionalist argument fails. But it does not follow that any attempt to prove the capitalist necessity of a reserve army—or, in another parlance, the existence of equilibrium involuntary unemployment—must likewise fail. The presumption that, at equilibrium, labour markets will clear rests on a number of common assumptions some of which are worth scrutinizing. One of them is that while the long-term demand for labour increases as wages fall, the long-term supply of labour decreases. The latter assumption is plausible enough for skilled labour: the less a particular skill is rewarded (relative to others), the less people will bother to acquire it. It is also plausible enough, even for unskilled labour, as long as there is a subsistence economy, an informal sector, to which workers can retreat as market wages drop. But under contemporary conditions and abstracting for a moment from all transfers, propertyless households have no choice but to sell their labour power and will, therefore, have to *increase* their supply of labour as the pay for a normal working day falls below subsistence. There is then no guarantee that the demand for labour will ever catch up with the supply, short of the point at which the supply dries up through starvation.[37] This argument suffices to invalidate an unquestioning faith in the automatic clearing of labour markets if capitalism were freed of minimum wage legislation and of the implicit minimum wages constituted by unemployment compensation and conditional minimum income provisions. But optimal capitalism will neither be transfer-free nor need to involve an implicit or explicit minimum wage at the subsistence level. What a substantial unconditional income would do is precisely to turn the labour market into a market similar (in this respect) to any other, by systematically making an alternative option available to the sellers. It would provide to contemporary workers what the traditional sector provided to their predecessors, and to the unskilled what working at a lower level of skill provides to the skilled. The higher the basic income, the more likely it is that the labour supply will unambiguously decrease as the wage rate falls. Optimal capitalism is thereby protected against one non-functionalist reason for believing a sizeable reserve army to be unavoidable under capitalist conditions.[38]

There are, however, a number of microeconomic arguments in support of the systematic presence of a reserve army, that would seem to apply even in the presence of a substantial basic income. Some of them are associated with the various versions of the efficiency-wage approach, already referred to (§ 4.4). These theories all rest on the assumption that profitability, and hence the equilibrium demand for labour, is not a monotonically decreasing function of the wage level, because the latter affects profits not only negatively as a cost, but also positively through its impact on productivity.[39] The consequence of this impact is that even in the absence of minimum wage legislation or trade union action, a capitalist labour market will fail to clear: the profit motive will not drive capitalists to exhaust the reserve army, for even though the labour cost would be lower at the market-clearing wage rate, the work effort would be less, indeed so much less that more would be lost than gained in the process. How large a reserve army can be expected as a result depends on a number of parameters, including, for example, the level and structure of replacement incomes or the ease with which existing technology permits the monitoring of work effort. Whatever the answer to this question, we here have a powerful set of arguments to the effect that persistent involuntary unemployment is intrinsic to capitalism. Yet, however large the deviation from the market-clearing wage that can be explained in this way, taking efficiency-wage arguments seriously does—arguably— nothing to strengthen the case in favour of socialism's superior economic efficiency.[40] The existence of involuntary unemployment or, equivalently, of employment rents, is here simply the counterpart of an efficient use of employed workers. Socialism's economic efficiency would be enhanced, not diminished, if firms were given the option of hiring people and offering wages in the most profitable fashion, and efficiency wages and their consequences would, therefore, need to be part of optimal socialism no less than of optimal capitalism.[41] Note, moreover, that in neither type of regime would real-freedom-for-all thereby legitimize massive joblessness and involuntary exclusion from the sphere of employment, for, as emphasized earlier (§ 4.5), the rents generated by efficiency-wage mechanisms need not be reflected in straight joblessness, but simply in the fact that some would like to work more hours or would prefer to swap their jobs for someone else's with no greater skill requirements. The point of providing as high a basic income as possible is precisely, under both types of regime, to give all maximal real possibilities to live the life they would like to lead, and, therefore, in particular to give those who attach particular importance to having a job, the real possibility of finding or creating one, be it at the low level of pay which the height of the unconditional basic income makes acceptable.

Finally, persistent involuntary unemployment could be attributed to the unavoidable presence of monopolistic practices in the labour market, with trade unions insisting on wages permanently above the market-clearing *and* efficiency levels, in their members' interests but at other workers' expense. This risk, which is just a more diffuse version of the problem raised by profit-squeeze-induced recessions (§ 6.4), pertains to any society, whether capitalist or socialist, that allows free collective bargaining. To prevent this risk from materializing, one could think of a permanent economy-wide incomes policy or of a compulsory generalization of workers' co-operatives along the lines discussed in the previous section. But even less radical transformations, such as limitation of the right to strike could go some way towards abolishing this source of static inefficiency. Unlike the right to form an association, in particular an independent trade union, the right to strike, that is, to have one's job frozen while staying away from it, is no part of formal freedom. Hence, whether under capitalism or socialism, real-libertarianism allows it to be restricted or even scrapped if this were to improve the opportunity dimension of real freedom by increasing the economy's efficiency and hence the highest feasible level of basic income. When entertaining the idea that optimal capitalism, or for that matter optimal socialism, should restrict the right to strike or get rid of it altogether, one must—needless to say—remain very cautious. Suggesting that such a step be taken in the name of real-freedom-for-all assumes great confidence in the power of universal suffrage, which itself was only conquered, in many places, through the pressure exercised by a succession of general strikes. There may be decisive indirect arguments, rooted in an analysis of the *de facto* balance of power in democratic regimes, in favour of protecting some appropriately specified right to strike. But this would be an indirect matter of strategy, not a direct matter of justice. Unlike the right to quit, or the right to an income if one quits, the right to strike is never an entailment of real-freedom-for-all. And recent labour history is replete with examples of particularistic strikes waged to defend or increase the privileges of powerful categories of well-paid workers. Long past are the days when the interests of organized labour could practically be identified with the imperatives of social justice. Hence, there should be nothing sacrosanct about the right to strike, and scrapping it can legitimately be considered, along with other potentially efficiency-increasing measures, as a way of improving a regime's performance in terms of real-freedom-for-all.

Might taking such a step be easier under (formal-freedom respecting) socialism than under capitalism? I cannot see why it would be. How acceptable and hence feasible it is to restrict the right to strike and the collective protection workers derive from it should rather depend on the extent to which each worker is individually protected through the real availability of sufficiently attractive alternatives, and hence, crucially, on the level of the basic income. Thus, if for some other reason one type of regime can be expected to yield a higher basic income, its economic efficiency and hence its potential for financing a higher basic income may be further increased as a result of thus being enabled to get rid of what constitutes not only a major source of lost working days, but also and more importantly, of labour market rigidity, and hence of misallocation of productive resources. If socialism enjoyed this advantage, it could, therefore, further increase it by gaining immunity from strikes. But discussing the reserve-army arguments—or indeed any of the other static-efficiency-based arguments in favour of socialism—has provided no independent reason of any weight for discrediting the presumption that the prior advantage is rather on the side of capitalism.

6.6 *Creative destruction*

The time has now come to remember that several of the most famous arguments in favour of socialism have focused on its superior dynamic efficiency, on its greater ability to generate new productive resources, rather than on its being better at using existing ones. For example, the theory of the falling rate of profit, when interpreted as a theory of breakdown rather than of crises, aims to show that capitalism is bound to become ever worse at accumulating capital, while the famous assertion, central to historical materialism, that the development of the productive forces tends to become 'fettered' under capitalism is most naturally interpreted as a claim about capitalism's systematically suboptimal choice of techniques. One may wonder, however, whether such arguments are relevant at all from a real-libertarian point of view. Accumulation and technical progress increase the productive potential of future generations. By doing so, they can no doubt improve the real freedom of the least-advantaged in those generations. But the saving required for accumulation and the research and development required for technical progress represent a cost to the present generation, a diversion of resources that could have been used to improve the situation of its worst off member. And it would, therefore, be illegitimate to keep this member's real freedom down in order to increase beyond this level the real freedom of the worst off in the next generation.[42] If it could be shown that, say, socialism is far better than capitalism in terms of dynamic efficiency thus conceived, it would follow that the real freedom that can be granted to the worst off in the current generation of a society that has been socialist for some generations is greater, *ceteris paribus*, than had it been capitalist all along. But the question is not whether it is better, from a real-libertarian perspective, that a society should *have been* socialist rather than capitalist for some generations, but whether it is better, for the sake of the real freedom of its (present or future) worst off member, that it should opt for socialism *now*.

And yet, from a real-libertarian perspective, dynamic efficiency considerations are of crucial importance. Remember that the unconditional income must be pitched at a level that is sustainable across generations. If there is demographic growth, it is obvious enough that this requires economic growth at the same pace, and hence that a regime which fosters accumulation and technical progress more than others do, *for a given current level of basic income*, will enjoy an important advantage. In a dynamically less efficient economy, the current level of basic income may prove unsustainable in the next, more numerous, generation, whereas it is not in the dynamically more efficient economy. Even in the absence of demographic growth, and hence in the absence of a (justice-based) need for net growth, dynamic efficiency is still of crucial importance. If, again for a given current level of basic income, one regime has a greater propensity to accumulate and innovate, and hence expand production, it follows that it has more leeway for increasing the basic income now above its current level and hence has the potential for sustaining a higher basic income across generations. Thus, the optimal regime—basic income level included—need not be the one with the highest rate of growth. With a stationary population, it need not even have a positive rate of growth. Yet, having a greater propensity to grow—displaying, subject to the usual constraints, a higher rate of accumulation and/or technical progress at given levels of basic income—provides a socio-economic regime with a highly relevant advantage in terms of real-freedom-for-all.[43] As we shall see later (§ 6.7), whether a particular socio-economic regime does better or worse than another in terms of dynamic efficiency so conceived may crucially depend on the level of basic income that features in the background of the comparison. Throughout the present section, however, I shall abstract from this possibility and tacitly assume that a regime's greater dynamic efficiency (its systematically higher rate of capital accumulation and/or technical progress) at, say, a zero level of basic income, means *ipso facto* that there will be more available for distribution in the form of a basic income.

Is there any reason to believe, first, that socialism systematically induces faster accumulation than capitalism? There was a time at which this could be taken for granted because of the Soviet regime's apparently far better performance in terms of growth.[44] Today, of course, tables have turned, and only theory can rescue the old presumption—if anything can. Several arguments have been constructed to show that capitalism has a systematic tendency to accumulate less than theoretically possible. One of them relies on the theory of the falling rate of profit and draws on the plausible assumption that the rate of profit constitutes the maximum rate of accumulation in order to conclude that capitalist accumulation will proceed at an ever-diminishing rate. But quite apart from the fatal flaws that affect the proof of the necessity of the alleged secular tendency, this argument raises, in the present context, the decisive objection that, if it were correct, it would similarly establish a falling rate of accumulation under socialism.[45] A more sophisticated argument, inspired by Lange (1936) and elaborated by Yunker (1986), gives a key role to a positive difference between the rate of saving determined by a democratically chosen social rate of discount and the one determined by the capital owners' self-interest. But it relies on a very shaky conjecture about the politically effective rate of time preference of the members of a democratic polity. Probably the most persuasive argument of this first category, variants of which have been developed by Lancaster (1973) and Przeworski and Wallerstein (1982), attempts to establish the dynamic inefficiency of (organized) capitalism by looking at it as a game between two groups of actors. Capital owners determine how profits are divided between investment and consumption, while (organized) workers determine how value added is divided between profits and wages. In such a context, it can be shown that the rate of accumulation will generally be suboptimal, because of the workers' lack of trust in the capitalists' propensity to reinvest what they have been allowed to keep. One will have recognized yet another facet of the basic phenomenon also reflected in profit-squeezed-induced recessions and union-caused structural unemployment and the associated static inefficiencies. Hence again the suggestion, if this source of dynamic inefficiency proved significant, that optimal capitalism should be shaped in a corporatist or co-operative direction (§ 6.4) or even possibly in a way that undercuts the relevance of collective bargaining (§ 6.5). At least in those capitalist economies in which, for some reason, such solutions proved unfeasible or unsuitable, it cannot be excluded that the public control over investment constitutive of socialism would provide the basis for a systematically higher rate of capital accumulation.

Whether this would translate into a higher propensity to grow—or in greater dynamic efficiency overall—depends on how the optimal version of each type of regime scores along the second dimension of dynamic efficiency, technical progress. More than any other, this is an area which has been feeding the empirical presumption in favour of capitalism's superior dynamic efficiency. The presumption has never been that, for deeply rooted reasons, capitalism is systematically better at accumulating, but that it is systematically better at innovating. It cannot be denied that capitalism's historical record on this count is rather impressive, not just—as Marx himself was keen to emphasize—compared to precapitalist regimes, but also—contrary to one of Marx's most central claims—compared to all past and present variants of socialism. Moreover, this plausible empirical generalization admits of a straightforward explanation which locates this advantage at the very core of what distinguishes capitalism from socialism. Under capitalism, specialization and subjection to market competition makes innovation a matter of life or death. This fosters technical progress both through an incentive mechanism and through a selection mechanism. The threat of falling profits and bankruptcy or absorption strongly motivates firms to keep looking for new products and more efficient processes and thereby enables them to overcome again and again managerial inertia, bureaucratic ossification, and workers' resistance to recurrent technological change. The muting of competition intrinsic to public ownership is bound to give socialism a lesser ability to overcome these powerful forces.[46] At the same time, capitalist competition keeps removing economic power from those who have proved unsuccessful innovators and unwise investors, while concentrating it in the hands of those who find and keep finding the cheapest ways of producing the goods that best satisfy demand. No similarly powerful selection mechanism regulates the allocation of the power to innovate under public ownership.[47]

Can this strong presumption in favour of capitalism be overturned, as Marx himself and many in the Marxist tradition firmly believed it could?[48] In the history of the debate on these issues, four main arguments have been used in support of the claim that technical progress can be expected to be faster under socialism than under capitalism. First, Marx himself bases his central thesis about the irrational nature of capitalism on the claim that capitalist relations of production *fetter* the development of the productive forces, in the sense that labour productivity grows less fast than it would under socialist relations. Why? Because competition forces capitalists to select techniques using a criterion of profit maximization that takes both the labour cost and the (profit-inclusive) capital cost into account, whereas socialist planners can choose them using a criterion of (dead and living) labour cost. As a result, so the argument goes, the techniques that prevail under capitalism will tend to be less capital-intensive and associated with a lower labour productivity than those prevailing under socialism. But this argument is fallacious, for it has been persuasively argued that in order to determine which technique should be used, rational socialist planners must not use labour values but weight differently labour of different periods, using a rate of interest that reflects the rate of accumulation and the rate of time preference. As a result, the techniques chosen under socialism will hardly differ, if at all, from those chosen under capitalism, where the rate of profit is used to weight past labour.[49]

A second influential argument has been offered by Oskar Lange (1937*a*: 128–33). In the debate between advocates of capitalism and socialism, the key issue is, according to him, whether real-life capitalism is compatible with sustained technical progress. His own answer is that it is not. Under monopoly capitalism there is a tendency to keep older machinery for longer, until it is fully depreciated, instead of being forced by intense competition to use the most advanced technology. 'When this state of things will have become unbearable, when its incompatibility with economic progress will have become obvious, and when it will be recognized that it is impossible to return to free competition, or to have successful public control of enterprises and of investment without taking them out of private hands, then socialism will remain as the only solution available.'[50] To this argument, Schumpeter's famous analysis of monopolistic competition, already referred to in connection with the static inefficiency associated with monopolies (§ 6.3), provides a powerful reply. 'The introduction of new methods of production and new commodities is hardly compatible with perfect—and perfectly prompt—competition from the start. And this means that the bulk of what we call economic progress is incompatible with it' (Schumpeter 1943: 105). Monopolistic competition creates better conditions for the creative destruction associated with capitalist innovation. The ever-present possibility of substitutes maintains a fair amount of pressure, even in the most concentrated industry, while the room to manœuvre opened up by market concentration can shelter the massive investments required by major breakthroughs.[51]

A third argument that is sometimes aired sees in the secrecy required by profit maximization a major hindrance to technical progress. By making technological knowledge available to all as soon as it has been produced, a socialist economy could innovate at a far faster rate. However, as pointed out by Schumpeter, Joan Robinson, and others, this argument ignores the feedback link from the diffusion to the production of technological knowledge. The pattern of the argument is the same as the one just applied to monopolistic practices: 'A system—any system, economic or other—that at *every* given point of time fully utilizes its possibilities to the best advantage may yet in the long run be inferior to a system that does so at *no* given point of time, because the latter's failure to do so may be a condition for the level or speed of long-run performance' (Schumpeter ibid. 83). The advantages a firm derives from using a technique or supplying a product that is not known to competitors account for much of what spurs a firm into allocating substantial resources in a way that will lead to innovations. By slowing down the diffusion of knowledge, the patent system makes sure that there is more knowledge to diffuse.[52]

Finally, a fourth and more recent argument stresses the fact that capitalists select methods of production which forgo improvements in productive efficiency in order to maintain their power over workers. This fact, Samuel Bowles (1985) claims, 'is fundamental to the Marxian assertion that the production potential of a society ("the forces of production") is inhibited (or "fettered") by the specifically institutional structure of the economy'. It does make a difference, in other words, whether capital hires labour or labour hires capital. As long as capital hires labour, technical progress will constantly be hindered by the capital owners' concern to choose the sort of machinery and work organization that will enable them adequately to control the workers' activity. In the present context, the main problem with this interesting argument is that it fails to provide a plausible ground for believing that such a departure from technical efficiency is not required for analogous reasons in a socialist context. Workers cannot simply be assumed to be more moral or altruistic under a different regime of capital ownership, and the degree to which their self-interest coincides with the firm's performance depends essentially on the latter's size and on the extent to which workers' pay includes a revenue-sharing component—as in the co-operatives and partnerships discussed earlier (§ 6.4), irrespective of whether the property regime is capitalist or socialist. Those in charge of choosing techniques in a socialist society will, therefore, have to take into account the risk of shirking, in a way that would not significantly differ from that characteristic of capitalism. Thus, even if one believes that 'conflict at the point of production' generates a major discrepancy between actual and optimal technical change, there is here again no serious hope that this may overturn the pro-capitalist presumption with which we started.[53]

Indeed, when discussing the issue of technical progress, authors sympathetic to socialism precisely recommend that socialist economies should introduce reforms that will bring their incentive structure closer to that of capitalism: they must decentralize decision-making, harden the budget constraint, allow firms to retain at least part of their profits.[54] This strongly suggests that there are ways in which optimal socialism could noticeably improve upon the performance, along this dimension, of actual socialist economies, even though the balance of the arguments reviewed does not warrant serious hope that, relative to optimal capitalism, this could turn a serious handicap into an advantage.[55]

6.7 Popular sovereignty

The previous sections were partly intended to illustrate how subtle, intricate, speculative, tentative the discussion of the relative efficiency of capitalism and socialism unavoidably needs to be, and to show how this discussion is affected by the choice of our real-libertarian criterion of assessment. But they were also meant to convey my own general impression, as a keen critical reader of an admittedly small portion of the vast literature that has a bearing on this issue. My overall impression is that it would be very hard indeed to overturn the strong, empirically supported and theoretically motivated, presumption in favour of capitalism's superior economic efficiency that formed our point of departure (§ 6.1). In particular, none of the possible advantages of socialism in terms of capital accumulation or various aspects of static efficiency offers a serious prospect of being able to offset the dynamic impulse capitalism owes to the imperative to innovate or perish. These advantages, as we have seen, are often the straight counterparts of key aspects of capitalism's efficiency (think of advertising or efficiency wages), or disappear when compared to some feasible form of capitalism (think of counter-cyclical state intervention or Weitzmanian partnerships), or rely in viciously circular fashion on the assumption that capitalism is bound to be perceived as unjust (think of the enforcement of capitalist property rights or the unavoidability of recurrent profit squeezes). Thus, I very much doubt that anything like a persuasive case can be made to the effect that socialism could boast, the historical evidence notwithstanding, greater economic efficiency than capitalism. This is not, and could not be, a tightly argued conclusion, only a conviction nourished by casual evidence and the less casual screening of scores of arguments. It is, therefore, no more, but no less, than a challenge to further evidence and further arguments.

Suppose, then, that optimal capitalism can safely be expected to be superior to optimal socialism in terms of economic efficiency. It may be tempting to conclude immediately that it will then also be superior as regards real-freedom-for-all. But this would be premature. From the concession of capitalism's superior economic efficiency it does *not* follow that the highest level of basic income that can be sustained under capitalism, subject to our constraints of formal freedom and undominated diversity, is greater than the highest sustainable level under socialism. Why not? One potential reason, already hinted at in passing, is that either or both of our constraints might be satisfiable at a significantly lower cost under socialism than under capitalism. Formal freedom, for example, would be cheaper to protect under socialism, other things being equal, if less police were needed to protect society's means of production when they are publicly owned than when they are privately owned (see § 6.3). And undominated diversity might be easier to achieve under socialism if a weaker pressure to consume created less need for targeted transfers to those with a low earning power (see § 6.2). But I have already indicated why I do not believe at least these versions of the first reason to hold much promise.

There is, however, a second reason for challenging the inference from economic efficiency to leximin real freedom which cannot be dismissed so easily. It relates to the crucial importance of *popular sovereignty*, defined as characterizing a political community whose options are constrained only by conditions, such as limited material resources, which are independent of anyone's will.[56] It follows from this definition that popular sovereignty is threatened, in particular, by the political community's individual members' discretion in using resources at their disposal. Paradigmatic illustrations are provided by socialist Chile, in so far as Allende's experiment came to an end as a result of the truck-owners' strike; by socialist France, in so far as the Mauroy Government's expansionary policies (in 1981) collapsed as a result of the French citizens' propensity to spend their increased purchasing power on foreign goods; or by the constraints on egalitarian wage policies that stem from the fact that the skilled workers trained at great expense in a comparatively egalitarian country may choose to emigrate to less egalitarian countries, where their skills command higher net wages.

But probably the main threat to popular sovereignty under capitalist conditions, and uncontroversially the one that is most relevant to the choice between capitalism and socialism, is the one that is rooted directly in the private ownership of the means of production.[57] Whether or not it is concentrated in few hands, whether or not those who own it are driven by purely selfish motives, private capital tends to move where profitability is highest and to be invested at a rate that depends on the level of profitability.[58] Now, even if the basic income were not financed at all out of capital income but entirely out of wages, so the argument goes, the effect on profits is bound to be negative. By taxing wages and—above all—by giving everyone a substantial unconditional income and thus strengthening the bargaining power of each individual worker, one forces capitalists to pay higher pre-tax wages and/or to provide more attractive working conditions. As a result, capitalists will invest less or invest elsewhere, and because innovation is closely tied to investment, technical progress will also suffer in the country concerned. Hence, the highest level of basic income sustainable under capitalism will be far lower than would be the case if investment behaviour were insensitive to the level of basic income—indeed quite possibly lower than under optimal socialism, despite the latter's admittedly inferior economic efficiency as discussed in the previous sections. Under socialism, society as a whole controls the allocation of the surplus and, if it decides to introduce a substantial basic income, it will not defeat its own decision by using capital in a way that makes such a grant unsustainable. Hence, even if one takes it for granted that socialism is economically less efficient than capitalism—that is, the maximum output achievable under capitalism (at some, possibly zero, level of basic income) is greater than the maximum output achievable under socialism—it may still be able to finance a higher basic income than capitalism could, thanks to its greater ability sustainably to allocate its output in the required way.[59] This provides, I believe, the strongest real-libertarian case against capitalism and therefore, for those committed to real-libertarianism or neighbouring positions, the strongest available defence of socialism.

It may be objected that even this strongest available defence is pretty weak if, as is argued by contemporary economic advocates of a basic income, the introduction of an unconditional income in the context of advanced capitalist societies would not depress but boost profitability. Quibbling about marginal tax rates, they argue, is of little significance, in regard to the massive contribution a basic income would make to rendering our economy more dynamic, less cripplingly rigid, less stiflingly conflict-ridden than it currently is, or would otherwise be. The main argument of this type stresses the crucial role a basic income would play, directly and indirectly, in fostering the flexibility of our economies.[60] With a significant unconditional income, individuals are enabled not only to bear but to make good use of repeated and protracted periods in which their market activities earn them little or nothing, for example as they retrain between two jobs, as they learn new skills on the job, as they keep old skills alive through part-time work in a period of (voluntarily or involuntarily) reduced professional activity, as they launch a new business, or as they undergo the vicissitudes of the market *qua* self-employed or workers in a profit-sharing enterprise. As a consequence and without the (often opaque, inhibiting, and costly) aid of special schemes, adjustments of all sorts are made easier, non-standard forms of enterprises such as labour–capital partnerships and workers' co-operatives are made more attractive, and an entrepreneurial spirit is encouraged throughout society. This direct and individual impact on the flexibility of the economy is further reinforced by an indirect, collective impact. If each individual worker is protected by the availability of a significant unconditional income *and* the employment possibilities the latter opens up, there is less justification for a number of regulations which currently constrain the labour market, such as restrictions on patterns of working-time or minimum wage legislations. The sort of flexibility which modern technology increasingly requires could, therefore, acceptably be traded by the labour movement against the income security provided by an unconditional income.

If, and in so far as, arguments of this sort can actually be sustained, the introduction of a basic income and the rise of its level do not constitute a liability but an asset in terms of profitability. Although the existence of such a marriage of justice and efficiency is, or would be, of great practical significance for someone committed to real-libertarianism in an advanced capitalist society, it does not yet do away with the pro-socialist argument. As the basic income increases—and especially once it starts increasing beyond the level of the conditional income guarantees it would gradually replace—it is bound to reach a point from which any attempt to raise it further would depress profitability, and may thereby trigger off a steady and damaging decrease in (domestic) investment. This is where the pro-socialist argument comes into its own, for a socialist country is not similarly constrained by the profitability criterion. This does not mean that a socialist society need not ensure that a sufficient part of the total product be left for investment—as we have seen (§ 6.6), the rate of accumulation matters to the sustainable achievement of leximin real freedom. Nor does it mean that the way in which a socialist society distributes the remaining part faces no constraint. Under (formal-freedom respecting) socialism too, distributing a higher proportion of total income in a contribution-insensitive way—in the form of an unconditional income and undominated-diversity-securing transfers—will not necessarily yield a higher amount in absolute terms because of reduced work incentives. But because a socialist society is not submitted to the constraint of making (domestic) investment sufficiently attractive to private capital owners, the absolute amount available for contribution-insensitive redistribution is likely to fall less steeply than under capitalism once it has become a substantial proportion of national income. Consequently, socialism may well have a significantly lower productive potential than capitalism—the total income its most favourable variant could sustainably generate may be far less than what is sustainably achievable under the most favourable variant of capitalism—and yet, thanks to the political community's direct control over society's surplus, its optimal variant may manage to raise the basic income sustainably above what is achievable under optimal capitalism. Owing to a crucial advantage in terms of popular sovereignty, socialism would outperform capitalism on real-libertarian standards.[61]

This argument looks particularly powerful, of course, in the context of an open economy with considerable transnational capital mobility. Then the credible threat that constrains redistributive measures is not just that, once profitability is under attack, capitalists will start consuming or hoarding a growing part of their profits. It is, far more disturbingly, that net investment will come to a halt and that even the current means of production will stop being replaced, as domestic profits are channelled abroad while foreign investment dries up. In such a context, the sort of corporatist pact discussed above as a way of checking various sources of static or dynamic inefficiency (§§ 6.4–6) is not exactly promising, as the party who would lose from the profitability-damaging pact is also the one who can most easily leave.[62] Nor would it help if the capitalist country concerned tried to impose tight restrictions on capital movement. Not only are there strong reasons to doubt that such measures would be effective, given the functioning of today's financial markets, the ubiquitous presence of multinational corporations, and the endless possibilities afforded by ingenious accounting. Even (indeed, especially) if they were effective, one would still have to account with the pre-emptive outflow that can hardly be avoided, given the prior debate which such tough measures are bound to necessitate in a real-libertarian-inspired and, therefore, (for instrumental reasons) democratic country. In order to repatriate at least part of the capital thus lost—and also in order to keep attracting foreign capital despite the new rules—the country concerned would have to offer levels of profitability in excess (owing to a risk premium) of what was previously needed to retain it. Moreover, even if it could act so swiftly and effectively that it would not suffer from much capital outflow despite the lower profitability, it would still be vulnerable to the departure of skilled labour which would indirectly suffer from the lowering of profitability (as well as directly from higher tax rates) and could not be retained through analogous means save at the cost of violating the constraint of formal freedom. Most fundamentally, as long as it was subjected to the world division of labour, no limitation of factor mobility would free the country from the constraint of competitiveness: if it was to keep acquiring the foreign goods it needed, it would have to keep producing goods the outside world wanted to buy at a cost it was willing to pay. If it did not keep pace with its competitors, it would have to expend ever more resources in order to be able to afford its essential imports. The standard of living of its citizens would suffer as a result, and hence also the level of basic income it could sustain.

In such a context, there seems to be no way in which a capitalist country could viably push the level of its basic income far above what is best for its overall profitability. At first sight, this completes and strengthens the case for socialism sketched above. But on closer inspection, not all of what I have just said is good news for the advocates of socialism. To start with, the transition problem I mentioned applies *a fortiori*, and in a more acute form, to any capitalist country that contemplates moving even further, for this sort of reason, into the grey area that separates capitalism from socialism. Even if there are feasible variants of socialism that sustainably yield a higher basic income than optimal capitalism, none of them may be accessible from capitalism, because of the permanent costs of the massive capital flight that would precede the transition. But let us leave the transition problem aside, either by assuming that the transition to socialism (through socialization of the bulk of the means of production) might take capitalists by surprise or by considering a country that is already socialist. Even though preventing the outflow of capital is now no longer a problem, the extent to which economic performance can be sacrificed for the benefit of a higher basic income is still very limited. Not only would good profitability prospects make it possible to attract private foreign investment. Not only would the country have to come up with a level of economic performance and a distribution of the latter's benefits that enabled it to retain precious skilled labour: socialism is crucially different from collectivism in this respect. Above all, a socialist country immersed in the world market would have to mind its competitiveness just about as much as would a capitalist one, for fear of losing its customers or of managing to keep them only at the cost of a steadily falling standard of living. So, in the world market we have come to live in, there is *some* leeway to be gained from a better grip on domestic capital, but the constraints are hardly looser, as each country's ability to sustain a generous basic income is crucially dependent on its competitiveness, itself largely a function of the capital and skilled labour the country manages to keep or attract.

What about disconnection from the world market? Forgoing the possibility of acquiring foreign goods and technologies would no doubt depress the average standard of living. But might this not reinstate the popular sovereignty which socialism, or socialism alone, could not confer, thereby making a higher basic income viable despite a lower overall standard of living? This would ignore one constraint which real-libertarianism would not allow to be removed and whose full force is precisely most likely to make itself felt under the circumstances we are contemplating here: the need to retain those skilled workers who could realistically find far more attractive jobs abroad and could not legitimately be prevented either from being informed about the existence of these opportunities or from leaving the country in order to seize them. By cutting itself off, a country emancipates itself from the constraint of competitiveness. But it thereby also deprives itself of the benefits of world-wide division of labour and technological development, at the expense of its long-term ability to retain its own human capital and hence to fund a substantial basic income beyond the very short term.[63] So, all in all, there is no doubt something important to be said in favour of socialism on grounds of popular sovereignty. And under imaginable circumstances, the advantage optimal socialism would enjoy over optimal capitalism in this respect might be sufficient to topple the efficiency-based presumption in favour of the latter: under such circumstances, although the most output-oriented feasible variant of socialism may be unable sustainably to produce as much as the most output-oriented feasible variant of capitalism could, optimal socialism would still be able to sustain, under the constraints of formal freedom and undominated diversity, a higher level of basic income than optimal capitalism. But in the world we live in, the constraints that would remain after the hold over the means of production is secured look so strong that the advantage so gained would count for precious little.[64]

6.8 *Steering clear of Penguins Island*

So, is capitalism justified? Of course not—but it can be. Of course not, because although optimal capitalism can reasonably be expected to be superior, in terms of real-freedom-for-all, to optimal socialism, most variants of capitalism cannot, and many of them are blatantly far worse than optimal socialism would be. But capitalism *can* be justified, providing its tremendous productive potential is appropriately constrained and used in the service of real-freedom-for-all. However, some of what has just been said in the previous section contains worrying suggestions about what this is likely to lead to in the sort of world-wide market economy in which we now live. To spell this out, let us consider the right-wing use to which John Rawls's theory of justice is beginning to be put, as an ideological justification, not of further progress beyond advanced welfare state capitalism, but of a dramatic regression below it. What is the reasoning? Rawls proposes, roughly, that one should maximin socio-economic advantages subject to the respect of fundamental liberties. On what scale? Not on a world scale, but (at most) at the level of each particular well-ordered society.[65] In the sort of world sketched above, each country's independent pursuit of justice so conceived will tend to degenerate into a mad rush for competitiveness, as even the maintenance of current types and levels of welfare state provisions is threatened by an ever-fiercer competition for scarce factors of production and market shares. Rawls's justice as fairness, the concern for the fate of the worst off subject to the respect of fundamental liberties, would then justify ever-growing levels of inequality on the plausible factual assumption that, in this context, attempting to reduce them in order to improve the situation of the least-advantaged would have a long-term negative impact on the latter. This is the contemporary version of Anatole France's (1907: 83–4) *Penguins Island* argument: what the public interest demands, said the spokesman of the island's wealthy farmers to the assembled people, 'is that little should be asked from those who possess a lot; for otherwise the rich would be less rich and the poor would be poorer. The poor live off the wealth of the rich; this is why this wealth is sacred. Don't touch it, it would be gratuitous wickedness. Taking from the rich would not do you much good, for there are not many of them; and instead it would deprive you of all resources by thrusting the country into poverty.'[66] True, real-libertarianism differs from justice as fairness. But the formal-freedom-constrained leximinning of opportunities is sufficiently close to the fundamental-liberties-constrained maximinning of socio-economic advantages for it to raise strictly analogous worries. Far from replacing the welfare state's stingy and imprisoning means-tested benefits by a generous and liberating citizens' income, one will have the greatest difficulty in maintaining even only the targeted transfers required by undominated diversity. As the world market strengthens its grip, one seems to be facing ever-worse prospects for making any moral progress as measured by real-libertarian standards and heading instead for an ethical disaster as our species is whirled into the next millennium by anonymous forces totally insensitive to the imperatives of justice. Can this scenario be avoided? Can real-libertarianism be prevented from degenerating, along with Penguins Island Rawlsianism, into an ethical justification of the demise of the welfare state? I believe it can, providing it is supplemented by some combination of two strategies.

First, we must fully recognize the crucially important difference between a universal local leximin (or maximin) and a global one, between a leximin that applies to each country of the world taken separately and one that applies to the world as a whole. And having recognized the difference between the two interpretations, we must unambiguously opt for the latter. When speaking of real-freedom-for-all we must mean it: for *all*. In other words, we must pursue the objective of introducing substantial redistributive mechanisms on a world scale, indeed ultimately an individual basic income at the highest sustainable level for each human being. If only for pedestrian technical reasons—the unavailability of suitable computerized payment systems except in a small number of countries—this ideal is, of course, still far off the political agenda.[67] But it should not be dismissed too lightly as a wild utopia. Not only will disillusionment with both conventional aid and neo-liberal development policies slowly drive those who mean business about helping the poorest of the planet to consider policy packages that include the direct, permanent, and unconditional transfer of purchasing power. But several powerful trends converge to create pressures that could only be alleviated through substantial transnational redistribution. The nations of the world cannot but increasingly realize that they are subjected to the vagaries of the same markets, both for the factors they need to buy and for the products they need to sell. Moreover, they cannot but realize ever more vividly that they are polluting the same air and the same water and that their territories are vulnerable to immigration by the same world population. World pollution will not be kept at a tolerable level without systematic redistribution from the high polluters to the low polluters. Nor will one be able to contain the cost of defending the borders of the affluent world against the influx of economic refugees—and the cost of digesting the fraction that got through into the domestic population—without transnational redistributive policies that significantly and permanently reduce the pressure to migrate.

These pressures, of course, will not smoothly yield leximin real freedom on a world scale. The political feasibility of significant moves in this direction hinges, first, on the spreading of attitudes of tolerance and solidarity across national boundaries. If such attitudes are not widely shared, there is no hope that a conception of justice that embodies both equal respect and equal concern could ever shape future institutions on this scale. The role of the media is crucial in this process. So is that of many transnational non-governmental organizations, from Amnesty International and Greenpeace to religious organizations and movements, large and small, with a widely scattered following. The political feasibility of justice as equal respect and concern, however, is not only a matter of sufficiently widespread emotional adhesion, but also of institutional design. In this respect, there is a world of difference between institutions that amount to mutually advantageous bargaining between nations and institutions that approximate one-man-one-vote democracy on a world scale. Even though the former are, of course, better than settlement by war or the breakdown of co-operation, only the latter hold the promise of making fast progress towards strongly redistributive structures, while at the same time making their own contribution to the required emotional adhesion. Needless to say, such world democracy need not encompass all subject-matters. It is fully compatible with so-called subsidiarity, understood as the maximal decentralization of decision-making the subject-matter allows—which is often far greater than the one currently prevailing. But it will need to have a strong hold not only over fundamental liberties, the rules of international trade, and global environmental problems, but also over basic redistributive mechanisms. Such centralization would not be a damaging intrusion into the autonomy of particular political communities, but a necessary condition for protecting the latter's real freedom to make choices, in particular the choice of granting each of its members considerable real freedom, instead of being ruled by the iron laws of competitiveness.

World democracy, thus limited and instrumentally justified, is no doubt still very remote. But its idea can and should guide and motivate more modest moves, not only when designing world-wide institutions with more narrowly specified competences, but above all when designing transnational institutions on a regional scale. In order to prevent the competitive dismantling of the welfare states, it is, of course, sheer common sense not to wait for world democracy, or even any form of more limited world government, to be possible. Building larger democratic political communities, such as the European Union, is one significant way in which competitive pressures can be attenuated, and thus more leeway gained for the pursuit of the greatest real freedom for all, and at the same time an unprecedented opportunity for proving that massive and permanent interpersonal transfers across the boundaries of largely autonomous nations is not a mere pipe-dream. But then at this level too, institutional design is of crucial importance: there is far more to expect, in a real-libertarian perspective, from a powerful parliament working under the majority rule than from a powerful council of ministers whose decisions require unanimity. Transnational democracy, not international bargaining is the institutional tool for real-freedom-for-all.[68]

Thus roughly sketched, *democratic scale-lifting* is the first strategy that must be adopted both in order to protect and regain the fast-shrinking leeway for intranational redistribution and for its own sake, as there is no morally non-arbitrary boundary to our equal concern, save the limits of mankind itself.[69] This strategy is essential and urgent, but it will take a long time to create political entities of the right sort at the right level, to equip them with appropriate democratic institutions and to build both the political will and the concrete instruments without which substantial international redistribution will remain a utopia. But we cannot wait that long. The competitive pressure against existing intranational redistribution is mounting, and it would, therefore, be good if there were another strategy which would enable us to keep and regain at least part of the required leeway. I believe there is one, to some extent in tension with the first strategy but none the less usable in connection with it: *solidaristic patriotism.* Whether or not there exists some institutionalized solidarity on a world scale, there will be pressures on a political entity that aims for a level of internal solidarity more generous than the one that connects it to the surrounding environment, as its citizens will want to purchase from abroad goods whose price is less inflated by the weight of redistribution, and as the net contributors to its redistributive system may want to move the precious factors they control elsewhere in order to earn a higher net income. Now, to some extent, this problem might be handled by imposing social tariffs, which would cancel the advantage some countries derive from lower social protection, thereby making their products less competitive and consequently reducing their attractiveness to capital and skilled labour. But this raises considerable practical difficulties, if only because of the intrinsic contestability of any criterion for establishing such tariffs and the resulting risk of retaliatory moves and mutually detrimental protectionism. So, if the members of the high-solidarity entity considered are moved by purely opportunistic motives, this high solidarity will be under strong pressure, especially as a combination of technological and market-structure factors tend to concentrate an increasing proportion of pre-tax earnings in the pockets of a small proportion of the working population.[70] This pressure would be greatly alleviated, however, if one could bank on a strong commitment to the underlying solidaristic conception of justice on the part of those who are enabled by their skills and other assets to be net contributors. Pride in the collective project in which they are thereby involved would prevent them from being on the look-out for more lucrative prospects abroad or simply for the many loopholes that would enable them to avoid taxation on a significant fraction of their actual income. Consequently it would provide a sturdy protection against competitive downward levelling and a firm basis for the viability of high solidarity on a local level long before it becomes possible on a global level.

Solidaristic patriotism in this sense[71] is as absent from Rawls's own explicit vision as is democratic scale-lifting. In a well-ordered society, he asserts, there is a natural duty not to cheat the institutions that embody the shared conception of justice. So, tax-payers should not subvert the maximin redistributive set-up by evading in their private behaviour the taxes they have consented to at the political level. But then should there not also be a natural duty not to subvert the same set-up by opportunistically taking advantage of less redistributive regimes abroad?[72] Whatever Rawls should answer to this question, it is clear to me that if Rawlsianism is not to reduce to a rejuvenated Penguins Island discourse and if real-libertarianism is not similarly to degenerate into an ideological justification of the dismantling of the welfare state, room should be made, along with energetic scale-lifting, for such a patriotic strategy. Utopian fantasy once again? One can hardly expect the required dispositions to flourish as a spontaneous expression of universal human nature. They will have to be nurtured, preserved, encouraged, engineered into existence by specific social conditions, specific ways of organizing social life. But these conditions may not be that different from the conditions that are required anyway for the lasting political feasibility of high levels of solidarity. At this level, again, the specific design of democratic political institutions is important, and so is the empathy-enabling role of the media. But to provide the emotional basis for a strong allegiance to high solidarity in both public and private decisions, one most probably needs more, namely various institutions which systematically provide recurrent opportunities for more-than-superficial personal contacts between people from all categories of the same society. Perhaps social life should be so organized, for example, that people of all social groups would have no option but to grow up (if not at home) in the same crèches and the same schools or to be born and die (if not at home) in the same hospitals. Perhaps one should even introduce a compulsory public service whose explicit purpose may be, say, to look after the environment (and thereby to develop a lifelong environmental awareness) but whose most important function would be to erode the barriers that tend to form between social categories and to maintain a sufficient level of social cohesion.[73] Some of these institutions may turn out to be counterproductive, and their actual impact on the political and private commitment to high solidarity must, of course, be evaluated in the light of the most relevant experiments. This indicates none the less how real-libertarianism may be led to advocate in this indirect, instrumental way, institutional restrictions on freedom which it has no way of justifying directly,[74] and how it can thereby consistently take on board at least some of the anti-individualistic concerns commonly associated with contemporary communitarianism. It also illustrates how a concern with maximin or leximin need not take either political feasibility or individual motivation as given but can and should inspire attempts to shape institutions in such a way that they do not erode but promote the emotional basis of equal concern.

Democratic scale-lifting and solidaristic patriotism are essential to protect us against the risk of passively endorsing, along Penguins Island lines, the unravelling of the welfare state into increasingly stingy and targeted transfers. They are, therefore, two key tenets of the resolutely left-wing variant of Rawlsianism, the radical yet realistic brand of solidaristic liberalism which I would like to advocate. The third key tenet is, of course, the distinctive implication of real-libertarianism, the institution whose justification has turned out to form the core of this whole book: basic income as the centrepiece of a just socio-economic regime.[75] None of these tenets—as I have, for the third one, taken great trouble to show—goes beyond, nor remains below, the direct or indirect requirements of liberal justice in its best interpretation. I am not taking for granted that nothing matters in social life apart from the dictates of equal respect and equal concern. A society is not, by definition, better if and only if it is more just. But I honestly doubt that there is much to be gained along other dimensions I care about—the warmth of human relations, for example, or the preservation of the natural world—at the cost of a loss in terms of social justice. There is not much hope of making our society better in these other respects—and a sizeable danger of making it worse—by introducing institutions that embody an unequal respect for people's conceptions of the good life or an unequal concern for their interests. So, a good society is more than a just society, but there is little chance of making it better other than through measures that contribute, be it indirectly, to making it more just.

Duly supplemented by some combination of democratic scale-lifting and solidaristic patriotism, real-libertarianism provides, I believe, a coherent framework for relevant progressive thinking and action in a post-neo-liberal, post-communist twenty-first century. It claims to accommodate, as indicated from the onset, both a belief in the paramount importance of freedom and the conviction that capitalism, as we know it, is replete with unacceptable inequalities. The conclusion that emerges is that an earnest commitment to freedom—appropriately understood as real-freedom-for-all—does nothing to warrant complacency with the inequalities of existing capitalism. Nor does it give us any good reason—on plausible factual assumptions—to fight for socialism now. In the process of reaching this conclusion, the focus of discussion shifted away from the traditional question with which this book started—the choice between capitalism and socialism—towards other dimensions along which socio-economic regimes may vary. Key issues for the future are rather whether, when, and how one should introduce an unconditional basic income, attribute redistributive powers to supranational authorities, or constrain the organization of social life so as to nurture feelings of solidarity. These are the issues around which the crucial struggles of the future will be fought. It is the outcomes of these struggles that will determine the pace of progress towards more justice, towards greater real freedom for all.

Only success along this uncertain path can justify capitalism— if anything can.

NOTES

CHAPTER 1

1. In so far as their use is regulated by customary, mostly implicit rules, the 'commons' of traditional communities are not unowned (or commonly owned), but publicly owned in the sense specified.

2. In general, the depth of private or public ownership will not be the same for different portions of the stock of means of production, and the notion of scope of private or public ownership is thereby made rather imprecise. To deal rigorously with this general case, one could—following a suggestion by Ian Carter—construe the extent of private (or public) ownership of the means of production as its average depth, and speak of capitalism (or socialism) whenever this average lies beyond some threshold level. But the metric presuppositions of this proposal—how should the means of production be counted and how should the depth of the private versus public ownership over each of them be measured?—are far more demanding than what is required to be able to tell which means of production are 'essentially' privately (or publicly) owned, and whether they form 'the bulk' of a given society's stock.

3. Throughout the book, 'him or her' and 'his or her' are abbreviated to 'her'; 'he or she' to 'she'.

4. I shall not attempt to provide a full analysis of the bundle of rights which make up self-ownership. Only some components of this bundle, to which I shall return, matter to my argument. Let me only note at this stage that if a society is to guarantee full self-ownership to all its members, the latter must be defined in such a way that it does not allow people to sell themselves into slavery, whether to the State or to other people. Hence, there is at least one feature of standard ownership which even full self-ownership does not possess.

5. This is the distinct 'traditional democratic claim that equality of power is a better safeguard than inequality of power against excessive coercion' (Norman 1982: 106).

6. Closely related is the common conflation, in everyday political rhetorics, of democracy and liberalism. The importance of distinguishing these is legitimately stressed by right-wing liberals such as Friedrich Hayek: 'It is possible for a dictator to govern in a liberal way. And it is also possible that a democracy governs with a total lack of liberalism. My personal preference is for a liberal dictator and not for a democratic government lacking in liberalism.' (1981 interview quoted by Bowles and Gintis 1986: 11–12).

7. Thus, Plato (*Laws*, 11. 923) and Aristotle (*Politics* 8. 1337ª) both explicitly assert that the citizen does not belong to himself but to the political community.

8. Though not strictly equivalent to 'basic liberties' or 'human rights' as expressed, for example, in Rawls's first principle of justice or in the constitutions of liberal democracies, self-ownership is closely associated with most of them. In so far as liberalism can be characterized as the recognition of these liberties and of their priority , then the communitarian critique of liberalism can be construed—as it is, for example, by Allen Buchanan (1989)—as questioning precisely the modern idea of self-ownership. Objections to the expression 'self-ownership', on the ground that the ownership of oneself is significantly different from the ownership of a thing, can be compatible with an acceptance of the idea of self-ownership as characterized here.

9. Along similar lines, Cohen (1985*a*; 1986; 1995) challenges the flat denial of self-ownership which is a central tenet of the standard response to libertarianism from the Left, and argues that the intuitive appeal of self-ownership should be recognized and the implications of such recognition explored, even if in the end full self-ownership is to be rejected.

10. This reply shows how weak a notion self-ownership is—we shall return to this very shortly—but it does not turn it into a vacuous notion. True, self-ownership is not sufficient to allow a shoe cleaner to sell her services privately, but it is sufficient, in a law-abiding society, to protect her against being coerced, whether by another person or the State, into providing such services.

11. Not only has this sometimes been criticized in socialism. It has also been conceded by some of its most prominent advocates. Thus Karl Kautsky (quoted by Nove 1983: 198): 'Socialist production is irreconcilable with the full freedom of labour, i.e. with the freedom of the labourer to work when, where and how he wills.'

12. Whether freedom of occupational choice should be counted among the fundamental liberties covered, for example, by Rawls's first principle of justice, may be debatable (see Barry 1989: 399; Rawls 1990: §§ 13.6, 15.2). But the (formal) freedom to choose one's occupation cannot plausibly be dissociated from self-ownership.

13. Typical freedom-based onslaughts on egalitarianism have to be construed along these lines if they are to be plausible at all. (See e.g. Joseph and Sumption (1979: 47), quoted by Norman (1982: 83–4): 'Egalitarians rely for the achievement of their objectives on the coercive power of the state, as they are bound to do by the nature of the human material with which they deal. A society in which the choices fundamental to human existence are determined by coercion is not a free society. It follows irresistibly that egalitarians must choose between liberty and equality.') Even under this construal, however, they are meticulously challenged by Joseph Carens's (1981) 'essay in utopian politico-economic theory'.

14. This is why Rawls (1971: 270–4; 1982: 163; 1987: 14; 1990: § 51) can maintain that his theory of justice does not rule out 'liberal socialism' on a priori grounds. Even under an efficiency constraint, the latter can be fully consistent with the freedom of occupational choice implied by Rawls's first principle of justice.

15. Baker (1987: 80–1) provides a particularly explicit formulation of this conception: 'Capitalist property rights are not an issue of freedom versus equality, but of freedom for a few versus freedom for everyone. For everyone who really cares about freedom, the choice must be obvious. [. . .] There is a tradition in politics which asserts that property is connected with freedom: we can now see the sense in which that tradition is correct. For freedom is extended to everyone only in a socialist society. And a society is truly socialist only if control over productive resources is exercised democratically.' But the underlying conception of freedom is quite widespread. Thus Norman (1982: 99): socialist relations of production 'would constitute a society in which all would share equally in the making of decisions and choices about the organization and direction of economic activity, in place of a society in which most people have these choices and decisions made for them. They would, to that extent, constitute the equalization of freedom [. . .].'; or Goodin (1982: 156–7): 'The freedoms which property rights secure for one individual or group always come at the expense of another: the landowners' rights make me a trespasser; and had I right of way across his land, his liberty to cultivate as he pleases would be impaired. The distribution of property rights—and their redistribution—is necessarily a zero-sum game.'

16. As Leopold Kohr (1974: 50) puts it: 'For a person can be free only within the limits of a right that excludes the rights of all others. If he cannot exclude all others when it comes to making a decision, he cannot be free. [. . .] It makes no difference whether these other persons are natural persons, or corporate and public persons in whom he may himself have a share in his capacity as stockholder or citizen.' See also Cohen (1986: § 3), who stresses the importance of substantive versus merely formal self-ownership: 'How can I be said to own myself if I may do nothing without the agreement of others?'

17. See Rakowski (1991: 68–9) for a fuller argument leading to the same conclusion.

18. To use David Friedman's (1973: p. xii) formulation.

19. For present purposes, we can abstract from the complications arising from the violation of property rights and the consequent need for rectification.

20. This distinction between the weaker and the stronger interpretation of the notion of an entitlement (or backward-looking, or purely historical) principle is further discussed and illustrated in van der Veen and Van Parijs (1985: § 1). Rawls (1978: 65; 1990: § 14) suggests a similar distinction when characterizing his theory of justice as 'pure adjusted procedural' in reply to Nozick's charge that the Difference Principle involves constant meddling with people's voluntary transactions.

21. This contrast underlies the principled rejection of original-position arguments by those who believe in 'natural entitlements' (see e.g. Nozick 1974: 226–7).

22. Along the same lines, Cohen (1985a: 95–102) emphasizes that Nozick's proviso is just one among many possible choices of the relevant baseline for comparison. In Van Parijs (1991a: § 8.5), I argue that this point is of decisive importance for the defence of Rawls against Nozick.

23. That such a situation could in principle arise is obvious under the first ('up for grabs') variant of the criterion of original appropriation. For it—or something close to it—to arise also under the other three variants which some libertarians have proposed (Nozick's proviso, Brody's fair shares, Steiner's equal ownership), one needs to make additional assumptions—for example, that the island can only be made fertile by using manufactured tools also owned by the island owner. These three variants do not remove the basic defect, but by alleviating the symptoms, they make it somewhat less easy to bring the basic defect into sharp focus.

24. Similar critiques of the standard libertarian view of freedom are presented in sketchy form by Lindblom (1977: 46–7) and Sterba (1980: 117) for example, and have been developed more systematically in several papers by Cohen (1979*b*, 1981*b*, 1989*a*), from whom I took over the expression 'moralized conception of freedom'. See also Carter (1993: § 1.4) for a useful critical discussion of such conceptions.

25. This was, e.g., Machiavelli's position, as interpreted by Skinner (1984: 209–10).

26. A libertarian, according to Rothbard (1973: 23), 'regards conscription as slavery on a massive scale'.

27. The relation is undoubtedly far more complex. Reducing (or increasing) society's freedom from alien powers need by no means generate automatically a reduction (or increase) in its members' freedom. As Hayek (1960: 15) keenly emphasizes, 'though the concept of national freedom is analogous to that of individual freedom, it is not the same; and the striving for the first has not always enhanced the second. It has sometimes led people to prefer a despot of their own race to the liberal government of an alien majority; and it has often provided the pretext for ruthless restrictions of the individual liberty of the members of minorities.'

28. Realistic informational assumptions rule out the effective use of lump-sum taxes and subsidies, while realistic motivational assumptions (under current conditions) rule out a reliance on people's responsiveness to pre-tax-and-transfer income, as in Carens's (1981) interesting blueprint.

29. The importance of this distinction has been rightly stressed by a long lineage of authors. Thomas Hobbes (1651: 264–6), for example, distinguishes the 'liberty of the commonwealth' and the 'liberty of the subjects'; Friedrich Hayek (1960: 13) contrasts a 'free people' and a 'people of free men'; and Leopold Kohr (1974: 56) opposes a 'free society' to a 'society of free citizens'.

30. Alexis de Tocqueville (1856: 62) emphasizes a similar contrast between the citizens' 'participation in the management of public affairs' and the right for each of them 'to settle his own fate according to his wishes'. For a useful discussion of Constant and Tocqueville in this context, see Aron (1965: ch. 1).

31. 'And where would we find these guarantees [of private enjoyments] if we were to give up political liberty? To give it up, Sir, would be a madness similar to that of a man who, because he lives only on the first floor, would want to erect on sand a building without foundations' (Constant 1819: 289).

32. On this issue, in other words, I am entirely on the side of Mill (1848: 569): 'That there is, or ought to be, some space in human existence thus entrenched around, and sacred from authoritative intrusion, no one who professes the smallest regard to human freedom or dignity will call in question,' or Hayek (1960: 13): 'Freedom thus presupposes that the individual has some assured private sphere, that there is some set of circumstances in his environment with which others cannot interfere,' for example.

33. See, e.g. MacCallum (1967), Rawls (1971: 202–3), Goodin (1982: 151–2).

34. A label chosen by reference to Berlin's (1958: 139–40) classic treatment of this issue. See Arneson (1985) and Flathman (1987: ch. 2) for two extensive discussions of the same issue. Note that according to the definition of freedom that is here being discussed, one cannot only increase freedom without expanding the set of accessible options, one can also reduce freedom by expanding that set in a way that breeds a desire for something that is outside the expanded set. See Arneson (1985: 443) for an example and a thoughtful discussion.

35. See especially Skinner (1984: 212–17; 1990: 301–8), who invites us to recognize, following Machiavelli, that taking our civil duties (and not just our rights) seriously provides 'the only means of guaranteeing the very liberty we may seem to be giving up'. See also Pettit (1993) for further discussion.

36. As Elster (1982*b*: 228) puts it: 'Being a free man is to be free to do all the things that one autonomously wants to do.' See also M. Taylor (1982: 148–50), Levine (1984: 41–3) and Arneson (1985: 432–7) for useful discussions.

37. This label is partly motivated by a (pretty problematic) analytical connection sometimes asserted between either or both of these strategies and the 'liberty of the ancients' discussed in the previous section. Thus, Charles Taylor (1979: 181) believes that we cannot do 'what we really want' outside a self-governing society. 'It follows that we can only be free in such a society, and that being free is governing ourselves collectively according to this canonical form.'

38. This is the strategy towards which Isaiah Berlin (1969: pp. xxxviii–xl) seems to be leaning in reply to some criticisms of his initial formulation. See also Benn and Weinstein (1971: 210): 'to see the point of saying that one is (or is not) free to do X, we must be able to see that there is some point in doing it'; and Flathman (1987: 29): 'freedom consists in the absence of obstacles, not merely to my actual, but to my potential choices.'

39. It does make perfect sense to say, as Ian Carter aptly pointed out to me, that I am free to do a number of things which only insane people would want to do. But one can recognize this and still claim that making people free to do certain things which none of them might want to do adds nothing to their freedom. (The measure of the added freedoms is zero.) What matters here, however, is less the acceptance of the mild restriction involved in the 'what one might want to do' than the rejection of the alternative, far stronger restrictions ('what one wants to do', 'what one ought to want to do'). Those who, like Carter (1993), would feel more comfortable if one did away with

any restriction of this sort, could still concede that the freedom to do what one might want to do is the aspect of one's freedom that matters (perhaps proportionally to the likelihood of our wanting to do it?) as far as our ideal of a free society is concerned.

40. I am therefore not interested as such in 'pure negative freedom', defined as the absence of physical impediments to action brought about by other people (see e.g. by Steiner 1974 and 1983 and much of Carter 1993), unless one went so far as to assume that whatever an institutional set-up does not allow would be physically prevented if it were attempted. One implication of my approach is that I would evaluate identically two dictatorial regimes that would make its citizens behave in the same way even if the threatened sanctions were sheer (though perfectly effective) bluff in one case but not in the other. According to holders of the pure negative view, on the other hand, freedom would be far greater under the bluffer than under the dictator who means business.

41. For an analysis of this sort, see Elster (1982*a*: 365; 1983: § 1; 1985: 211–14), usefully discussed by Carling (1987). The option a (credible) threat suppresses is not what its realization would negate (say, continuing to live), but the combination of non-compliance with the request and non-realization of the threat. In another standard account of coercion (see Nozick 1969: 127–34; M. Taylor 1982: 14–19), threats are defined more broadly: whereas an offer consists in promising to make a person better off, relative to what would have been 'the normal and expected course of events', if she complies with what she is being requested to do, a *threat* is a promise to make that person worse off, relative to the same baseline. Threatening not to renew a labour contract if the employee does not agree to some tougher conditions would thus become a case of coercion despite the absence of (threat of) right violation. See Charles Lindblom's (1977: 48) assertion of the coercive nature of any threat to discontinue exchange relations.

42. Although Hayek's (1960: 20–1) own explicit definition does not exactly point in this direction ('By "coercion", we mean such control of the environment or circumstances of a person by another that, in order to avoid greater evil, he is forced to act not according to a coherent plan of his own but to serve the ends of another'), his concrete illustrations do support this interpretation ('The courtier living in the lap of luxury but at the beck and call of his prince may be much less free than a poor peasant or artisan [. . .]. In the sense in which we use the term, the penniless vagabond who lives precariously by constant improvisation is indeed freer than the conscripted soldier with all his security and relative comfort' (Hayek 1960: 17–18)).

43. For a helpful critique of Hayek on liberty, see Norman (1982: 87–90 and 1987: 38–9).

44. See J. M. Buchanan (1985: 9–10); Buchanan and Lomasky (1985: 17 n. 8). In a more recent article, Buchanan proposes what he says might be a way of reconciling 'positive' and 'negative' liberty. My 'liberties of disposition', he says, are measured by the number of alternative dispositions I can make with my endowment in exchange for other assets. They are, therefore, restricted

if some endowment owner denies me liberty of purchase, thus reducing the size of the choice-set that would otherwise represent the feasible options within my overall budget constraint (J. M. Buchanan 1987: 11–12) 'The size of the choice set is a function of both the legally protected endowment and the liberties to use or exercise this endowment. [. . .] The familiar budget set of the first person [with a $100 endowment] is larger than that of the second [with a $10 endowment] only on the implicit presumption that both have the same liberties of disposition' (ibid. 16). This is all fine and surely suggests that it is the actual size of the choice-set, as opposed to the nominal size of the endowment, that constitutes the most sensible interpretation of (real) freedom. But this is not the conclusion drawn by Buchanan, for 'liberty' (*tout court*) turns out to be nothing but the liberties of disposition (ibid. 12). Hence: 'A person who, say, holds legal claim to a piece of land but who is also highly restricted in the set of potential buyers (leasers) *clearly has less liberty* than the person who holds legal claim only to his own labor power but who remains totally unrestricted as to the uses to which his labor power may be put' (ibid. 16, my emphasis). Is this so obvious? And if it were, is it supposed to follow that owning an estate (even with restricted uses) adds nothing to one's freedom, or that the fact that no one is willing to hire one's (unrestrictedly owned) labour power, owing to some disability, makes no difference to one's freedom?

45. This conception of real freedom, which has been implicit all along, is very close to Amartya Sen's approach. According to Sen (1990*d*), 'if we really do think it is important that a person should be able to lead the life that he or she would choose, then it is the general category of positive freedom [defined by what, everything considered, a person can achieve] with which we have to be concerned'. Freedom is concerned 'with the *real opportunity* that we have to accomplish what we value' (Sen 1992: 31, his emphasis). I could have followed his suggestion that 'the category of capabilities is the natural candidate for reflecting the idea of freedom to do' (Sen 1984: 316; see also 1985: ch. 7; 1992: ch. 3). However, as I shall want to contrast permissions and abilities as two sets of factors affecting the size of the opportunity-set, the term 'opportunity' seemed more appropriate. See Cohen (1990: § 3) and Sen (1990*b*: § 3.2) for a clarifying discussion of Sen's notion of capability.

46. This distinction between formal and real freedom obviously echoes a long tradition of similar distinctions. In particular, it occupies a prominent position in the tool box of many critics of capitalism. Thus, according to Tawney (1952: 228), 'there is no such thing as freedom in the abstract [. . .]. Whatever else the conception may imply, it involves a power of choice between alternatives, a choice which is *real*, not merely *nominal*, between alternatives which exist in fact, not only on paper.' In the same vein, Norman (1982: 90–4) stresses that freedom is more than non-coercion and includes the various things that enable us to make choices—wealth, power, education—and Levine (1984: ch. 1) offers a thorough discussion of the essentially parallel distinction between liberty and capacity-freedom. In the liberal tradition, there is a greater concern not to lump together these two dimensions of

freedom under a single label. This was already the case with Kant's (1793:§ 2) distinction between *Freiheit* and *Selbständigkeit.* Contemporary liberals often phrase the distinction in terms of liberty versus its value. Thus, Isaiah Berlin (1969: pp. xlv–xlvi) acknowledges that, in his 'Two concepts of liberty', he 'should perhaps have stressed (save that [he] thought this too obvious to need saying) the failure of such [*laissez-faire*] systems to provide the minimum conditions in which alone any degree of significant "negative" liberty can be exercised by individuals or groups, and without which it is of little or no value to those who may theoretically possess it. For what are rights without the power to implement them?' This rhetorical question echoes a very similar one in his earlier essay: 'Without adequate conditions for the use of freedom, what is the value of freedom?', which was, however, followed by the warning that 'nothing is gained by a confusion of terms' (Berlin 1958: 124–5). Rawls (1971: 204) has obviously heeded this warning: 'The inability to take advantage of one's rights and opportunities as a result of poverty and ignorance, and a lack of means generally, is sometimes counted among the constraints definitive of liberty. I shall not, however, say this, but rather I shall think of these things as affecting the worth of liberty, the value to individuals of the rights that the first principle defines.' Though not abolished, the significance of the terminological issue is of course greatly reduced if, unlike Hayek or Buchanan, one hastens to add to a 'formal' definition, the emphatic assertion that freedom, thus defined, is worthless in the absence of conditions that turn it into what others may wish to call (real) freedom. There need not be any substantive issue between the ideal of a really free society and that of a formally free society in which formal freedom is worth having.

47. By this I mean the question of whether we are talking about opportunities 'at the start' or at any given point in time. I shall return at length to this important issue in due course (§§ 2.5, 4.2, 5.8).

48. All of these conditions have been widely discussed in the literature. Thus, Berlin (1958: 122–3) moves from a characterization of unfreedom as entailing 'deliberate interference' to one where other human beings are said to interfere 'with or without the intention of doing so'; Sterba (1980: 115–16) contrasts his own characterization of a freedom-restricting obstacle as 'any intentional or unintentional act of commission for which others are morally responsible' with its broader characterization by Macpherson (1973: 95–119) as 'any humanly alterable condition that prevents a person from doing something'; and, according to C. Taylor (1979: 175–6), the key issue is whether or not there can be internal rather than just external obstacles to freedom.

49. There are, of course, some inabilities (e.g. to travel faster than light) that cannot be abolished (because they derive from physical laws) nor need compensating (because they are shared by all). But it is no inconvenience to subsume them under the general notion of unfreedom, since anyway the freest *possible* society is not expected to do anything about them.

50. Thus, to the question of whether property can be a chain, rather than a source of freedom, we need not agree with Kohr's (1974: 54) categorical

dismissal: 'Whatever our attitude towards happiness, there can be therefore only one answer as far as freedom is concerned. What deprives us of it, what enslaves us, is not property but the absence of it.' If possessing property, or a particular form of property, can induce desires—rapaciousness, addiction to comfort?—which the person can no longer get rid of, however hard she tries, then property might indeed reduce as well as increase freedom.

51. The position held here is therefore close to the (allegedly untenable) 'halfway position' described by Charles Taylor (1979: 184–6) in his defence of full-blown positive freedom. Despite admitting that desires can be a source of unfreedom, it remains fully on the opportunity side of Taylor's (1979: 177–8) opportunity–exercise divide. See also Flathman (1987: ch. 2) for a useful discussion.

52. For the sake of simplicity, I shall stick to this strict leximin formulation in the sequel, but I would gladly settle for a softening of the leximin along the following lines: a negligible, or hardly noticeable improvement in the opportunities of the worst off does not justify a massive worsening of the situation of many or all higher up the scale. Such a softening is parallel to the softening of the priority rules to be discussed shortly (and raises similar, though somewhat easier, issues of measurement). It seems to me to provide the most satisfactory way of handling the objection that maximin condones intuitively absurd sacrifices of opportunities (or welfare, or primary goods, or whatever). See Rawls (1990: § 19) for an alternative response based on the idea that, as a matter of fact, the sort of situation that is being assumed in the objection does not arise.

53. What would count as a mild restriction might be characterized, e.g., as one to which everyone would agree when looking as an intelligent and sober adult at all the relevant facts (this may apply to the paternalistic restrictions), or as one to which everyone would consent if it could be part of an enforceable insurance contract (this may apply to compulsory vaccination and help: see Sugden 1982: 211). But the examples of compulsory voting and demographic restraint show that I would probably be willing to go beyond this.

54. All this clearly takes for granted that some meaningful metric of opportunities can be worked out. This question will be the focus of attention in the next three chapters.

55. See e.g. Rawls (1971, 1993*a*), Dworkin (1981*b*, 1990), Sen (1985, 1992), Arneson (1989, 1990*a*), and even Cohen (1989*b*, 1990). So characterized, solidaristic or equal-concern conceptions of justice may advocate strict equality or aggregate maximization rather than maximin, focus on outcomes rather than opportunities, and ascribe no priority to the protection of formal freedom.

56. For those who see justice as the only or primary virtue of social institutions, this postulate entails the view that the State has no other purpose, or no more important purpose, than the maintenance of rules and the provision of facilities that make it possible for each individual to pursue her own goals— as opposed to the realization of some collective project, such as national

expansion or the transformation of man. To use the terminology suggested by Oakeshott (1975: ch. 3), society is then to be conceived as a *societas* (on the pattern of the relations between nations), not as a *universitas* (on the pattern of an association defined by a common goal). A free society, as characterized here, must be a *societas* but only corresponds to one of the many interpretations of the form this *societas* should take.

57. I realize that neutrality, anti-perfectionism, impartiality, equal respect, etc. should not be lumped together too readily. (See Larmore (1987), Goodin and Reeve (eds.) (1989), and Da Silveira (1994) for careful discussions of the relevant distinctions.) But for the purposes of this book, the formulation already adopted here will suffice. I return briefly to this issue in the final section (§ 6.8).

58. Despite the various similarities pointed out, there are significant differences with Rawls's position. Thus, the priority rules are softened, formal freedom does not coincide with the respect of the fundamental liberties governed by Rawls's first principle and leximin opportunity lumps together the two components of Rawls's second principle. This book makes no pretence to offer, let alone to defend, a fully worked-out alternative to Rawls's theory of justice. Only divergences relating to the second principle will be seriously examined and argued for. What the exact nature and significance of these divergences are will emerge as we proceed.

CHAPTER 2

1. This points to an important difference with the 'capitalist road to communism' approach of van der Veen and Van Parijs (1986a). The reasons beyond this difference are expounded in §§ 4.1–2.

2. Organizations and scholars from thirteen West European countries joined in the mid-1980s to form the Basic Income European Network (BIEN). Information about the state of the discussion can be found in Walter (1989) and in recent issues of BIEN's newsletter.

3. The expression 'basic income' was first used (it seems) in a sense akin to the current one, by Jan Tinbergen (1953), and its Dutch equivalent gained wide currency in the Netherlands as from the mid-1970s. In English, it started being used as from the early 1980s by Hermione Parker (1982), and was later selected for naming both the Basic Income Research Group (founded in London in 1984, renamed 'Citizens Income Study Centre' in 1992) and BIEN (founded in Louvain-la-Neuve in 1986).

4. Assertions of a close link between basic income and some strong notion of freedom—in particular the freedom not to live a life of submission to someone else's will—are quite common in the long intellectual history of basic income. See Johnson (1971: 184), Brittan (1973: 202–5), Fromm (1976: 218), and Adler-Karlsson (1979: 61) for some paradigmatic formulations.

5. See Jordan *et al.* (1992) for an illuminating description of this aspect of the

unemployment trap on the basis of interviews with some of those caught in it.

6. Only under the assumption just stated that no control is needed for other reasons. If such control is needed (and, even on real-libertarian grounds, there are historical circumstances under which it may be needed: see § 3.5) the administrative-cost argument may go the other way, and this *may* be sufficient to offset the other two considerations, and hence justify a means-tested form of guaranteed minimum income.

7. A scheme of this type is discussed, though not actually proposed, by Salverda (1984). Though not as extreme, one of the schemes considered in the appendix to Meade (1989) involves regressive taxation, with low earners facing higher tax rates than high earners, putatively for their own benefit. (This scheme makes it possible to have less dissuasive marginal tax rates in the crucial middle range, and thereby to boost the sustainable tax yield.)

8. The problem with residence-insensitivity is not that the resulting scheme is too stingy with people who have grown up in a poor area (as objected by Arneson 1992*b*: 504). An unconditional redistribution of wealth will precisely make it far less costly to them to keep living close to 'their friends and family and other valuable social contacts'. The problem is rather that the scheme does not make more income available to (the poorest among) those who happen to have grown up in a more expensive part of the country, or whose area happens to have grown more expensive. This raises a problem because it may seem important that people should be enabled to keep living close to the sites and the people to which they are emotionally attached. But this is not legitimate, according to the perspective here spelt out, if it must happen at the cost of making a lesser amount available to some others, who happen to live in cheaper areas but might want to move. Leximin real freedom is not to be confused with leximin welfare. I shall soften somewhat this harsh stance when discussing some objections to undominated diversity in § 3.6.

9. I am here taking for granted that our picture of the just society leaves room for self-interested individual choices, and hence for the justification of incentive payments by an appeal to a maximin principle. See Van Parijs (1993*b*) for an extensive discussion of Cohen's (1992) arguments to the contrary.

10. If the levels of the tax rates and of the basic income affect—positively or negatively—the amount of resources required to secure the protection of formal freedom (e.g. to keep the streets safe), the criterion must be adjusted accordingly. What needs to be maximized is the tax yield net of the requisites of formal freedom protection.

11. A more radical way of integrating the demographic aspect, suggested by Rakowski (1991: 153–4, 166), would consist in requiring parents to provide the 'basic stipend' to their children, as they themselves have received it from their parents, or, more conveniently perhaps, in getting the State to pay the stipend and then to claim it back through taxation of the parents' incomes. This would amount to a system of large negative child benefits—and pave the way for terminally shrinking societies?

12. Or perhaps the highest average *lifetime* basic income. A (formal-freedom-respecting) measure that would have no other effect than to increase the average number of economically unproductive years (e.g. by cheapening the access to life-prolonging technologies for the elderly) would be neutral in terms of the latter criterion, but negative in terms of the former. Note that it is theoretically possible with either criterion that the optimal structure should take the form of large child benefits and nothing else, or of a large basic pension and nothing else.

13. The latter view corresponds to the *solidarisme* advocated at the turn of the century by such authors as Léon Bourgeois (1902) and Célestin Bouglé (1907) (see Tanghe 1989: 74–6 for a recent account), while the former has been worked out by Hartwick (1977) or Barry (1979, 1983) but can be traced back to Colins (1835) (see Cunliffe 1987 for a recent account).

14. I shall return to this proposition at greater length in § 6.6.

15. An early expression of such a view is arguably to be found in Kant's (1793: 151; 1797: 433) emphasis on *Selbständigkeit*. Powerful freedom-based pleas for a wide spread of productive property can also be found in the writings of the British 'libertarian catholic' Hilaire Belloc (1912), of Leopold Kohr (esp. 1974: 63), and of his disciple Ivan Illich (esp. 1978: 94–5). Tibor Liska's 'entrepreneurial socialism', where people can bid with their share of social capital for the right to use society's means of production, is similarly defended on the ground that it 'guarantees the highest degree of human freedom' (Szécky 1982: 94).

16. Whether the basic income should be given to people *in the form of* (individual) productive wealth must be sharply distinguished from whether *their entitlement* to the basic income should be based on their being (joint) owners of society's productive wealth, for example as a result of holding equal shares in society's private corporations or, more simply, as a consequence of public ownership. The fact that the grant is a dividend on productive wealth does not force one to pay it in the form of productive wealth. Whether in Cole's (1929, 1944), Lange's (1936), Meade's (1938, 1989), Yunker's (1977), or Roemer's (1992, 1993) version, the 'social dividend' is generally meant to be paid in cash.

17. This aspect of the argument for basic income is particularly stressed by Nooteboom (1986) and Meade (1989). It is a direct corollary of the second advantage of basic income over means-tested schemes delineated at § 2.2.

18. Goodin (1982: 151) is close to making this point when observing that, unlike the welfare state's typical adjustments of final distributions, 'statutory guarantees of a certain future stream of income might, in effect if not in name, produce much the same result [as a redistribution of formal titles to the means of production]'. And a basic income would easily fit into Rawls's (1990: § 51.3) picture of a 'property-owning democracy', which 'insur[es] the widespread ownership of productive assets and human capital at the *beginning* of each period', in contrast to welfare-state capitalism, which 'redistribut[es] income to those with less at the end of each period, so to speak'. In Ch. 4, I shall return at far greater length to the question of whether Rawls's

theory of justice, and in particular his Difference Principle, warrant a basic income.

19. Bearing in mind that the level of public expenditure required effectively to protect formal freedom (e.g. the police force required to keep urban centres safe) cannot be assumed to be given independently of the overall level of basic income, the structure of taxation, and other features of the socio-economic regime.

20. Note that a justification by leximin real freedom does not only require that there should be a positive impact (via productivity) on the highest sustainable level of the grant, but that it should be an optimal impact. No other public use of the resources thus allocated must have a more favourable impact. Nor must, of course (in a capitalist context), the private use to which the resources would otherwise be put—this is why it is essential that a positive externality should be involved. Note, further, that the externalities concerned must specifically affect the sustainable level of the cash grant (or possibly in-kind provision of the third kind, to be considered below) and that they must be more effectively produced by universal than by selective free provision (unlike the cases of higher education or research grants).

21. The underlying assumption is that the variety of things people in the society concerned *actually want* to have or do after due consideration ('in their right minds') provides a sensible approximation of the variety of things they *might want* to have or do. It is only on the basis of this assumption that one can simply infer, as I do here, from the cheaper satisfaction of actual unanimous desire to a greater real freedom. This very same assumption plays a key role in the way in which Ch. 3 interprets leximin real freedom when the assumption of identical abilities is relaxed.

22. Bear in mind that you do not need to walk, ride, or drive in order to 'consume' a street. You can 'consume' it by having your rubbish collected or by staring at the traffic. Nor do you need to walk in a park or on a footpath for you to 'consume' them. If you care about your grandmother or your grandson, it is enough that they do. Even so, of course, for each particular street or walking area, most of society's members can confidently say that they will never 'consume' it. Its free provision, therefore, by reducing the cash grant given to all, can plausibly be said to reduce most people's freedom to do whatever they might want to do. However, everyone actually uses some streets directly and some others indirectly. The lumping together under one heading of many items which a more fine-grained classification would distinguish is essential for the argument to go through. But then, why should one want to restrict this lumping together to such 'natural' categories as streets, walking areas, or the air one breathes in various places? Could free access to the beach in one place not be 'compensated' by free access to the mountain in another, or better air in one place by better street lights in another, or indeed by free culture or sport? There is no a priori limit to the packages that can be made. A minimal constraint is that each good in the package should be such that paid access to it is costly to administer, and that taken together the goods in the package sufficiently meet the wants of each

person for her real freedom (to do what she might want to do) to be increased as a result of the free provision of the package.

23. This third real-libertarian case for in-kind universal provision (in particular of environmental goods) sheds some light on why claiming a cash basic income on grounds of justice is today more plausible than ever before. One reason is no doubt that increased heterogeneity in life plans has increased the number of meaningful uses to which environmental goods could be put. Another is the rapid erosion of the in-kind basic income available to each person in the form of a costlessly accessible enjoyable environment. Thus, while environmental protection (say, spring water preservation) is one way of giving a basic income, environmental destruction is one reason why a cash basic income (say, to pay for mineral water bottles) needs giving.

24. Thurow (1977) mentions three categories of reasons for preferring in-kind transfers: (1) metapreferences for the equal distribution of certain goods, (2) lapses in consumer sovereignty, (3) concern with the transmission of certain values. A very small subset of Thurow's first and third categories are sub-sumed under my first heading (formal freedom must be guaranteed to all, and one way of doing this may be by sponsoring, say, civic education). If a real-libertarian standpoint makes any sense at all, Thurow's second category can-not justify giving part of the basic income in kind rather than in cash to all members of society, even though it may justify doing so for some of them who lack the mental conditions for the exercise of freedom: it does make sense to provide food and shelter rather than cash to the mentally handi-capped or the mentally deranged. For analogous reasons, in addition to the externality argument mentioned earlier, it does make sense to provide free education to children. This is a pretty strong form of paternalism of course, but restricted to where it belongs. Thurow's typology ignores (though I believe it should include) my second and third categories. It also ignores what may be the most frequent argument for justifying in-kind welfare benefits (subsidized low-quality housing, free soup-kitchen): that they will be better at filtering out the 'undeserving', those who are not truly needy, because of the stigma attached to collecting them (see e.g. Lang and Weiss 1990; Besley 1990). From a real-libertarian standpoint, such an argument is largely irrele-vant, as the aim of the transfer scheme is not to trace as accurately as possible the 'deserving' or the 'truly needy', but to make everyone as really free as possible. It is not completely irrelevant, though, as we shall see in § 3.5.

25. Suppose industrial production involving river pollution raises the possible level of the cash grant. But it makes it more difficult, perhaps even impossi-ble, to fish any trout in it. What does leximin freedom require? If being able to fish trout is something no one in the society 'might not want' to buy for less than the increment in the grant made possible by the polluting produc-tion, then the pollution must definitely stop, whether through shut down or substitution of a cleaner technology. On the other hand, if some do not attach the slightest importance to trout fishing, leximin freedom requires that the pollution should continue until the trout fishermen manage to raise enough money to buy some anti-pollution device. The full justification of

this response requires the argument about the metric of real freedom to be presented at § 2.6

26. Let us bear in mind that at this stage people are presumed not to differ significantly in terms of internal resources. In reality, of course, they do. In order to deal with this general case, I shall not propose (for reasons to be presented in the next chapter) to extend the insurance approach from the future to the past by counterfactually dropping a veil of ignorance over people's present internal endowments. I shall rather be assuming that the criterion for correcting inequalities in endowments (to be presented, again, in Ch. 3) has been appropriately applied before the insurance reasoning takes off. For an insightful and far more thorough discussion of equalization versus counterfactual insurance in health matters, see Rakowski 1991: chs. 4 and 6).

27. Possibly modulated according to age, but then only if this is required to compensate for variation in people's internal resources (e.g. less physical strength, marketable skills, or political connections as they grow old)—a possibility still assumed away at this stage (see Ch. 3).

28. If those living longer receive a higher grant (when totalled over their whole lives), are we then not faced with a case of expensive taste, where those who take care of themselves sufficiently well to keep living long after they have stopped being net contributors impose an unfair burden on the others, just as would those who give birth to lazy or crippled offspring. In either case, however, the adoption of a strictly individualistic perspective forbids one to penalize, by giving them a lesser basic income, the people who would not exist were it not for the 'expensive tastes' of others.

29. I owe this formulation of the objection to Hillel Steiner.

30. Arneson (1992*b*: 510) is therefore justified in observing that 'the call for an unconditional basic income grant represents a compromise with paternalism, not a repudiation of it'. But this compromise need not be represented, contrary to what he suggests (ibid. 509–10) as a move away from a real-libertarian or option-oriented perspective to a welfarist or outcome-oriented one. What characterizes justice remains a fair distribution of options, not of what people make with them. But our being concerned with points of departure rather than final achievements does not prevent us from guaranteeing the recurrent possibility of fresh starts. Of course, the shorter the time-span between fresh starts, the less difference it makes to concentrate on options rather than outcomes. But the difference never vanishes altogether.

31. We could simplify further by assuming a single-period world, in which case the basic income would take the form of a one-off endowment and renting would amount to buying. But it will be convenient to speak about changes, rather than just differences, in the price structure, and I shall therefore forgo this simplification.

32. This suggestion is strictly analogous to Dworkin's (1981*b*: 248–9) auctioning of the resources of a desert island to immigrants, each previously supplied with an equal number of clamshells. Dworkin's parable is further discussed and defended by Rakowski (1991: 69–72). It was strikingly anticipated by the

French philosopher François Huet (1853: 258–9). In a book in which he tries to reconcile socialism and Christianity, Huet asks his readers to imagine a situation in which a number of shipwrecked people arrive on a desert island. 'They are all able-bodied, trained to various occupations and each of them has taken a partner with him.' On the island, there is not just soil, plants, and animals, but also houses and tools left by a population that has now gone. The island is then partitioned into 'bundles of equal value', a lottery takes place, followed by voluntary swapping in order to 'correct the mistakes of the lottery', and in particular to ensure that tools will end up in the hands of those who can put them to the best use. Along with Huet and Dworkin, I am not too bothered by the possibility of situations in which competitive equilibria are not unique (e.g. because of income effects making the demand for some good a non-monotonic function of its price)—which does not affect the argument below—or do not exist (e.g. because of increasing returns to scale)—which is admittedly more embarrassing but fortunately seldom realistic.

33. See e.g. M. Taylor (1982: 150–2), who draws on Steiner's (1974) analysis of the concept of pure negative freedom.

34. See Pattanaik and Xu (1990) for an axiomatic defence of the option-counting variant, and Steiner (1977, 1983, 1994) and Carter (1993) for an elaboration and defence of the spatio-temporal variant.

35. And provided by Arneson (1989, 1990a) in his thoughtful defence of equal opportunity for welfare.

36. See e.g. Dworkin (1981a: § 8), Rawls (1982: § 4), for classic formulations of the general critique of welfarism on this ground, and Rakowski (1991: 44–52) for a more comprehensive critical discussion of Arneson's approach from a similar perspective.

37. I return below (§ 3.7) to this approach in the context of a discussion of various objections to my own preferred alternative, and show how, under some interpretations, the two approaches converge.

38. In his more recent writings, Dworkin (1987, 1989) lays great emphasis on the key role of opportunity costs as the metric of equality.

39. This crucial, though 'non-welfarist', role of preferences has been fully acknowledged from the start by Dworkin (1981b: 289, 338). One implication he also emphasizes is that equality of (heterogeneous) resources cannot be defined without making use of some market or market-like mechanism, which enables people's tastes to be expressed and aggregated. Without such a mechanism, it is impossible to say whether 'equal' amounts of resources are being allocated to each person's life.

40. In the case of produced goods, the fact that many other people want them too may make them less expensive as a result of economies of scale. Interestingly, this possibility is invoked by de Jouvenel (1952: 38-9) in his plea against income egalitarianism: 'It is clear that those goods and services in demand by greater collections of individuals will be provided to those individuals more cheaply than other goods and services wanted by smaller collections of individuals will be provided by these latter. The satisfaction of minority wants

will be more expensive than the satisfaction of majority wants. Members of a minority will be discriminated against.' So be it—at least if, as argued here, what fairness requires is equality in the value of bundles, not in their welfare potentials.

41. See Foley (1967: § 4), Kolm (1972: ch. 2), Varian (1974, 1975) for some classic treatments; Fleurbaey (1994) and Arnsperger (1994) for helpful recent surveys; and Kolm (1994) for a direct connection between envy-freeness and equal (real) freedom.

42. In Dworkin's (1981*b*: 285–7) initial article, satisfaction of the no-envy test seemed to be viewed as an attractive property that happened to be met by the outcome of the auction procedure by which equality was defined. In some of his more recent writings (esp. Dworkin 1987: § 3A), however, he rather seems to view it as providing the very definition of equality: 'Roughly, [equality of resources] stipulates that an ideal egalitarian distribution is one that satisfies an appropriately complex version of the "envy" test: no one will envy the property assigned to or controlled by any other person.' Note that if equality is defined by the auction procedure, it is correct to say that one needs something like a market to even *make sense* of the ideal of equality. But it is not if equality is defined by envy-freeness, even though something like a market may then still be necessary as a *means* for achieving or approximating equality.

43. To see this, suppose Very Funny wants only cliffs in her bundle and nothing else—no beaches or blackberries. The other Funnies care for cliffs more moderately and end up with other goods as well. With an equal number of clamshells to all and competitive pricing, Very Funny can acquire, say, 100 units of cliff. Had she been given double the number of clamshells the others had been given, she would have been able to acquire far more units of cliff and would have done so. Yet, others with less exclusive tastes would still not have envied her bundle. Thus, envy-freeness can be satisfied without equality, as characterized by the procedure.

44. See e.g. Varian (1975). This holds for the pure distribution case, but also for a (perfect foresight) production economy if the resources to which envy-freeness applies are those present at the start: participants in the auction simply take their production as well as their consumption plans into account when making their bids. The full implications of this important restriction to initial endowments will appear in Ch. 4.

45. See Varian (1976), generalized by Champsaur and Laroque (1981). The relevance of this theorem in the present context is pointed out by Varian (1985: 113–14).

46. This is at any rate the strategy I offer to counter Arneson's (1985: 448) negative conclusion that 'judgements of comparative freedom are unable to bear the weight that is often placed on them in the strife of ideological debate'.

47. This is, in its simplest version, the objection spelt out by Arneson (1992*b*: 503-6). A more complex version of the objection relates specifically to the fact that one opportunity-set may contain more income but less leisure than

the other and hence to the choice for an unconditional versus a work-related minimum income. I shall return to it at length in Ch. 4.

48. This is the principal way in which the treatment of externalities—the prevention of public nuisances and provision of public goods—whose relevance is rightly stressed by Arneson (ibid. 506) should be accommodated in this approach. It enables us to avoid the absurd implication that more pollution is always fine as long as it does not hinder the level of production, and thereby the level of the highest sustainable cash basic income.

49. There is another (less problematic) way in which tastes or attitudes differentially fostered by various socio-economic regimes affect the choice between them. For example, if the operation of some regime favours more (or erodes less) a widespread work ethic or a pervasive spirit of co-operation—which is crucially different both from imposing anti-parasite laws or forced labour (in violation of self-ownership) and from subjecting the right to the basic income to some willingness-to-work condition (in violation of non-discrimination)—the highest sustainable level of basic income will be far higher, *ceteris paribus*, than under other regimes. There is a key difference between dispositions and even duties on the one hand, and institutional obligations on the other. And it is therefore conceivable that a real-libertarian case could be made for some type of regime because of the ethos it tends to generate. This possibility will be further illustrated in § 6.2.

50. This approach takes account of the fact that in a less egalitarian regime the minimum income may give access to poorer quality housing because the wealthier can afford larger or more homes. But it does not take into account the fact that with what is assessed as the same minimum income in real terms one may feel more frustrated, envious, ashamed, unhappy in a less egalitarian than in a more egalitarian regime (see e.g. Rawls (1971: 546) or Grey (1973: 321), for hints in this direction), or in an inegalitarian regime with more class mobility than in a more caste-like one. Hard luck: maximum real freedom for all does not always coincide with maximum happiness for all. This comment should sound less harsh, however, once the constraint of undominated diversity is introduced in the next chapter.

CHAPTER 3

1. I use these terms interchangeably in a broad sense that covers both capacities to function and capacities for welfare (see Cohen 1989*b*: 918–9). I prefer to use the term 'endowments' where others might have used, for example, 'resources', 'opportunities', or 'capacities' to stress the restriction to what people have been 'given', whether at the start or later on, whether intentionally or unwittingly, whether in the form of external goods and purchasing power or as bodily and mental features.

2. Possessing an expensive taste is relevantly distinct from being stuck with one, i.e. from failing to possess the capacity to get rid of it. This distinction will prove important further on.

3. Equivalently, one can imagine that each of the n Polypolitans is given, in the form of a tradable share, $1/n$ of each external good and of each person's talents.

4. We could equivalently model the problem in such a way that some people would not bother to buy all their own leisure and would rather abandon some of it to other people, who would allocate it to its most productive use (or sell it to firms that would do so), since they would anyway do exactly the same with it if they had bought it themselves.

5. Or, equivalently, as giving everyone a grant matching the per capita value of all endowments, while taxing at a rate of 100% those who happen to hold those endowments. Akerlof (1978) points out some advantages such a system of 'tagged' transfers possesses over a negative income tax system, without claiming that the overall balance of advantages is in its favour.

6. If talents were identical, this difficulty would not arise, because there would be no reason to depart from equality of external endowments. Nor would it arise if tastes were identical, for if both care for racing and not for singing, the good runner will have to compensate the good singer up to the point where both will feel equivalence is reached. Classic discussions of the nature of the problem and how it might be tackled can be found in Pazner and Schmeidler (1974) and Varian (1975: 152–3). The general conditions under which there exist envy-free allocations have now been thoroughly studied. See e.g. Thomson (1994), Fleurbaey (1994), and Arnsperger (1994) for helpful surveys of the literature.

7. Providing, of course, the abilities in relation to which people's implicit incomes are defined coincide with the 'received' talents which are supposed to be up for bids in the auction. This is taken for granted by Varian (1985: 111–13) in his discussion of Dworkin (1981*b*). However, the market price of someone's leisure, i.e. the earning power associated to her current abilities, does not generally coincide with the earning power associated with her talents, i.e. to that part or aspect of her abilities which has been 'given' to her. At first sight, the latter seems necessarily inferior to the former, since it only concerns a subset or incipient stage of abilities. But the opposite is the case, for in the context of the auction, the counterfactual earning power that must be equalized is not the one associated to people's talents if they had been left undeveloped but the one associated to those same talents when developed and used in the most productive fashion. It is each person's maximally developed potential, given her internal endowment, that must be equalized.

8. She and her—it may be worth repeating here—are used as genderless abbreviations.

9. Lonely and Lovely resemble Dworkin's Deborah and Ernest in relevant respects. The second objection does not play such a central role in Dworkin's motivation for his own proposal, even though its relevance is implicitly acknowledged in the fact that Dworkin finds it necessary (as we shall see in § 3.4) to introduce a separate device for dealing with handicaps, whether or not these affect people's productive abilities.

10. Dworkin suggests three further arguments for discarding the extended auction which I find less convincing. First, he points out that we are not 'able to find some way of identifying, in any person's wealth at any particular time, the component traceable to different talents as distinguished from different ambitions' (Dworkin 1981*b*: 313). However, a similar problem arises, and is assumed to be solved, in the case of external resources. People's ambitions do not leave external any more than internal resources unimproved and combine them all together to generate their wealth. This does not in principle prevent the counterfactual auction from yielding a competitive price for either. Secondly, Dworkin stresses the 'reciprocal influence that talents and ambitions exercise on each other' (ibid.). But similarly, while your ambitions determine which external resources you will bid for, if any, in the auction, the external resources you actually possess will affect your ambitions (you'll want to become a botanist because of the many flowers in the garden of the family house you have inherited). True, there is a difference. Unlike your external resources, you cannot (much?) help having the talents you actually have. And it makes, therefore, little sense to ask yourself what your preferences might have been without them when bidding for the various resources, whereas it does make some sense to abstract from the external resources actually allotted to you. But this does not prevent the auction from applying to talents. All it requires is that the bidders should be able to say, given their preferences (which they have in part because of the internal—but also the external—resources they possess in the real world), how much they would give for the opportunity to possess, use, and develop the various sorts of talents. Thirdly, one rough way of describing the auction for external resources consists in viewing it as a counterfactual determination of what people's incomes would be if they had been allocated the same amount of these resources. But, Dworkin (1981*b*: 314) points out, it is impossible to determine, for each person, what 'income he would have had if, counterfactually, talents for production had all been equal'. And even if we do not agree with him that 'in a world in which everyone could play sexy roles in films with equal authority, there would probably be no [. . .] films', it must be recognized that trying to imagine what the distribution of income (or earning power) would look like in such a world is a hopeless business. What is required in the auction (for both internal and external resources), however, is not that everyone should possess (either before or after) an equal amount of each resource, but an equal tradable title to each resource. The counterfactual exercise remains rather adventurous. But it is not meaningless. It is, as it happens, exactly the sort of exercise in terms of which Roemer (1982*a*) defines his notions of capitalist (external resources) and socialist (internal resources) exploitation (see § 5.7).

11. It has been the object of a close critique by John Roemer, which I discuss in App. 1.

12. Note that this implies that risk-averse people interested in maximum leisure subject to subsistence will choose a level of coverage (in terms of *earning power*) that *exceeds* the subsistence level. Otherwise, they would end up

having to work nearly full-time in order to reach subsistence with very poor talents, while having to work far less with abundant talents.

13. One might think of objecting that Dworkin here got himself into unnecessary trouble, for in order to avoid the difficulty he sees with the thick-veil insurance scheme, there is no need to restrict compensation narrowly to the lack of lucrative talents. Just as one can let people know that they like growing pumpkins and are good at it without telling them whether anyone is interested in buying them, similarly, could one not let them know that they can curl their tongue, and how much they enjoy doing it, but not to what extent this can constitute a source of power, prestige, or affection in their particular community? The point is that knowledge of one's talents (in addition to one's tastes) need not convey all the non-pecuniary advantages attached to them, any more than it conveys all its pecuniary advantages. Unfortunately, this strategy does not lead very far, for there are many talents—arguably, beauty, charm, or wit—which do not mean anything apart from these non-pecuniary advantages they convey (can you be funny if no one finds you funny?). It makes no sense, therefore, to assume knowledge of their presence, but not of the associated advantages.

14. In the formulation of Dworkin (1981*b*), not altered nor qualified in Dworkin's later writings on equality.

15. At least in a certain world. Under uncertainty, on the other hand, there is no reason why luck should systematically lead the film star to be envied rather than to envy.

16. This might provide a fair reconstruction of what Sen (1984: 323) presents as his central criticism of Dworkin's approach: 'Indeed, to see the interpersonal variations of the mappings from resources to capabilities as due only to handicaps of some people is to underestimate the general nature of the problem. As was already mentioned, depending on our body size, metabolism, temperament, social conditions, etc., the translation of resources into the ability to do things does vary substantially from person to person and from community to community, and to ignore this is to miss out on an important general dimension of moral concern.' To be fair to Dworkin, one must concede that his concern with the equalization of capabilities does not boil down to a compensation for handicaps. But to the extent that he actually goes beyond such compensation, he does so in a biased way, by completely ignoring any 'ability to do things' (of the type Sen has in mind) that is not matched by an ability to make money.

17. Note that if this is objectionable, so is—at least prima facie and in a first best world—any form of income tax (as opposed to a lump-sum tax). For an income tax is bound to treat differently, because of different behaviours stemming from different tastes, people with identical talents. If correct, this point would be most damaging for the claim put forward in the previous chapter, as the ban on income taxation would contradict advocating the highest sustainable basic income. This constitutes one version of the central issue that will occupy us in the next chapter.

18. Dworkin (1981*b*: 302) forcefully argues against a conception that would

allow for insurance against tastes that lead to a less-than-average level of welfare: if one abstracts from one's tastes, how could one possibly decide how much to insure for?

19. More formally, it fails what Fleurbaey (1994: § 4) calls the 'strict-pairwise-compensation test', which requires two people to receive equal external endowments if their internal endowments are identical. A different formulation of basically the same objection can be found in Rakowski (1991: 135–7).

20. Fleurbaey (1994: § 4) shows, for example, that there is no criterion that can meet simultaneously the condition of strict pairwise compensation that has just been shown to be violated by Dworkin's proposals and a condition of 'full pairwise compensation' which requires that two people with identical preference schedules should achieve the same level of welfare. This is an interesting impossibility result, but one that is irrelevant to our resolutely non-welfarist approach.

21. Internal endowments must here be understood, as they have been all along, as referring to the capacities (or lack of them) people owe to their genetic equipment or their environment over their whole lifetimes. It is not because the internal endowment of a dying 95-year-old is worse in all respects than that of a healthy teenager, that the former person's endowment can be said to be dominated by the latter's, as she may have enjoyed a splendid health and possessed enviable talents for most of her life. Dominance only occurs when in view of what is known or can be predicted about a person's past and future internal circumstances, everyone finds her lifetime endowment worse than that of another person. This implies, of course, that a person who is crippled by an accident may suddenly become entitled to a specific transfer, but also that the amount of the transfer required to cancel dominance will be higher if a person is crippled at 20 than at 90. (This touches directly on the legitimacy of using expensive techniques to keep a person alive or fit beyond a certain age at society's expense.) It further follows that assessments will have to be revised in the light of developments in the availability and costs of medical technology, or in the community's taste pattern (which may e.g. turn something into a 'handicap' which was not previously one, or affect the level of transfer required to cancel dominance). These remarks supplement the real-libertarian justification of an extensive free (or nearly free) health insurance system initiated in § 2.4. The articulation between the veil-of-ignorance approach sketched there (under the assumption of equal endowments) and undominated diversity (across different endowments) would need to be spelt out far more than I can do here. For extensive relevant discussions, see Rakowski (1991: chs. 4 and 6), who rightly argues, in particular, that undominated diversity cannot be the sole yardstick for assistance in matters of health care (ibid. 97).

22. Hence, contrary to what Ackerman (1980: 132) suggests, showing that 'I have the ability to do some good things better than you, and vice versa' is generally not sufficient to be able to conclude that there is no dominance.

23. Genetic engineering, if not ruled out by powerful second-best arguments, should use a lottery such that 'the only embryo distributions that can be

forbidden are those in which at least one member of the set genetically dominates at least one other member of the set. Thus it is perfectly possible that a blind embryo will be brought into existence in a perfectly liberal world—so long as it has other attributes that permit it to establish a relation of undominated diversity with each and every one of the fellow citizens with which it will share the planet' (ibid. 120).

24. Even on this criterion, the boundary between a handicap and a lack of talent which does not qualify as such is to some extent technologically and culturally relative (short-sightedness or a low IQ may count as handicaps in some societies though not in others). But the underlying distinction is a more precise formulation of what Dworkin (1981*b*: 299, 316) has in mind when referring to 'ordinary handicaps' or to 'the risks against which most people would insure in a general way' and, therefore, of the intuition behind the central distinction of his hybrid scheme.

25. The reason for the reversal of at least one person's preferences may, but need not, be that the transfer is being used to regain the missing capacity (say, through an eye operation). The approach presented here is not capacity-focused in the narrow sense this would imply. But it is capacity-focused in the sense that the transfers are not required to compensate for a welfare deficit, but to make people able to do (in the broadest sense) at least one thing which others could not do.

26. Note that the maximum amount that can be sustainably redistributed in a differentiated way need not be the same as the highest amount that can be sustainably redistributed in a uniform way. It may be higher, because it provides stronger incentives to work to the talented (they are not given the option of remaining idle). And it may be lower because of the greater simplicity of a basic income and its contribution to a more flexible economy. See Akerlof (1978) and Van Parijs (1990) on efficiency arguments for and against targeting, and see Suplicy (ed.) (1992) on the important closely related question of how unconditional the minimum income guarantee should be in a less-developed country such as Brazil.

27. I do not have the option of excluding this possibility by arguing—as does Arneson (1989: 89–90), for example—that it would be unfair to regard Lovely as responsible for the fact that she has a taste for her own (as it happens, expensive) leisure. In contrast with the blind with a taste for seeing (given the assumptions made earlier in this section), there is, by assumption, at least one preference schedule genuinely available that would make Lovely better off than people in Lonely's position. It is not 'her fault' that she has the talents she has, but it is 'her fault' that she has no taste for using the possibilities they give her. The criterion of undominated diversity is fully consistent with people having less leisure by virtue of their talents, just as it is fully consistent with people having less income by virtue of their lack of talents. What it does exclude—indeed, what it amounts to excluding—is that one should *necessarily* (i.e. irrespective of the available preference schedule one picks) have less welfare by virtue of one's talents or lack thereof.

28. This seems to me a more direct and general way of getting to Dworkin's

(1981*b*: 321) main practical conclusion: 'The lower the income level chosen as the covered risk, the better the argument becomes that most people, given the chance to buy insurance on equal terms would in fact buy at that level. The argument becomes compelling, I think, well above the level of income presently used to trigger transfer payments for unemployment or minimum wage levels in either Britain or the United States.' There is an earning power that is so low that anyone would prefer practically any situation with a higher earning power. Under such circumstances, our scheme requires that the basic income should be reduced, possibly to zero, to finance a transfer system targeted to those with low earning powers. This approach is more general because the compensation for 'ordinary handicaps' is derived in exactly the same way.

29. See App. 2, for a more rigorous characterization of these conditions.

30. See App. 3, for a more formal treatment of the links between undominated diversity and related notions, and Fleurbaey (1994) for an illuminating axiomatic discussion.

31. The approach offered here can therefore be viewed as a special case of what is being explored by Amartya Sen (1985: ch. 7; 1992: ch. 5) in connection with the valuation of capability-sets. Comparisons are here assumed to operate straight over the capability sets associated with comprehensive endowments—which amounts to bypassing the question of whether or not the value of a capability-set, i.e. a set of accessible functionings, is reducible to that of its best element (Sen 1985: 67–9). The fact that these comparisons, in a diverse society, often conflict and that our procedure therefore yields only a partial ordering is no embarrassment whatever on Sen's view. For there is 'no compulsion to rank the capability sets completely': 'In comparing the advantages of two persons, it is perfectly possible to say that *neither* is clearly more advantaged than the other.' Going beyond the intersection partial ordering is only possible 'at the cost of some arbitrariness' (Sen 1985: 66–7; also Sen 1992: 7, 133–4). For further documentation of the proximity between Sen's approach and what is being proposed here, see especially his recent discussion with Rawls, where the possibility of providing a partial ranking of capability-sets that 'can be based on superiority in terms of each of the relevant comprehensive doctrines' (Sen 1990*a*: 119 n. 22; 1992: 84 n. 25) plays a crucial role and also, most explicitly, his response to an earlier version of this chapter (Sen 1990*b*: 460–3).

32. This looks like a point of disagreement with Ackerman (1980: 120), who is concerned to achieve 'undominated diversity with each and every one of the fellow citizens with which it will share the planet', but ceases to be one if one ascribes to him the cosmopolitan assumption that we are henceforth all part of a single global community.

33. I borrow this example from Arneson (1992*a*: § 5).

34. This is why, under plausible factual assumptions, the respect of undominated diversity is consistent with a basic income that is insensitive to cost-of-living differences between different areas (see § 2.2).

35. Hence choosing this strategy would not make the criterion of undominated

diversity vacuous, contrary to what is suggested by Rakowski (1991: 96–7) in his (too) brief and (too) dismissive discussion of undominated diversity.

36. At least providing the preferences by reference to which equal opportunity for welfare is defined are not deemed 'inaccessible'—as sometimes suggested by Arneson (see esp. 1992*a*: § 5)—if the only reason for not adopting them is that 'it would be unreasonable from the point of view of [our] current values to adopt [them]'. This would bring back the strong version of the expensive-taste objection.

37. This argument is congruent with G. A. Cohen's (1989*b*: 920–1) shift from the one-dimensional metric of equal opportunity for welfare to the multidimensional metric of 'equal access to advantage'.

38. This provides, it seems to me, an adequate riposte to Alexander and Schwarzschild's (1987: 100–2) central objection to Dworkin, that there is no 'neutral' distinction between needs and wants, and hence that 'for anyone who takes neutrality seriously, handicaps, cravings and expensive tastes are on a par with one another' (ibid. 101). It is no doubt abstractly conceivable, as they point out, that someone with particular religious beliefs *might* value blindness as a sign of Divine Grace (and hence not as a handicap). But using the conceptions of a good life (and of what is required for it) that are *actually* (and genuinely) held in the society considered in order to assess dominance seems to me a sensible thing to do, as the aim is to consider the full range of preferences for the choice of which people can plausibly be held responsible.

39. This indicates how our criterion can accommodate Amartya Sen's insistence that applying the principle of 'equality of basic capabilities' is bound to be culture-dependent (e.g. Sen 1980: 368), and his dissatisfaction with the goods metric on the ground that it is insensitive not just to differences in abilities but also to differences in the 'social demands of particular customs' (e.g. Sen 1985: 28).

40. The universe of preference schedules that is being taken into account need not in principle coincide with the scale on which redistribution is being considered. But I doubt that the question of distributive justice has ever been, and can ever be, seriously raised in a society that is not either culturally homogeneous, or knit together by sufficiently sizeable flows of information and people across its component cultural traditions.

41. A related but distinct—and, for my present purposes irrelevant—objection is that the implied level of compensation is politically unrealistic. See e.g. Dworkin (1981*b*: 300–1) on Sen (1980).

42. If the level of the unconditional income has already been driven down to zero when this point is reached, this potential universal gain may simply be due to the adverse incentives generated by increased taxation. If it has not, this may be due to the fact that transfers distributed in an unconditional way (i.e. as a basic income) are simpler to administer, do not generate incentives to hide one's capacities (e.g. to pretend to be involuntarily unemployed or unfit for work), and arguably increase economic efficiency by fostering labour flexibility and spreading an entrepreneurial spirit. (As previously mentioned in n. 26, however, there may also be more to sustainably redistribute in a

differentiated than in an undifferentiated way.) I am here taking for granted that undominated diversity can be pursued through income taxation as well as through lump-sum taxation (of less than the level of basic income), since I depict this pursuit as consisting in diverting resources from the funding of a basic income at the highest sustainable level, without any principled restriction on the tax base. As already mentioned in n. 17, this is at least prima facie inconsistent with the last objection made to Dworkin (about the unequal treatment of identically talented people) and raises a crucial issue that will occupy us throughout Ch. 4.

43. Do these two qualifications concede too much, at the expense of the handicapped? Let us bear in mind that for the latter, receiving resources in the form of a basic income rather than as targeted transfers has advantages too. Transfers one owes to the inadequacy of one's internal endowment tend to involve a stigma, a blow to one's self-respect, and often also, owing to the imperfect detection of talents and handicaps, a 'disability trap', that is partly removed as a higher unconditional income makes some conditional transfers dispensable.

44. It is only under those circumstances that the implications here drawn from a concern with undominated diversity would coincide with those drawn by Ackerman (1980: 268 n. 2), who argues against universal systems, such as a negative income tax, on the ground that they are too favourable to 'healthy proletarians': 'it would be best to design a more complex strategy that, despite heavy administrative costs, tries to identify severely handicapped citizens entitled to aid levels that are far more generous than those prevailing under the typical negative income tax proposal.' Outside those circumstances, I argue, justice requires that both types of system be combined.

45. Because the maximization of basic income needs to operate under the constraint of undominated diversity, special attention will have to be given to various policies that may make the constraint significantly easier to meet. Universal provision in kind (such as preventive medicine), specific provision in kind to the handicapped (say, access to public transport), or to those who would otherwise become handicapped (e.g. special educational aid to the slow learners), the promotion of a spirit of tactful and effective help to those with special needs are just a few examples. This implies that economic efficiency is not the sole important consideration that must guide the shaping of health care and educational systems from a real-libertarian standpoint.

46. This argument, discussed, for example, by Grey (1973: 317–20), is in my view the best defence of a maximin principle against Harsanyi-like original-position utilitarians. Rawls (1990: § 28.1) himself insists that he has never claimed that maximin was adequate in all circumstances of risk or uncertainty: 'The only question is whether, given the highly special, indeed unique, conditions of the original position, the maximin rule is a useful heuristic rule of thumb for the parties to use to organize their deliberations.' Roemer (1985*b*: 165) must have come close to seeing the strength of this point when contrasting the case where people want to insure against fluctuations of their skill level

and the case where 'after the die is cast, each person will be either of high or of low skill for his whole life'.

47. I assume, for simplicity's sake, that we are in a certain world. Tastes being given, each endowment is associated with one level of welfare. If uncertain events were allowed to disturb this simple association, the most natural extension would consist of evaluating each endowment by the level of welfare it would yield under the worst possible circumstances.

48. As meticulously shown by Cohen (1989*b*: § 4), Dworkin is not always clear as to whether his central distinction is one of identity v. circumstances, capacities v. preferences, or choice v. (brute) luck. But I believe what he says can consistently be reconstructed along the lines sketched here.

49. Alexander and Schwarzschild (1987: § 3C) similarly reject Roemer's critique of Dworkin because of its deterministic presuppositions.

CHAPTER 4

1. See the discussion of expensive tastes in §§ 2.6 and 3.7.

2. The substance of the following important objection has been formulated by Steiner (1986) and Cohen (1987) in a way that made it unescapable. Both raise the objection in connection with van der Veen and Van Parijs's (1986*b*: 726–7) handling of Elster's (1986: 719) main ethical charge that 'most workers would, correctly in [his] opinion, see the proposal as a recipe for exploitation of the industrious by the lazy'.

3. If there is only one Lazy and one Crazy, this is of course not true, as Crazy's work would no longer finance the grant. But if there are many Crazies, this holds for any one of them taking the others' choices as given.

4. This strategy is envisaged, but eventually rejected, by Robert van der Veen (1991: 204–7), in his own reply to the Steiner–Cohen critique of van der Veen and Van Parijs (1986*b*). Abstracting from rather feeble externality-based arguments, reliance on perfectionistic premises is even more obviously required to justify the 'Marxian' criterion of maximization of basic income *as a proportion* of average income, be it at the expense of its absolute level. This point is discussed more fully in Van Parijs (1992: 17–21) and Van Parijs (1993*a*: 195–8).

5. See Roemer (1989*a*: esp. theorem 8), for a relevant formal discussion.

6. Jeroen Knijff (private communication, 11 Aug. 1993) rightly ticked me off for conceding too rashly that maximin actual income generally diverges from maximum basic income. In an opulent society (in the technical sense of Ch. 3, App. 2), this cannot be taken for granted. In a less than opulent society, however, it *is* plausible to conjecture that some appropriately designed conditional schemes would yield a higher minimum income. In such a society, therefore, the arguments adduced below are needed to provide a Rawlsian justification of the highest feasible basic income, though not necessarily as a full substitute for the conditional income guarantee. The constraint of

undominated diversity, which requires that everyone's potential income should reach at least the subsistence level (§ 3.5), implicitly provides a way of balancing a concern with income and a concern with the other dimensions of socio-economic advantage.

7. From the most sketchy to the most developed, explicitly Rawlsian justifications of basic income along these lines can be found in Brittan (1988: 301), Van Parijs (1991*a*: § 8.7), and Byrne (1993: ch. 2).

8. See Rawls (1990: § 51.3). His emphasis.

9. See Musgrave (1974: 630, 632). Richard Arneson's 'equal opportunity for welfare', discussed and rejected above (§ 3.7) constitutes a sophisticated variant of Musgrave's 'equality of potential welfare'.

10. Rawls (1988: 257). See also, more elliptically, Rawls (1974: 654). By turning to this response, Rawls is discarding another possibility which one might think his framework provided. His 'principle of fairness' requires each individual 'to do his part' as defined by the rules of a just basic structure (Rawls 1971: 111–12). But interpreting such an obligation as an obligation to work would be entirely *ad hoc* under the initial formulation of the Difference Principle. Hence Rawls's sensible preference for the proposed reformulation.

11. See the Appendix to this chapter.

12. See Lerner (1936) and Lange (1937*b*: 143–4). See also Suzumura (1987), for a more general formal analysis.

13. See David Purdy's (1990: § 3) witty presentation of a case for basic income grounded in part on the endless contestability of any solution to such difficulties, in part on the impossibility of designing, at a reasonable cost (in terms of both resources and liberties), a scheme that would significantly improve the fit between income and a normatively meaningful notion of work. See also Goodin's (1992) partly parallel argument for a basic income as a 'minimally presumptuous social policy'.

14. Rawls's proposal thus appears to imply a particularly strong version of the principle 'To each according to her labour', in so far as it requires (abstracting from incentive effects that may require one to settle for less on maximin grounds) the whole of the social product to be distributed in strict proportion to labour. Weaker versions only require, for example, that anyone working more should have a higher income than anyone not working at all, or that the reward for work should exactly compensate workers for the effort involved in working (and training for it). See § 5.6 for further discussion.

15. The strategy presented in the following section is, I believe, the only satisfactory one. James Sterba (1980: 43–6, 120–1) is struggling with the same problem when trying to settle the conflict between 'Hard Toilers' and 'Free Riders'. He ends up justifying an unconditional basic income at a level just sufficient to meet the normal costs of living in society. But his (original-position-type) argument leaves this conclusion poorly protected both against the challenge that some work could be demanded as a counterpart and against the claim that, in a sufficiently affluent society, the basic income could legitimately be higher than this bare minimum.

16. Or, within the framework of Dworkin's (1981*b*: 283–90) parable, it is the

income given by the equal amount of clamshells each immigrant receives in order to bid for the resources found on the island. According to Dworkin (1981*b*: 304–6), 'an equal share of resources should be devoted to the life of each person. [. . .] It would therefore violate equality of resources if the community were to redistribute [the hard worker's] wealth, say, at the end of each year.' This is fully consistent, however, with taxing the hard worker to finance the basic income, providing the tax does not exceed the rent on the external resources on which her hard work operates.

17. The determination of such equilibrium prices or rents requires that one abstract from improvements performed on the particular asset by members of the current generation (e.g. a piece of land without the coal mine dug in it, but with the coal found in it, or perhaps the probability of finding it), but not from any improvement performed, even by the current generation, on neighbouring assets. In principle, account must be taken of everyone's plans in the process of determining the value of any asset.

18. In a world in which Crazies need no land (or any other scarce asset), a positive basic income would really mean an appropriation of part of the exclusive product of Crazy's labour. Lazy's basic income would constitute his positive endowment. But Crazy, in this case, would receive a negative endowment over the period, as the income taxed away in order to finance Lazy's and her own basic incomes would not match the value of anything she appropriates.

19. See Dworkin (1981*b*: 306): 'Of course, Adrian [a close kin of Crazy's] might actually enjoy his hard work, so that he makes no sacrifice. He prefers working hard to anything else. But this cannot provide any argument, under equality of resources, that he should gain less in money or other goods by his work than if he hated every minute of it, any more than it argues against charging someone a low price for lettuce, which he actually prefers to truffles.' Note, however, that if it were work, rather than income, that all Crazies were in love with, and if there were enough Crazies around, land would be turned into a toy (while remaining a tool), and competition for its appropriation might conceivably drive the Crazies' incomes below the Lazies'.

20. If it were, we would be considering the position held by Hillel Steiner (1994: ch. 8), in the tradition of Thomas Paine (1796), Henry George (1879), Léon Walras (1896), and others, which favours an equal distribution of the competitive rent of *natural* resources. When the guiding notion is a concern with people's real freedom, not the respect of their (so-called) natural rights, there is no ground for making a sharp distinction between produced and unproduced assets. Note, however, that Steiner (1992: 83–6) narrows the gap between the two approaches by assimilating bequests (but not gifts) to natural resources.

21. In the particular context of our Lazy-Crazy situation, therefore, whereas Rawls's strategy consisted in modifying the list of socio-economic advantages by adding leisure to wealth and income, Dworkin's strategy consists of dropping income and leaving only wealth.

22. Justifications of this type have been offered, for example, by Thomas Paine

(1796: 620)—not altogether consistently with his main rationale (in terms of common land ownership)—and by a long series of socialist thinkers, from François Huet (1853), César De Paepe (see Cunliffe 1987), and Edward Bellamy (1888, 1897) to George D. H. Cole (1935, 1944) and Tibor Liska (1990).

23. This objection was put to me by Erik Schokkaert (in 1989) and by Ronald Dworkin (in 1991). The issue it raises is discussed at length, and handled very differently, by Rakowski (1991: 155–66).

24. A distinct but related objection is that many gifts and bequests specifically made in order to benefit someone could be treated on a par with other rewards of a person's activities, and hence assimilated, not to her endowments, but to the other products of her ambition. I shall rely on this very analogy to argue, conversely, that a significant part of the reward for work should be treated as a (self-interested) gift, and hence assimilated to a person's endowment. The argument used there (§ 4.6) to refute the objection that more than the endowment part of a wage risks being taxed away can also be used here in order to refute the parallel objection that gift or inheritance taxes are treating the more ambitious unfairly. See Rakowski (1991: ch. 7) for a more thorough discussion of (and divergent view on) the underlying issues.

25. I take this elaboration of the criterion to be consistent with Dworkin's (1981*b*: 331) incidental suggestion that he would be willing to abandon strict equality in favour of some analogue of a difference principle applied to resources.

26. See Daussun (1986), tables 71 and 95. Underreporting can of course safely be assumed to be pervasive. (Total private wealth is estimated to be about three times the GNP. With a life expectancy of about 75 years and a strong concentration of wealth in the older cohorts, this should lead to gifts and bequests at least twice as high as the 3 per cent quoted.) But this is hardly relevant, as it can even more safely be assumed that underreporting would reach unprecedented peaks if the taxation of wealth transfers were dramatically increased beyond the current level. Other countries perform even worse than France, with wealth transfer taxes at 0.20 per cent of GNP in the United Kingdom, for example, and at 0.17 per cent in the United States (1984 figures, same source).

27. A publicly owned art collection, which only the rich bother to visit, would presumably provide a more persuasive example.

28. In several of G. D. H. Cole's (e.g. 1944: 306) formulations of the case for a social dividend, for example, more emphasis is laid on inherited technology than on inherited capital. The same ethical intuition is also very present in contemporary justifications of basic income. For typical examples, see Duboin (1988) and Oubridge (1990).

29. In the next section, I defend a roundabout way of locating and capturing a further (and massive) part of our common technological inheritance.

30. In the following discussion, I shall be assuming a capitalist context. I shall consider much later (§ 6.1) how the conclusions of this discussion apply in a socialist context as well.

31. I return to the problem raised by externalities and externality-based free-riding in § 5.2 below and, at more length, in Van Parijs (1996a: §§ 1–3).

32. See Lindbeck and Snower (1985, 1988) and Akerlof and Yellen (1986), for useful surveys of microeconomic equilibrium-unemployment theories in general, and efficiency-wage theories in particular, respectively. It is this sort of theory that I shall primarily have in mind in the following pages. Insider–outsider and efficiency-wage models have the great advantage, in the present context, of contradicting the common claim that the inequality of endowments with which this section is concerned would go away if, as those who make this claim usually recommend, the labour market were left to its own devices. One particularly relevant special case covers the *involuntary* unemployment that is generated by the existence of some form of (means-tested, work-tested) minimum income guarantee called forth by a concern for undominated diversity. Even in the absence of a matching statutory minimum wage, unemployment will be generated in such a context not because people would not take jobs that paid less than this income guarantee (they may be forced to by virtue of the latter's conditionality), but because their work motivation would be so poor that employers would not find it worth their while to employ them. Because of this efficiency-wage mechanism, the unemployment that stems from the existence of a conditional minimum income guarantee can be largely involuntary, and hence give rise to employment rents that are up for redistribution, rather than only voluntary unemployment, which does not have this implication.

33. Are jobs really assets people are endowed with, rather than something they manage to achieve by applying energetically, getting up early, standing in the queue, etc.? If this prevents your job from being part of your endowment, then the huge estate you inherited from the aunt whose favours you spent some time courting is no part of it either. I shall indicate below (§ 4.6) how the practical implementation of the idea that job assets should be redistributed is protected against taxing more than the gift or rent component of jobs. See also Van Parijs (1993a: ch. 6) for further discussion of the crucial relevance of job assets for a theory of social classes relevant to today's world.

34. Such a job voucher system is suggested, independently of Dworkin's auction-based notion of equal resources, in stimulating papers by Bert Hamminga (1983, 1988, 1995).

35. As it will be used here, the notion of rent is coextensive with the appropriation of an asset in short supply. It is crucially narrower than the notion of consumer or producer surplus. Schor and Bowles's (1987: 584–5) concept of employment rent is similarly meant to measure the extent of job scarcity. It is empirically estimated by the cost of job loss, more precisely by the difference between current earnings and the expected income during the year following employment termination (the average of future earnings and income-replacing social welfare benefits, weighted by the expected duration of unemployment). For two more thorough discussions of the notion of rent, both in connection with David Gauthier's use of the latter, see Mack (1992) and Van Parijs (1995a: §§ 5–6).

36. There is a wide variety of possible mechanisms, some more contingent (e.g. social security contributions calculated per worker rather than per working hour), some more intrinsic (relating e.g. to hiring, training, and firing costs, to the risk of bottlenecks, etc.), that may account for such a negative impact. I discuss what I believe to be the most important among them in Van Parijs (1991*b*).

37. This is *not* equivalent to turning the involuntarily unemployed into voluntary unemployed: one effect of the bribes will be to induce some of the employed to take parental or sabbatical leave or to retire early, thus making some jobs available to the involuntarily unemployed.

38. This second premiss can be challenged. For example, various reasons (cost of on-the-job training, efficiency-wage argument, etc.) may contribute to the creation of new jobs badly affecting average productivity, in such a way that the workers' net income will be lower under the employer-bribing strategy than under the basic-income strategy. However, I make here the less favourable assumption that both the subsidizing of wages and the distribution of selective benefits is a 'cheaper' way of getting to full employment than introduction of a basic income.

39. The intuition is akin to the one that underlies James Meade's (1984: 140) 'attempt to devise wage-setting institutions which would allow the real wage rate to fall to the extent necessary to provide employment opportunities to all who sought them, but to combine this with fiscal and other institutions which ensured that directly or indirectly everyone enjoyed a fair share of the profits earned on the robots, computers and tapes, and indeed on profits in general'. The same justification remains present in the more recent formulations of his social dividend proposal (Meade 1989, 1993).

40. In other words, it is possible to combine the abolition of the *ex ante* rent (which is reflected in the price people are willing to pay for the job and hence matters to distributive justice) with the preservation of the *ex post* rent (which constitutes the sanction and hence affects the work effort) by issuing bonds that are lost without compensation by a dismissed worker. This possibility was pointed out to me by Sam Bowles.

41. Moreover, should our concern with leximin real freedom not lead us to reject this whole scheme? The net external endowment of a worker dismissed from a highly valued job will be far lower than that of anyone else. Indeed, it may even be negative. (The price paid, possibly on credit, for the job, may easily exceed the level of the person's basic income and her income from other external assets.)

42. At least under conditions under which deviations from the package of measures that maximizes profit is not disastrous. I shall return (§ 6.7) to the crucial role played, under contemporary conditions, by the profitability constraint.

43. These arguments are reviewed in Van Parijs (1990). See also § 6.7.

44. See e.g. Stiglitz (1987), Bowles and Gintis (1988).

45. This is the view implicitly adopted by Dworkin (1981*b*), who makes no distinction between internal resources and job-based resources. Indeed, by

calling his compensation scheme 'underemployment insurance' (ibid. 314), he strongly suggests that jobs and talents should be treated in the same fashion. In Ch. 3, I have argued against Dworkin's proposal for 'equalizing' talents in favour of a criterion of undominated diversity. But the question remains of why the principle that is deemed adequate to 'equalize' talents should not also be used to 'equalize' job assets.

46. See e.g. Lindbeck and Snower (1985) for a discussion and refinement of this definition.

47. This is a fairly accurate stylized representation of the strong real-life correlation between educational level and unemployment rate. (For some striking figures, see Rees 1986.) Educational level, of course, is no direct reflection of genetic talent. But let us not forget that our notion of internal endowment encompasses any aspect of a person's non-transferable equipment given to her, whether by nature or her family or her social background. And educational level is, no doubt, strongly affected by talent in this broad sense. For one interesting explanation of why one should expect this to be the case, see Akerlof's (1981) jobs-as-dam-sites argument, which shows that under some plausible conditions, firms will find it in their interest to exhaust more talented labour, while leaving some untalented labour unused despite high wage differentials. Indeed, some less-talented labour may remain unemployed at any positive wage rate despite positive net productivity, as long as some more-talented labour is available.

48. I owe this puzzling objection to Erik Schokkaert.

49. It is not the same, no doubt, for an employer to work with her employee as for an employee to work with her employer. But then is it the same for a woman to live with a man as for a man to live with a woman? (Surely, it is not only an auction for gay partners that seems, even conceptually, inappropriate!)

50. The fact that scarcity, rather than inherited technology or productive capital, provides the key criterion for the redistribution of job assets does not mean that technological progress and capital accumulation are irrelevant. Job scarcity may arise despite an unchanged number of jobs, an unchanged number of people, unchanged tastes, and an unchanged condition of the jobless, just because innovation and accumulation make having a job increasingly rewarding.

CHAPTER 5

1. From the beginning, the term 'exploitation' had strongly normative connotations: Thus we read in the influential *Doctrine de Saint-Simon* (published in 1830 by Saint-Simon's disciples in their journal *L'Organisateur*): 'Nowadays, the entire work force is exploited by those whose property it uses; the managers themselves are subjected to this exploitation in their relations with the owners, but to an incomparably smaller extent; and they

participate in turn in the privileges of exploitation whose weight falls entirely on the workers' (quoted in Ansart 1984: 34). Whether Marx himself used the notion of exploitation in order to condemn capitalism morally, and indeed whether he engaged in any form of ethical argument at all, are controversial exegetical issues in which I do not have the slightest desire—nor fortunately the slightest need—to get involved. See Geras (1984), Lukes (1985), and Peffer (1990) for useful surveys of the large literature on these issues.

2. Along these lines, see e.g. Cohen (1983c: 444–5), Reiman (1989: 299).

3. Which is not to say that the overexploitation of natural resources is not relevant to the assessment of socio-economic regimes (it has in fact already been discussed in § 2.3), nor that our dealings with members of other species do not raise important ethical issues. The latter, however, have little to do with the 'exploitation of man by man' and belong to the large set of issues that apply in pretty much the same way to all liberal conceptions of justice and will not be discussed here.

4. What profit-motivated organizations 'exploit', in the various forms of 'consumer exploitation' explored by e.g. Giordan (1978), are 'our emotions', our 'needs and desires', our 'uncertainties', etc. Exploiting *someone* nearly always refers to the benefit derived from a person's work.

5. That both a work condition and a benefit condition must be imposed if the flow of counterexamples to his own definition of exploitation is to be stemmed is explicitly recognized by Roemer (1989b: 260, 265), who incorporates into his definition of exploitation the requirement that the exploiters should 'gain by virtue of the labor of' the exploited.

6. When it can be defined, the labour value of the surplus product is called the *surplus value*. And exploitation could then also be defined as the production of surplus value. There is, however, no need to bring in the concept of value at this stage (see § 5.5). The more general definition of exploitation in terms of surplus product does everything the surplus value definition would do in the simple world we are considering.

7. Strictly speaking, Marx's (1867: 230–2) most explicit definition of exploitation makes the latter coextensive with the production of a surplus. The 'ratio of surplus labour time to necessary labour time', he says, provides a direct and exact 'expression of the degree of exploitation of labour by capital or of the worker by the capitalist', necessary labour time being defined as the time in which workers 'obtain the means of subsistence required for (their) own maintenance and continuous reproduction' and surplus labour time as the difference between total and necessary labour time. As long as wages do not exceed subsistence requirements, this definition makes perfect sense. But once they do—a possibility that must be contemplated by anyone who does not tautologically define the 'value of labour power' (i.e. the labour time required for a worker's reproduction) by what the real wage happens to be— it leads to absurd consequences: workers are exploited to exactly the same extent, for example, whether the surplus is consumed entirely by themselves or entirely by the capitalists. Marx (ibid. 556) states elsewhere that surplus labour can be called unpaid labour, and that the ratio of unpaid to paid labour

can be viewed as a 'popular expression' of the ratio of surplus to necessary labour time, which strongly suggests that in the event of a discrepancy between what workers need and what they get, only the latter is relevant to the assessment of exploitation. This narrower definition is of course the one that prevails almost universally in the literature.

8. This view is taken for granted in the close connection standardly established between the rate of exploitation and the ratio of profits to wages: however large a share of profits is accumulated, all profits enter the numerator of the rate of exploitation. Without such a connection, Morishima's (1973: 53–4) 'fundamental Marxian theorem' would fail, and it would not make the slightest sense to take the rate of accumulation as a proxy for the rate of exploitation (as proposed e.g. by A. E. Buchanan 1979: 135–6). This choice is not unanimous, however. Thus, von Weizsäcker (1973: 252–3, 261–4) and Elster (1985: 177–9) restrict exploitation to the use of the surplus either for the capitalists' current consumption or in order to boost their future consumption.

9. In these cases, those who consume the surplus product are just the beneficiaries of exploitation. In other cases, where I give up part of what I appropriate because of being subjected to someone's power (say, that of a tax-collecting despot), the beneficiaries are joint exploiters, or even sole exploiters if they let me keep nothing of the surplus product.

10. In this sense, it is correct to say, as does Terray (1985: 20), for example, that the key criterion for exploitation is not whether the capitalists consume anything, but whether the surplus is 'used according to [the workers'] will'. What, however, if the capitalists can only decide how the surplus is to be used because the workers know they are going to use it the way they themselves see fit? It may not be absurd to view social democracy as a system in which an electoral majority of workers *could* appropriate the whole of the product but find it expedient to leave part of it to the capitalists on the assumption that they will use it so as to expand the potential for workers' future consumption efficiently (see Przeworski 1985: ch. 5). I shall return to this interpretation in § 6.7.

11. This is why exploitation, though an essentially distributive concept, is not purely distributive: the existence of exploitation in our potato example cannot simply be read from the distribution of the net product, or of the benefits derived from production, between workers and non-workers, but some 'extraction' mechanism, to be characterized shortly, must be at work. An alternative, in my view less general, way of characterizing the not purely distributive nature of exploitation is proposed by Carling (1984: 9–10) in terms of 'moral sociology' or norms which determine what kinds of individual can be exploiters or exploitees.

12. In order to keep such situations exploitation-free, Roemer (1989*b*: 258–9, 265) postulates the *absence of consumption externalities*: the invalid does not exploit the rest of society 'because the invalid's welfare enters the utility function of the rest of society'. But this proposal does not exclude enough: using Sen's (1977: 95–7) classic distinction, if the altruistic transfer stems

from 'commitment' rather than 'sympathy', a genuine gift does not involve any consumption externality. And it also excludes far more than I guess Roemer wants to exclude: what I shall discuss below under the heading of free-riding typically relies on consumption externalities.

13. I shall thereby deliberately deviate from the terminology recommended by libertarians such as John Hospers (1971: 236), who wants exploitation confined to the coercive case: 'To use the same word "exploitation" to cover robbery by marauding gangs (or by government) on the one hand, and conditions of employment in a free market on the other is more than being guilty of semantic sloppiness—it is to use words deliberately to mislead people into a false picture of the facts.' Conversely, but for symmetric reasons, Elster (1983: § 1) proposed to contrast (uncoercive) exploitation with (coercive) extortion—a proposal he later abandoned (Elster 1985: 167–8) in favour of the broader definition adopted here. Steiner's (1984) 'liberal' conception of exploitation is a complex compound of Hospers's and (the earlier) Elster's: although the exploitative transaction itself must be uncoerced, the circumstances which make it mutually beneficial must have been decisively affected by coercion (typically through the prevention of some transactions between the exploitee and third parties) for the transaction to qualify as exploitative.

14. As pointed out in the earlier discussion of coercion (§ 1.6), one must be careful when characterizing feudal exploitation as coercive (or opportunity-set-restricting) and capitalist exploitation as uncoercive (or opportunity-set-expanding). The shrinking or swelling of opportunity-sets is always relative to a background of property rights. Even in Elster's (1982*a*: 365) example of sexual favours (coercively) requested in exchange for not impairing normal promotion versus (uncoercively) requested in exchange for granting extra promotion, the distinction relies, as emphasized by Carling (1984: 18–21), on the pre-existence of a right to normal, not to extra, promotion. But if this is the case, should not feudal exploitation be viewed as uncoercive? In the relevant system of property rights, the duty to perform a corvée is inseparable from the right to cultivate a plot of land, and the enforcement of this duty (by the lord and his soldiers) does not make feudal exploitation any more coercive than the enforcement of a capitalist contract (by the courts and the police) makes capitalist exploitation coercive. The only way to make the distinction stick is to assume some trans-historical right to self-ownership, which is violated by the feudal serf's ties to her land, but respected by the capitalist workers' right to leave their jobs.

15. I therefore also reject, and need to reject for my purposes, a definition of exploitation as benefiting by harming suggested by e.g. David Friedman (1973: 61) and also, in an interesting extended variant, by David Gauthier (1986: 11): interest in one's fellows 'becomes a source of exploitation if it induces persons to acquiesce in institutions and practices that but for their fellow-feelings would be costly to them. Feminist thought has surely made this, perhaps the core form of human exploitation, clear to us.' See also Hampton (1991) for further discussion. As will soon be obvious, I am not ruling out that affection can be a source of exploitation, but it is essential for

the notion of exploitation we need that it should not be restricted to cases where the exploitee is being harmed, even in this extended sense.

16. This position is explicitly shared by e.g. Roemer (1989b: 261): 'economic actors can be exploited even if they have viable alternatives to the exploitative relationship.' Characterizations of exploitation which do require compulsion in this sense (or either compulsion or coercion) are implied or proposed by e.g. Glyn (1979: 335), Arneson (1981: 213), Wood (1981: 232), van der Veen (1984: 118), Smith (1985), etc.

17. Note that it is perfectly possible for advocates of a substantial basic income to defend it as part of a struggle against exploitation, without defining exploitation in such a way that a substantial basic income would, by definition, abolish exploitation. See e.g. Jordan (1985: 13): 'A basic income scheme which gave a generous, unconditional guaranteed income to all citizens would not end all forms of exploitation; but it would be a new bulwark against the major forms of exploitation which exist within the present system. [. . .] It could [. . .] provide a platform for a new advance in the battle against exploitation of all kinds.'

18. See e.g. Arneson (1981: 224): 'Exploitation is roughly a matter of being taken advantage of by someone who has power over you.' This view must be sharply distinguished from an account of exploitation, represented by e.g. Tucker (1963: 322), Wood (1972: 281–2), Hodgson (1980: 263–7), and Reiman (1989), which makes exploitation a matter of power, understood as domination or control *within the production process*. If I let you work on my plot on condition that I keep some of the potatoes you grow, I exploit you according to the view under discussion, even if I abstain from any interference with the way in which you choose to produce: you decide what techniques you use, what rhythm you impose yourself, who else you work with, etc. This view is fully consistent with Marx's (1867: 232) own canonical formulation of the rate or extent of exploitation, or with his explicit recognition that rent and interest earners, not just capitalist entrepreneurs, are exploiters (see e.g. Marx 1894: 594, 829). Hence, the complaint that Marxian exploitation is just a deviation from a zero-interest regime and 'has nothing whatsoever to do with the property relations or power relations *inside or outside* the workplace' (Ellerman 1983: 331–2) is half correct, but no more.

19. See, e.g. M. Taylor (1982: §§ 1–2) for an illuminating analysis.

20. In the Marxist tradition, exploitation is often defined by reference to this single power base. Thus, for example, Kolakowski (1978: 333): 'Exploitation consists in the fact that society has no control over the use of the surplus product, and that its distribution is in the hands of those who have an exclusive power of decision as to the use of the means of production'; and Hodgson (1980: 268): 'Expropriation is the appropriation of the surplus product by the class that owns the means of production.'

21. 'Two hundred grenadiers have erected the obelisk of Luqsor in a few hours; can you imagine that one man could have managed this in two hundred days? Well, cultivating a desert, building a house, running a manufacture is like erecting an obelisk or moving a mountain. [. . .] The capitalist, it is being said,

paid the workers' *days*; to be precise, one should say that the capitalist has paid as many times *one day* as he has employed workers each day, which is not at all the same thing. For he has failed to pay for this enormous force that results from the workers' unity and harmony, from the convergence and simultaneity of their efforts' (Proudhon 1840: 215).

22. I am here referring to knowledge as a productive asset. Knowledge, like tools, can also be used in a coercive way: this yields the possibility of blackmail-based exploitation (see Carling 1984: 22).

23. This brings out how weak the proposed concept of power is. However, a more restrictive answer to the background-clearing question of what it involves to *take* advantage of someone's work, would not significantly affect the central argument of this chapter, which is about what it involves to take *unfair* advantage of someone's work.

24. Even this pretty narrow room left for genuine gifts may be judged excessive. Suppose you are Pharao and I believe you are God. I am therefore willing to do for you far more than you expect of me, not because of any benefit I expect from doing so, but out of gratitude for your having given me life and many things besides. (See Godelier (1978: 179–81) on the Peruvian peasants' unextinguishable 'debt' towards the Inca.) Should we not say that this can be exploitation all the same, because my keenness to give up part of my product, however unqualified, rests on what we know, or are pretty confident, is an illusion, namely the belief that you, Pharao, are God? Similarly, if the reason I grow your potatoes and sew your socks is my sincere and firm belief that this is the part of the natural role assigned to my caste or gender, should we not say that I am being exploited even if failure to perform my duty would not be (nor would be expected to be) sanctioned by any penalty—not even by your displeasure or the disapproval of my peer group? The move that is suggested by these examples would make the concept of exploitation uncomfortably dependent on some objective standards about true beliefs and genuine duties. (If only uncontroversial truths and duties were accepted, all room for genuine gifts would be wiped out.) I shall therefore prefer to stick to a definition of exploitation that makes power a necessary condition of it.

25. Alan Carling (1987 and 1991: ch. 11) provides an entertaining and illuminating formal analysis of similar examples. See also Elster (1983: § 1) and Van Parijs (1995*a*: § 1).

26. In David Gauthier's (1986: 96) terminology, 'a free-rider obtains a benefit without paying all or part of its cost', whereas 'a parasite in obtaining a benefit displaces all or part of the cost onto some other persons'. A lighthouse and industrial pollution are offered as paradigmatic examples of free-riding and parasitism, respectively. I am suggesting that parasitism should be construed as a subcase of free-riding, where the benefit consists at least partly in the processing of a cost inflicted by the free-rider on the producers of the benefit. Pollution, therefore, is an example, only if the polluter needs clean air that would not be forthcoming without the action taken by others at their own expense (and in their own interest) in order to purify the polluted air.

27. Note, however, that the latter situation could be construed as one in which I owe my ability to benefit from your work to sanctions imposed on you by third parties: your caring so much for a tidy house merely reflects your fear of being disapproved of by those who would blame you (your peers and relatives about whose judgement you care, not me), if the house were not tidy. Could this therefore be understood as a case of putative exploitation where the beneficiary (me) does not coincide with the exploiter (your peer group), though a case significantly different from that which would arise if a capitalist gave away all his profits to his old mother (see § 5.1)?

28. I hereby open the possibility of externality-based (and not just power-based) exploitation. One counterintuitive implication is that it becomes conceivable to exploit past generations: I can enjoy the sight of flowers planted by your great-grandfather as well as by you. (Power-based exploitation of past generations is impossible because the sanctions we control cannot affect the behaviour of someone who is no longer around.) If this is found embarrassing, perhaps one could stipulate that exploitation must refer to a relation of some permanence between the exploiter and the exploitee—as required, for example, by Reiman (1989: 302) and Hampton (1991: § 4). Also, allowing for externality-based exploitation opens the possibility that I may be exploiting you even if the only benefit I am deriving from your work is the purely altruistic pleasure I take in knowing about the pleasure that you derive from it yourself. To avoid this, one could try to impose an *ad hoc* restriction on the nature of the benefit extracted or, more wisely, await the criterion of 'unfairness' to solve this problem as a special case.

29. Labour contributions must refer to labour performed in the current period. The return on capital accumulated thanks to earlier labour does not count as appropriation by virtue of one's labour contribution. Interest-free savings, on the other hand, do not count as appropriation of part of the net product, even if they enable the saver to consume part of it, but as a pure exchange between equivalent bundles. (Hence, pensioners need not be exploiters.)

30. This is an advantage of some significance given the role played by the reliance on labour value in the critique of exploitation-based approaches. See e.g. Nozick (1974: 253): 'With the crumbling of the labor theory of value, the underpinning of [Marxist economics'] particular theory of exploitation dissolves.'

31. Space or land, for example, are at least as necessary to production as labour is. And food, being required to reproduce labour power, must therefore be basic if labour is. Many versions of this argument against the selection of labour value can be found in the existing literature, from Wicksteed (1884: 711–14) to Wolff (1981: 102–3). Morishima's (1973: 53–4) 'fundamental Marxian theorem', which states that the rate of profit is positive if and only if the rate of exploitation (expressed in terms of labour value) is positive can therefore be formulated using any other basic good as a numeraire. As clearly explained by Gintis and Bowles (1981), Wolff (1981: 94–101), Roemer (1982*a*: 186-8) and others, the key underlying condition is the supposition

that the economy is productive enough to yield an output that does more than replace its means of production, including labour power.

32. Contrary to what is sometimes asserted, e.g. by Armstrong, Glyn, and Harrison (1978: 23) and Glyn (1979: 335).

33. Here is Crocker's (1972: 205) formulation: 'I propose that the necessary and sufficient condition of exploitation is that there be a surplus product which is under the control of a group which does not include all the producers of that surplus.' The very same conception is also casually used, for example, by Barbara Wood (1985: 270) reporting on Fritz Schumacher's feelings towards the National Coal Board: 'Nationalization, by placing ownership in the hands of the nation, removed the danger of *exploitation* and other excesses perpetrated by private greed and meant that the workers were contributing not to an individual's wealth but toward the nation as a whole *of which they were a part*' (my emphasis). My formulation only differs from these by adding 'and only them' at the end of Crocker's formula in order to accommodate the following difficulty: if I am reckoned to be exploited if I am the sole worker and produce on my own the whole of the surplus product over which nineteen other people have full control, then surely I am also exploited if I, as the only worker, produce the whole of the surplus product which the twenty of us jointly decide how to use.

34. Except in the far-fetched case that can be illustrated as follows. Consider a community of farmers. Part of the product is paid in wages, while the rest is collectively appropriated by all workers. There is no exploitation according to Crocker's definition, but appropriation *qua* non-worker may be present: it may be by virtue of constituting the local community, not by virtue of contributing to the product, that all workers are involved in the control of the surplus product. Note, incidentally, that even when it is only by virtue of their work that workers are *allowed* to control the surplus product, it need not be by virtue of their work only that they are *able* to control as much surplus as they do. Other communities of workers earning similar wages for similar work may have no surplus product left because of the inferior nature of the natural resources (or capital, or technologies) they have to work on. (This fact is closely related to a decisive argument against this whole approach: see the end of § 5.4).

35. To spell out more explicitly the connection with the dilemma sketched at § 5.2: Appropriation *qua* non-worker is far weaker than appropriation *by* non-worker—which is what gives this approach some bite on capitalism—but still far stronger than appropriation *tout court*—which is what enables it to spare (the formal sector of) socialism—at least potentially. We shall see later that the room left for exploitation-free regimes is extremely narrow.

36. According to e.g. Alec Nove (1983: 207, 212), for example, the income allocated to working owner-managers in the small private firms of his 'feasible socialism' is not 'unearned income': 'there would be no exploitation except in so far as a working owner-manager derives additional income from his employees (but then I exploit the secretary who is typing this page).' Carver (1987: § 3) also stresses the difficulty presented by owner-managers for the

related view that exploiting consists in benefiting from the worker's labour 'by virtue of being an owner'.

37. Nozick (1974: 253), who sees this as a major defect of the Marxian concept of exploitation.

38. See e.g. Rae and Daudt (1976) on the Ostrogorski paradox, and Przeworski and Wallerstein (1986), more generally, on the political limits to popular sovereignty.

39. Along these lines, see e.g. Arneson (1981: 226) and A. Buchanan (1985: 99). Under democratic socialism, Crocker (1972: 212) replies, 'decisions throughout the society would be made by agreement or voting, but majority rule would have lost its character as rule over the minority since differences would no longer reflect fundamental antagonisms of social position'. But what characterizes such a 'fundamental antagonism' except (begging the question) being rooted in the conflict between capital and labour? Depending on what skills they possess, what positions they occupy, what part of the country they live in, what conception of the good life they have, different categories of workers may have 'fundamentally opposed' interests.

40. Not only would that worker not be exploited given our definition of what it means to be *unfairly* taken advantage of. She would not even be taken advantage of (see § 5.1), since the exploiter would not benefit from her work.

41. For example, wages far in excess of productivity—say, smoking cigars in a cosy office for a fat salary—may systematically correspond to the final and coveted stage of a career structured in such a way as to optimally boost productivity at earlier stages (see e.g. Lazear 1979 and Malcomson 1984).

42. The distinction between patterned and entitlement principles of justice goes back to Nozick (1974: 150–60). The distinction between a strong and weak sense of entitlement was introduced earlier, § 1.3.

43. See e.g. Dobb (1973: 137–8) and Reeve (1987) for a discussion of Ricardian socialism. And see e.g., Proudhon (1840: 152): 'Here is what I propose: the worker keeps, even after having received his wage, a natural right of ownership over the thing he has produced.'

44. Thus e.g., Proudhon (1846: 107–8): 'It is labour, and labour alone, which produces all the elements of wealth, and which combines them up to their last molecules . . .'

45. The contribution of capital to production is clearly recognized by Proudhon (1840: 200): 'The truth is that neither the Earth is productive, nor labour is productive, nor capital is productive; production is the outcome of these three elements, all three necessary but, taken separately, sterile.' In his most explicit passage, Marx (1880: 359) is somewhat more ambiguous, as it is not entirely clear whether he is referring to the capitalist *qua* manager (and hence worker) or *qua* capital owner ('I present the capitalist as a necessary functionary of capitalist production, and show at length that he does not only 'deduct' or 'rob' but forces the production of surplus value, and thus helps create what is to be deducted.'). Elsewhere, however, Marx (1875) unambiguously dismisses the Gotha Programme's claim that 'labour is the source

of all wealth and culture' and asserts that 'nature is just as much the source of use values as labour'. (See Young (1978) for an extensive exegetical discussion.) That labour is not the sole creator of the product is generally recognized by contemporary Marxists. See e.g. Yunker (1977: 97), Cohen (1979*a*: 152), Arneson (1981: 214), Levine (1984: 87), A. Buchanan (1985: 13), etc. This claim has to be sharply distinguished from the claim that only labour determines the *value* of the product. As clearly explained by Cohen (1979*a*: 153–7; 1983*b*: 313–14; 1985*c*: § 4), quite apart from being even less defensible than the former, the latter claim is altogether irrelevant to the present discussion.

46. See e.g. Elster (1978*a*: 10–11; 1978*b*: 105). This argument is abandoned, however, in Elster's (1985: § 4.3) discussion of the ethics of exploitation.

47. Suppose Pat and Sam produce equal amounts of corn this year. Pat makes bread and cake, and eats it all. Sam makes bread and keeps the rest of the corn as seed for next year. What is at stake is the specific contribution made to next year's product by Sam's decision to use some corn as seed instead of cake.

48. Along the same lines, see Arnold (1985: 101–2). In an uncertain world, as Arnold (ibid. 100) also points out, capital owners further contribute to (useful) production by speculating about what consumers (and intermediate consumers) want. Whether they take investment decisions themselves or delegate them to someone else, whether they have had to think hard or are just lucky, people who invest in successful enterprises can also claim on this ground to be among the joint creators of the product.

49. See Cohen (1983*b*: 316–17; 1983*c*: 443–5; 1985*a*: 98–9; 1986*a*: 87–90). Elsewhere, Cohen (1979*a*: 151–2, 1983*b*: 314) also proposes another strategy which rests on a distinction between *contributing* to the creation of something and *participating* in it. Even though capitalists contribute to production, they do not participate in it (at any rate *qua* savers, not *qua* entrepreneurs). Only labour involves active personal participation. And this is what matters. But why? Perhaps because only active participation needs incentives, or because only active participation involves a deserving effort. Even assuming these two assertions to be true, they cannot provide us with what we need because they both take us away from the domain of entitlement principles, which we are investigating here as a possible ethical basis for the notion of exploitation, in the direction of either consequentialist principles (the efficient pursuit of some social objective) or patterned principles (e.g., 'To each according to her efforts'), to which we shall turn later on. In any case, the success of the other strategy proposed by Cohen, and discussed in the main text, would make this one pointless. (Why bother to discuss whether or not capital is productive in the right sense if capitalists are not entitled to it anyway?)

50. David Gauthier's (1986) interpretation of distributive justice in terms of equal (or maximin) relative benefit can be viewed as a sophisticated extension of the approach considered in this section and shares its crucial defects. I discuss it at length in Van Parijs (1995*a*).

51. This definition is suggested by Marx's (1867: 232) assimilation of the rate of

exploitation to what he calls the rate of surplus value—only suggested, and not entailed, because Marx assumes a dichotomic world of non-saving workers and non-working capitalists. For explicit and rigorous formulations of this definition, see e.g., von Weizsäcker (1973: 247) and Roemer (1985*a*: 30). It is sometimes asserted (e.g. by Steiner 1987: 135) that any conception of exploitation rests on some notion of unequal exchange of value, with differences then stemming from differences between the value concepts adopted. This is true when the key concept of unfairness is understood in terms of unequal exchange as it is in the (Lutheran) approach explored here, but not when it is understood either in terms of entitlements, as in the Lockean approach explored earlier or in terms of opportunities, as in the Roemerian approach explored later.

52. The latter is chosen, for example, by Morishima (1973: 184–6) and von Weizsäcker (1973: 265–7). Although Marx clearly indicated that the labour value of a good does not refer to the amount of labour that actually went into its production, he did not himself unambiguously choose between the average and the minimum interpretation.

53. See Armstrong, Glyn, and Harrison (1978: 4–6). Another advantage is that it makes it a necessary truth that the total value produced in a given period is equal to the total amount of labour performed in that period. (Under the minimum definition, total value is generally less than total labour.)

54. The opposite choice is made e.g. by De Vroey (1982) and Gouverneur (1983: ch. 2).

55. This view is forcefully defended by e.g. Folbre (1982: 317–18) and Reiman (1989: 311–12).

56. For presentations of the problem and discussions of possible solutions, see e.g. Steedman (1977: 150–83) and Armstrong, Glyn, and Harrison (1978: 6–11).

57. It is sometimes suggested (e.g. by Glyn 1979: 339–40; or Hodgson 1980: 257) that this difficulty could be avoided by stipulating that the concept of exploitation should only be applied to a country's workforce as a whole. But if the country trades with the outside world, the problem that arises at the level of an individual or firm arises again at the level of a country. Moreover, with an appropriately broad concept of work, there is hardly anyone in the country who does not belong to the workforce, and the total labour value which it appropriates will therefore tend to be equal to the total labour it contributes.

58. See Morishima's (1973: 190–3) neat formalization of Hilferding's (1904) original proposal, and Rowthorn (1973) for useful further discussion.

59. See Holländer (1982) and Steedman (1985) for clarifying discussions.

60. An important difference with the Lockean conception is that pure workers can be not only exploited but also exploiters, because of variations in wage rates and productivity levels. The latter implication is sometimes regarded as a major embarrassment for a conception of exploitation. Thus, Bettelheim (1969: 327, 331–2) criticizes Emmanuel's conception of exploitation as unequal exchange on the ground that it has this implication—which

Emmanuel (1975: 412–15) implicitly recognizes would be embarrassing but wrongly attributes to the misguided use of national values (average labour times calculated on a country-by-country basis) rather than world values (which he rightly thinks provide the appropriate standard). For another example, see Glyn's (1979: 338–40) option for a conception of exploitation of the Lockean type, which cannot turn the workers of a rich country into exploiters. Although a close class-exploitation correspondence may be important if exploitation is to be relevant for the analysis of social conflict, it is by no means essential for our normative purposes, and there is therefore no reason to impose it as a desideratum, let alone as a requirement, for an adequate notion of exploitation. Indeed, some (such as von Weizsäcker 1973: 279-80) argue that it is an advantage of such a definition that it enables us to capture the (quantitatively larger) exploitation of workers by workers stemming from the need for material work incentives. For a rigorous analysis of the (narrow) conditions under which the labour-hiring/labour-selling class divide coincides with the exploiter/exploited divide, see Roemer (1982*a*: 268–70).

61. This only concerns, of course, the formal economic sphere and could make no claim to abolishing *ipso facto*, e.g. love-based exploitation in the private sphere. Moreover, one cannot avoid the difficult question of how the surplus product collectively (and democratically) appropriated by all workers is to be treated in each worker's labour-value balance.

62. There is nothing originally Lutheran about this doctrine, strongly rooted in the scholastic (and in particular Thomistic) tradition. In the 'Treatise on Contracts and Usury', in which he makes one of the first attempts to make room for a legitimate return to capital, the French lawyer Carolus Molinaeus summarizes the doctrine as follows: 'in commutative justice one man should not receive more from another than he gave him in value' (Comble and Norton (eds.) 1991: 51).

63. For a clear formulation of the underlying ethical principle, see e.g. Morishima and Catephores (1978: 41–2): since workers exchange *t* hours of labour for the value of a commodity bundle which corresponds to an amount of labour smaller than *t*, 'the actual contract is therefore always unfair and not on equal terms between the capitalists and the workers [. . .].' The same ethical principle is also explicitly invoked, for example, by Bertrand Russell (1932: 28): 'Every human being, of necessity, consumes in the course of his life a certain amount of the produce of human labour. Assuming, as we may, that labour is on the whole disagreeable, it is unjust that a man should consume more than he produces.'

64. This distinguishes the conception under discussion from Pigou's (1920: 511–19) 'neo-classical' conception of exploitation as (downward) deviation from what real wages would be under perfect competition. The contrast between these two conceptions is emphasized by e.g. Robinson (1942: 21–2), Bronfenbrenner (1971: 196–7), Persky and Tsang (1974), Elster (1978*a*: 8–11). In a more Pigovian spirit, see Kolm's (1969) notion of international exploitation, which requires the exploiting country to manipulate prices

through private monopolies or monopsonies or through tariffs and subsidies.

65. The same holds for the 'commercial exploitation of poor countries' to which Marx (1863: 106) briefly alludes and for Emmanuel's (1969) 'unequal exchange' between countries, as made clear, in particular, by his discussion of the Ricardian theory of comparative advantage (ibid. 137–9).

66. The former difficulty is stressed by e.g. Glyn (1979: 342–3) and Cohen (1983*b*: 324); the latter by Elster (1985: 174).

67. One could attempt to reduce the size of the grey area by stipulating that someone is exploited as soon as the only bundles of goods she could appropriate with her income either contain less labour value than she contributes *or do not enable her to subsist* (the only bundles with more labour value she could afford consist of e.g. haircuts and massages but not food). It is most unlikely, however, that the grey area would shrink much as a result.

68. Note, however, that income is only appropriate to assess exploitation if it accurately expresses purchasing power. The exploited may be systematically prevented from making the best 'available' use of whatever income they have, e.g. because of price discrimination against them or because of systematically inferior information, and uncorrected income data are then insufficient to assess the existence and extent of exploitation.

69. That is, unless the (Lutheran) unequal exchange approach is reduced back to a variant of the (Lockean) 'right to the fruit of one's labour' approach, rather than developed, as proposed here, into a conception of unfair co-operation. The two directions in which the ethical intuitions underlying the notion of exploitation can be construed are well expressed by Mill (1848: 253–4): 'In a cooperative industrial association, is it just or not that talent or skill should give a title to superior remuneration? On the negative side of the question, it is argued that whoever does the best he can, deserves equally well . . . . On the contrary side, it is contended that society receives more from the efficient worker; . . . that a greater share of the joint result is actually his work, and not allowing his claim to it is a kind of robbery'.

70. In the appendix to Emmanuel's book, Bettelheim (1969: 297–8) characterizes unequal exchange between countries as an exchange of less for more labour value. But Emmanuel (1975: 351, 407) himself emphatically rejects this interpretation. Once freed of the considerable confusion that surrounds it, the implicit ethical basis of the 'unequal exchange' approach in development theory also amounts to condemning a mismatch between labour performed and income received, whether owing to differences in productivity (even in a perfectly competitive world) or to obstacles to both labour and capital mobility (which make it possible for equally productive labour to be unequally rewarded). See Barry (1979: 64–7), Roemer (1983*a*), and Van Parijs (1993*a*: 143–6) on the ethics and economics of unequal exchange between countries.

71. A principle very close, incidentally, to the one we have seen (§ 4.2) is implied by Rawls's solution to the Crazy–Lazy challenge. From the fact that it could be rejected as an adequate expression of the real-libertarian approach one

cannot infer, of course, that it must be rejected as a way of articulating the ethical challenge to that approach

72. Barry (1979: 74–6) and Arneson (1981: 211) make parallel points. Note that suffering unfair treatment according to the principle 'To each according to her labour' is not only consistent with deriving a benefit from the work of those unfairly well treated (as just illustrated). It is also consistent with earning more than one would (after adjustment to the new situation) if the unfairness were suppressed. Giving disproportionately high wages to those at the top of the promotion ladder, for example, may boost performance to such an extent that even those at the bottom of the ladder earn more than they would if proportionality were strictly adhered to.

73. In an interesting interpretation of the Marxian principle 'To each according to his labour contribution', van der Veen (1978: 458–61) also combines the length of labour and its quality—which can be understood, at least roughly, as the inverse of its disutility. But he dissociates the two dimensions and holds the view that labour should be rewarded according to its length, while labour quality must be distributed in maximin fashion i.e. so as to maximize the quality of the worst job. I can see no good reason, however, for allowing no trade-off between length and disutility, nor for bringing the maximin criterion into the interpretation of the quoted principle. A consistent *alternative* principle could require the minimaxing of labour contributions (subject to some subsistence constraint i.e. the minimization of the disutility associated with the worst job, characterized by both length and quality). This principle is closely linked to the 'Marxian' criterion of relative basic income maximization to which I return (at n. 80).

74. Put more generally: if marginal disutility is—plausibly—increasing, the nth hour of (say, daily) work can justly claim a reward that exceeds the one earned by the same person for the $(n - 1)$th hour. In the present context, it is obviously average (or total), and not marginal disutility which is relevant to determine the just rate of pay. For suppose we both incur the same disutility from spending the day cleaning windows, even though we incur it according to a very different time pattern. You find it moderately bothersome from the early morning, whereas I enjoy it most of the day but badly resent it in the late afternoon. Yet, paying me far more than you for this reason would obviously be unjust.

75. That appeal to this more general principle underlies the notion of exploitation is asserted, for example, by Mancur Olson (1965: 29), who justifies his use of the term to refer to the 'exploitation of the great by the small' (see § 5.2) by pointing out that it is 'commonly used to describe situations where there is a disproportion between the benefits and sacrifices of different people'.

76. Kolm (1975) speaks of the exploitation *of workers* through inflation to refer to a situation in which, owing to unanticipated inflation, small savers are paid a negative real rate of interest by the capitalists who borrow from them. But, whatever the implicit criterion of fairness that is being used, this cannot constitute exploitation as minimally characterized (§§ 5.1–2), since it is *qua*

savers, not *qua* workers, that the recipients of negative real interests are being unfairly treated.

77. The classic statement of the interpretation of interest as 'the reward of the sacrifice involved in the waiting for the enjoyment of material resources' is by Alfred Marshall (1890: 191–4). For an explicitly apologetic use of this interpretation, see e.g. David Friedman (1973: 83): '[The capitalist] himself bears a cost, since he too would rather have the money to do with as he wishes, instead of having it tied up and released slowly over a period of time. It is perfectly reasonable that he should receive something for his contribution.' This sacrifice-based argument in support of capital's claim on a Lutheran background is crucially distinct from the contribution-based argument examined earlier in a Lockean framework (§ 5.4).

78. Suppose I save a couple of ECUs a year because that corresponds to all the consumption I can afford to forgo at a welfare cost to me that does not exceed the rate of interest, while your wealth enables you to invest a million ECUs a year before you reach the ECU which you could not divert from your current consumption without adversely affecting your welfare more than the expected interest would enhance it. Your capital and mine both get a reward per unit which is equal to our marginal disutility. Yet, because you are able to save so many more ECUs, and most of them with a minute welfare cost to yourself, your average disutility from saving is negligible compared to mine, and the reward you get for the saving you do is therefore completely out of proportion with the sacrifice you are making.

79. I am here leaving aside the argument that the dynamics of power relations under socialism will systematically prevent this potential from being actualized. As we shall see shortly, whether or not this argument is correct does not matter for our present purposes.

80. This criterion corresponds to the most straightforward version of the 'capitalist road to communism' suggested by van der Veen and Van Parijs (1986a). My reasons for rejecting it in favour of the real-libertarian criterion of *absolute* basic income maximization are sketched in § 4.1 and explained more fully in Van Parijs (1992: 17–21; 1993a: 196–7).

81. See also Carling (1991: 139–44, 359), who considers welfare egalitarianism as the best rationale for Marx's combined needs-contribution principle.

82. Such an egalitarianism (including a compensation of labour contributions on the basis of individually undifferentiated assessments) is developed by Baker (1987, 1992). For critical discussions of this approach, see Carens (1985), Barry (1992), and Van Parijs (1993b).

83. See Homans (1961: esp. 72–8, 232–64) and Deutsch (1985) for the original formulation and a useful overview of the social-psychological approach; Shepelak and Alwin (1986), Schokkaert and Overlaet (1989), and D. Miller (1992) for instructive analyses of survey data.

84. See David Miller's (1989) desert-based defence of market socialism.

85. Equivocation between the stronger and weaker versions of the principle of distribution 'according to' effort is quite common. Thus, George Homans's (1961: 75) own canonical statement: 'A man in an exchange relation with

another will expect that the rewards of each man be *proportional* to his costs—*the greater* the rewards, *the greater* the costs—and that the net rewards, or profits, of each man be *proportional* to his investments—*the greater* the investments, *the greater* the profits' (my emphases).

86. Should such risk-generated disruptions be legitimized for other than efficiency reasons? This raises the status of what Dworkin (1981*b*: 293) calls *option luck* (as opposed to brute luck), i.e. of gambles which people are fully free not to take (see § 3.5 above). According to Dworkin, option luck, unlike brute luck, does not need to be corrected. But the effort involved in taking the gamble (if any) is the same whether one wins or loses, and option luck would therefore generate discrepancies between efforts and rewards even in the absence of maximin considerations. Option luck is not, of course, confined to explicit lotteries. It is also exemplified by the inheritance I receive as a result of taking the trouble to visit an old lady or by the job I get as a result of bothering to respond to an advertisement. No doubt losers should bear the cost of their choices (the efforts deployed in vain). But should what the winners get not be assimilated to gifts they receive, and hence swell the pool of resources to be distributed equally among all (see § 4.2)? According to my understanding of the real-libertarian approach (and consistently with my treatment of capital income in § 4.6), it should be treated on the same footing as gifts to the extent that not everyone has an (equal) opportunity to get it. People can take gambles and benefit from option luck, but it is legitimate to tax entirely the benefit thereby gained (assessed, as usual, in terms of opportunity costs), even though it would only be expedient to do so in the absence of maximin considerations. Hence, option luck does create legitimate discrepancies between effort and income, but only because maximin considerations allow differential rewards to be attached to gambles.

87. My own moral intuitions about the pairing of effort and benefit are strongly dichotomic, depending on whether the context is a particular co-operative interaction (e.g. the parents' participation in the organization of the children's school party) or the basic structure that determines people's rights and real opportunities, in particular to participate in such interactions. Free-riding may well be exploitative in the former context—with 'To each according to her effort' or perhaps Gauthier's 'equal relative benefit' or something else again as the underlying criterion of fairness—even though the free-riding of basic income beneficiaries (see § 5.2) is not. The present enquiry focuses exclusively on macro-social justice.

88. When answering this question, it is crucial to bear in mind that the equalization of opportunities involved in real-freedom-for-all is of a particularly far-reaching brand. Not only is it not restricted to 'given talents', as in a 'starting-gate conception of justice' or in Rawls's principle of fair equality of opportunity, but by making job and other rents part of people's endowments (and hence up for redistribution), it reaches a great deal of what is commonly located on the side of outcomes rather than of opportunities.

89. I shall return in § 6.8 to the question of how much space is left for arguments of this type.

90. Another advantage repeatedly stressed by Roemer is that it truly dispenses with any use of the concept of labour value.

91. See e.g. Marx (1867: 249): 'Whenever a part of society possesses the monopoly of the means of production, the labourer, free or unfree, must add to the working time necessary for his own maintenance an extra working time in order to produce the means of subsistence for the owners of the means of production.' Before Roemer, van der Veen (1978: 438) suggested this approach when characterizing exploitation as 'a kind of social injustice which is based on unjust—often unequal—distributions of property rights to scarce factors'.

92. This difficulty is acknowledged by Roemer (1982*a*: 219; 1982*c*: 392; 1982*d*: 285), who mentions it as one key reason for preferring the equal-distribution formulation to be considered below (Roemer 1989*b*: 262).

93. This difficulty too is now recognized by Roemer (ibid.) and viewed by him as a reason for preferring the equal-distribution definition to the withdrawal definition.

94. Similarly, if it is the case that, owing to the loss of the benefits they currently receive, the unemployed would become worse off as a result of withdrawal with a per capita share of the means of production (while the rest of society would become better off), they are capitalist exploiters according to the proposed definition, even if they own no capital whatsoever. It is no doubt conceivable that the unemployed may become better off—and the rest of society worse off—as a result of such a withdrawal, as they would no longer be denied access to the means of production. Indeed, this possibility is taken for granted by Roemer (1982*d*: 297), who sees it as an advantage of his definition that the unemployed would then qualify as exploited. My point here is simply that *if* an unemployed worker were better off with her (sufficiently high) benefit than with a (sufficiently low) equal share of the means of production, she would be—oddly—a capitalist exploiter according to the proposed definition even if she possessed no capital.

95. For example, Roemer (1982*a*: 219–26) made an elaborate attempt to cover the case of increasing returns by introducing the notions of 'vulnerable individual' and 'canonical exploited coalition'.

96. The cases mentioned do not exhaust the anomalies generated by the withdrawal definition. Elster (1982*a*: 367–9) offers a rather far-fetched example in which withdrawal puts an end to a positive externality which one coalition derived from the sheer presence of another. This sort of counterexample too can conceivably be dealt with in an *ad hoc* fashion, for example by requiring, as Roemer (1989*b*: 258) proposes, that consumption externalities be ignored. But getting rid of the withdrawal aspect of the counterfactual definition is a far more effective strategy.

97. A similar formulation can be found in van der Veen (1982: 41–3). Roemer (1989*b*: 262–3) has recently stressed the advantages of this definition over his initial one.

98. In the actual implementation of his withdrawal criterion, however, Roemer (as we shall see, rightly) disregards such dynamic considerations. See his

definition of the characteristic function of the relevant games in Roemer (1982*a*: 196–7).

99. This difficulty is hinted at by Roemer (1989*b*: 263). One used to think that this possibility, first demonstrated by Wassily Leontief in 1936 and referred to as the *transfer paradox*, could only arise, assuming standard preferences on the part of the agents involved, if the equilibrium to which the economy was supposed to move was unstable—and therefore *de facto* unreachable. Kolm (1969: 870–2) showed that this restriction does not hold as soon as the assumption of perfect competition is relaxed to allow for some (incomplete) control of the terms of trade by the 'victim' of the redistribution. More recently, Donsimoni and Polemarchakis (1985) have shown that the transfer paradox and the related phenomena of *advantageous* and *disadvantageous reallocation* (see Guesnerie and Laffont 1978)—which occur when both the 'beneficiary' and 'the victim' are made better or worse off, respectively, by the redistribution—can also affect stable equilibria in a perfectly competitive context. This point is of course altogether distinct from the more obvious one that aid can be detrimental to the aided country because of a suboptimal use of the transferred resources. The transfer paradox holds even if it is assumed that the transferred resources are put to the best possible use.

100. To illustrate, imagine first that I have the rare skill of beautifully painting eyelashes and that all those whose income goes up thanks to the equalization of wealth use their additional income to buy my services. My income is likely to rise even if I had to give up much of my wealth, of which I had more than the average before equalization took place. According to the equal-distribution definition, I am—oddly—capitalistically exploited in the initial situation, despite my possessing more than average wealth. Imagine next that the rare skill just mentioned is the only one I have, and that all my customers would vanish as soon as equalization chops off the top of the pyramid of wealth. My income may well drop as a result even if I had no wealth whatsoever at the start and therefore derive a considerable direct benefit from wealth equalization. In that case, according to the equal-distribution definition, I am a capitalist exploiter in the initial situation in spite of my poverty.

101. As John Roemer pointed out to me, this difficulty (along with the transfer paradox) is inherent in any price-dependent characterization of the counterfactual situation. It has, therefore, provided motivation for his price-independent withdrawal criterion, even though it might just as well motivate other price-independent criteria, such as one using Shapley values. Of course, nothing but a price-dependent exercise could yield an answer to the question of what would happen if wealth were equalized in a market economy. Abstracting from the change in prices does not force us, however, to give up the attempt to capture a causal notion—as we would if we went for Shapley values. What we should—and are about to—do, is focus on the specific income effect of the redistribution of wealth.

102. Elster (1982*a*: § 2) claims more radically that the causal concept of

exploitation cannot be adequately expressed by counterfactuals. However, his specific argument (which only substantiates the claim that the satisfaction of Roemer's counterfactual is not sufficient for exploitation, using the externality example referred to in n. 96) does not hinge on the general discrepancy between causal and counterfactual claims, but on the particular (withdrawal) formulation of the latter. In his reply to Elster, Roemer (1982c: 391) makes the right concession but for the wrong reason: '[Elster's] general point is that the counterfactual technique of the withdrawal criterion can never fully capture the kind of causality which we think is necessary for a diagnosis of exploitation. I agree: as a fully general, satisfactory definition, the game-theoretic approach falters.' The game-theoretical approach does falter for a reason touched upon by Elster, but this reason is not the general inadequacy of counterfactual formulations, but the specific inadequacy of its withdrawal version.

103. This is the sort of exercise in which Yunker (1977: 104–13) is involved when trying to 'ascertain for what proportion of the population an equal distribution of the property return in the form of a social dividend would be—in an immediate financial sense—preferable to the unequal distribution of property return currently prevailing under capitalism'. He subsequently attempts to take the effect on savings (one aspect of the efficiency effect) into account and concludes: 'for the vast majority of the population, distribution of the property return in the form of a social dividend would constitute a modest—but appreciable and immediate—financial improvement' (ibid. 129).

104. Strictly speaking, this shorthand expression is incorrect. If wealth happens to be inversely correlated to the other determinants of income distribution (e.g. skills), its unequal distribution actually has an equalizing effect on the distribution of income. If instead there is either independence or a positive correlation between the main determinants—as is more likely—'wealth-based inequality' is not too misleading a formula.

105. In this case, the game-theoretical (or withdrawal) formulation has the advantage of bringing out an interesting connection between the notion of feudal exploitation and the neo-classical or Pigovian notion of exploitation as deviation from marginal-product remuneration (see § 5.5). As the number of agents increases, there is a convergence between the 'Debreu core' of an economy (i.e. the set of all allocations such that no coalition can improve its lot by withdrawing), in terms of which feudal exploitation has been defined, and its 'Ostroy core' (i.e. the set of all allocations such that no coalition can worsen the lot of its complement by withdrawing), which captures the notion of marginal product. Under perfect competition, in other words, a worker is feudally exploited if and only if she is neo-classically exploited. See Roemer (1982a: 207–8) for a short discussion.

106. All this assumes that the serfs 'owned' their land and tools in some well-defined sense. As Roemer (e.g. 1982b: 93) is well aware, however, the exact nature of the serfs' ownership rights over their means of production (and over themselves) is a rather complicated matter.

107. See Roemer (1982*a*: 215–16; 1982*b*: 98) and Roemer (1982*a*: 279–81), respectively. The first label is justified by the fact that, according to Marx's scenario, skills are supposed to keep commanding higher wages at the first, or 'socialist', stage of the communist society (see § 5.6).

108. Feudal exploitation fails to imply capitalist exploitation when, by an extra-ordinary coincidence, the impact of feudal bondage on income happens to be exactly offset by the impact of wealth inequality (and analogously for the other implications mentioned). This does not mean that it is (virtually) impossible for someone to be a feudal exploiter without also being a capi-talist, socialist, and needs exploiter. No fluke is needed for the impact of wealth, skills, or needs inequalities to overcompensate the impact of feudal bondage on income. The unwelcome implications pointed out here are hid-den in Roemer's discussion because he analyses capitalist, socialist, and needs exploitation on the background of formal freedom for all; socialist exploitation in a context in which capital is collectively owned; and needs exploitation in a context in which all productive assets have been equalized (or their effects neutralized).

109. The revised typology also enables us to express more elegantly Roemer's (1982*a*: 283; 1982*b*: 98–100; 1982*c*: 382–3) historical–materialist claim that 'history progresses by successively eliminating the entitlements of individ-uals to various forms of property, in a certain order': as modes of produc-tion succeed one another, a ban is being imposed on a growing number of types of exploitation: first feudal exploitation (capitalism), next wealth exploitation (socialism), and finally skills and health exploitation (commu-nism).

110. See Van Parijs (1993*a*: 123–8 and 142–8) on the relevance of job-based and citizenship-based exploitation, respectively. Wright (1985*a*; 1985*b*) simi-larly argues for the central importance of organization-based exploitation in socialist societies.

111. Such an open-ended notion of exploitation is sketched by Ackerman (1980: 241–5), who insists—against the 'radical folks who . . . typically speak as if exploited and exploiter can be neatly sorted out into two grand classes con-taining all humanity'—that access to wealth, power, or education is affected in a non-overlapping way by several factors such as handicapped v. normal, white v. black, male v. female, etc.

112. This discrepancy between Roemer's approach and the usual one may sound surprising, given the importance Roemer (1982*a*: 202–6; 1982*b*: 94–6) gives to the equivalence between 'capitalist exploitation', as defined by his coun-terfactual characterization, and 'Marxian exploitation' understood as the unequal exchange of labour value: an agent would be better off as a result of wealth equalization if and only if she commands more labour value through her income than she contributes to production through her work. As pointed out earlier (§ 5.5), a non-worker who gets anything is bound to be a beneficiary of unequal exchange and hence a Marxian exploiter in this sense. Given the equivalence just stated, why is she not also bound to be a capitalist exploiter in Roemer's sense? Here is the explanation. For the

equivalence statement to hold, one does not only need to assume that market equilibrium obtains (no coercion, no entrepreneurial profits, etc.), but also that all agents are identical as regards both their skills and their preferences. The assumption that all markets clear gets rid of the possibility that our poor rentier may be involuntarily unemployed. And the possibility that she may be voluntarily unemployed is taken care of by the assumption that all workers are identical: either no one will work, and there will be no work for our rentier to take advantage of, or all will work, and there will be no idle rentier. Once these assumptions are lifted, the equivalence breaks down, and it is possible for a net value appropriator such as our rentier to be capitalistically exploited according to Roemer's definition.

113. This distinction is made most explicitly in Roemer (1982*d*: 299–300). In order to capture the benefit aspect, he suggested adding a condition of 'dependence' of the exploiter on the exploitee (Roemer 1982*d*: 285). In order to capture the power aspect, he suggested adding a condition of 'dominance' (Roemer 1982*a*: 195, 237; 1982*b*: 91–2). In order to capture the work aspect, he suggested adding the condition that the exploiter should be 'gaining by virtue of the labour' of the exploitee (Roemer 1989*b*: 260). Even without such supplements, Roemer's notion of exploitation could legitimately claim to characterize various ways of 'exploiting'—or taking advantage of—*one's superior position*. The intuitively uncomfortable clash is, of course, with the distinct notion of 'exploitation of man by man', which has been at the core of the socialist critique of capitalism—and therefore also of this chapter.

114. This proposition should be qualified as regards the special case of health exploitation. Unlike the other types of exploitation mentioned by Roemer, health exploitation does not point to factors which ought not to affect the distribution of income, but rather to a factor (inequality of needs) whose impact on material welfare ought to be neutralized by the distribution of income. This implies some patterning of the latter. But the distribution of material welfare remains entirely unpatterned even when the imperative of abolishing health exploitation is taken on board.

115. For a more precise statement of this point and an analysis of its implications for a general typology of theories of justice, see van der Veen and Van Parijs (1985).

116. See e.g. Yunker (1977: 133): 'The clearest, most immediate, and most obvious social improvement from socialism would be the abrogation of the pathologically unequal distribution of unearned property return under capitalism. Most of the other things that many socialists put forward as the 'advantages' of socialism are not necessarily connected with socialism in that the problem can be solved without socialism and/or socialism will not necessarily solve the problem.' The latter claim must be qualified, however, if we allow for democratic wealth exploitation (see § 5.3).

117. See Roemer (1983*c*: 381–3). That the possibility of such a clean path should be given due weight was already emphasized by Cohen (1981*a*) and Arneson (1981: 204).

118. For fuller accounts, see Elster (1985: 226–9) and Roemer (1989*a*: 159–63).

119. As emphasized by Roemer (1989*a*) in his discussion of the advantages of public ownership over equal division private ownership, attempts to realize justice through private ownership with equal starts may be thwarted by a 'private ownership externality'. But the lesson to be drawn is simply that 'there would have to be frequent or continuous redistributions to adjust for the private property externalities that come about from the use of markets' (Roemer ibid. 178). And it is, of course, such continuous redistribution that turns out to be justified, for reasons to be recalled shortly, once the implications of equality of endowments are consistently worked out.

120. Roemer (1982*a*: 241) himself points in this direction with his notion of 'socially necessary' exploitation, as I argue elsewhere (Van Parijs 1991*a*: § 3.6).

121. In recent writings, Roemer is driven towards this conclusion, though not all the way. He recognizes that according to his approach those who would choose to do no work and consume no more than their equal share of a publicly owned economy's profits would not be exploiters. After having thrown in that '[his] intuitions are not firm in cases where preferences differ', he then proposes 'an alternative approach to defining exploitation when agents' preferences differ', where exploitation turns out to consist in disproportionality between income and labour expended (as in § 5.6). But he insists: 'I can see no persuasive argument for adopting one of these characterizations of exploitation as the unique "correct" one' (Roemer 1989*b*: 264–5). Rather than going against the grain of his own perspective (as he would if he opted for this Lutheran regression), he now seems to have come to terms with the idea that his approach to wealth exploitation has great affinity with the justification of a basic income. His most recent blueprints of a desirable and feasible market socialism incorporate an unconditional social dividend: 'The social dividend will be a form of guaranteed income, or what some European writers have called a universal grant. I prefer not to call it a grant, since it is not a gift, which 'grant' connotes: it is that part of the national income which is not distributed as wages or interest, but which belongs to the people as owners of the means of production. Of course, a society such as the one I am describing might decide to distribute profits in some other way to people, such as in proportion to the value of labor they have expended, but I personally would oppose that proposal' (Roemer 1992: 453–4).

CHAPTER 6

1. For a closely related though more general reason, we do not need to worry about the different nature of the tax base under capitalism and socialism. Had our argument restricted the legitimate tax base to transferred external wealth (as feared in § 4.3), we would have been embarrassed by the fact that, under socialism, a far greater share of society's wealth is never transferred

from one person to another. But since all formal-freedom-respecting ways of sustainably channelling social wealth into a basic income and dominated-diversity-reducing transfers are legitimate in a capitalist economy (§ 4.6), nothing prevents a socialist economy from financing a basic income at the highest sustainable level through a direct reduction in the wages paid by state-owned firms rather than by using tax tools, subject to the usual constraints of formal freedom and predictability. One incidental implication is that it is quite appropriate to extend the meaning of the term 'social dividend', originally used to refer to the distributed part of profits on publicly owned capital (see e.g. Cole 1929, Lange 1936, Yunker 1977, Meade 1989, Van Trier 1989) to make it coextensive with basic income (as in e.g. Collard 1980, A. Miller 1983, and Standing 1989).

2. It is discussed by e.g. Hayek (1960: 137), Okun (1975: 38-9), A. Buchanan (1985: 78), and Levine (1984: 44–6).

3. See e.g. A. Buchanan's (1982: 21–35) discussion of the 'distortion of desire' under capitalism.

4. I am not questioning here the validity of this explanation. Capitalism's bias towards a longer working week could also be interpreted as the outcome of the capitalists' efforts to economize on the rents paid to workers in order to secure their subjection. (See Bowles and Gintis 1990.)

5. This objection is raised and discussed by Cohen (1978: 317–20) himself.

6. As argued by e.g. A. Buchanan (1985: 28).

7. In his lively presentation of the dynamics of monopolistic competition, Martin Weitzman (1984: 33–6) further points out that 'these and other forms of non-price competition can be taken to undesirable extremes, but they do account for a substantial part of the richness, dynamism, diversity, and, yes, quality of economic life under capitalism'. A positive impact on the diversity of the products offered for consumption, here stressed by Weitzman, is consistent with—indeed possibly conducive to—a negative impact on the diversity of attitudes to the trade-off between income and leisure, as stressed in the argument under consideration.

8. This needs to be qualified somewhat in the light of § 3.6: the preferences of the minority must, in the relevant sense, be 'available' to the others.

9. As suggested by Arneson (1990*b*: 53) in a different context, an increase in the economic feasibility of generous redistribution may go hand in hand with a decrease in its political feasibility. Because of a modified trade-off between leisure and income, more people want to work at any given level of basic income, but less people want to vote for a basic income. Political support, however, is too significantly mediated by 'ideology'—in particular fairness criteria—and political success too strongly affected by institutional factors, for any direct inference to be possible from the structure of self interest to political feasibility. I shall briefly return (§ 6.8) to this important question.

10. A similar job is usefully performed by Przeworski (1991: ch.3) along lines broadly consonant with the view presented here.

11. See e.g. Sweezy (1942: 54–5, 270–2) and Robinson (1942: 78–80) for classic statements of this point as parts of the Marxian critique of capitalism.

12. Only a far weaker result (a presumption of second-best efficiency) can be established when there is just one firm. The standard reference is Baumol, Panzar, and Willig (1982). See also Baumol (1982) and Spence (1983) for useful shorter presentations.

13. Along the same lines, see Brus (1966: 21–2) and Kornai (1981: 132–3) and, more crudely, Weston (ed.) (1986: 5, 29): 'It is time that greens accepted that it is capitalism rather than industrialism as such which is at the heart of the problems they address.'

14. As Przeworski (1991: ch.3) puts it: 'Capitalism is not any less, or more, capable than socialism of handling all the situations in which social rates of return diverge from private ones.' Erik Wright (personal communication, Sept. 1989) objects: 'If a capitalist society had the power to effectively mimic all the waste-reducing planning that it would have if it actually owned outright all of the means of production, then *of course* socialism would offer no advantages with respect to planning. But capitalism, under those conditions, becomes an extremely thin type of private ownership.' I agree that subjecting the behaviour of private firms to environmental legislation moves us some distance towards the grey area (see § 1.1). But it need not be far more invasive than a legislation aimed at protecting property rights, and therefore constitutes only a modest step that, taken on its own, should still leave us a long way from the grey area.

15. See McKean (1975: 101–6).

16. This is related to part of the (often rather confused) debate about so-called unproductive activities, sometimes understood as coinciding with circulation (as opposed to production) activities (see e.g. Gouverneur 1983: 109–10). Part of the confusion that affects this debate derives from the fact that unproductive activities are also sometimes understood as activities which are 'unproductive of value' because of their non-market nature. See De Vroey (1982: 51–6) for a useful survey of the uses of the expression.

17. I shall return to this sort of argument, in connection with Habermas's version of capitalist crisis theory (§ 6.4). The rebuttal holds, in particular, for the interesting variant of the argument that relates to the capitalists' need to use control labour and devices in order to make sure that labour is extracted from labour power (see e.g. Bowles and Gintis 1990). I shall return to a corollary of this variant in connection with technical progress (§ 6.6).

18. A similar conclusion holds for what Schumpeter (1943: 197-9) saw as 'one of the most significant titles of superiority that can be advanced in favour of the socialist plan': in a capitalist society, collective objectives can only be pursued through a struggle between state officials and profit-propelled individuals and firms, most conspicuously in the field of taxation. This does not only imply that some labour needs to be devoted to the collection of taxes and the enforcement of regulations, but also that individuals and firms are induced to allocate their resources in suboptimal fashion (the deadweight loss from taxation is just one aspect of this), and to develop a variety of lobbying and protective activities (think of lawyer services). See Krueger (1974) on the economics of rent seeking. Once state intervention is recognized to be

indispensable—as it certainly is under optimal capitalism—it is, of course, important to take this sort of phenomenon into account in assessing capitalism's static efficiency. But here again, it is hard to see how this could feed a case for socialism: implicit taxation through lower gross wages generates economic effects parallel to explicit taxation, and as soon as gains and losses are decentralized in order to provide adequate incentives (see § 6.6), publicly owned firms and state institutions are driven into the same sort of game as under capitalism, and the extent of waste due to protective or lobbying activities is then less a function of the property regime than of the design of legal and political institutions. (To what extent can the elaboration, interpretation, and implementation of economic legislation be influenced by lobbying? To what extent does the law offer loopholes and opportunities which it would be profitable to hire lawyers to exploit to the full?)

19. This point was persuasively brought to my attention by Hillel Steiner. Standard cost-benefit analyses of advertising tend to ignore this whole dimension.

20. Although the 'anarchy of capitalist production' has featured prominently in the socialist critique of capitalism, its role has been downplayed (into a 'complicating' or 'precipitating' factor) by the latter's most articulate exponents. See e.g. Robinson (1942: 44–6), Mandel (1962: 15–28), and Morishima (1973: 126–8).

21. See Marx's (1885: 391–518) theory of the business cycle, as reconstructed by e.g. Sweezy (1942: 75–9, 163–4) or Morishima (1973: 105–28).

22. Moreover, planned economies too are subject to these sorts of adjustment. It is misleading to say that, whereas capitalist production is 'for exchange', socialist production is 'directly for use'. Some form of mediation between resources and needs is required in any regime that relies on an extensive division of labour. And the socialist mediation generates mismatches between supply and demand and, if all goes well, reallocations of labour involving temporary underemployment which, though less visible, are comparable to those that characterize capitalism. See Roland (1989) for an illuminating analysis.

23. See e.g. Alcaly (1978), Shaikh (1978), Weisskopf (1978), and Elster (1985: § 3.4) for useful historical surveys of radical crisis theories. I am here leaving entirely aside the fatally flawed 'falling-rate-of-profit theory of crisis'. In Van Parijs (1993a: chs. 3–4) I discuss extensively the many unsuccessful attempts to rescue it.

24. This argument goes back to a number of pre-Marxian critics of capitalism (see Bleaney 1976 and, more briefly, Shaikh 1978: 222–4). Marx himself is ambivalent about it. On the one hand, he describes the underconsumption of the masses as the 'ultimate cause' of capitalist crises (1894: 568). On the other hand, he dismisses any explanation of crises by a lack of effective demand as a 'pure tautology' (1885: 409–10). Modern exponents of this argument include Sweezy (1942) and Mandel (1962).

25. One variant of the approach connects closely the tendency towards crises of underconsumption to the development of monopoly capitalism. The

argument is then that monopolies are reluctant to use the surplus they generate, because using it to boost output in their own industry would 'spoil the market' and investing in a more competitive sector would depress even more its rate of profit. (See e.g. Sweezy 1942: 275–7, Mandel 1962: 229–35.) But this twist in the argument does little to strengthen it. First, investment in the monopoly sector can consist in capital deepening or in the development of new products, rather than in capital widening at the risk of spoiling the market. Secondly, investment in a more competitive industry will remain attractive as long as the rate of profit is positive.

26. These features are associated with the regime called Fordism by the 'regulation school' (Aglietta 1976, Lipietz 1979, De Vroey 1984, Boyer 1987, etc.). They are sometimes explained 'functionally', precisely by their ability to reduce the risk of major crises. But the relevance of this analysis does not hinge on the operation of any 'functional necessity'.

27. In the absence of a basic income, workers may have overwhelming incentives to upset the working of the system by striking a tacit deal with their employers: their compliance and collaboration would be at the price of the firm owners taking a greater part of the shock in case of downward fluctuations and thereby colluding to turn an apparent share system (possibly legally enforced) at least partly into a *de facto* wage system, with negative consequences on the firm's hiring policy. With a high basic income, on the other hand, the further, non-externality-based advantages of the share system (especially the effect on workers' productivity of their becoming residual claimants) may so offset the risk-sharing advantages of the wage system that adopting the former would Pareto-dominate the latter at the level of many firms (i.e. both the workers and the capital owners of many firms would prefer it) and that no legal arrangement would be needed to encourage or impose it.

28. Early formulations of a profit-squeeze approach can be found in Bauer (1913), Sweezy (1942: ch. 9), and Kalecki (1943), and even in Marx (1867: 641–9, 661; 1894: 529–30) himself, even though he also says that 'there is nothing so stupid' as such an approach. More recent variants include Goodwin (1967), Glyn and Sutcliffe (1971, 1972), Nell (1972), Boddy and Crotty (1975), Rowthorn (1976), Itoh (1980), Bowles (1983), Bowles, Gordon, and Weisskopf (1985), Boyer (1991), etc. Different variants emphasize different factors and focus on different periods or countries. The brief account just given is, of course, only a simplified rendering of the core scenario common to them all.

29. The argument needs to be modulated to fit e.g. the degree to which markets are monopolistic and the strength of international competition. Here again, I reconstruct and simplify the core of some Marxist analyses of the 'fiscal crisis' (e.g. O'Connor 1973: esp. 205–11) or of the 'inflation crisis' (e.g. Rowthorn 1977). There is more than a superficial resemblance with some 'bourgeois' analyses, such as Brittan's (1975) or Bacon and Eltis's (1976).

30. For reasons strictly analogous to those spelt out by Lancaster (1973) in his demonstration of the 'dynamic inefficiency of capitalism' (see § 6.6 herein).

31. See Garrett and Lange (1986), as interpreted by Przeworski (1987: 22). For empirical evidence as to the workers' willingness to exercise self-restraint, see e.g. Visser and Pellikaan (1985).

32. This is the core of Claus Offe's (1972: esp. 100–1) and Jürgen Habermas's (esp. 1973: 58–9, 76–7, 98, 113, 130; also 1985: 6–8) 'legitimacy-crisis' thesis, a variant of which can also be found, for example, in O'Connor (1973: 49–50). Habermas (esp. 1973: 68–71, 89–96, 106–9) further argues that there is no way in which this legitimacy crisis could be significantly alleviated by active pro-growth state intervention, first because of a 'rationality crisis' that stems mainly from the government's vulnerability to the pressure of sectoral interests and holds down the State's effectiveness at boosting productivity, and secondly because of a 'motivation crisis' that weakens people's commitment to a performance-oriented professional ethos, to a consumption-oriented possessive individualism, and to a civic privatism that dispenses with active participation. The central intuition behind the legitimacy crisis thesis was shared in the 1970s by a wide range of authors, from Fred Hirsch (see esp. 1977: 174) to Samuel Brittan (esp. 1975: 258–61, 267–72).

33. Of course, the organized working class's acceptance of the legitimacy of a substantial basic income (see § 4.6) is here presupposed in the case of optimal capitalism, as it would need to be in the case of optimal socialism.

34. This standard difficulty of 'market socialism' is usefully discussed by e.g. Vanek (1970), Fehr (1988), and Drèze (1989).

35. In the sense of Ch. 3, App. 1. The stronger condition of opulence need not be met for a significant basic income to be viable, and hence the following considerations to be relevant.

36. See Elster's (1982c: 470–1) illuminating game-theoretical analysis of the capitalists' predicament.

37. If the demand for labour rises fast enough as wages fall, it might, of course, catch up even a (mildly) rising supply. But recognizing this possibility does not take us far towards the serene confidence in the virtues of the labour market which one could muster if the labour supply could be assumed to decrease monotonically as wages fall. Note that the 'backward bend' of the supply curve on which this argument relies is distinct from the one commonly talked about in development economics. What is relevant here is not that people want to work less and less as the wage rate goes up beyond a certain threshold (with the possible consequence that the supply of labour falls short of demand whatever the wage), but that they want to work more and more as the wage rate goes down below a certain threshold (with the possible consequence that the supply of labour remains greater than demand whatever the wage). In both cases, however, the income effect is assumed to start outweighing the substitution effect as from a certain point.

38. The highest sustainable basic income is, of course, most likely to generate a considerable shortfall from full-time employment for all able-bodied citizens at their most productive occupation, and hence to imply a lower level of output than would be achievable under some alternative arrangement. But although this can plausibly be interpreted as a negative impact on the

regime's static efficiency (through a negative impact on its mobilization of existing resources), this cannot, of course, be used as an argument against a regime that incorporates such a basic income, since static efficiency is only relevant, in the present context, to the extent that it affects the level to which a basic income can sustainably be raised.

39. In addition to the 'Hobbesian' version—which views the efficiency wage as a way of making dismissal a more painful sanction—and to the 'Maussian' version—which views the efficiency wage as a countergift-inducing gift—both briefly presented earlier (§ 4.4), there is a 'Malthusian' variant which simply views the efficiency wage as a way of securing a better health for workers (see Bowles 1985, Akerlof 1982, and Leibenstein 1963, respectively, for typical illustrations).

40. On the other hand, it may strengthen the case in favour of labour management, and hence in favour of the co-operative variant of capitalism discussed in the previous section or some analogous public-ownership regime. See Bowles and Gintis (1993) for an interesting argument to this effect.

41. Other microeconomic theories of equilibrium involuntary unemployment under competitive conditions are equally unpromising. The insider–outsider approach, for example, also briefly referred to earlier (§ 4.4), applies to any society in which workers are and remain the owners of their labour power, hence to formal-freedom-respecting socialism (not to collectivism) just as much as to formal-freedom-respecting capitalism.

42. With the usual qualification (see § 1.8) that a negligible deterioration of the situation of the worst off may be justified by a huge increase in the situation of some of the better-off.

43. It hardly needs saying that the growth potential must be understood in a sense that takes adequate account of environmental externalities and the depletion of natural resources (see § 2.3).

44. Henry Wallich (1960), for example, talks of 'the cost of freedom' in the title of his book because he believed that a lower economic growth was the price capitalism had to pay for the sake of preserving freedom.

45. See Van Parijs (1993a: 37–85) for an extensive discussion of this theory and of the lessons to be drawn from the debates it gave rise to.

46. True, the functioning of large capitalist corporations, where much of capitalist technical progress is being made, has more in common with that of socialist bureaucracies than with that of a lone producer directly submitted to the discipline of the market. Yet it is the ultimate subjection to the sanctions of the market that keeps giving the 'functionaries of capital', from the top to the bottom of the hierarchy, both the self-interested energy and the rhetorical weaponry that enable them to fight inertia effectively.

47. This selection dimension of dynamic efficiency is emphasized by e.g. Arnold (1985: 98). As Oskar Lange (1937a: 131) had already pointed out, this advantage is reduced under monopoly capitalism, to the extent that the capitalists' or managers' lobbying qualities are becoming as important as their qualities as economizers.

48. This belief must have inspired Lenin in a 1919 speech quoted by Brus (1987:

346–7): 'Labour productivity is what is most important, decisive for the victory of the new social order. Capitalism generated a level of labour productivity unheard of in conditions of serfdom. Capitalism can be and will be finally defeated because socialism generates new, much higher labour productivity.'

49. See von Weizsäcker and Samuelson (1971), Samuelson (1982), Roemer (1983b), Elster (1985: §§ 3.22, 5.1.3), and Van Parijs (1993a: 158–60) for more extensive critical discussions of this argument.

50. Variants of this argument soon became part of the stock-in-trade of the critique of capitalism. See e.g. Sweezy (1942: 276–7) or Mandel (1962: 107–14).

51. Schumpeter is not saying that the more concentrated the market structure, the better: 'It is certainly as conceivable that an all-pervading cartel system might sabotage all progress as it is that it might realize, with smaller social and private costs, all that perfect competition is supposed to realize' (Schumpeter 1943: 91). But he persuasively argues that concentration as such is very far from being, necessarily, a bad thing for technical progress.

52. For brief statements of the same argument, see e.g. Brus (1966: 21–2), Robinson (1956: 87), Okun (1975: 57–8), Elster and Moene (eds.) (1989: § 1).

53. For further discussion, see e.g. Gordon (1976: 22–6), Drago (1986: 76–86), Bowles and Gintis (1990). I do not wish to deny that the workers' feelings about the legitimacy of the system they are working in may significantly affect their propensity to shirk. But if this is a crucial premiss, then we are here again (see § 6.3 on policing activities and § 6.4 on the legitimacy crisis) begging the question by taking for granted in the course of the argument what the conclusion might establish—namely, the ethical superiority of socialism over capitalism.

54. See e.g. Brus (1966), Kornai (1981), and Roland (1989).

55. A broadly similar remark applies to a workers' co-operative economy. As in a labour-owned firm the workers' fate is heavily dependent on the firm's success, there will be a strong bias against risky business, and hence against innovation. In order to mitigate this bias, the ownership structure can be brought closer to the standard variant of capitalism, as proposed by e.g. Meade (1989).

56. This is approximately the definition offered by Przeworski and Wallerstein (1986) in their illuminating analysis.

57. Here is a strong statement of the superiority claimed for socialism on this ground: 'It is necessary to recognize that private ownership of the means of production is severely limited in its freedom of choice of objectives, because it is compelled to be profit-seeking, and tends to take a narrow and selfish view of things. Public ownership gives complete freedom in the choice of objectives and can therefore be used for any purpose that may be chosen. While private ownership is an instrument that by itself largely determines the ends for which it can be employed, public ownership is an instrument, the ends of which are completely undetermined' (Schumacher 1959, quoted by Ward 1985: 271–2). See also Przeworski's (1991: ch. 3) sharp contrast between the blueprint of capitalism (fundamentally irrational because

technically feasible distributions of welfare are made inaccessible by the private owners' right to withdraw their endowments from productive uses) and the blueprint of socialism or rather, in my terminology, of collectivism (which fully controls all resources and can therefore reach the outer utility possibility frontier).

58. This is the most general form taken by the threat to popular sovereignty under capitalist conditions. A more specific (but far from negligible) form is rooted in the private ownership of the media (see e.g. Dunn 1984: 15–16). The influence of the media on the outcome of elections may prevent a democratic capitalist society from doing what a large majority of its members would like it to do. This is another illustration of what is sometimes referred to e.g. in connection with the legitimacy crisis discussion (see § 6.4), as a contradiction between capitalism and democracy. Other threats to popular sovereignty, however, may derive from difficulties inherent in the democratic political process, such as the Condorcet paradox or the Ostrogorski paradox (see § 5.3). See Przeworski and Wallerstein (1986) for a comprehensive survey.

59. One version of this argument is at the core of Wright's (1986) and Roland's (1988) critiques of the feasibility of basic income capitalism, and another can be constructed from Sam Bowles's (1992) illuminating formal analysis.

60. Different variants of this argument, briefly referred to earlier (§ 4.6), have been developed by Guy Standing (1986, 1989), Bart Nooteboom (1986), and James Meade (1989: § 3). Another, more speculative, argument (suggested to me by Sam Bowles) emphasizes the costly conflicts increasingly generated in our economies, as a result of the growing importance of environmental externalities and of wealth held in the form of information rather than of material goods—and hence of property rights that are very difficult to define and enforce. Markets can handle sharp conflicts of interest, but only if the uncertainty surrounding legitimate claims remains limited. As the two trends mentioned are likely to persist, it will become increasingly difficult to make sure that whoever is responsible for wealth destruction (creation) actually pays (is paid) for the damage (benefit) caused. To forestall economically damaging chaos, one will then have to drastically reduce what is at stake in the market game, i.e. to make an increasing part of people's material welfare depend on society's overall productivity rather than on their individual contribution. A basic income is a natural way of institutionalizing this solution. See Van Parijs (1990) for further discussion of the relevance of economic arguments.

61. Consistently with my earlier emphasis on the distinction between individual and societal freedom (§ 1.4), nothing in this argument relies on making popular sovereignty a value in itself. Its possibly crucial importance is of a purely instrumental nature, in the service of *individual* real freedom for all.

62. Of course, for that party too, leaving would be worse than the pre-pact situation, but the cost would be even greater for the other parties, who do not have the option to leave. The latter will therefore agree not to have the (profitability-damaging, basic-income-boosting) pact, unless of course,

driven along by an irrepressible sense of injustice, they 'irrationally' drive the profit-seeking investors away—a possibility which, in some contexts, should not be neglected, as neatly illustrated by the experiments on 'ultimatum bargaining' (see e.g. Güth 1988).

63. The sharpness of this constraint obviously depends on such factors as the geographical and linguistic proximity of the countries in which better jobs would be available, their readiness to welcome skilled immigrants, and above all the extent to which the carriers of the country's human capital are guided exclusively by the maximization of their net incomes. I return to this last factor in the next section.

64. Conversations with Susan Strange persuaded me of the narrow limitations, in today's world, of popular-sovereignty-based arguments for socialism.

65. At most, because not all well-ordered societies need to adopt a liberal theory of justice. Some may adopt a perfectionistic one, which need not incorporate the list of fundamental liberties (and their priority) nor anything like the Difference Principle. The most explicit statement about these issues is Rawls (1993*b*). Several other authors, such as Beitz (1979), Pogge (1989, 1994), and Barry (1989, 1994), who are also committed to some variant of the Difference Principle, defend instead a global interpretation akin to the one advocated here.

66. I am grateful to Serge-Christophe Kolm for having drawn my attention to this paradigmatic expression of right-wing Rawlsianism *avant la lettre*.

67. Which does not prevent some people from advocating it. For example, the Dutch artist Pieter Kooistra (1983) has been pleading for years for a 'U.N. income for all people'; Gunnar Adler-Karlsson (1990) argues (mainly on grounds of factor mobility) that a world basic income is the only realistic possibility, but that it would require, as a quid pro quo, an effective limitation of population growth in Third World countries; and the idea of a world basic pension financed by the rich countries is occasionally aired as a way of simultaneously fighting Third World poverty and excessive demographic growth.

68. I further develop and illustrate several aspects of this argument in Van Parijs (1996*b*).

69. An alternative strategy for the pursuit of international justice would be to count on the migration of people, which, together with the migration of capital and the spreading of technologies, would gradually but powerfully redistribute opportunities downwards from the not-so-rich in the rich countries to many even less rich in poor countries. For several strong reasons, however, massive economically motivated migration is far less appropriate than massive inter-individual redistribution as a way of equalizing (or leximinning) opportunities: it would not improve, and may well worsen, the situation of the poorest in the poor countries; it would relieve the pressure for 'responsible' demographic policies in each country; it would generate large negative externalities through the destruction of local communities both in the country of departure and in the country of arrival; it would create additional constraints on intranational redistribution; and it would undermine social

cohesion which, for indirect reasons to be explored shortly, matters greatly to the viable realization of leximin real freedom. For extremely useful food for thought in this area, see esp. Barry and Goodin (eds.) (1992) and Carens (forthcoming).

70. This has been increasingly the case in the last two decades or so in most advanced capitalist countries. See e.g. Atkinson (1993) for relevant data. Kaus (1992) takes this trend and its irreversibility as the point of departure of his plea for a replacement of the attempt to achieve greater equality ('money liberalism') by an attempt to protect certain spheres of life from the intrusion of income inequalities ('civic liberalism'). I shall argue that some version of the latter is important to salvage the former.

71. The choice of words is, of course, meant to convey a close connection with the notion of a solidaristic or equal-concern conception of justice introduced in § 1.8.

72. I discuss these questions at length in the last two sections of Van Parijs (1993*b*).

73. To this extent, I would concede to André Gorz (1985, 1988, 1992) that the viable introduction of a substantial basic income might require the parallel introduction of some sort of public service. But it must be clear that the argument is neither about economic viability (a compulsory public service of sizeable length would *reduce* the economic potential for financing a substantial basic income), nor about ethical justification (Chs. 3 and 4 have taken great trouble to show that, under appropriate circumstances specified in § 3.8, justice requires that each member of society be entitled to a substantial income irrespective of any contribution), but about the sociological conditions for widespread allegiance to solidaristic justice.

74. Other examples were given much earlier (§ 1.4) in connection with the restriction of freedom for the sake of freedom.

75. This third tenet of my resolutely left-wing variant of Rawlsianism cannot count any more than the first two on Rawls's own explicit endorsement. Indeed, his explicit disagreement with it was discussed in detail earlier on (§ 4.2). None the less I believe that, along with the first two tenets, it is far from being totally alien to Rawls's approach. Support for this view can be found e.g. in Rawls's fullest description of property-owning democracy, his own favourite regime, which he contrasts with (firmly criticized) welfare-state capitalism in terms of *ex ante* endowments versus *ex post* corrections, while assuming (over-optimistically, in my view, under present conditions) that an appropriate distribution of bequests and human capital endowments could be sufficient to guarantee the great majority of people a decent standard of living (see Rawls 1990: § 51). Further, James Meade, Rawls's 'economic guru' (Barry 1989: 394), from whom he borrowed, in particular, the very notion of a property-owning democracy (see Meade 1964), has recently become one of the most influential advocates of basic income in the economic profession (see Meade 1989, 1990, 1993). Finally, after I presented an ancestor of Chapter 4 as a lecture at Harvard (in April 1990), Rawls commented that if there were permanently not enough jobs around, he might (or

perhaps even would?) go along with my conclusion. Like the first two tenets, the third one would of course be far less important if we lived in the world in which Rawls is implicitly assuming we live (and in doing so he was basically right until not so long ago): a world of nations hardly constrained by international competition and in which every able-bodied person could reasonably expect to find, after some affordable training, a job that paid enough to feed a family. I am reasonably confident that a full realization of the changes that have been taking place in the world economy would turn Rawls into a full-blown left-wing Rawlsian, as characterized.

REFERENCES

ACKERMAN, BRUCE A. (1980), *Social Justice in the Liberal State*, New Haven, Conn., Yale University Press.

ADLER-KARLSSON, GUNNAR (1979), 'Probleme des Wirtschaftswachstums und der Wirtschaftsgesinnung: Utopie eines besseren Lebens', *Mitteilungsdienst der Verbraucherzentrale NRW*, 23: 40–63.

—— (1990), 'Towards a World Citizen Income', paper presented at the Third European Conference on Basic Income, Florence: European University Institute.

AGLIETTA, MICHEL (1976), *Régulation et crises du capitalisme: L'Exemple des États-Unis*, Paris: Calmann-Lévy.

AKERLOF, GEORGE A. (1978), 'The Economics of "Tagging" as Applied to the Optimal Income Tax, Welfare Programs, and Manpower Planning', in G. A. Akerlof, *An Economic Theorist's Book of Tales*, Cambridge: Cambridge University Press (1984), 45–68.

—— (1981), 'Jobs as Dam Sites', in G. A. Akerlof, *An Economic Theorist's Book of Tales*, Cambridge: Cambridge University Press (1984), 101–22.

—— (1982), 'Labor Contracts as Partial Gift Exchange', in G. A. Akerlof, *An Economic Theorist's Book of Tales*, Cambridge: Cambridge University Press (1984), 145–74.

—— and YELLEN, JANET L. (1986), 'Introduction', in *Efficiency Wage Models of the Labor Market*, Cambridge: Cambridge University Press, 1–22.

ALCALY, R. E. (1978), 'An Introduction to Marxian Crisis Theory', in *Radical Perspectives on the Economic Crisis of Monopoly Capitalism*, New York: Union for Radical Political Economics, 15–22.

ALEXANDER, LARRY, and SCHWARZSCHILD, MAIMON (1987), 'Liberalism, Neutrality, and Equality of Welfare vs. Equality of Resources', in *Philosophy and Public Affairs*, 16: 85–110.

ANSART, PIERRE (ed.) (1984), *Proudhon: Textes et débats*, Paris: Livre de Poche.

ARISTOTLE. *Politics*, ed. H. Rackam, London: Heinemann.

ARMSTRONG, PHILLIP, GLYN, ANDREW, and HARRISON, JOHN (1978), 'In Defence of Value: A Reply to Ian Steedman', *Capital and Class*, 5: 1–31.

ARNESON, RICHARD J. (1981), 'What's Wrong with Exploitation?', *Ethics*, 91:202–27.

—— (1985), 'Freedom and Desire', *Canadian Journal of Philosophy*, 15: 425–48.

—— (1989), 'Equality and Equal Opportunity for Welfare', *Philosophical Studies*, 56: 77–93.

—— (1990a), 'Liberalism, Distributive Subjectivism, and Equal Opportunity for Welfare', *Philosophy and Public Affairs*, 19: 158–94.

—— (1990b), 'Is Work Special? Justice and the Distribution of Employment', *American Political Science Review*, 84: 49–64.

ARNESON, RICHARD J. (1991), 'A Defense of Equal Opportunity for Welfare', *Philosophical Studies*, 62: 187–95.

—— (1992*a*), 'Property Rights in Persons', *Social Philosophy and Policy*, 9: 201–30.

—— (1992*b*), 'Is Socialism Dead? A Comment on Market Socialism and Basic Income Capitalism', *Ethics*, 102: 485–511.

ARNOLD, N. SCOTT (1985), 'Capitalists and the Ethics of Contribution', *Canadian Journal of Philosophy*, 15: 87–102.

ARNSPERGER, CHRISTIAN (1994), 'Envy–Freeness and Distributive Justice', *Journal of Economic Surveys*, 8: 155–86.

ARON, RAYMOND (1965), *Essai sur les libertés*, Paris: Librairie Générale Française (1976).

ATKINSON, ANTHONY B. (1993), 'What is Happening to the Distribution of Income in the UK?', STICERD Working Paper WSP/87.

BACON, ROBERT and ELTIS, WALTER (1976), *Britain's Economic Problem: Too Few Producers*, London: Macmillan (1978).

BAKER, JOHN (1987), *Arguing for Equality*, London: Verso Books.

—— (1992), 'An Egalitarian Case for Basic Income', in P. Van Parijs (ed.), *Arguing for Basic Income: Ethical Foundations for a Radical Reform*, London: Verso, 101–27.

BARRY, BRIAN (1979), 'Justice as Reciprocity', in E. Kamenka and A. E. S. Tay (eds.), *Justice*, London: Edward Arnold, 50–78.

—— (1983), 'Intergenerational Justice in Energy Policy', in D. MacLean and P. G. Brown (eds.), *Energy and the Future*, Totowa, NJ: Rowman & Littlefield, 15–30.

—— (1989), *Theories of Justice*, Hemel-Hempstead: Harvester-Wheatsheaf.

—— (1992), 'Equality Yes, Basic Income No', in P. Van Parijs (ed.), *Arguing for Basic Income: Ethical Foundations for a Radical Reform*, London: Verso, 128–40.

—— (1994), 'Dirty Work in the Original Position', paper presented at the conference, 'The Ethics of Nationalism', The University of Illinois at Urbana-Champaign (Apr. 1994).

—— and GOODIN, ROBERT (eds.) (1992), *Free Movement: Ethical Issues in the Transnational Migration of People and Money*, Hemel-Hempstead: Harvester-Wheatsheaf; and University Park: Pennsylvania State University Press.

BAUER, OTTO (1913), 'Die Akkumulation des Kapitals', *Die Neue Zeit*, 31: 831–8, 862–74.

BAUMOL, WILLIAM J. (1982), 'Contestable Markets: An Uprising in the Theory of Industry Structure', *American Economic Review*, 72: 1–15.

—— PANZAR, J. C., and WILLIG, R. D. (1982), *Contestable Markets and the Theory of Industry Structure*, New York: Harcourt, Brace, Jovanovitch.

BECKER, GARY (1981), *A Treatise on the Family*, Cambridge, Mass.: Harvard University Press.

BEITZ, CHARLES (1979), *Political Theory and International Relations*, Princeton, NJ: Princeton University Press.

BELLAMY, EDWARD (1888), *Looking Backward*, Boston: Houghton Mifflin (1966).

—— (1897), *Equality*, New York: Appleton & Co.

BELLOC, HILAIRE (1912), *The Servile State*, Indianapolis: Liberty Press (1977).

BENN, STANLEY I. and WEINSTEIN, WILLIAM (1971), 'Being Free to Act and Being a Free Man', *Mind*, 80: 194–211.

BERLIN, ISAIAH (1958), 'Two Concepts of Liberty', in I. Berlin, *Four Essays on Liberty*, Oxford: Oxford University Press (1979), 118–72.

—— (1969), 'Introduction', in I. Berlin, *Four Essays on Liberty*, Oxford: Oxford University Press (1979), pp. ix–lxiii.

BESLEY, TIMOTHY (1990), 'Means Testing versus Universal Provision in Poverty Alleviation Programmes', *Economica*, 57: 119–29.

BETTELHEIM, CHARLES (1969), 'Remarques théoriques', appendix to A. Emmanuel, *L'Échange inégal*, Paris: Maspero (1975), 295–341.

BLEANEY, MICHAEL (1976), *Underconsumption Theories: A History and Critical Analysis*, New York: International Publishers.

BODDY, R. and CROTTY, J. (1975), 'Class Conflict and Macro-Policy: The Political Business Cycle', *Review of Radical Political Economics*, 7: 1–19.

BOUGLÉ, CÉLESTIN (1907), *Le Solidarisme*, Paris: Giard & Brère.

BOURGEOIS, LÉON (1902), *Solidarité*, Paris: Armand Colin.

BOWLES, SAMUEL (1983), 'The Post-Keynesian Capital-Labor Stalemate', *Socialist Review*, 65: 45–74.

—— (1985), 'The Production Process in a Competitive Economy: Walrasian, Neo-Hobbesian and Marxian Models', *American Economic Review*, 75: 16–36.

—— (1992), 'Is Income Security Possible in a Capitalist Economy: A Micro-Economic Analysis of the Basic Income Grant', *European Journal of Political Economy*, 8: 557–78.

—— and GINTIS, HERBERT (1986), *Democracy and Capitalism*, London: Routledge.

—— (1988), 'Contested Exchange: Political Economy and Modern Economic Theory', *American Economic Review*, 78: 145–50.

—— (1990), 'Contested Exchange: New Microfoundations for the Political Economy of Capitalism', *Politics and Society* 18: 165–222.

—— (1993), 'The Democratic Firm: An Agency-Theoretic Evaluation', in S. Bowles, H. Gintis, and B. Gustafson (eds.), *Markets and Democracy*, Cambridge: Cambridge University Press, 13–39.

—— GORDON, DAVID M., and WEISSKOPF, THOMAS E. (1985), *Beyond the Waste Land: A Democratic Alternative to Economic Decline*, New York: Anchor Press.

BOYER, ROBERT (1987), *La Théorie de la régulation*, Paris: La Découverte.

—— (1991), *Justice sociale et performances économiques: De l'alliance cachée au conflit ouvert?*, Paris: CEPREMAP, Working paper 9135.

BRITTAN, SAMUEL (1973), *Capitalism and the Permissive Society*, London: Macmillan. (Abridged in *A Restatement of Economic Liberalism*, London: Macmillan (1988), 1–209.)

BRITTAN, SAMUEL (1975), 'The Politics of Excessive Expectations', in S. Brittan, *The Economic Consequences of Democracy*, London: Temple Smith (1977), 247–78.

—— (1988), *A Restatement of Economic Liberalism*, London: Macmillan.

BRODY, BARUCH (1983), 'Redistribution without Egalitarianism', *Social Philosophy and Policy*, 1: 71–87.

BRONFENBRENNER, M. (1971), *Income Distribution Theory*, London: Macmillan.

BRUS, WLODIMIERZ (1966), 'Economic Incentives, Technical Progress and the Evolution of the Socialist Economic System', in W. Brus, *The Economics and Politics of Socialism*, London: Routledge & Kegan Paul (1973), 21–30.

—— (1987), 'A Note on Socialism's Claim to Economic Rationality', in G. Fink, G. Pöll, and M. Riese (eds.), *Economic Theory, Political Power and Social Justice: Festschrift Kazimierz Laski*, Vienna: Springer, 345–57.

BUCHANAN, ALLEN E. (1979), 'Exploitation, Alienation and Injustice', *Canadian Journal of Philosophy*, 9: 121–39.

—— (1982), *Marx and Justice: The Radical Critique of Liberalism*, Totowa, NJ: Rowman & Littlefield.

—— (1985), *Ethics, Efficiency and the Market*, Totowa, NJ: Rowman & Allanheld.

—— (1989), 'Assessing the Communitarian Critique of Liberalism', *Ethics*, 99: 852–82.

BUCHANAN, JAMES M. (1985), *The Limits of Liberty*, Chicago: University of Chicago Press.

—— (1987), 'Towards the Simple Economics of Natural Liberty: An Exploratory Analysis', *Kyklos*, 40: 3–20.

—— and LOMASKY, LOREN E. (1985), 'The Matrix of Contractarian Justice', in E. F. Paul, F. D. Miller, and J. Paul (eds.), *Liberty and Equality*, Oxford: Blackwell, 12–32.

BYRNE, STEVEN E. (1993), *A Rawlsian Argument for Basic Income*, University College Dublin: Department of Politics, MA thesis.

CARENS, JOSEPH H. (1981), *Equality, Moral Incentives and the Market: An Essay in Utopian Politico-Economic Theory*, Chicago, Ill.: University of Chicago Press.

—— (1985), 'Compensatory Justice and Social Institutions', *Economics and Philosophy*, 1: 39–67.

—— (forthcoming), *Immigration and Political Community*.

CARLING, ALAN (1984), 'Exploitation: A Calculus of Dissent?', University of Bradford: School of Interdisciplinary Human Studies.

—— (1987), 'Exploitation, Extortion and Oppression', *Political Studies*, 35: 173–88.

—— (1991), *Social Division*, London: Verso.

CARTER, IAN (1993), *The Measurement of Freedom*, Florence: European University Institute, Ph.D. thesis.

CARVER, TERRELL (1987), 'Marx's Political Theory of Exploitation', in A. Reeve (ed.), *Modern Theories of Exploitation*, London: Sage, 68–79.

CHAMPSAUR, PAUL and LAROQUE, GUY (1981), 'Fair Allocations in Large Economies', *Journal of Economic Theory*, 25: 269–82.

COHEN, G. A. (1978), *Karl Marx's Theory of History*, Oxford: Oxford University Press.

—— (1979*a*), 'The Labour Theory of Value and the Concept of Exploitation', in M. Cohen, T. Nagel, and T. Scanlon (eds.), *Marx, Justice and History*, Princeton, NJ: Princeton University Press (1980), 135–57.

—— (1979*b*), 'Capitalism, Freedom and the Proletariat', in A. Ryan (ed.), *The Idea of Freedom: Essays in Honour of Isaiah Berlin*, Oxford: Oxford University Press, 9–25.

—— (1981*a*), 'Freedom, Justice and Capitalism', *New Left Review*, 126: 3–18.

—— (1981*b*), 'Illusions about Private Property and Freedom', in J. Mepham and D. Ruben (eds.), *Issues in Marxist Philosophy*, Hassocks, Harvester Press, iv. 223–42.

—— (1983*a*), 'The Structure of Proletarian Unfreedom', *Philosophy and Public Affairs*, 12: 3–33.

—— (1983*b*), 'More on Exploitation and the Labour Theory of Value', *Inquiry*, 26: 309–31.

—— (1983*c*), Review of Wood (1981), *Mind*, 92: 440–5.

—— (1985*a*), 'Nozick on Appropriation', *New Left Review*, 150: 89–105.

—— (1985*b*), 'Marx and Locke on Land and Labour', *Proceedings of the British Academy*, 71: 357–88.

—— (1986), 'Self-Ownership, World-Ownership and Equality, Part II', *Social Philosophy and Policy*, 3: 77–96.

—— (1987), 'Comments on the Universal Grant Proposal', Oxford: All Souls College, unpublished note.

—— (1989*a*), 'Are Freedom and Equality Compatible?', in J. Elster and K. O. Moene (eds.), *Alternatives to Capitalism*, Cambridge: Cambridge University Press, 113–26.

—— (1989*b*), 'On the Currency of Egalitarian Justice', *Ethics*, 99: 906–44.

—— (1990), 'Equality of What? On Welfare, Goods and Capabilities', *Recherches Économiques de Louvain*, 56: 357–82.

—— (1992), 'Incentives, Inequality and Community', in *The Tanner Lectures on Human Values*, Salt Lake City: University of Utah Press, xiii. 261–329.

—— (1995), *Self-Ownership, Freedom and Equality*, Cambridge: Cambridge University Press.

COLE, GEORGE D. H. (1929), *The Next Ten Years in British Social and Economic Policy*, London: Macmillan.

—— (1935), *Principles of Economic Planning*, London: Macmillan.

—— (1944), *Money: its Present and Future*, London: Cassel & Co.

COLINS, HENRI (1835), *Du Pacte social et de la liberté politique considérés comme complément moral de l'homme*, Paris: Montardier.

COLLARD, DAVID (1980), 'Social Dividend and Negative Income Tax', C. Sandford, C. Pond, and R. Walker (eds.), *Taxation and Social Policy*, London: Heinemann, 190–202.

COMBLE, JERRY and NORTON, EDGAR (eds.) (1991), *Economic Justice in Perspective*, Englewood Cliffs: Prentice-Hall.

CONSTANT, BENJAMIN (1819), 'De la liberté des anciens comparée à celle des modernes', in B. Constant, *De l'esprit de conquête et de l'usurpation*, Paris: Flammarion (1986), 265–91.

CROCKER, LAWRENCE (1972), 'Marx's Concept of Exploitation', *Social Theory and Practice*, 1: 201–15.

CUNLIFFE, JOHN (1987), 'A Mutualist Theory of Exploitation?', in A. Reeve (ed.), *Modern Theories of Exploitation*, London: Sage, 53–67.

DA SILVEIRA, PABLO (1994), *Neutralité et enseignement dans une société pluraliste: Arguments pour un perfectionnisme modeste*, Université catholique de Louvain: Institut supérieur de philosophie, Ph.D. thesis.

DAUSSUN, ROBERT (1986), 'Le Rapport du Conseil des impôts relatif à l'imposition du capital', *Les Notes Bleues du Ministères de l'Economie, des Finances et de la Privatisation*, 307: 1–7.

DEUTSCH, MORTON (1985), *Distributive Justice*, New Haven, Conn.: Yale University Press.

DE VROEY, MICHEL (1982), 'On the Obsolescence of the Marxian Theory of Value: A Critical Review', *Capital and Class*, 17: 34–59.

—— (1984), 'A Regulation Approach Interpretation of the Contemporary Crisis', *Capital and Class*, 23: 45–66.

DE JOUVENEL, BERTRAND (1952), *The Ethics of Redistribution*, Indianapolis: Liberty Press (1990).

DOBB, MAURICE (1973), *Theories of Value and Distribution since Adam Smith*, Cambridge: Cambridge University Press (1981).

DOLAN, E. G. (1971), 'Alienation, Freedom and Economic Organization', *Journal of Political Economy*, 79: 1084–94.

DONSIMONI, M. P. and POLEMARCHAKIS, H. M. (1985), 'Variations in Endowments and Utilities', Louvain-la-Neuve: CORE Discussion Paper 8530.

DRAGO, R. (1986), 'Capitalism and Efficiency: A Review and Appraisal of the Recent Discussion', *Review of Radical Political Economics*, 18: 71–92.

DRÈZE, JACQUES (1989), *Labour.Management, Contracts and Capital Markets*, Oxford: Blackwell.

DUBOIN, MARIE-LOUISE (1988), 'Guaranteed Income as an Inheritance', in A. G. Miller (ed.), *Proceedings of the First International Conference on Basic Income*, London: BIRG; Antwerp: BIEN, 134–45.

DUNN, JOHN (1984), *The Politics of Socialism*, Cambridge: Cambridge University Press.

DWORKIN, RONALD (1981a) 'What is Equality? Part I. Equality of Welfare', *Philosophy and Public Affairs*, 10: 185–246.

—— (1981b), 'What is Equality? Part II. Equality of Resources', *Philosophy and Public Affairs*, 10: 283–345.

—— (1987), 'What is Equality? Part 3: The Place of Liberty', *Iowa Law Review*, 73: 1–54.

—— (1989), 'What is Equality? Part 4: Political Equality', *University of San Francisco Law Review*, 22: 1–30.

—— (1990), 'Foundations of Liberal Equality', in G.B. Peterson (ed.), *The Tanner Lectures on Human Values*, Salt Lake City: University of Utah Press, xi. 1–119.

ELLERMAN, D. P. (1983), 'Marxian Exploitation Theory: A Brief Exposition, Analysis, and Critique', *The Philosophical Forum*, 14: 315–33.

ELSTER, JON (1978a), 'Exploring Exploitation', *Journal of Peace Research*, 15: 3–17.

—— (1978b), *Logic and Society: Contradictions and Possible Worlds*, Chichester: Wiley & Sons.

—— (1982a), 'Roemer versus Roemer', *Politics and Society*, 11: 363–74.

—— (1982b), 'Sour Grapes: Utilitarianism and the Genesis of Wants', in A. K. Sen and B. Williams (eds.), *Utilitarianism and Beyond*, Cambridge: Cambridge University Press, 219–38.

—— (1982c), 'Marxism, Functionalism and Game Theory', *Theory and Society*, 11: 453–82.

—— (1983), 'Exploitation, Freedom and Justice', *Nomos*, 26: 277–304.

—— (1985), *Making Sense of Marx*, Cambridge: Cambridge University Press.

—— (1986), 'Comment on van der Veen and Van Parijs', *Theory & Society*, 15: 709–22.

—— (1989), *Solomonic Judgements*, Cambridge: Cambridge University Press.

—— and MOENE, KARL OVE (eds.) (1989), *Alternatives to Capitalism*, Cambridge: Cambridge University Press.

EMMANUEL, ARGHIRI (1969), *L'Échange inégal: Essai sur les antagonismes dans les rapports internationaux*, Paris: Maspero (1975).

—— (1975), 'Réponse à Charles Bettelheim', appendix to A. Emmanuel, *L'Échange inégal*, Paris: Maspero, 342–415.

ENGELS, FRIEDRICH (1873), *Zur Wohnungsfrage*, in K. Marx and F. Engels, *Werke*, Berlin: Dietz (1959), xviii. 211–321.

FEHR, ERNST (1988), *Ökonomische Theorie der Selbstverwaltung und Gewinnbeteiligung*, Frankfurt: Campus.

FLATHMAN, R. E. (1987), *The Philosophy and Politics of Freedom*, Chicago: University of Chicago Press.

FLEURBAEY, MARC (1991), 'On Fair Compensation', University of California (Davis): Department of Economics.

—— (1994), 'L'Absence d'envie dans une problématique post-welfariste', *Recherches économiques de Louvain*, 60: 9–42.

FOLBRE, NANCY (1982), 'Exploitation Comes Home: A Critique of the Marxian Theory of Family Labour', *Cambridge Journal of Economics*, 6: 317–29.

FOLEY, DUNCAN K. (1967), 'Resource Allocation and the Public Sector', *Yale Economic Essays*, 7: 45–98.

FRANCE, ANATOLE (1907), *L'Île des Pingouins*, Paris: Calmann-Lévy, 1980.

FRIED, CHARLES (1983), 'Distributive Justice', *Social Philosophy and Policy*, 1: 45–59.

FRIEDMAN, DAVID (1973), *The Machinery of Freedom: Guide to Radical Capitalism*, New Rochelle, (NY): Arlington House (1978).

FRIEDMAN, MILTON (1962), *Capitalism and Freedom*, Chicago: University of Chicago Press.

FROMM, ERICH (1976), *To Be or To Have?*, New York: Harper.

GARRETT G. and LANGE P. (1986), 'Economic Growth in Capitalist Democracies 1974–1982', *World Politics*, 38: 517–45.

GAUTHIER, DAVID (1986), *Morals by Agreement*, Oxford: Oxford University Press.

GEORGE, HENRY (1879), *Progress and Poverty*, London: Hogarth Press (1953).

GERAS, NORMAN (1984), 'The Controversy about Marx and Justice', *Philosophica*, 33: 33–86 (repr. in *New Left Review*, 150, 1985).

GINTIS, HERBERT and BOWLES, SAMUEL (1981), 'Structure and Practice in the Labor Theory of Value', *Review of Radical Political Economics*, 12: 1–26.

GIORDAN, M. (1978), *How to be Exploited . . . and How to Avoid It*, London: Temple Smith.

GLYN, ANDREW (1979), 'The Rate of Exploitation and Contemporary Capitalism', *Hitotsubashi Economic Review*, 10: 334–46.

—— and SUTCLIFFE, BOB (1971), 'The Critical Condition of British Capitalism', *New Left Review*, 66: 3–33.

—— (1972) *British Capitalism, Workers and the Profit Squeeze*, London: Penguin.

GODELIER, MAURICE (1978), 'La Part idéale du réel: Essai sur l'idéologique', *L'Homme*, 18: 155–88.

GOODIN, ROBERT E. (1982), 'Freedom and the Welfare State', *Journal of Social Policy*, 11: 149–76.

—— (1992), 'Toward a Minimally Presumptuous Social Policy', in P. Van Parijs (ed.), *Arguing for Basic Income: Ethical foundations for a Radical Reform*, London: Verso, 195–214.

—— and REEVE, A. (eds.) (1989), *Liberal Neutrality*, London: Routledge.

GOODWIN, RICHARD M. (1967), 'A Growth Cycle', in E. K. Hunt and J. G. Schwartz (eds.), *A Critique of Economic Theory*, Harmondsworth: Penguin (1972), 442–9.

GORDON, DAVID M. (1976), 'Capitalist Efficiency and Socialist Efficiency', *Monthly Review*, 28: 19–39.

GORZ, ANDRÉ (1985), 'L'Allocation universelle: Version de droite et version de gauche', *La Revue Nouvelle*, 81: 419–28.

—— (1988), *Métamorphoses du Travail: Quête du sens*, Paris: Galilée.

—— (1992), 'On the Difference between Society and Community, and Why Basic Income Cannot by Itself Confer Full Membership of Either', in P. Van Parijs (ed.), *Arguing for Basic Income*, London: Verso, 178–84.

GOUVERNEUR, JACQUES (1983), *Contemporary Capitalism and Market Economics*, Oxford: Martin Robertson.

GREY, THOMAS C. (1973), 'The First Virtue', *Stanford Law Review*, 25: 286–327.

GUESNERIE, ROBERT and LAFFONT, JEAN-JACQUES (1978), 'Advantageous Reallocation of Initial Endowments', *Econometrica*, 46: 835–41.

GÜTH, WERNER (1988), 'Ultimatum Bargaining for a Shrinking Cake: An Experimental Analysis', *Lecture Notes in Economics and Mathematical Systems*, 314: 111–128.

HABERMAS, JÜRGEN (1973), *Legitimationsprobleme im Spätkapitalismus*, Frankfurt: Suhrkamp.

—— (1985), 'Die neue Unübersichtlichkeit: Die Krise des Wohlfahrtsstaates und die Erschöpfung utopischer Energien', *Merkur*, 39: 1–14.

HAMMINGA, BERT (1983), 'Opstaan voor iemand misstaat niemand', *Maandschrift Economie*, 47, 395–410.

—— (1988), 'Arbeid en moraal in de spiegel van een utopie', in W. Goddijn et al., *Aftellen tot 2000*, Tilburg: Tilburg University Press, 4–25.

—— (1995), 'Could Jobs be like Cars and Concerts?', *Journal of Political Philosophy*, 3: 23–33.

HAMPTON, JEAN (1991), 'Varieties of the Social Contract', paper presented at a Conference on Contractarianism, European University Institute, Florence (Apr. 1991).

HARTWICK, JOHN (1977), 'Intergenerational Equity and the Investing of Rents from Exhaustible Resources', *American Economic Review*, 66: 972–4.

HAYEK, FRIEDRICH A. (1960), *The Constitution of Liberty*, London: Routledge & Kegan Paul.

HILFERDING, RUDOLF (1904), *Boehm-Bawerks Marx-Kritik*, Vienna: Ignaz Brand.

HIRSCH, FRED (1977), *Social Limits to Growth*, London: Routledge & Kegan Paul.

HOBBES, THOMAS (1651), *Leviathan*, Harmondsworth: Penguin (1968).

HODGSKIN, THOMAS (1825), *Labour Defended against Capital, or the Unproductiveness of Capital Proved*, London.

HODGSON, GEOFFREY (1980), 'A Theory of Exploitation without the Labour Theory of Value', *Science and Society*, 44: 257–73.

HOLLÄNDER, HEINZ (1982), 'Class Antagonism, Exploitation and the Labour Theory of Value', *Economic Journal*, 92: 868–85.

HOMANS, GEORGE C. (1961), *Social Behaviour: Its Elementary Forms*, London: Routledge & Kegan Paul (1973).

HOSPERS, JOHN (1971), *Libertarianism: A Political Philosophy whose Time has Come*, Santa Barbara, Calif.: Reason Press.

HUET, FRANÇOIS (1853), *Le Règne social du christianisme*, Paris: Firmin Didot; Brussels: Decq.

ILLICH, IVAN (1978), *The Right to Useful Unemployment*, London: Marion Boyars.

—— (1981) *Shadow Work*, London: Marion Boyars.

ITOH, MAKOTO (1980), *Value and Crisis*, London: Pluto Press.

ITURBE, I. and NIETO, J. (1992), 'On Fair Allocations and Monetary Compensations', Universitat Autonoma de Barcelona: Department of Economics.

JAY, PETER (1977), 'The Workers' Co-operative Economy', in A. Clayre (ed.), *The Political Economy of Co-operation and Participation*, Oxford: Oxford University Press (1980), 9–45.

JOHNSON, WARREN A. (1971), 'The Guaranteed Income as an Environmental Measure', in H. E. Daly (ed.), *Toward a Steady-State Economy*, San Francisco: Freeman (1973), 175–89.

JORDAN, BILL (1985), 'Exploitation and Basic Incomes', *BIRG Bulletin*, 4: 12–13.

—— JAMES, SIMON, KAY, HELEN, and REDLEY, MARCUS (1992), *Trapped in Poverty? Labour-Market Decisions in Low-Income Households*, London: Routledge.

JOSEPH, KEITH and SUMPTION, JONATHAN (1979), *Equality*, London: John Murray.

KALECKI, MICHAEL (1943), 'Political Aspects of Full Employment', in M. Kalecki, *Selected Essays on the Dynamics of the Capitalist Economy*, Cambridge: Cambridge University Press.

KANT, IMMANUEL (1793), 'Über den Gemeinspruch: Das mag in der Theorie richtig sein, taugt aber nicht für die Praxis', in W. Weischedel (ed.), *Werkausgabe*, Frankfurt: Suhrkamp (1977), xi. 125–72.

—— (1797), *Die Metaphysik der Sitten*, in W. Weischedel (ed.), *Werkausgabe*, Frankfurt: Suhrkamp (1977), viii. 305–634.

KAUS, MICKEY (1992), *The End of Equality*, New York: Basic Books.

KIRZNER, ISRAEL M. (1978), 'Entrepreneurship, Entitlement and Economic Justice', in J. Paul (ed.), *Reading Nozick*, Totowa NJ: Rowman & Littlefield (1981), 383–401.

KOHR, LEOPOLD (1974), 'Property and Freedom', in S. L. Blumenfeld (ed.), *Property in a Humane Economy*, La Salle, Ill.: Open Court, 47–70.

KOLAKOWSKI, LESZEK (1978), *Main Currents of Marxism*, i, Oxford: Oxford University Press.

KOLM, SERGE-CHRISTOPHE (1969), 'L'Exploitation des nations par les nations', *Revue économique*, 20: 851–72.

—— (1972), *Justice et equité*, Paris: CNRS.

—— (1975), 'L'Exploitation par l'inflation', *Les Temps modernes*, 351: 454–481.

—— (1994), 'L'Égalité de la liberté', *Recherches économiques de Louvain*, 60: 81–6.

KOOISTRA, PIETER (1983), *Voor*, Amsterdam: Stichting UNO-inkomen voor alle mensen.

KORNAI, JANOS (1981), 'Efficiency and the Principles of Socialist Ethics', in J. Kornai, *Contradictions and Dilemmas: Studies in the Socialist Economy and Society*, Cambridge, Mass.: MIT Press (1986), 124–38.

KRUEGER, ANN O. (1974), 'The Political Economy of the Rent-seeking Society', *American Economic Review*, 64: 291–303.

LANCASTER, KURT (1973), 'The Dynamic Inefficiency of Capitalism', *Journal of Political Economy*, 81: 1092–109.

LANG, KEVIN and WEISS, ANDREW (1990), 'Tagging, Stigma and Basic Income Guarantees', paper presented at the Conference 'Basic Income Guarantees: a New Welfare Strategy?', University of Wisconsin, Madison, (Apr. 1990).

LANGE, OSKAR (1936), 'On the Economic Theory of Socialism. Part I', *Review of Economic Studies*, 4: 53–71.

—— (1937a), 'On the Economic Theory of Socialism. Part II', *Review of Economic Studies*, 5: 123–42.

—— (1937*b*), 'Mr Lerner's Note on Socialist Economics', *Review of Economic Studies*, 5: 143–4.

LARMORE, CHARLES (1987), *Patterns of Moral Complexity*, Cambridge: Cambridge University Press.

LAZEAR, E. P. (1979), 'Why is there Mandatory Retirement?', *Journal of Political Economy*, 87: 1261–84.

LEIBENSTEIN, HARVEY (1963), 'The Theory of Underemployment in Densely Populated Backward Areas', in G. A Akerlof and Janet L. Yellen (eds.), *Efficiency Wage Models of the Labor Market*, Cambridge: Cambridge University Press (1986), 22–40.

LERNER, ABBA (1936), 'A Note on Socialist Economics', *Review of Economic Studies*, 4: 72–6.

LEVINE, ANDREW (1984), *Arguing for Socialism: Theoretical Considerations*, London: Routledge & Kegan Paul.

LINDBECK, ASSAR and SNOWER, DENNIS J. (1985), 'Explanations of Unemployment', *Oxford Review of Economic Policy*, 1: 34–59.

—— (1988), *The Insider–Outsider Theory of Employment and Unemployment*, Cambridge, Mass.: MIT Press.

LINDBLOM, CHARLES E. (1977), *Politics and Markets*, New York: Basic Books.

LIPIETZ, ALAIN (1979), *Crise et Inflation: Pourquoi?*, Paris: Maspero.

LISKA, TIBOR (1990), 'The Reform of Property Relations: A Proposal for Entrepreneurial Socialism Based on Personal-Social Property Relations', paper presented at the Third International Conference on Basic Income, Florence (Sept. 1990).

LOCKE, JOHN (1690), *Of Civil Government*, London: Dent & Sons (1924).

LUKES, STEVEN (1985), *Marxism and Morality*, Oxford: Oxford University Press.

MACCALLUM, GERALD C. (1967), 'Negative and Positive Freedom', *Philosophical Review*, 74: 312–34.

MACK, ERIC (1992), 'Gauthier on Rights and Economic Rents', *Social Philosophy and Policy*, 9: 171–200.

MCKEAN, R. N. (1975), 'Property Rights, Pollution and Power', in R. T. Selden (ed.), *Capitalism and Freedom: Problems and Prospects*, Charlottesville: University Press of Virginia, 92–127.

MACPHERSON, CRAWFORD B. (1973), *Democratic Theory*, Oxford: Oxford University Press.

MALCOMSON, JAMES M. (1984), 'Work Incentives, Hierarchy, and Internal Labor Markets', *Journal of Political Economy*, 92: 486–507.

MANDEL, ERNEST (1962), *Traité d'économie marxiste*, iii, Paris: Union Générale d'Édition (1969).

MARSHALL, ALFRED (1890), *Principles of Economics*, London: Macmillan (1961).

MARX, KARL (1863), *Theorien über den Mehrwert*, iii, Berlin: Dietz (1960).

—— (1867), *Das Kapital*, i, Berlin: Dietz (1962).

—— (1875), 'Randglossen zum Programm der deutschen Arbeiterpartei', in K. Marx and F. Engels, *Werke* xix, Berlin: Dietz (1962), 15–32.

MARX, KARL (1880), 'Randglossen zu Adolf Wagners "Lehrbuch der politischen Oekonomie"', in K. Marx and F. Engels, *Werke* xix, Berlin, Dietz (1962), 355–83.
—— (1885), *Das Kapital*, ii, Berlin: Dietz (1963).
—— (1894), *Das Kapital*, iii, Berlin: Dietz (1964).
MEADE, JAMES E. (1938), *Consumers' Credits and Unemployment*, Oxford: Oxford University Press.
—— (1964), *Efficiency, Equality and the Ownership of Property*, London: Allen & Unwin.
—— (1984), 'Full Employment, New Technologies and the Distribution of Income', *Journal of Social Policy*, 13: 129–46.
—— (1989), *Agathotopia: The Economics of Partnership*, Aberdeen: Aberdeen University Press.
—— (1990), 'Can we Learn a "Third Way" from the Agathotopians?', in A. B. Atkinson (ed.), *Alternatives to Capitalism: The Economics of Partnership*, Basingstoke: Macmillan (1993), 9–23.
—— (1993), *Liberty, Equality and Efficiency*, London: Macmillan.
MILL, JOHN STUART (1848), *Principles of Political Economy*, London: Longmans, Green & Co. (1904).
—— (1859), *On Liberty*, Harmondsworth: Penguin (1974).
MILLER, ANNE G. (1983), *In Praise of Social Dividends*, Heriot-Watt University (Edinburgh): Department of Economics, Working Paper 83.1.
MILLER, DAVID (1989), *Market, State and Community: Theoretical Foundations of Market Socialism*, Oxford: Oxford University Press.
—— (1992), 'Distributive Justice: What the People Think', *Ethics*, 102: 555–93.
MORE, THOMAS (1516), *Utopia*, Harmondsworth: Penguin (1978).
MORISHIMA, MICHIO (1973), *Marx's Economics: A Dual Theory of Value and Growth*, Cambridge: Cambridge University Press.
—— and CATEPHORES, GEORGE (1978), *Value, Exploitation and Growth: Marx in the Light of Modern Economic Theory*, London: McGraw-Hill.
MUSGRAVE, RICHARD A. (1974), 'Maximin, Uncertainty, and the Leisure Trade-off', *Quarterly Journal of Economics*, 88: 625–32.
NELL, EDWARD J. (1972), 'Profit Erosion in the United States: An Introductory Essay', in A. Glyn and B. Sutcliffe *Capitalism in Crisis*, New York: Random House (1972), pp. vii–xxxix.
NOOTEBOOM, BART (1986), 'Basic Income as a Basis for Small Business', *International Small Business Journal*, 5 (3): 10–18.
NORMAN, RICHARD (1982), 'Does Equality Destroy Liberty?', in Keith Graham (ed.), *Contemporary Political Philosophy: Radical Studies*, Cambridge: Cambridge University Press, 83–109.
—— (1987), *Free and Equal*, Oxford: Oxford University Press.
NOVE, ALEC (1983), *The Economics of Feasible Socialism*, London: George Allen & Unwin.
NOZICK, ROBERT (1969), 'Coercion', in P. Laslett, W. G. Runciman, and Q. Skinner (eds.), *Philosophy, Politics and Society*, Oxford: Blackwell, 101–35.
—— (1974), *Anarchy, State and Utopia*, Oxford: Blackwell.

OAKESHOTT, MICHAEL (1975), *On Human Conduct*, Oxford: Oxford University Press.

O'CONNOR, JAMES (1973), *The Fiscal Crisis of the State*, New York: St Martin's Press.

OFFE, CLAUS (1972), *Strukturprobleme des kapitalistischen Staats*, Frankfurt am Main: Suhrkamp (1975).

OKUN, ARTHUR M. (1975), *Equality and Efficiency: The Big Tradeoff*, Washington, DC: The Brookings Institution.

OLSON, MANCUR (1965), *The Logic of Collective Action: Public Goods and the Theory of Groups*, Cambridge, Mass.: Harvard University Press.

ORWELL, GEORGE (1945), *Animal Farm*, London: Secker & Warburg.

OUBRIDGE, VICTOR (1990), 'Basic Income and Industrial Development: An Employer's Viewpoint', *BIRG Bulletin*, 11: 28–30.

PAINE, THOMAS (1796), 'Agrarian Justice', in P.F. Foner (ed.), *The Life and Major Writings of Thomas Paine*, Secaucus, NJ: Citadel Press (1974), 605–23.

PARKER, HERMIONE (1982), 'Basic Income Guarantee Scheme: Synopsis', in *The Structure of Personal Income Taxation and Income Support* (House of Commons, Treasury and Civil Service Committee), London: HMSO (21 July 1982), 424–53.

PATTANAIK, PRASANTA and XU, YONGSHENG (1990), 'On Ranking Opportunity Sets in Terms of Freedom of Choice', *Recherches économiques de Louvain*, 56: 383–90.

PAZNER, E. A. and SCHMEIDLER, D. (1974), 'A Difficulty in the Concept of Fairness', *Review of Economic Studies*, 41: 441–3.

PEFFER, R. G. (1990), *Marxism, Morality and Social Justice*, Princeton NJ: Princeton University Press.

PERSKY, J. and TSANG, H. (1974), 'Pigouvian Exploitation of Labor', *Review of Economics and Statistics*, 56: 52–7.

PETTIT, PHILIP (1993), 'Negative Liberty, Liberal and Republican', *European Journal of Philosophy*, 1: 15–38.

PIGOU, A. C. (1920), *The Economics of Welfare*, London: Macmillan.

PLATO, *Laws*, ed. R. G. Bury, London: Heinemann.

POGGE, THOMAS W. (1989), *Realizing Rawls*, Ithaca, NY: Cornell University Press.

—— (1994), 'An Egalitarian Law of Peoples', paper presented at the conference 'The Ethics of Nationalism', University of Illinois at Urbana-Champaign (Apr. 1994).

PROUDHON, PIERRE-JEAN-JOSEPH (1840), *Qu'est-ce que la propriété?*, Paris: Rivière.

—— (1846), *Système des contradictions économiques, ou Philosophie de la misère*, i, Paris: Rivière.

PRZEWORSKI, ADAM (1985), *Capitalism and Social Democracy*, Cambridge: Cambridge University Press.

—— (1987), *Capitalism, Democracy, Pacts*, University of Chicago: Department of Political Science.

PRZEWORSKI, ADAM (1991), *Democracy and Markets*, Cambridge: Cambridge University Press.

—— and WALLERSTEIN, MICHAEL (1982), 'The Structure of Class Conflict in Democratic Capitalist Countries', *American Political Science Review*, 76: 215–36.

—— (1986), 'Popular Sovereignty, State Autonomy and Private Property', *Archives européennes de sociologie*, 27: 215–59.

PURDY, DAVID (1990), 'Work, Ethics and Social Policy: A Moral Tale', paper presented at the Third International Conference on Basic Income, Florence (Sept. 1990).

RAE, DOUGLAS W. and DAUDT, HANS (1976), 'The Ostrogorski Paradox: A Peculiarity of Compound Majority Decision', *European Journal of Political Research*, 4: 391–8.

RAKOWSKI, ERIC (1991), *Equal Justice*, Oxford: Oxford University Press.

RAWLS, JOHN (1971), *A Theory of Justice*, Oxford: Oxford University Press (1972).

—— (1974), 'Reply to Alexander and Musgrave', *Quarterly Journal of Economics*, 88: 633–55.

—— (1978), 'The Basic Structure as Subject', in A. I. Goldman and J. Kim (eds.), *Values and Morals*, Dordrecht: Reidel, 47–61.

—— (1982), 'Social Unity and Primary Goods', in A. Sen and B. Williams (eds.), *Utilitarianism and Beyond*, Cambridge: Cambridge University Press (1982), 159–86.

—— (1987), 'The Idea of an Overlapping Consensus', *Oxford Journal for Legal Studies*, 7: 1–25.

—— (1988), 'The Priority of Right and Ideas of the Good', *Philosophy and Public Affairs*, 17: 251–76.

—— (1990), 'Justice as Fairness: A Restatement', Harvard University: Department of Philosophy, unpublished lecture notes.

—— (1993*a*), *Political Liberalism*, New York: Columbia University Press.

—— (1993*b*), 'The Law of Peoples', in S. Shute and S. Hurley (eds.), *On Human Rights*, New York: Basic Books, 41–82.

REES, ALBERT (1986), 'An Essay on Youth Unemployment', *Journal of Economic Literature*, 24: 613–28.

REEVE, ANDREW (1987), 'Thomas Hodgskin and John Bray: Free Exchange and Equal Exchange', in A. Reeve (ed.), *Modern Theories of Exploitation*, London: Sage, 30–52.

REIMAN, JEFFREY (1989), 'An Alternative to "Distributive" Marxism: Further Thoughts on Cohen, Roemer and Exploitation', *Canadian Journal of Philosophy*, suppl. 15: 299–331.

ROBINSON, JOAN (1942), *An Essay on Marxian Economics*, New York: St Martin's Press (1976).

—— (1956) *The Accumulation of Capital*, London: Macmillan.

ROEMER, JOHN E. (1982*a*), *A General Theory of Exploitation and Class*, Cambridge, Mass.: Harvard University Press.

—— (1982*b*), 'Exploitation, Alternatives and Socialism', *Economic Journal*, 92: 87–107.

—— (1982c), 'Reply', *Politics and Society*, 11: 375–94.

—— (1982d), 'Property Relations vs. Surplus Value in Marxian Exploitation', *Philosophy and Public Affairs*, 11: 281–313.

—— (1983a), 'Unequal Exchange, Labor Migrations and International Capital Flows: A Theoretical Synthesis', in P. Desai (ed.), *Marxism, the Soviet Economy and Central Planning*, Cambridge, Mass.: MIT Press, 34–60.

—— (1983b), *Choice of Technique under Capitalism, Socialism and Nirvana: Reply to Samuelson*, University of California (Davis): Department of Economics, Working Paper 213.

—— (1983c), 'Are Socialist Ethics Consistent with Efficiency?', *Philosophical Forum*, 14: 369–88.

—— (1985a), 'Why should Marxists be Interested in Exploitation?', in B. Chavance (ed.), *Marx en perspective*, Paris: Éditions de l'École des Hautes Études en Sciences Sociales, 29–50.

—— (1985b), 'Equality of Talent', *Economics and Philosophy*, 1: 151–87.

—— (1986), 'Equality of Resources Implies Equality of Welfare', *Quarterly Journal of Economics*, 100: 751–84.

—— (1988), *Free to Lose*, London: Radius Books.

—— (1989a), 'Public Ownership and Private Property Externalities', in J. Elster and K. O. Moene (eds.), *Alternatives to Capitalism*, Cambridge: Cambridge University Press, 159–79.

—— (1989b), 'Second Thoughts on Property Relations and Exploitation', *Canadian Journal of Philosophy*, suppl. 15: 257–66.

—— (1992), 'The Morality and Efficiency of Market Socialism', *Ethics*, 102: 448–64.

—— (1993), *A Future for Socialism*, Cambridge, Mass.: Harvard University Press; London: Verso.

ROLAND, GÉRARD (1988), 'Why Socialism Needs Basic Income, why Basic Income Needs Socialism', in Anne G. Miller (ed.), *Proceedings of the First International Conference on Basic Income*, London: BIRG; Antwerp: BIEN, 94–105.

—— (1989), *Économie politique du système soviétique*, Paris: L'Harmattan.

ROTHBARD, MURRAY N. (1973), *For a New Liberty: The Libertarian Manifesto*, New York: Collier (1978).

ROUSSEAU, JEAN-JACQUES (1762), *Du contrat social*, Paris: Garnier-Flammarion (1966).

ROWTHORN, ROBERT B. (1973), 'Skilled Labour in the Marxist System', in R. B. Rowthorn, *Capitalism, Conflict and Inflation: Essays in Political Economy*, London: Lawrence & Wishart (1980), 231–49.

—— (1976), 'Mandel's "Late Capitalism"', *New Left Review*, 98: 59–83.

—— (1977), 'Conflict, Inflation and Money', in R. B. Rowthorn, *Capitalism, Conflict and Inflation*, London: Lawrence & Wishart (1980), 148–81.

RUSSELL, BERTRAND (1932), 'In Praise of Idleness', in V. Richards (ed.), *Why Work?*, London: Freedom Press (1983), 25–34.

SALVERDA, WIM (1984), 'Basisinkomen en inkomensverdeling: De financiële uitvoerbaarheid van een basisinkomen', *Tijdschrift voor Politieke Ekonomie*, 8: 9–41.

SAMUELSON, PAUL A. (1982), 'The Normative and Positivistic Inferiority of Marx's Value Paradigm', *Southern Economic Journal*, 49: 11–18.

SCHOKKAERT, ERIK and OVERLAET, B. (1989), 'Moral Intuitions and Economic Models of Distributive Justice', *Social Choice and Welfare*, 6: 19–31.

SCHOR, JULIET B. and BOWLES, SAMUEL (1987), 'Employment Rents and the Incidence of Strikes', *Review of Economics and Statistics*, 69: 584–92.

SCHUMACHER, E. F. (1959), 'Is the Ownership Debate Closed?', *Socialist Commentary* (Feb. 1959).

SCHUMPETER, JOSEPH A. (1943), *Capitalism, Socialism and Democracy*, London: Allen & Unwin (1976).

SEN, AMARTYA (1977), 'Rational Fools: A Critique of the Behavioural Foundations of Economic Theory', in A. Sen, *Choice, Welfare and Measurement*, Oxford: Blackwell (1982), 84–106.

—— (1980), 'Equality of What?', in S. M. McMurrin (ed.), *Liberty, Equality and Law*, Salt Lake City: University of Utah Press (1987), 137–62. (Also in A. Sen, *Choice, Welfare and Measurement*, Oxford: Blackwell (1982), 353–69.)

—— (1984), 'Rights and Capabilities', in A. Sen, *Resources, Values and Development*, Oxford: Oxford University Press (1984), 307–24.

—— (1985), *Commodities and Capabilities*, Amsterdam: North-Holland.

—— (1990*a*), 'Justice: Means versus Freedoms', *Philosophy and Public Affairs*, 19: 111–21.

—— (1990*b*), 'Welfare, Freedom and Social Choice: A Reply', *Recherches Économiques de Louvain*, 56: 451–86.

—— (1990*d*), 'Individual Freedom as Social Commitment', *New York Review of Books* (14 June 1990), 49–54.

—— (1992), *Inequality Reexamined*, Oxford: Oxford University Press.

SHAIKH, ANWAR (1978), 'An Introduction to the History of Crisis Theories', in *Radical Perspectives on the Economic Crisis of Monopoly Capitalism*, New York: Union for Radical Political Economics, 219–41.

SHEPELAK, N. J. and ALWIN, D. F. (1986), 'Beliefs about Inequality and Perceptions of Distributive Justice', *American Sociological Review*, 51: 30–46.

SKINNER, QUENTIN (1984), 'The Idea of Negative Liberty: Philosophical and Historical Perspectives', in R. Rorty, J. B. Schneewind, and Q. Skinner (eds.), *Philosophy in History*, Cambridge: Cambridge University Press, 193–221.

—— (1990), 'The Republican Ideal of Political Liberty', in G. Bock, Q. Skinner, and M. Viroli (eds.), *Machiavelli and Republicanism*, Cambridge: Cambridge University Press, 293–309.

SMITH, GEOFFREY W. (1985), 'Marxian Exploitation as Coercive Justice', University of Lancaster: Department of Politics, unpublished.

SPENCE, M. (1983), 'Contestable Markets and the Theory of Industry Structure: A Review Article', *Journal of Economic Literature*, 21: 981–90.

STANDING, GUY (1986), 'Meshing Labour Flexibility with Security: An Answer to Mass Unemployment?', *International Labour Review*, 125: 87–106.

—— (1989), *European Unemployment, Insecurity and Flexibility: A Social Dividend Solution*, Geneva: International Labour Office, Working Paper.

STEEDMAN, IAN (1977), *Marx after Sraffa*, London: New Left Books.

—— (1985) 'Heterogeneous Labour, Money Wages and Marx's Theory', in B. Chavance (ed.), *Marx en perspective*, Paris: Éditions de l'École des Hautes Études en Sciences Sociales, 475–94.

STEINER, HILLEL (1974), 'Individual Liberty', *Proceedings of the Aristotelian Society*, 75: 33–50.

—— (1977), 'The Structure of a Set of Compossible Rights', *Journal of Philosophy*, 74: 767–75.

—— (1981), 'Liberty and Equality', *Political Studies*, 29: 555–69.

—— (1983), 'How Free: Computing Personal Liberty', in A. Phillips-Griffiths (ed.), *Of Liberty*, Cambridge: Cambridge University Press, 73–89.

—— (1984), 'A Liberal Theory of Exploitation', *Ethics*, 94: 225–41.

—— (1986), 'Comment on van der Veen and Van Parijs's Reply', University of Manchester: Department of Government, unpublished note (Sept. 1986).

—— (1987), 'Exploitation: A Liberal Theory Amended, Defended and Extended', in A. Reeve (ed.), *Modern Theories of Exploitation*, London: Sage, 132–48.

—— (1988), 'Capitalism and Equal Starts', in J. Paul *et al.* (eds.), *Equal Opportunity*, Oxford: Blackwell, 49–72.

—— (1992), 'Three Just Taxes', in P. Van Parijs (ed.), *Arguing for Basic Income*, London: Verso, 81–92.

—— (1994), *An Essay on Rights*, Oxford: Blackwell.

STERBA, JAMES P. (1980), *The Demands of Justice*, Notre Dame, Ind.: University of Indiana Press.

STIGLITZ, JOSEPH (1987), 'The Causes and Consequences of the Dependence of Quality on Price', *Journal of Economic Literature*, 25: 1–48.

SUGDEN, ROBERT (1982), 'Hard Luck Stories: The Problem of the Uninsured in a Laissez-faire Society', *Journal of Social Policy*, 11: 201–16.

SUPLICY, EDUARDO (ed.) (1992), *Programa de garantia de renda mínima*, Brasilia: Senado Federal.

SUZUMURA, K. (1987), 'Equity and Incentives: Homans' Theory of Distributive Justice Reconsidered', Hitotsubashi University, Institute of Economic Research, Working Paper.

SWEEZY, PAUL M. (1942), *The Theory of Capitalist Development*, New York: Monthly Review Press, 1970.

SZÉCKY, JANOS (1982), 'Entrepreneurial Socialism at the Experimental Stage', *The New Hungarian Quarterly*, 87: 93–8.

TANGHE, FERNAND (1989), *Le Droit au travail entre histoire et utopie: De la répression de la mendicité à l'allocation universelle*, Brussels: Publications des Facultés Universitaires Saint-Louis; Florence: Publications de l'Institut Universitaire Européen.

TAWNEY, RICHARD H. (1952), *Equality*, London: Allen & Unwin (1964).

TAYLOR, CHARLES (1979), 'What's Wrong with Negative Liberty?', in A. Ryan (ed.), *The Idea of Freedom*, Oxford: Oxford University Press, 175–93.

TAYLOR, CHARLES (1988) 'Le Juste et le bien', *Revue de Métaphysique et de Morale*, 83: 33–56.

TAYLOR, MICHAEL (1982), *Community, Anarchy and Liberty*, Cambridge: Cambridge University Press.

TERRAY, EMMANUEL (1985), 'Exploitation et domination dans la pensée de Marx', in B. Chavance (ed.), *Marx en perspective*, Paris: Éditions de l'École des Hautes Études en Sciences Sociales, 15–28.

THOMSON, WILLIAM (1994), 'L'Absence d'envie: une introduction', *Recherches économiques de Louvain*, 60: 43–62.

THUROW, LESTER C. (1977), 'Government Expenditures: Cash or In-Kind Aid?', in G. Dworkin, G. Bermant, and P. G. Brown (eds.), *Market and Morals*, New York: Wiley, 85–106.

TINBERGEN, JAN (1946), *Redelijke Inkomensverdeling*, Haarlem: De Gulden Pers.

—— (1953), *Economic Policy: Principles and Design*, Amsterdam: North-Holland.

TOCQUEVILLE, ALEXIS DE (1856), *L'Ancien Régime et la Révolution*, ii, Paris: Gallimard (1953).

TUCKER, R. C. (1963), 'Marx and Distributive Justice', in C. Friedrich and J. W. Chapman (eds.), *Nomos VI: Justice*, 306–25.

VAN DER VEEN, ROBERT J. (1978), 'Property, Exploitation, Justice: an Inquiry into their Relationship in the Work of Nozick, Rawls and Marx', *Acta Politica*, 13: 433–65 (repr. in van der Veen (1991), 217–50).

—— (1982), 'A Critique of John Roemer's General Theory of Exploitation', Universiteit van Amsterdam: Economisch Seminarium, unpublished manuscript.

—— (1984), 'The Marxian Ideal of Freedom and the Problem of Justice', *Philosophica*, 34: 103–26 (repr. in van der Veen (1991), 277–301).

—— (1991), *Between Exploitation and Communism. Explorations in the Marxian Theory of Justice and Freedom*, Groningen: Wolters-Noordhoff.

—— and VAN PARIJS, PHILIPPE (1985), 'Entitlement Theories of Justice: From Nozick to Roemer and Beyond', *Economics and Philosophy*, 1: 69–81.

—— (1986a), 'A Capitalist Road to Communism', *Theory and Society*, 15: 635–55. (Rev. as ch. 8 of Van Parijs (1993a), 155–75.)

—— (1986b), 'Universal Grants versus Socialism: Reply to Six Critics', *Theory and Society*, 15: 723–57. (Rev. as ch. 9 of Van Parijs (1993a), 176–210.)

VANEK, JAROSLAV (1970), *The General Theory of Self-Managed Market Economies*, Ithaca: Cornell University Press.

VAN PARIJS, PHILIPPE (1990), 'The Second Marriage of Justice and Efficiency', *Journal of Social Policy*, 19: 1–25. (Also in P. Van Parijs (ed.), *Arguing for Basic Income*, London: Verso (1992), 215–40.)

—— (1991a), *Qu'est-ce qu'une société juste?*, Paris: Le Seuil.

—— (1991b), 'Basic Income: A Green Strategy for the New Europe', in S. Parkin (ed.), *Green Light on Europe*, London: Heretic Books, 166–76.

—— (1992), 'Competing Justifications of Basic Income', in P. Van Parijs (ed.), *Arguing for Basic Income*, London: Verso, 1–43.

—— (1993a), *Marxism Recycled*, Cambridge: Cambridge University Press.

—— (1993*b*), 'Rawlsians, Christians and Patriots. Maximin Justice and Individual Ethics', *European Journal of Philosophy* 1, 309–42.

—— (1996*a*), 'Free Riding versus Rent Sharing. Why Even David Gauthier should Support a Basic Income', in F. Farina, F. Hahn and S. Vanucci (eds.), *Ethics, Rationality and Economic Behaviour,* Oxford: Oxford University Press 159–81.

—— (1996*b*), 'Justice and Democracy: Are they Incompatible?', *Journal of Political Philosophy,* 4: 101–17.

VAN TRIER, WALTER (1989), *Who Framed Social Dividend? A Tale of the Unexpected,* Universitaire Faculteiten Sint-Ignatius Antwerpen: SESO, rapport 89/230.

VARIAN, HAL (1974), 'Equity, Envy and Efficiency', *Journal of Economic Theory,* 9: 63–91.

—— (1975), 'Distributive Justice, Welfare Economics and the Theory of Fairness', in F. Hahn & M. Hollis (eds.), *Philosophy and Economic Theory,* Oxford: Oxford University Press (1979), 135–64.

—— (1976), 'Two Problems in the Theory of Fairness', *Journal of Public Economics,* 5: 249–60.

—— (1985), 'Dworkin on Equality of Resources', *Economics and Philosophy,* 1: 110–25.

VISSER, PATRICE E. and PELLIKAAN, HUUB (1985), 'Overlegeconomie en speltheorie', *Beleid en Maatschappij,* 12: 45–54.

VOLTAIRE (1766), 'Le Philosophe ignorant', in Voltaire, *Mélanges,* Paris: Gallimard (1961), 877.

VON WEIZSÄCKER, CHRISTIAN C. (1973), 'Modern Capital Theory and the Concept of Exploitation', *Kyklos* 26: 245–81.

—— and SAMUELSON, PAUL A. (1971), 'A New Labour Theory of Value for Rational Planning through Use of the Bourgeois Profit Rate', *Proceedings of the National Academy of Sciences,* 68, 1192–4.

WALLICH, HENRY (1960), *The Cost of Freedom: A New Look at Capitalism,* New York: Harper & Brothers.

WALRAS, LÉON (1896), *Études d'économie sociale,* Lausanne: Rouge; Paris: Pichon & Durand-Auzias (1936).

WALTER, TONY (1989), *Basic Income: Freedom from Poverty, Freedom from Work,* London: Marion Boyars.

WARD, BARBARA (1985), *Alias Papa: A Life of Fritz Schumacher,* Oxford: Oxford University Press.

WEISSKOPF, THOMAS E. (1978), 'Marxist Perspectives on Cyclical Crises', in *Radical Perspectives on the Economic Crisis of Monopoly Capitalism,* New York: Union for Radical Political Economics, 241–60.

WEITZMAN, MARTIN L. (1984), *The Share Economy: Conquering Stagflation,* Cambridge, Mass.: Harvard University Press.

WESTON, JOE (ed.) (1986), *Red and Green: The New Politics of the Environment,* London: Pluto Press.

WICKSTEED, P. H. (1884), 'The Marxian Theory of Value', in P. H. Wicksteed *The Common Sense of Political Economy,* London: George Routledge and Sons, 1933, ii. 705–33.

WOLFF, ROBERT PAUL (1981), 'A Critique and Reinterpretation of Marx's Labor Theory of Value', *Philosophy and Public Affairs* 10, 89–120.

WOOD, ALLEN W. (1972), 'The Marxian Critique of Justice', in M. Cohen, T. Nagel, and T. Scanlon (eds), *Marx, Justice and History,* Princeton: Princeton University Press (1980), 3–41.

—— (1981), *Karl Marx*, London: Routlege & Kegan Paul.

WOOD, BARBARA (1985), *Alias Papa. A Biography of Fritz Schumacher*, Oxford: Oxford University Press.

WRIGHT, ERIK O. (1985*a*), 'A General Framework for Class Analysis', *Politics and Society,* 13: 385–423.

—— (1985*b*), *Classes*, London: New Left Books.

—— (1986), 'Why Something like Socialism Is Necessary for the Transition to Communism', *Theory and Society* 15, 657–72.

YOUNG, GARY (1978), 'Justice and Capitalist Production: Marx and Bourgeois Ideology', *Canadian Journal of Philosophy,* 8: 421–54.

YUNKER, JAMES A. (1977), 'The Social Dividend under Market Socialism', *Annals of Public and Co-operative Economy,* 48: 91–133.

—— (1986), 'A Market Socialist Critique of Capitalism's Dynamic Performance', *Journal of Economic Issues*, 20, 63–86.

INDEX OF NAMES

INDEX OF SUBJECTS